Living Space

Michael E. Veal

LIVING SPACE

John Coltrane, Miles Davis,
and Free Jazz,
from Analog to Digital

Wesleyan University Press   Middletown, Connecticut

Wesleyan University Press
Middletown CT 06459
www.wesleyan.edu/wespress
© 2024 Michael E. Veal
All rights reserved
Manufactured in the United States of America
Designed by Mindy Basinger Hill / Typeset in Minion Pro

Library of Congress Cataloging-in-Publication Data

Names: Veal, Michael E., author.

Title: Living space : John Coltrane, Miles Davis, and free jazz,
from analog to digital / Michael E. Veal.

Description: Middletown, Connecticut : Wesleyan University Press,
2024. | Series: Music/culture | Includes bibliographical references
and index. | Summary: "A musical study of free jazz, specifically John
Coltrane's controversial 'late period' and Miles Davis's long-neglected
'Lost Quintet,' bringing jazz into dialogue with experimental currents
in analysis of architecture and photography." — Provided by publisher.

Other titles: Music/culture.

Identifiers: LCCN 2023036472 (print) | LCCN 2023036473 (ebook) |
ISBN 9780819569196 (cloth) | ISBN 9780819569202 (trade paperback) |
ISBN 9780819500892 (ebook)

Subjects: LCSH: Free jazz—History and criticism. | Coltrane, John,
1926–1967—Criticism and interpretation. | Davis, Miles—
Criticism and interpretation.

Classification: LCC ML3506.V4 2024 (print) | LCC ML3506 (ebook) |
DDC 781.65/6—dc23/eng/20230809

LC record available at https://lccn.loc.gov/2023036472
LC ebook record available at https://lccn.loc.gov/2023036473

5   4   3   2   1

All the creative fields of life are closely linked to each other.

Lazslo Moholy-Nagy, cited in Ingrid Pfeiffer and Max Hollein, Laszlo Moholy-Nagy: Retrospective *(Munich: Prestel, 2009)*

I'm free to sing my song, though it gets out of time.

Rolling Stones, from "I'm Free"

There is no such thing as "our
universe," only degrees of the swinging, what
does not swing is nothing, and nothing swings
when it wants to.

*Amiri Baraka, from "J. Said, 'Our Whole Universe is Generated by a Rhythm,'"
from* Later Trane *(Candia, NH: John LeBow, 2003)*

He who has ears to hear, let him hear.

Gospel of St. Matthew 15:11

CONTENTS

ACKNOWLEDGMENTS

Love and thanks to my family and close friends: Mom and Dad, Liebechen, Mascha Deneke, Uncle Perce and Aunt Liz, Uncle Vann and Aunt Faye, Fritz and Christiane Deneke, Eva, Jens, Janos, Noah, Pia, Celine and Brother Ben, Ike and Renee, Baby Elephant and family, Brim Holder, R2 and Moms, Fleetwood, Donna Bilak, Olive, Tone-Ray, Kate Pruitt and family, Lucy and Antoine, Ingi-Mai Loorand, Yomi, Pet-Ra, Greg and AJ, the Quinto Kid and Susan, Dorothea, Darnell and Niecy and family, Joan-Ann Bostic, Luke, Barb, Man Smith, Hank and Felicia, Carmel, Luciana Parisi, Ra Kohlmann, Tamara, Groove Maneuvers, R. Casper Willis, Ilana Wind, Uncle Ojayé and family, Kris Gunsalus, Billdane, Tonya Williams-Saunders and family, Darryl Madison and family, Kim Aiken and family, Earl Bolden and family, Lauralito, Melissa Coren, Norbu, Rachael, Ellen Koehlings and Pete Lilly, and all the Veals, Smiths, Colemans and Tysons.

I would like to acknowledge my colleagues in the Departments of Music, African-American Studies, American Studies, and African Studies at Yale University. I would also like to acknowledge our wonderful office staff in the Department of Music, including Kristine Kinsella, Jennifer Gambaccini-Denillo, Susan Penney, and Elaine Culmo.

The book has benefitted immensely from gratifying conversations with various colleagues, friends, and associates from various fields and practices who read over the text, offered ideas, or assisted in other ways, including Elizabeth Alexander, Magdalyn Asimakis, Paul Austerlitz, Chris Becker, Renée Barbre (Yale University), Michael Benedikt (University of Texas, Austin), Franya Berkman, Ethan Braun, Daphne Brooks (Yale University), David P. Brown (University of Illinois, Chicago), Melvin Butler (University of Miami), Will Calhoun, Timothy Carter (University of North Carolina, Chapel Hill), Eric Charry (Wesleyan University), Matthew Clayton (University of Pennsylvania), Richard Cohn (Yale University),

Kwami Coleman (New York University), Steve Coleman, Jade Conlee (Yale University), Carolyn Cooper (University of the West Indies, Mona), Manthia Diawara (New York University), Nicholas Forster, Terri Francis (University of Indiana), Wills Glasspiegel (Yale University), Daniel Goldberg (Yale University), Sumanth Gopinath (University of Minnesota), Jocelyne Guilbault (University of California, Berkeley), Marc Hannaford, Diedra Harris-Kelley (Romare Bearden Foundation), Daniel Harrison (Yale University), Jay Hoggard (Wesleyan University), Aaron Jackson (Yale University), Kellie Jones (Columbia University), Brian Kane (Yale University), Emily Laber (City University of New York Graduate Center), George Lewis (Columbia University), Nick Lloyd, Tony Lombardozzi (Wesleyan University), Carlos Martinez (Universidad de los Lagos, Chile), Miya Masaoka, N. Serra M'bana, Achille Mbembe (University of the Witwatersrand), Ingrid Monson (Harvard University), Ras Moshe, Fred Moten (New York University), David Novak (University of California, Santa Barbara), Luciana Parisi (Duke University), Mrs. Alaknanda Patel, Rehana Patel (Wesleyan University), Marc Perlman (Brown University), John Peters (Yale University), Eve Poudriér (University of British Columbia), Ian Quinn (Yale University), Mark Rakatansky (Columbia University), Andrea Ray (Parsons School of Design), Carmel Raz (Max Planck Institute), Anthony Reed (Vanderbilt University), Petra Richterova (Savannah College of Art and Design), Joseph Salem (University of Victoria), Florian Sautter, Kamala Schelling, Matthias Schönenbäumer (Deichtorhallen Hamburg), Matthew Schulman (University of Oklahoma), Stanley Scott, Whitney Slaten (Bard College), Mark Slobin (Wesleyan University), Tyshawn Sorey (University of Pennsylvania), Zachary Stewart (Yale University), Didier Sylvain, John Szwed (Columbia University), Greg Tate, Michael Tenzer (University of British Columbia), Jason Vigneri-Beane (Pratt Institute), Chris Washburne (Columbia University), Salim Washington, Laura Wexler (Yale University), Mark Wilder (Sony Records), Deborah Wilson (Columbia University), Mabel Wilson (Columbia University), and Sheron Wray (University of California, Irvine). My sincerest apologies to anyone whose name I have forgotten here!

I would like to acknowledge the brilliant students in four iterations of my "Jazz and Architecture" seminar, in which we were able to explore several of these ideas in depth: Monica Chen, Stephanie Cheng, Michael Cohen, Michael Cruciger, Pek Shi Bao, D. J. Stanfill, and Cyril Zhang (2011); Zak Blickensderfer, Alex Chen, Nick Henriquez, Ben Houston-Edwards, Josh Isenstein, Catherine Jameson, Brooke Levin, Nate McNair, Brittney Sooksengdao, Rain Tsong, Noelle Villa, and Elisabed Zhvania (2012); Ade Ben-Salahuddin, Colin Hemez, Eric

Margolis, Julia Medina, Noelle McPhail, and Zachary Sekoff (2014); and Alexa Schor, Franklin She, Beza Tessema, Ted Wayland, and Peter Yu (2020).

I would like to give a big shout-out to my musician colleagues: members of the Aqua Ife Big Band, the Armillary Sphere, and all the members of Burnt Sugar, as well as Ed Byrne, Tony Lombardozzi, Anthony "Topi" Peterson, Michele Rose-woman, and Sensei Bruce Williams.

I would like to thank Parker Smathers for bringing this book to Wesleyan University Press and the press's chief editor Suzanna Tamminen for believing in this project over the longest of hauls. Special thanks also to Jordan D. Thomas for designing such a beautiful cover for the book; to Dr. Guthrie Ramsey, Arthur Jafa, and Fred Moten for the blurbs; to Hannah Krasikov for shepherding the book through the production process; and to Chris Dodge for the great indexing.

Deep thanks and appreciation to my research assistants for this (and other) projects: Clifton Boyd, Lauren Frankel, Danielle Ward-Griffin, Clare Eng, Joseph Marquez, Marissa Moore, Matthew Mendez, Holly Chung. Special thanks to Jade Conlee, and extra special thanks to Chloe Smith.

I offer heartfelt thanks to my colleagues in the Columbia University Jazz Study Group which, more than any other space, has provided a rigorous, supportive, and inspiring forum in which scholars and practitioners of jazz can exchange ideas. I am very proud to be affiliated with this brilliant and special group of scholars, musicians, colleagues, and friends: Kwami Coleman, C. Daniel Dawson, Krin Gabbard, Maxine Gordon, Farah Jasmine Griffin, Brent Hayes-Edwards, Vijay Iyer, Aaron Johnson, Diedra Harris-Kelley, Wolfram Knauer, George Lewis, Yulanda McKenzie-Grant, Jason Moran, Fred Moten, Robert O'Meally, Imani Owens, Chris Washburne, and Salim Washington. I am especially grateful for the opportunities the center provided to present earlier versions of this material at Columbia University in 2009, in three 2016 lectures as Louis Armstrong Visiting Professor, and in 2018 as the leader of our meeting on the theme of connections between jazz and architecture.

Very special thanks to Gudrun Geest and Geest Digital-Perspektiven for the "Morphing Grid" animation project we completed in 2015. Thanks also to the members of ArchitekturSalon in Hamburg, Germany, who graciously hosted my jazz-architecture lecture in 2015.

Special thanks to the following people who have been especially helpful, gener-ous, and/or supportive throughout this project and/or throughout my career in general, in ways too numerous to detail here: Gage Averill, Ellen Rosand, Gary Tomlinson, Robert O'Meally, Guthrie Ramsey, Hazel Carby, Manthia Diawara,

George Lewis, Paul Gilroy, Farah Jasmine Griffin, Jay Hoggard, Ingrid Monson, Bennett Paster, Kay Kaufman Shelemay, Robert Farris Thompson, Bob Belden, Eisenman Architects, Chris Becker, Aaron Cohen, Carolyn Cooper, Jack and Lydia DeJohnette, Detlef Diedrichsen and the staff at Haus der Kulturen der Welt, Michael Denning, Justin Faye, Jacqueline Goldsby, Sumanth Gopinath, Drew Greis, Zaha Hadid Architects, Daniel Harrison, Amy Hungerford, Arthur Jafa, Gerald Jaynes, John Klaess, Emily Laber, Steve Lantner, Lewis LoCicero, Kathryn Lofton, Sally Mann, Portia Maultsby, Marcus Miller, Anja Nitz, Alondra Nelson, Mrs. Alaknanda Patel, Rehana Patel, Eve Poudrier, Andrea Ray, Spencer Richards, Petra Richterova, Wayne and Carolina Shorter, Barbara Shailor, Mark Slobin, Robert Steptoe, Parker Smathers, the Estate of Louis Stettner, John Szwed, Tichy Ocean Foundation, Olakunle Tejuoso, McCoy Tyner, Danilo Udovicki, DvM, Avraham Wachmann, Chris Washburne, Deborah Wilson, Ken Wissoker, and Craig Wright. My sincerest apologies if I have left anyone out.

This book is dedicated to the memories of Greg Tate (1957–2021), Lawrence "Butch" Morris (1947–2013), and Robert Farris Thompson (1932–2021), three paradigm-shifting super-spirits who cleared the path that I and so many others continue to tread and who heightened the sky in which I and so many others continue to try to fly.

Living Space

INTRODUCTION
Through the Looking Glass

Babel-17. It's being automatically transcribed so I can study it later . . .
I prerecorded some messages and I'm sending them out now.
Maybe they'll get through.[1]

Samuel Delany

In the spring of 1959, Miles Davis assembled a group of musicians at Columbia Recording Studios in New York City to record *Kind of Blue*, the album that would become the biggest-selling and most celebrated album of his long career. On hand with him for the series of recording dates was a lineup of modern jazz luminaries—alto saxophonist Julian "Cannonball" Adderley, tenor saxophonist John Coltrane, pianists Bill Evans and Wynton Kelly, bassist Paul Chambers, and drummer Jimmy Cobb. Even though *Kind of Blue* was essentially a fairly skeletal collection of hard-bop vignettes, those vignettes were subtly shaded with Impressionist harmonies, non-Western music, gospel, and blues, and it was this unique palette that enabled it to become one of the most heralded works of recorded American music. In particular, the album stands as a high point of the collaboration between Davis and John Coltrane.

The achievement represented by *Kind of Blue* has been chronicled numerous times, most notably in books by Ashley Kahn, Eric Nisenson, and Farah Jasmine Griffin and Salim Washington.[2] This book can be seen as following two distinct but interwoven trajectories out of that storied moment. From the point that Coltrane and Davis parted ways in 1960, they would follow radically different paths, and as the decade progressed, both of these paths would reshape jazz irrevocably. Coltrane's odyssey through what became known as "free jazz," which began around 1965, brought stylistic (r)evolution and chaos in equal measure. Miles's spearheading of "jazz-rock fusion," which began in earnest in 1968, opened a door through which jazz's ongoing dialogue with the popular tradition could be regenerated, engaging both high and low ideas of creativity, community, and commerce. Born of a particularly turbulent episode in American history, however, the music of Coltrane from 1964 to 1967 and of Miles's "Lost Quintet" during 1968 and 1969 has been by turns demonized, dismissed, deemphasized, or just plain misunderstood. And while there are several reasons for this (some of which I will discuss below), their creativity undeniably reflected, on one hand, a new, Space Age understanding of the human, and on the other, an era of challenge to prevailing social, political, and cultural norms, a period that has been discredited during fifty subsequent years of an America that has swung politically to the right. The observations I offer in this book are, in a way, acknowledgments, invocations, and affirmations of the utopian imaginings that shaped and powered their art during this period, and in fact the term "utopia" turns up frequently throughout this book, used to provide context uniting constructions of rhythm with visions of society.

MULTIPLE JUPITERS

When things break down, they tend to do so spectacularly. I don't just mean that bridges fall down, that ships sink, that cities are leveled by earthquakes. I mean that we may be left with stunningly rich patterns, sometimes on an awesome scale.[3]

Philip Ball, from The Self-Made Tapestry

It always kills me how people say John lost his mind after 1964. When they get freaked out by the exterior elements, they're missing a vast inner detail.[4]

Ravi Coltrane

When John Coltrane recorded his landmark album *Ascension* in the summer of 1965, the title perfectly evoked the later phase of his career, devoted as it was to one of the most intense and concentrated spells of stylistic evolution in the history of jazz. Within a two-year time span beginning in mid-1965, Coltrane and his musicians traversed the nether regions of jazz improvisation with the force and velocity of a rocket—deconstructing, and ultimately reconstructing, the structural conventions upon which jazz performance had rested for more than half a century. On albums like *Ascension* (1965), *Sun Ship* (1965), and *Om* (1966), the mechanics of modern jazz were melted down into a cauldron of marathon-length collective improvisation, often rendered at an extreme of emotional intensity, using a concept of melody based as much in a language of screams, cries, growls, and abstract pitch formulae as it was in any traditional concept of melody, with the entire band seeming to float in a turbulent rhythmic space, unmoored from an underlying beat that would unify the ensemble.

Coltrane was in fact distilling a radically new jazz language, but this understanding of his later music as an act of distillation has by no means been shared by all jazz musicians, listeners, or scholars. At the time of his passing in July 1967, the prevailing opinion was that *Coltrane himself* had deconstructed, losing his bearings due to his increasingly avant-gardist predilections that led first to the dissolution of his "Classic Quartet" in late 1965, followed by a year and a half of musical confusion with his second quintet. Sometimes, the narrative is more benevolently worded along the lines that Coltrane "died in the midst of yet another provocative chapter within his endless musical quest." Regardless of the wording, the sentiments are consistent: Coltrane was the unquestioned saxophone virtuoso of his generation, but his final music left even many of his most ardent supporters puzzled.[5] Even Lewis Porter, whose 1998 biography *John Coltrane: His Life and Music* is generally considered the authoritative and most sympathetically written account, depicts Coltrane of this period as "confused about his musical direction."[6] Meanwhile, the recordings from this period issued during Coltrane's lifetime—including *Ascension*, *Om*, and *Live at the Village Vanguard Again*—are considered among the most controversial and inscrutable jazz recordings of the 1960s. By most accounts, then, the final two years of Coltrane's life are considered to sound a bizarre footnote to an otherwise towering and unassailable musical contribution. Like the encrypted codes described by sci-fi writer Samuel Delany in the epigraph that opened this introduction, Coltrane's late works generally continue to float like a space capsule above the normative reasoning of jazz, awaiting their decoding within—or beyond—that musical territory.

———

Given that it refers to a mere two-year interval in his career, the term "late-period John Coltrane" can be partially understood as a rhetorical contrivance that demonstrates just how much virtual media (such as sound recording) and the language of commerce can influence our perception of time and history. Had Coltrane lived longer, these two years might have seemed a mere blip on his career timeline. Given that it immediately preceded his passing, however, the music created during those two years has come to bear the weight of a final, career-summarizing statement. Furthermore, Coltrane's aesthetic choices and changes in band personnel in this period do, taken as a whole, comprise a distinct stylistic phase in his musical evolution.

A good deal of the confusion surrounding this period of Coltrane's work stems from the delayed availability of many of his later recordings. The saxophonist was in the recording studio fairly frequently between early 1965 and early 1967, but several of the most musically revealing recordings were not made available until after his passing. The recordings documenting the final, transformative months of the original Coltrane quartet in the spring and summer of 1965, for example (including, but not limited to *Transition*, *Sun Ship*, and *First Meditations*), were not released until 1970, 1971, and 1977, respectively. Of the studio recordings he made with his final band during the first half of 1967, none had been made commercially available at the time of his death. *Expression* was recorded in February of that year and released a few months after his passing. *Interstellar Space* was recorded the same month, but released seven years later in 1974. *Stellar Regions* was also recorded in February 1967, but not released until 1995. Even today, at the time of writing, there are apparently other studio sessions from 1966 and 1967 that remain unreleased.[7]

There are three main reasons that it has taken such a long time for this material to reach the listening public. First, Coltrane's frequent recording sessions during this period exceeded the market demand, resulting in a substantial backlog of unreleased material. Second, the saxophonist probably viewed at least some of these sessions as experiments more than as finished, release-ready works (this might be a reason why, as his productivity accelerated during mid-1965, a number of pieces remained either untitled or generically titled).[8] Third, Coltrane's posthumous affairs were handled by his widow Alice, and her schedule of staggered releases suggests a deliberate strategy to maximize the Coltrane estate's income over the long term. The strategy was well executed in commercial terms, but it also obscured the details of her husband's musical evolution, given that crucial developmental stages went unheard by so many for so long.

It is not surprising that an artist of Coltrane's creative energy would record more than his record company was able to release in the short term. But this delay in releasing his recordings profoundly affected the reception of his music during his lifetime. Since few listeners were privy to the developmental stages in his later music, concert audiences of his time were often forced to confront radically unfamiliar sounds without the preparation of prior, graduated exposure via commercial recordings. The extant anecdotes of hostile audiences, disgruntled club owners, and disillusioned reviewers might seem petty and small-minded in light of Coltrane's now-canonical status. But they are understandable in the context of his times, when we consider (for example) the staggering stylistic distance traveled between his commercially successful 1961 cover of Rodgers and Hammerstein's "My Favorite Things" and his radical remodelings of the same tune that were released on later live albums like *Live at the Village Vanguard Again* (recorded in 1966) or *The Olatunji Concert* (recorded in 1967). That distance, which rendered the original barely recognizable, might be compared to a highly literary romance novel subsequently reconceived as a work of experimental science fiction, and it's doubtful that *any* audience in any genre or tradition would have been easily able to reconcile such aesthetic extremes.

What remains unclear, through all of the attempts to unravel this complex music, is how Coltrane himself conceptualized his stylistic decisions. Like his former employer Miles Davis, Coltrane was not a musician given to extensive verbal explications of his music (this is one reason that collectors have treasured every fragmentary snippet of Coltrane's North Carolina drawl or Miles's reptilian rasp preserved as studio chatter). Similar to Miles, he preferred to choose the musicians best suited for the tasks at hand, give them vague, schematic instructions, and let the solutions to various musical problems be worked out intuitively, in the act of performance. For whatever reasons, none of the main musicians involved in Coltrane's final phase—including saxophonist Pharoah Sanders, pianists McCoy Tyner and Alice Coltrane, bassist Jimmy Garrison, and drummers Elvin Jones and Rashied Ali—ever went on record with any extensive discussion of the mechanics of Coltrane's later music.

The unsurprising result of this cumulative silence has been that the reception history of Coltrane's later music has remained cloudy, convoluted, and contentious, with opinions often strongly polarized and polemically voiced. Those who advocate for his work up until mid-1965 are typically hostile to or dismissive of his post-1965 music, while those who advocate for his post-1965 music are often indifferent to his earlier music. This has had consequences for the overall understanding of his music; the rigorously achieved concepts embedded within his later music have not been nearly as well articulated as those associated with his earlier music, such as the "Coltrane system of chord substitutions," the "sheets of sound" approach to saxophone improvisation, the modal approach to jazz harmony, and others.

One goal of this book is to render the concepts in Coltrane's later music a bit more transparent, albeit in a way that is as poetic and evocative as it is starkly analytical. In the absence of clearly articulated musical explanations, a number of speculative interpretations about the motivations behind Coltrane's late work have been advanced, all of which are relevant, to one degree or another, to the content of his late music. These tend to center on the racial and political situation in the United States in the 1960s, on Coltrane's alleged experimentation with psychedelic drugs in the last years of his life, on his interest in non-Western forms of music and spirituality (particularly, those of South Asia and West Africa), and on the state of his health. "Living Space," the first of two extended essays in this book, takes its title from a 1965 piece by Coltrane, synthesizing the above perspectives and others into a narrative that presents Coltrane's late music as a logical and organic extension of his earlier work—however fevered in its exploration—and a visceral reflection of the times in which it was conceived. The keyboardist, composer, and bandleader Sun Ra (1914–1993) factors into this essay as an important influence shadowing Coltrane's musical evolution during the period.

———

My own interest in Coltrane's music began to consolidate around 1984, when my college buddy (and pianist) Steve Lantner gave me a cassette of the live version of the saxophonist's *A Love Supreme* suite, recorded in France during the summer of 1965 (Steve also introduced me to later Coltrane works such as *Interstellar Space* and *Expression*). The same year, another college buddy (and tenor saxophonist) named Mike Hamilton had shocked me by singing Coltrane's entire twenty-seven-minute solo, note for note, from the famous version of "One Down, One Up" recorded at the Half Note in New York City the same year (Mike told me he had memorized the solo by listening to it every night as he fell asleep). In the following years, I immersed myself more deeply in Coltrane's music which, among other things, ultimately inspired me to begin playing the soprano saxophone. But what I consider to be a fuller understanding of his later music really consolidated a quarter-century later, while I was living in Berlin during the summer of 2009, and I bought a vinyl copy of the 1978 compilation *The Mastery of John Coltrane, Volume 3: Jupiter Variation*.[9] This record, which documents music Coltrane recorded during the last seven months of his life, was one I had seen numerous times over the years but for one reason or another had neglected to buy. Nevertheless, I had always been intrigued by the title *Jupiter Variation*—did it mean that Coltrane was somehow imagining multiple Jupiters as a theme for some sci-fi take on free jazz? Was the planet being "versioned" into multiplicity like a piece of Jamaican dub music? Or was it being serially repeated and refracted through different color lenses or screens, like a Warhol print? I eventually realized that the titling was actually much more prosaic, merely referring to an alternate take of Coltrane's 1967 piece "Jupiter." But the particular track that caught my ear that day in Berlin was the equally prosaically titled "Number One" (recorded in March 1967), which can be heard as a revisiting of a piece Coltrane had recorded in August 1965 called "Sun Ship"—at least from the standpoint of a core motif that is central to both improvisations. From the first seconds, I was captivated by the ensemble's graceful flow, the rhythm section of pianist Alice Coltrane, bassist Jimmy Garrison, and drummer Rashied Ali shadowing every move of Coltrane's pan-tonal improvisation as they navigated their way through the curves and contours of metrically free space. More than any piece of late Coltrane I had heard to this point, "Number One" made a convincing argument that the saxophonist had successfully consolidated the new direction that seemed to erupt so suddenly in the summer of 1965. It was this piece that inspired me to hear his last months, at their moments of greatest clarity, as a concretization of the initial breakthroughs of that summer, and to connect the dots backward through the previous eighteen months of musical evolution. Late Coltrane recordings like "Number One" have inspired me to argue that the shift in his music was actually the final phase of a deliberate, purposeful, and accelerated—if sometimes inscrutable—trajectory that (for the purposes of my own argument) began with the influential 1959 composition "Giant Steps" (the harmonic ideas of which, I argue, eventually had profound rhythmic consequences). It continued through his work in the modal jazz idiom, and culminated in his final work in the free jazz idiom. This idea in turn makes a more fundamental assertion regarding how we understand so-called free jazz within the evolution of Coltrane's music, within the broader historical scope of jazz history, and within the history of Afro-diasporic music and culture.

It is in this light that I use the image of "Multiple Jupiters" to evoke the cultural and cosmological visions embedded in this music. On one hand, it is a heavily textured sound of abstracted drone-based sonorities derived equally from the African American sacred tradition and South Asian classical traditions. It is powered by extraordinarily complex pitch equations deployed as mediums of mathematical contemplation and cosmological reflection. It unfolds in time atop equally complex equations of Africanist drumming that radically expand the concept of meter in order to beat back the legacy of American slavery by asserting the drum as a sonic-psychic anchor of Afro-diasporic, historical consciousness. The issue of "free meter"—music played without reference to an underlying beat—is central to both extended essays and one of the core themes of this book.

LOST IN SPACE

We went out and out, beyond the Rim until the Sun was just a bright star behind—then even not particularly bright. We were braking, on the point of turning back . . . And then we saw the first reef . . .[10]

Frederik Pohl and Jack Williamson

I hope this material becomes available now, with all the technology and people bootlegging and so forth. And I hope that people will try to locate these recordings and listen to them with fresh ears and maybe find some gems in it that they didn't know existed.[11]

Jack DeJohnette

Miles Davis began his own dramatic musical transition a year after Coltrane's passing. The Lost Quintet—sometimes also referred to as the "Third Miles Davis Quintet"—was the last of the stable jazz quintets assembled by Miles during the 1960s. This band, which existed for a year and a half from early 1968 to late 1969, included Miles on trumpet, Wayne Shorter on tenor and soprano saxophones, Chick Corea on electric piano, David Holland on acoustic and electric basses, and Jack DeJohnette on drums. Dubbed the "Lost Quintet" in a 1989 article by Peter Keepnews, it was so described because, although it formed the core of the expanded ensemble Miles assembled to record the landmark 1970 album *Bitches Brew*, it never recorded a formal studio album as a quintet.[12] The only existing recorded documents of the band are a batch of live recordings of varying provenance and even more varied sonic fidelity, the best known of which were recorded during two European concert tours in 1969. Given that the band's existence was relatively brief, its notoriety is largely based on these recorded documents.[13] The challenge in writing their story lies partly in the analysis of musical structure, but equally in the necessity of decoding a musical archive that has been scattered among lo-fi audience recordings and captured radio broadcasts of equally low fidelity.

The first time I heard the Lost Quintet was sometime during the early 1980s, on a cassette tape given to me by another one of my college music buddies, the bassist Michael Rivard.[14] The tape was simply labeled "Holland 69" (the precise location was the De Doelen concert hall in Rotterdam, Netherlands, on November 5, 1969). I was fascinated right away but, as in the case of Coltrane's late music, it took years—decades, even—for me to digest this music. My impressions at the time were of a very dense, abstract music that, while clearly inspired by the rock and funk of the late sixties, actually sounded closer to free jazz than anything I had previously associated with Miles Davis. In some ways, in fact, it was surprisingly similar to some of the later music of John Coltrane. The music spun by in a dizzying tapestry of obliquely rendered themes and morphing moods, with brief passages of abstracted swing and funk rhythms bracketing extended passages of impassioned free-meter playing. The band's sound was dense and its performance style intense, drawing on traditional modes of jazz virtuosity, the extended playing techniques of the jazz avant-garde, and, in the case of electric pianist Chick Corea, a limited use of electronics. This is by no means to assert Miles as a leader of the jazz avant-garde but rather to use the Lost Quintet as a way of positioning him more accurately in relationship to a movement about which he had expressed so much disdain and dismissal.[15]

It was difficult to find much information about this group at the time, but a somewhat clearer picture began to emerge for me around the time that Keepnews's essay was first published, as semi-authorized recordings of their performances began to turn up on the commercial market in the US. Keepnews's article was the first to give the Lost Quintet a clearly defined identity within Miles's body of work and was apparently the first time this unit had been written about since the glowing reviews of their performances twenty years earlier.[16] Despite the strong impression this band made on both audiences and musicians in its day, however, most of the subsequent writings on Miles give the Lost Quintet, at most, passing mention. To date, it hasn't made its way into jazz history textbooks, or even the typical college course devoted to Miles Davis. Even more strikingly, it has been only fleetingly mentioned in the full-length biographies of the trumpeter, including those specifically devoted to Miles's electric period, such as Paul Tingen's *Miles Beyond* (2001),[17] Philip Freeman's *Running the Voodoo Down* (2005),[18] Victor Svorinich's *Listen to This* (2006), and George Grella's *Bitches Brew* (2015).[19] I don't intend, in any way, to demean the works of the above authors, all of which are excellent pieces of research and writing. I simply mean to call attention to the way that this band, appraised by so many listeners as the equal (and direct extension) of Miles's previous and legendary quintets, has continued to haunt the history of Miles Davis and of modern jazz in general as a phantom. The reason for this is clear, however. Jazz history is generally constructed around sound recordings, and the so-named "Lost" Quintet never recorded a formal studio album around which any kind of history could be written. In any case, this lacuna was finally addressed in 2017 with the publication of Bob Gluck's *The Miles Davis Lost Quintet and Other Revolutionary Ensembles*, a preliminary attempt to document the band's brief existence and one in which, similar to this book, discussion of the Lost Quintet comprises *part* of a book as opposed to an entire book. In this book, the issue of "unofficial" sound recordings, with all of their attendant sonic anomalies, is central to the extended essay on Miles Davis and, to a lesser extent, the essay on John Coltrane.

The writing of history is as much an act of interpretation as it is one of documentation, and, as such, older histories will always and inevitably beget newer histories—especially in the case of a complex and iconic figure such as Miles Davis. As such, there will probably be no shortage of Miles-related biographies, analyses, and interpretations for the foreseeable future. Nonetheless, all of these brief, partial narratives raise the question of whether the one-and-a-half-year existence of the Lost Quintet, like the final two years of Coltrane's career, really warrants more extensive treatment than it has been given to date. Is isolating the third quintet as a discrete period of Miles's music an organic way of understanding what was, in reality, a very fluid period in his career? I would argue that it is because, as the last of his ensembles that conformed to the standard quintet format of modern jazz, the Lost Quintet allows us to clarify a pivotal moment in the evolution of Miles and of modern jazz. The very quintet concept, in fact, allows us to trace his musical trajectory backward into the mainstream jazz and first-generation avant-garde of the 1960s while allowing us to simultaneously understand the way it functioned as a laboratory for the second-generation jazz avant-garde, jazz-rock fusion, and the concept albums of the 1970s. It is this fertile period, stretching from Miles's albums *Filles de Kilimanjaro* (1968) to *Bitches Brew* (1970), that is the topic of this book's second extended essay, "Electricity Was Just Another Color." And similar to Sun Ra's influence on John Coltrane's later music, the blues-rock guitarist Jimi Hendrix (1942–1970) emerges as a critically important shadow influence on Miles's music during this period.

As an image, "Just Another Color" is particularly meant to evoke the Fender

Rhodes electric piano as the defining sonority of the Lost Quintet and to high-light the way Miles's adoption of this instrument facilitated both continuity and transformation within his late-1960s music. It is also my own way of simultane-ously acknowledging and transcending some of the well-worn debates in the conversations around his music. The Fender Rhodes is often stereotyped as a sixties/seventies jazz instrument that symbolized the birth of jazz-rock fusion. In reality, it was a keyboard instrument of the Space Age on which the entire history of jazz pianism could be reimagined. Framing the discussion around this instru-ment helps expand the frame of reference in several directions, transcending the tired, dichotomized debates about "free versus straight-ahead," "free versus fusion," or "fusion versus straight-ahead," and so on.

This dichotomy of funk and freedom is central to the narrative of the Lost Quintet. The *Bitches Brew* album, recorded in August 1969 and released to great fanfare and controversy in March 1970, ultimately demonstrates that the quintet was in fact not entirely "lost" since Shorter, Corea, Holland, and DeJohnette formed the core of the expanded ensemble that recorded that album. The Miles essay in this book could easily have been constructed around the canonical *Bitches Brew*, but I chose to orient it around the Lost Quintet's eighteen months as a live performing unit. Not only does this help clarify Miles's relationship with both jazz-rock fusion and the jazz avant-garde, but it also chronicles a moment in the late 1960s and early 1970s when the mainstream, avant-garde, and fusion camps were in potent and productive dialogue with each other, as well as a mo-ment when Miles was successfully adapting his previous role as a black culture hero to this transformative era in the music.

―――――

"Living Space" and "Electricity Was Just Another Color" are the core chapters of this book, extended essays that unfold as chronological narratives concerned with the evolution of musical style, and interpolated with biographical, socio-contextual, historical, and intermedial artistic perspectives. These chapters will likely be of most interest to jazz scholars, jazz musicians, music scholars, and aficionados of Coltrane and Miles. At its core, however, the book as a whole is shaped around two dominant sonic themes. The first is the music-analytical issue of how the music of Miles and especially Coltrane can help us understand the mechanics of the type of jazz played without reference to an underlying metric pulse. Throughout the book I generally use the terms "free meter" and "metrically free" interchangeably to refer to this rhythmic sensibility, and, given the book's emphasis on rhythm, I pay particular attention to drummers and drumming. The second theme is a consideration of how the recorded archives of Coltrane and especially Miles—with all of their sonic anomalies—can help articulate the issue of free meter, as well as how they can inspire us to reconsider the sonic terms upon which we understand the jazz recording. In this light, I would also suggest that these chapters serve as de facto listening companions, relying on sonic description and various visual metaphors drawn from other artistic mediums to open up new ways of listening to these complex musics.

JAZZ IN AND OUT OF TIME (AND SPACE)

> I don't think you always have to play in time . . . There's a way
> of playing where you can play with no time . . . That's what I feel is
> *heaven*, being able to be that free, spiritual, musical.[20]
>
> *Sonny Rollins*

Free meter. Rubato. The feeling of floating in musical time, untethered from an underlying beat. The move into metrically free playing was one of the most dramatic and transformative developments of 1960s jazz, although its roots run deeply throughout African and Afro-diasporic cultural history. But the general lack of a shared or standardized language with which to discuss this type of music, plus the physical discomfort it sometimes creates in listeners accustomed to metered music, have been among the main obstacles to the understanding and appreciation of the new jazz-based structures of the 1960s and 1970s. Jazz musicians have had their various ways of discussing this trait, several of which I cite in this book. A number of ethnomusicologists have also grappled with the issue of free meter, including Richard Widdess (in relation to the free-meter *alap* in Indian classical music)[21] and a more comprehensive, cross-cultural overview by Martin Clayton.[22] Meanwhile, several music theorists have addressed this concept specifically in relation to jazz (they typically refer to it as "non-isochronous meter"), including scholars such as Fernando Benadon (2009)[23] and Richard Ashley (2002).[24] While I cite some of these ideas at various point in this text, I have also drawn on the language and imagery of architecture to help articulate my observations.

Why architecture? The discourse of architecture serves several purposes throughout this book. Most immediately, it has helped me develop a way of thinking through the issue of free meter in jazz. A number of architects, in fact, have suggested that it is through a discourse of *rhythm* that fields of music and architecture can be brought closest to each other. Recent works by authors such as Eric Goldemberg (2011)[25] and Karen Franck (2016)[26] have asserted *rhythm* and *time* as central parameters of architectural experience. Architecture's morphological (shape), topological (surface), and spatial imagery also provides a vivid, visceral set of descriptive analogies that can be used to discuss musical structures, while the discourse of space(s) in particular ultimately allows my musical observations to open out onto society. If the artist Romare Bearden once wrote, "Spatial structures are the architecture for describing the visible world," I am asserting spatial thinking in this book as an equally potent descriptor of the audible world.[27]

As Hal Foster has written, architecture has moved over the course of several decades from a field of interest to only practitioners and theorists, to a field that now interfaces with other fields, practices, and discourses and that even substantially interfaces with contemporary popular culture.[28] And this has provided a context for my own attempts to create a more specific interface between architecture and jazz. In the broadest picture, in fact, this book peripherally reflects the "spatial turn" in the humanities (inspired by the work of theorists/ philosophers such as Michel de Certeau, Gaston Bachelard, and Henri Lefebvre) and the different ways that the discourse of space has manifested in humanistic scholarship.[29]

I often tell my students that there are two ways an artistic language can evolve. The first way is that it is extended internally, according to its own established rules and procedures. The second way is that it is extended externally, forced to operate according to the rules of a different artistic medium—for example, poetry reconceived as music, literature reconceived as painting, etc. The same point can be made about musical analysis, and in this book I have tried to draw from modes of thinking both native and foreign to jazz and to music in general. It would be highly impractical for me to try to articulate my insights without using standard musical terminology and ways of talking about rhythm that have been developed by musicians and music scholars. But the language and concepts associated with architecture have also helped me illustrate musical ideas that might not necessarily find easy expression through the traditional language(s) of music.

In the introduction to his 1995 book *Studies in Tectonic Culture*, the architect/ architectural historian Kenneth Frampton presents the practice of architecture as having been alternately understood in different periods as *the act of building* and/or *the act of articulating space.*[30] Both of these interrelated understandings of architecture have furnished valuable insights for this book's focus on jazz rhythm and rhythmic structures. Frampton's understanding of architecture as *the act of building* helps articulate jazz rhythm and structure (i.e., the interrelationship of ensemble parts) via a sensibility of *design* and *construction* that I ultimately root in Africanist aesthetics and practices—aesthetics and practices that have been at times radically transformed in the African diaspora in general and the United States in particular. Meanwhile, Frampton's understanding of architecture *as a manipulation of space* helps depict the way these rhythmic designs can in turn be used (in conjunction with other musical parameters) to articulate social space. Throughout this book, I alternate between these understandings of architecture to support and/or illuminate my various micro- and macro-musical observations and analyses.

Beyond Frampton's basic binary, there are actually a number of ways that architecture and its subthemes of spaces, shapes, and surfaces can be "conjugated" to generate different modes of musical insight. It can be used morphologically, to suggest similarities in forms and structures between the two mediums. It can be used acoustically, to narrate the sonic characteristics of different physical spaces, and musicians' ways of sonically negotiating those spaces through their arrangement of sounds (i.e., "playing the room"). It can be used socioculturally, to delineate the different social and cultural "spaces" within which music derives its meaning. It can be used metaphorically, such as when literary figures like Wilson Harris and Nathaniel Mackey assert the structures of Haitian *vodun* music (Harris) or the low register ostinati of many forms of black dance music (Mackey) as *cathedrals* within which radical and exalted forms of cultural, political, and spiritual consciousness thrive.[31] Finally, it can be used conceptually, to provide a geometric abstraction of musical operations in the manner of music theorists such as Richard Cohn, Dmitri Tymozcko, and Godfried Touissant.[32] Viewed from one perspective, in fact, my way of thinking is not so different from the geometrically driven work of theorists like Cohn and Tymozcko. In the end, however, I felt that the humanly habitable geometries of architecture opened out onto society more directly than the cerebral shapes, spaces, and surfaces of geometrically driven music theory. This ultimately made it easier for me to bring micromusical concerns of structure into dialogue with macromusical concerns of politics and society. And ultimately, as an ethnomusicologist who understands musical sound and society as mutually constitutive, this was the most compelling line of interpretation for my own project. This theme of jazz and architecture is explored in more detail in chapter 1, "Space, Shape, Surface, and the Urban as Modes of Jazz Consciousness," a chapter that will likely be of most relevance to readers interested in intermedial thinking as a way of articulating musical concepts.

Chapter 2 ("Curvilinearity, Swing, and the Spline") fuses rhythmic and architectural thinking to introduce the concept of the "Africanist Grid," a model I invoke throughout this book as a way of focusing the idea of a rhythm pattern as being something *assembled* or *constructed*, while providing historical and cultural context for a particular way of assembling and manipulating musical sounds that is rooted in West Africa and prevalent across the Black Atlantic cultural sphere. The discussion of the African roots of jazz has been fraught territory, typically ebbing and flowing in accordance with the level of anti-black racism in the United States, African American sentiments about Africa, Euro-American ignorance of/indifference to Africa, and Africa's status in the world at large. This has had profound consequences for jazz theory. The truth is that the cultural reference points for jazz do not only lie within Europe. They lie equally in West Africa, but the African reference points have been obscured in the United States for two main reasons. First and most obvious is the history of slavery and its resolute attempt to destroy any and all traces of African cultural practices. In the end, the plantocracy didn't succeed in eradicating the African element; they only succeeded in destroying its explicit cultural referents. The second is the reality that many of the African source practices were uncodified in Africa itself (at least in written form) and without literate traditions of music theory and music history, it was very difficult for them to survive the Middle Passage in any explicitly articulated form. This left the African element to roam American culture as what I call a "conceptual stealth element," powerfully Africanizing American cultural forms—across racial categories—while divorced from identifiable ancestral source cultures such as Wolof, Yoruba, Ewe, Mandinka, etc. What this means in relation to the history and analysis of jazz is that, aside from generically identifiable Africanist traits, it is very difficult to articulate the music's African-derived concepts with the cultural specificity of the European-derived elements.

But in keeping with my own political/cultural belief that African Americans will never be properly oriented within the world until we cultivate an informed understanding of our African cultural roots, I am asserting the Africanist component here as central to an accurate understanding of jazz as a sonic and philosophical system. And that is because jazz itself will never be properly understood until its African component has been properly elucidated beyond the stereotypical narratives of blue notes, pentatonicism, and rhythmic vitality. And if the goal is to counteract the Eurocentric bias in an analytical understanding of the music, this can also be accomplished without subsuming Afro-diasporic history into African "master race" narratives. It is simply a matter of understanding the Black Atlantic cultural sphere as an ongoing musical/cultural conversation.[33] After all, African musical traditions would themselves undergo numerous and profound transformations during the nineteenth and twentieth centuries as a result of their encounter with Afro-diasporic musical traditions. The "Curvilinearity" chapter will interest readers who desire to understand (and analyze) jazz within the constellation of Black Atlantic musics. And ultimately, this book's rhythmic discourse is projected through the architectural sensibility of design and expanded to the scale of the utopian visions of Civil Rights and decolonization, inspiring us to understand rhythm as a powerful medium of world making.

JAZZ IN AND OUT OF FOCUS

I could only understand it as irrational and devoid of meaning,
and so I walked away from it, confused and titillated.[34]

Rosa Menkman

The only resolution to the problem of noncommunication
was to incorporate it within the system.[35]

Friedrich Kittler

If this book's "spatial" discourse ultimately services my sonic-analytical thinking in the sphere of rhythm, the third chapter (" 'We No Longer Consider Them Damaged' ") is in dialogue with the discourse around photography, in order to service sonic-analytical thinking from a different angle. A substantial body of literature already exists surveying photographic traces of jazz—portraits, album covers, significant locales, etc. But my interest lies more in photography as an analogue to sound recording, a parallel virtualizing technology with its attendant aesthetic anomalies and conceptual issues. The third chapter explores these anomalies in relation to what I refer to throughout this book as the "alter-archives" of jazz—the network of unofficial recordings that are sometimes sold commercially as so-called bootlegs and that in other instances circulate through unofficial channels such as tape-trading networks and internet blog sites. While usually illegal, both informally and commercially circulated versions of recorded jazz have periodically been able to flourish—more easily, in a sense, than unauthorized recordings of more lucrative forms of popular music. This is because jazz bootlegs exploit a sphere of the music industry that is not particularly lucrative and in which the financial stakes (and consequently, surveillance by the music industry) are correspondingly low.

The significance of these unofficial recordings to jazz should not be surprising. As the rock historian Clinton Heylin noted in his history of bootlegs, "Jazz buffs . . . tended to prize live performances over and above recordings achieved in a studio. As a music founded on improvisation, each jazz performance was intrinsically unique . . . Jazz was an obvious medium for someone smitten with the bootleg mentality."[36] In taking us along the same conceptual corridors mapped out by alternate takes, deleted film scenes, artists' sketchbooks, or authors' drafts, these recordings allow us to piece together a more complete evolutionary narrative of an art form that is by definition in perpetual flux. The truth is that all of these sound recordings have played a crucial, if unacknowledged role in constructions of jazz knowledge and jazz history. More importantly, many significant recordings of John Coltrane, and especially of Miles Davis's Lost Quintet, have only been available through these unofficial channels, and this book would have been inconceivable without them.

Central to my own narrative, however, is the fact that many of these recordings are of low fidelity and as such, only of interest to the most committed fans, musicians, collectors and scholars. As "ruins" of both the industrial documentation and social circulation of music, the mixed bag of information they present has ensured their consignment to a status of secondary, inferior, flawed, and unsalable documents for all but the most avid devotees, and their value has been ambiguous within a jazz tradition that is strongly shaped by sound recordings and that places so much value on the ostensibly "accurate" depiction of musical events. The question then becomes to what extent these recordings—marred by analog distortion, digital glitches, and radio signal interference—can be recuperated and made productive for the purpose of analysis, history, interpretation, or even pleasurable listening. Or, as Eliot Bates writes, "What are the implications of the musical work when we consider machine-additions, the inevitable degeneration or playback malfunction, along with environmental interpretations?"[37] Initially I had no choice but to deal with such recordings and the issues they raised, due to the value of their musical content. Over time, however, my attitude changed, and my immersion gradually became less a matter of force and more a matter of choice as I began to develop a feel for the hidden potentials of these recordings.

My discussion here is underpinned by the work of scholars such as Bates and David Novak, who have discussed distortion and "glitch" phenomena in relation to various musical practices and traditions.[38] Bates defines "glitch" broadly as *sonic phenomena resulting from malfunctions in music playback technology*.[39] "As individual copies increasingly degrade," he writes, "what we end up with are skips, pops, and glitches that express not the voice of the composer, but rather the voice of the technology itself."[40]

Like most musicians of my own generation, which might be called the "cassette generation," my life's musical soundscape has been intimately shaped by these recordings, which have often circulated through various trading networks that evolved around the easy portability of the audiocassette. These are networks devoted not only to recordings of live jazz performances, but also (to use examples of trading cultures I have been a part of over the years) to hip-hop tapes made at parties and from radio broadcasts around New York City in the 1970s and 1980s, tapes made at Jamaican sound-system dances, the tape-trading culture of the Grateful Dead, cheaply reproduced commercial cassettes obtained in foreign lands, and ethnomusicological field recordings from various parts of the world. In the context of increasing standardization and centralization in the music industry, bootlegs and traded tapes acquired a very seductive outlaw character, and it was the audiocassette's ease of reproduction and portability that led to the explosion of music trading that in turn laid the foundation for the digital age culture of file sharing.[41] This same convenience led to the formation of new and intersectional communities of taste. In this light, it is worth noting that I obtained my own earliest recordings of Miles Davis's Lost Quintet not through the jazz network, but from collectors in other networks who happened to have some jazz in their collections.[42]

The deeper I ventured into this project, in fact, the more I realized that the ears I bring are even more generationally coded than what is signified by cassette culture. This is to say that any electric guitarist, bassist, or keyboardist who came of age between the 1970s and 1990s will remember the way the soundscape of those decades was textured by commercially produced distortion devices such as Electro-Harmonix's Big Muff, Dallas-Arbiter's Fuzz Face, Univox's Super Fuzz, ProCo's RAT, and others. Similarly, anyone present during the early days of hip-hop will remember how the skips and scratches of distressed vinyl record surfaces sampled by artists and producers were gradually embraced as part of the genre's sonic identity. Finally, the emergence of "glitch" culture in the 1990s and its take on the variable sonic fidelities of both analog and digital media opened a portal for a new mode of listening to sound recordings. David Novak has used the term "remediation" to discuss the ways that the same information manifests across successive modes of technology.[43] And if, as Novak asserts, the cross-media circulation of sound recordings has opened up new channels for experimental listening, it has also opened new opportunities for musical analysis. Today, smart phones are fitted with filter apps that give digital photographs the low-resolution appearance of earlier analog formats; hearing the age of analog recording through digital ears similarly allows us to embrace lo-fi and distortion as sonic prisms through which to experience the sound of recorded jazz in a new way.[44]

Similarly to the way that my interest in architecture influenced my articulation of rhythmic ideas, my immersion in the language and history of photography helped transform what initially seemed like an intractable stumbling block into a constellation of new opportunities for jazz history, analysis, and interpretation, inspiring me to use the centrality of chance in the history of photography in order to "loft" the composite culture of recorded jazz sound up to the profound levels of expression attained by jazz improvisation. In "'We No Longer Consider Them Damaged'" and throughout the text, I use ideas and images from photography (and, to a lesser extent, film) as analogies that help problematize the status of sound recordings in the construction of jazz history, to reconsider the terms upon which we understand the jazz recording as an aesthetic object, and to think through the relationship between concepts of jazz sound and the broader social/cultural/political ethos. As Michael Pickering and Emily Keightley have written in *Photography, Music and Memory*, sound recording and photography closely parallel each other as mediums of social remembering and social envisioning.[45] Photography's processes of mechanical reproduction, its history of innovation-by-accident, and its language of visual capture are potent thematic and conceptual metaphors through which to make sense of the continuously morphing traces of recorded jazz as it travels across networks of jazz players and listeners, and across successive technological eras of sonic capture. And if the easy portability of sound recordings is mirrored by the similar circulation of "vernacular" genres of photography, a number of "high art" photographers also pass through these pages, including Miroslav Tichý, Josef Sudek, Keith and Chandra Calhoun, Daido Moriyama, Monica Carocci, Ming Smith, Spencer Richards, Hart Leroy Bibbs, and Sally Mann. All of these artists pursue highly idiosyncratic photographic practices that embrace distortion and disfiguration as central compositional techniques. Their work has been a reference point for other artists and scholars of filmmaking, photography, and media such as John Akomfrah, Arthur Jafa,

Robin Kelsey, Hito Steyerl, and others who also pass through these pages. The most immediately relevant to my ideas would probably be Akomfrah, his cohorts in the Black Audio Film Collective, and artist/filmmaker Jafa, both of whom have explored, in various ways, interwoven issues of archives, distortion, and fidelity and their relationship to black history.[46] Throughout, I use the work of these artists and scholars to help theorize the implications of degraded audio signals as they manifest throughout jazz's alter-archive, listening in to the occult dimensions of sound recordings for their ability to intimate black pasts and futures.

Viewed narrowly, it may seem ethically problematic to embrace "outsider" recordings that the original creators never intended, nor would they have sanctioned. But from Andy Warhol's and Roy Lichtenstein's painstaking duplication of commercial iconography, to Robert Rauschenberg's silk-screening of previously produced images and his use of found objects, to Richard Serra's industrially fabricated monoliths, to Jean-Michel Basquiat's xeroxed surfaces, the concept of the "hand" of the artist has in fact become very complex and contested over the course of the twentieth century.[47] In one way of thinking, then, recuperating these recordings as art objects is consistent with the contested and contingent nature of authorship in contemporary art, and engaging them becomes less a matter of veracity and more a matter of interpretation and aesthetics. More concretely, the music-analytical conclusions I draw from these recordings are a way of finding a productive midpoint between the ideas of sound recording as documentary and sound recording as fantasy. To be clear: these recordings were not *deliberately* produced to sound the way they now sound; my creative engagement with their various sound worlds in this book is my own interpretive strategy. By using photographic metaphors, concepts, and contexts to retroactively force the Lost Quintet's alter-archives into a sphere populated by the "corrupted" sonic values of hip-hop, dub, experimental music, and their stylistic progeny, we are inspired to take them at face value—as art objects, so to speak—embracing the aesthetic, psycho-emotional, music-analytical, and sociopolitical implications of recorded sounds that seem to corrode, crumble, or evaporate at the margins of perceptibility.

The artist and theorist Hito Steyerl has written that "the poor image tends toward abstraction," and distorted sound recordings and experimental photography are considered throughout this text as comparable modes of abstraction, albeit generated in different ways and with different intentions (including sometimes, as we will see, unintentionally).[48] The third chapter also takes a brief detour through several recordings of the bebop progenitor Charlie Parker, setting the stage for a journey through the alter-archives of his acolytes John Coltrane and Miles Davis. In the scholarly sense, this book partially reflects the current interest in archives, the way archival presences and absences can be made productive, and the way digital culture has transformed our understanding of the kinds of sources that are useful to our thinking as scholars and practitioners.[49] In the world of jazz commerce, on the other hand, it ponders an alternate trajectory to thirty years of neoliberal restructuring of media (manifesting in jazz as deluxe, digitally sanitized box sets and boutique reissues) that, as Steyerl notes, rendered less mainstream/more experimental arts much less visible and accessible. Steyerl quotes the Cuban film theorist Juan García Espinosa, whose essay "For an Imperfect Cinema" argues that technically precise aesthetics can sometimes serve elitist or reactionary ends.[50] David Novak, meanwhile, has asserted, "Home taping is killing music (but saving noise)."[51] The chapter "'We No Longer Consider Them Damaged'" embraces the philosophies of scholars like Espinosa and Novak, embracing noise as a positive and regenerative value for jazz. This will likely be of most relevance to readers interested in a critical history of sound recording in jazz, and in the relationship between sound recording and film as two representational mediums, as well as those curious about sounding their way out of several decades of encrusted jazz conservatism.

———

With a slight squint of the eyes, then, this book might be considered a work of music theory disguised as art history and/or science fiction. And while intermedial thinking like this—whether bringing music into dialogue with architecture, photography, or other media—has often been met with resistance and skepticism from within established discourses, this mode of inquiry is really nothing new in jazz. When John Coltrane's drummer Elvin Jones became frustrated with the direction the band's music was taking in late 1965, for example, he famously quipped that "only poets can understand it."[52] In his sarcasm, however, Jones was unwittingly proposing an intermedial space of musical understanding. In 1995, the late musicologist Samuel Floyd founded *Lenox Avenue*, a journal devoted entirely to exploring relationships between different black arts.[53] In his 2017 study *Epistrophies*, Brent Hayes-Edwards traced the diffusion of jazz energy through a variety of literary and poetic practices.[54] Meanwhile, artists and collectives as diverse as Duke Ellington, Cecil Taylor, Sun Ra, Steve Lacy, Geri Allen, the Black Artist's Group, the Association for the Advancement of Creative Musicians, John

Zorn, Jane Ira Bloom, Steve Coleman, Sam Newsome, Greg Osby, Jason Moran, and many others have experimented with combinations of jazz and other art forms—dance, film, visual arts, literature, and beyond.

Today, when musicians, music scholars, architects, and practitioners of other art forms and ideas are beginning to find a degree of common ground within academia and within the increasingly multimedia spaces of the art world, these practices and discourses have moved much closer to each other. The International Institute for Critical Studies in Improvisation, for example, is devoted to investigating the ways that the concept of improvisation manifests across a wide spectrum of musical and nonmusical practices (including architecture and urban studies), opening another kind of space for intermedial dialogues.[55] Columbia University's Center for Jazz Studies has been a powerfully generative space for the so-called New Jazz Studies and a substantial amount of research on jazz's relationship with other arts as well as its manifestations outside the sphere of music. With ideological roots in the 1960s (but disciplinary roots in the 1990s), the New Jazz Studies is one of a number of fields that have used literary methods to broaden the discourse around jazz (and black music in general), with the result that "musical analysis" can be situated in any domain of culture—literature, film, visual art, dance, speech, humor, politics, cuisine, to take a few examples—that interfaces with the musical or extramusical reality of jazz. In fact, it could be argued that the rise of New Jazz Studies was an organic response to the increasingly narrow theorization of jazz in academic music departments where its discourse was increasingly shaped by music theorists, music historians, and ethnomusicologists. Meanwhile, recent book-length works by imaginative player-scholars, such as David Borgo's *Sync or Swarm: Improvising Music in a Complex Age*[56] (2005), Stephon Alexander's *The Jazz of Physics* (2016),[57] and several essays by saxophonist Steve Coleman also reflect this trend, helping to move the jazz conversation beyond its older analytical, biographical, and discographical foci, and situating it within a broader range of artistic and intellectual discourses.[58] In one way of reading, however, the design of this book is fairly conservative at its core; it is organized along the poles of chronology and biography, while the sound studies/archival argument extends out of the jazz studies emphasis on discographical research and the spatial and photographic arguments broaden the concept of musical analysis.

As this book neared completion and the proverbial "big picture" came into sharper focus, I realized that its poetics of rhythm, spatiality, and distortion had grown organically out of my previous work, none of which was particularly concerned with jazz. Architects, and especially builders of streamlined objects such as aircraft and boats, use the term "lofting" to describe a process in which curved, aerodynamic surfaces are extrapolated from foundational measurements. The term has resonance here, as the concerns of this book represent an expansion, or "lofting" of ideas out the conceptual environment of my earlier projects. In particular, my 2007 study of Jamaican dub music explored that genre's intersection of groove-based music and spatializing sound-processing technologies (such as synthetic reverberation and delay), helping to lay a crucial foundation for the rhythmic/spatial orientation of this book.[59] A volume I co-edited on the Sublime Frequencies recording label (2015) was equally important in that it explored the aesthetics of sound recordings, the idea of distortion as a productive prism through which to hear culture, and cassette culture as a portal for encountering the world's musics.[60] It might initially seem incongruous to some to bring figures such as the Jamaican recording engineers King Tubby or Lee "Scratch" Perry into dialogue with jazz virtuosi like Coltrane and Miles—not to mention contemporary architects like Zaha Hadid or Peter Eisenman. It might seem absurd or transgressive to bring the hard-won technical virtuosity of musicians like Miles Davis, John Coltrane, and Charlie Parker into deliberate dialogue with vinyl surface noise and faulty radio signals. In radically different ways, however, they are all connected within the constellation of dramatic post–World War II transformations in politics, culture, and technology, which manifested across the arts.

RACE, ANALYSIS, AND INTERPRETATION

I'd like to address a broader challenge having to do with putting *musical sound* (understood in fairly traditionalist terms) at the center of this project, in the current intellectual and political climate. One element at the heart of the ongoing reconsideration of many of the core assumptions of the field of music theory, for example, is the contested issue of formalist analysis. Similar to what took place in the New Musicology of the 1980s and 1990s, formalist analysis of music (i.e., analyzing a musical work solely on the basis of its sonic elements) is being attacked as the insular, exclusionary, and elitist domain of privileged white men.[61] I myself am neither a white man nor a music theorist, but I *am* a musically trained person, a music scholar, and a musician. So the question becomes: What is the value and relevance of foregrounding these sonic issues as an African American man? Could anything be less fashionable in the current climate than formalist observation funneled through often inscrutable architectural and photographic theory (themselves often heavily raced), brought to bear on the work of two cisgender, heterosexual male musicians? Or are there other ways of thinking through those apparent contradictions?

One way of addressing this question is by understanding even the most abstract forms of creativity through the prism of the personal. Musical innovation is not only the result of manipulating the materials of sound. It also takes place at the intersection of every kind of social relationship, including friendships and intimate partnerships. The storied relationships of Louis Armstrong and Lil Hardin, Stanley Turrentine and Shirley Scott, Randy Weston and Melba Liston, or Don and Moki Cherry—among many others—are testaments to the fact that jazz innovation has often flown along the contours of relationships in which friends, lovers, or partners doubled as collaborators or crucial sounding boards. Music was central to the relationship between John and Alice Coltrane, for example. They encountered each other as professional musicians and evolved together as sonic and spiritual seekers, with Alice eventually joining her husband's band as pianist, while creating her own compelling body of work. Her creative open-mindedness and supportive, sympathetic presence were undoubtedly crucial during a period in which John's increasingly unconventional music was confounding as many listeners as it was converting. Miles Davis's wife Betty, meanwhile, was an innovative and influential creative artist in her own right who helped redirect her husband's music as powerfully as John Coltrane, Gil Evans, and Wayne Shorter had earlier in his career. Like Alice Coltrane's contribution to the radical free jazz innovations of John Coltrane, Betty Davis's hand in the redirection of Miles's career enables us to think through the question of innovation from a different angle. Is innovation something that only takes place in the public sphere, or is the intimate sphere equally fertile ground for innovation? Are artistic insights only generated within artistic spheres, or can they be generated in the intimate sphere, and transposed into the realm of artistic practice? How can we more accurately trace the complex threads of influence that have shaped this music, from the most public to the most private spheres?

One of the most pronounced contrasts in this book, in this line of thinking, is between the relationships that these two musicians enjoyed with romantic partners who were also important creative interlocutors. By all accounts, John Coltrane was a sensitive person raised in a close-knit, nurturing family environment that was tragically shattered by a series of unexpected deaths and, aside from a period of heroin and alcohol addiction, music was the force that he used to process and transcend his emotional pain.[62] His wife Alice Coltrane was a brilliant musical partner who could go as deeply into the music as he could, and was an important sounding board for many of his most experimental, controversial ideas. After his passing, she spent the rest of her career extending ideas they had developed together, while carefully safeguarding her late husband's musical legacy. Miles Davis, on the other hand, was also a deeply sensitive person, but one who had been raised in a family environment of conflict and violence.[63] Like Coltrane, he also struggled with drug addiction and, while his music was a realm in which he could express his vulnerability, he seemed to rely on physical and emotional abuse of his romantic partners as a way of processing his own emotional pain. The recollections of his most significant romantic partners (Frances Davis, Betty Davis, and Cicely Tyson) all paint portraits of a brilliant artist and highly sensitive human being whose redeeming qualities had been distorted by his chemical dependencies, but whose deepest addictions were to self-destruction and the spiritual destruction of the women who loved him. So in addition to modulating the male-centeredness of the jazz narratives that form the core of this book, acknowledging the centrality and contributions of Alice Coltrane and Betty Davis paints a more nuanced and accurate portrait of the creative process and of these musicians as human beings, with recordings such as *First Meditations* and *In A Silent Way* heard as sonic maps of emotional intimacies that also manifested as musical innovation.

A second way of addressing the race-theory equation is through the disciplinary equation. Even though this is not a work of ethnography per se, it still reflects the core methodologies and philosophical principles of ethnomusicology, and might provide one answer to the conundrum currently posed at the intersection of race and musical-analytical thinking. The truth is that the broader, metamusical themes of African culture, the trans-Atlantic slave trade, Civil Rights, Black Power, Pan-Africanism, African independence, the Space Age, globalization, gender, sexuality, and mass incarceration are present throughout this book. But they are addressed through musicians' manipulation of sonic elements like minor key vamps, drones, symmetrical scales, ostinati, and different rhythmic languages. In this light, it is my training as an ethnomusicologist that has provided one helpful mode of resolution, since even the most music-analytically-minded ethnomusicologists have tended to understand sound and society as mutually constitutive. The curator Magdalyn Asimakis once suggested to me that a work of art (and, by extension, an act of analysis) should ideally address three issues: the technical, the political, and the conceptual. I have found that tripartite scheme helpful while writing this book: the intermedial mode of analysis essentially helps mediate between these three priorities, allowing me to do justice to the sound material while also gesturing outward toward human stories, history, culture, other forms of artistic expression, and ideas from outside of the realm of music. That observation is also germane to the language I use. I would encourage those readers unfamiliar with musical terminology to read the analytical passages as forms of poetry, gleaning meaning by merely surfing the imagery and rhetorical slopes of the prose. After all, any descriptive language is nothing but a set of metaphors in the end, and in any case, the Amiri Baraka–Nathaniel Mackey–Fred Moten triumvirate's poetic resignification of music theoretical language—itself rooted in the political struggles of the 1960s and the desire of black writers to reclaim the discourse around jazz—has opened a space for a sensual experience of ostensibly technical texts.

Finally, the political/cultural imperative is significant. Unlike the Western classical tradition, which has been exhaustively documented through long-standing traditions of music history and music theory, the vast majority of jazz will never be documented, simply vanishing into the air after being played. Thus, there is a concrete political imperative involved in documenting *who* did *what, when,* and *how.* I would further assert that forty years of police brutality, mass incarceration, chemical warfare, and gentrification (not to mention the corporatizing of jazz) have severely undermined the post–World War II ideal of the jazz musician as cultural hero. Put more simply: if half of the country cannot abide by the reality of a black president, what chance does a black saxophonist or trumpeter have? It's not surprising that, in recent years, jazz has been so frequently derided as America's "least popular" or "most hated" music.[64] Outside of the United States, meanwhile, jazz continues to be recognized as one of America's greatest cultural exports. This book embraces the challenge of deeper musical understanding as a way of asserting the continued (and conflicted) power, beauty, and relevance of jazz—including its avant-garde—in these embattled times.

RHYTHM, RACE, AND OUTER SPACE

The sonic utopias proposed by Coltrane and Miles in the 1960s were generated in the context of Civil Rights, Black Power, African independence, and other narratives of black self-determination.[65] But it is crucially important to note that they were also generated in the context of the Space Age: the age of the Apollo and Sputnik space exploration projects, and the explosion of science fiction—or what

Kodwo Eshun has referred to as the "futures industry"—in popular culture.[66] With Americans of the 1960s thus accruing innumerable hours of zero-gravity experience via films such as *2001: A Space Odyssey*, and television programs like *Star Trek*, *Lost in Space*, and the ongoing broadcasts of the Apollo missions, it is unsurprising that flotation was a pervasive sensation in the popular culture of the 1960s. This had profound implications for not only politics and culture, but equally for musical *sound*. Although (with the exception of Sun Ra and, to a lesser extent, Alice Coltrane) the Afrofuturist discourse has been rarely brought to bear on jazz, it is a fitting frame for the music discussed in this book. The outer-space theme is relevant to both Coltrane and Miles, with particular implications for my discussion of rhythm. Not being a reader of science fiction, for example, I had never heard of Frederik Pohl and Jack Williamson's 1963 novel *The Reefs of Space* until I happened upon it in a used bookstore. But the image immediately appealed to my sonic-analytical instincts.[67] Outer space exists in most of our imaginations as a network of (ostensibly solid) celestial bodies interspersed across vast regions of empty space. Reefs, on the other hand, are solid, terrestrial formations that exist within aquatic environments of fluidity and flow. The fusion of these two environments in Pohl and Williamson's title served me well in relation to the music of both late Coltrane and the Lost Quintet, with the idea of reefs inspiring me to develop this book's rhythmic discourse from a dialectic of passages of "solid" repetitive meter that cyclically consolidate and dissolve within both Coltrane's and Miles's exploration of fluid, amorphous rhythmic spaces.

While the icons, iconography, and works of Afro-inflected science fiction appear intermittently throughout this book, the energies of politics, protests, planets, and spaceships primarily manifest in the music-analytical passages that discuss the ways that Coltrane and Miles used instruments, rhythms, chords, scales, pitch intervals, and sonic textures as mediums for cosmological imaginings, and to leverage African and Afro-diasporic pasts and futures to forge new freedoms here on Earth. Free-meter rhythm is imagined as a metaphor for the escape from earthly histories of racial and political oppression, while the textures and timbres of the Fender Rhodes electric piano evoke the bleeping electronic sounds of science fiction, and the distorted degeneration of recorded sound conjures the exotic atmospheres of other worlds, whether of the historical past, or the imagined (and utopian) extraterrestrial future. As such, those musical sensations were in turn implicated in the broader concept of "world building" that was as strongly predicated on the imaginings of artists as it was on more obviously "political," economic, or technological agents. These interwoven themes of rhythm, race, noise, and space are marbled throughout the book and shape the concluding chapter, "A Liquid Feeling Emerges."

But in the context of the standpoint of the "Second Deconstruction" that African Americans are currently fighting against, as well as the neocolonization of Africa, these political realities of the post–World War II decades sometimes seem so remote as to suggest that they only ever existed in the imagination. That is one reason the excerpts of authors like Samuel Delany, Tracy K. Smith, and Jorge Luis Borges have provided part of the spiritual aura of this project. Delany's literary fashioning of alternate worlds and societies has always struck me as an off-planet projection of his growing up in deindustrializing New York during one of the city's most fertile, creative, and socially flexible eras—this is, of course, the same time period and setting in which Coltrane and Miles flourished. I've excerpted passages from Tracy K. Smith's *Life on Mars* at points because, like Coltrane (explicitly) on *Interstellar Space* or Miles (implicitly) on *Bitches Brew*, Smith provides a bluesy, emotional inflection of the interstellar theme. Meanwhile, Borges's complex, labyrinthine narratives such as "Tlön, Uqbar, Orbis Tertius" draw on a range of archival sources—some real, some imagined, some invented—in the creation of incredibly rich narratives that are in fact models of how the entire concept of archives can be radically reimagined.[68] This, of course, is ultimately a mere metaphor for how the world itself can be reimagined.

If using these sources to amplify these historical resonances sometimes seems akin to fashioning an imaginary history from scratch, or from scattered clues, this long, reconstructive gaze is precisely the point. The saxophonist Steve Lacy, commenting on the music of Thelonious Monk, once likened Monk's music to the looking glass in Lewis Carroll's classic children's story *Alice in Wonderland*: if one stared long and hard enough, another world would emerge on the other side of the glass. The jazz innovations of the late 1960s are precisely this "other side" of the looking glass. At first glance, all the proportions and perspectives seem distorted. But after a while, it becomes clear that there is in fact a vibrant—and viable—world on the other side of that glass. I have stared long and hard—throughout decades of post-1980 war against African American people via legislation, mass incarceration, communities carpet bombed with crack and sociopathic forms of popular music, police brutality, and gentrification—and this book represents the world that I've glimpsed on that other side. And if the ideas in this book come from various sources, in the end I have merely tried, to use the words of Borges, "to be sincere to the plot, to the dream."[69] In addition to its political and economic dimensions, that dream was also a liberation of imagination: the freedom to engage with other cultural ways of being, as well as to envision entirely new worlds and to fashion entirely new forms of culture. The plot was a Space Age musical manifestation of pan-Africanist cultural connection, powered by radical reformulations of black rhythm and sound, now refracted into unexpected spaces of radical freedom and possibility for us in the twenty-first century.

NOTES

1. Delany, Samuel. *Babel-17*. New York: Knopf, 1966, 105.

2. See the following sources: Kahn, Ashley. *Kind of Blue: The Making of the Miles Davis Masterpiece*. New York: Da Capo, 2000. Griffin, Farah J., and Salim Washington. *Clawing at the Limits of Cool: Miles Davis, John Coltrane, and the Greatest Jazz Collaboration Ever*. New York: St. Martin's Press, 2008. Nisenson, Eric. *The Making of Kind of Blue: Miles Davis and His Masterpiece*. New York: St. Martin's, 2013.

3. Ball, Philip. *The Self-Made Tapestry: Pattern Formation in Nature*. London: Oxford University Press, 1998, 140.

4. Ravi Coltrane quoted in Kahn, Ashley. *The House That Trane Built: The Story of Impulse Records*. London: Granta, 2006, 263.

5. Leonard Brown's edited volume *John Coltrane and Black America's Quest for Freedom: Spirituality and the Music* (Oxford: Oxford University Press, 2010) contains a number of insightful essays that address Coltrane's later music, in part or whole. See especially Salim Washington's essay "Don't Let the Devil (Make You) Lose Your Joy: A Look at Late Coltrane."

6. See Porter, Lewis. *John Coltrane: His Life and Music*. Ann Arbor: University of Michigan Press, 1999, 292.

7. Various published sources indicate studio sessions occurred on April 21 and 28, 1966 and February 27, March 29, and May 17, 1967.

8 Ashley Kahn's *A Love Supreme: The Story of John Coltrane's Signature Album* (Penguin, 2003) provides a detailed chronology of Coltrane's recording activities between 1961 and 1967.

9. Coltrane, John. *The Mastery of John Coltrane, Volume 3: Jupiter Variation*. Impulse IA 9360. Originally released 1978.

10. Pohl, Frederick, and Jack Williamson. *The Reefs of Space*. New York: Ballantine, 1964, 51.

11. Jack DeJohnette, interview with the author, Woodstock, New York, November 2009.

12. See Peter Keepnews's essay, "The Lost Quintet." In *A Miles Davis Reader*, edited by Bill Kirchner. Washington, DC: Smithsonian Institution Press, 1997.

13. In 2008, the company Jazz Shots released a DVD titled *Miles Davis Quintet Live in Rome and Copenhagen 1969* (Jazz Shots 2869080). Unfortunately, this release suffers from

poor programming, sequencing, and sound/video quality, but it at least makes some of the Lost Quintet's work available on the commercial market. Hopefully, higher-quality releases will follow.

14. The cassette was given to me by the electric bassist Michael Rivard, leader of the Boston-based collective Club D'Elf and formerly of the Either/Orchestra.

15. See, for example: Martin Jr., Waldo. "Miles Davis and the 1960s Avant-Garde." In *Miles Davis and American Culture*, edited by Gerald Early. St. Louis: Missouri Historical Society Press, 2001.

16. Keepnews, "The Lost Quintet."

17. See Tingen, Paul. *Miles Beyond: The Electric Explorations of Miles Davis, 1967–1991.* New York: Billboard Books, 2001, 112–13.

18. See Freeman, Philip. *Running the Voodoo Down: The Electric Music of Miles Davis.* San Francisco: Backbeat, 2005, 23, 48–49.

19. Grella, George Jr. *Bitches Brew*. New York: Bloomsbury, 2015.

20. Rollins, as quoted in Ratliff, Ben. *The Jazz Ear: Conversations over Music.* New York: Times Books, 2008, 41.

21. Widdess, Richard. "Involving the Performers in Transcription and Analysis: A Collaborative Approach to Dhrupad." *Ethnomusicology* 38, no. 1 (Winter 1994): 58–79.

22. Clayton, Martin R. L. "Free Rhythm: Ethnomusicology and the Study of Music Without Metre." *Bulletin of the School of Oriental and African Studies* 59, no. 2 (1996): 323–32.

23. Benadon, Fernando. "Gridless Beats." *Perspectives of New Music* 47, no. 1 (2009): 135 64. See also Benadon, Fernando. "Speech Rhythms and Metric Frames." In *International Conference on Mathematics and Computation in Music* #3, edited by Elaine Chew, Adrian Childs, and Ching-Hua Chuan, 22–31. Berlin: Springer, 2009.

24. Ashley, Richard. "Don't Change a Hair for Me: The Art of Jazz Rubato." *Music Perception* 19, no. 3 (2002): 311–32.

25. Goldemberg, Eric. *Pulsation in Architecture*. Plantation, FL: J. Ross Publishing, 2011.

26. Franck, Karen. *Architecture Timed: Designing with Time in Mind*. London: Architectural Design, 2016.

27. Bearden, Romare, with Carl Holty. *The Painter's Mind: A Study of the Relations of Structure and Space in Painting*. New York: Crown, 1969, 87.

28. Foster, Hal. *The Art-Architecture Complex*. London: Verso, 2011.

29. For sources on the spatial turn in the humanities, see the following texts: De Certeau, Michel. "Walking in the City." In *The Practice of Everyday Life*. Berkeley: University of California Press, 1984. Bachelard, Gaston. *The Poetics of Space*. Boston: Beacon Press, 1969. Lefebvre, Henri. *The Production of Space*. Cambridge: Blackwell, 1991. For more general overviews, see Crang, Mike and Nigel Thrift. *Thinking Space*. New York: Routledge, 2000; and Warf, Barney and Santa Arias. *The Spatial Turn: Interdisciplinary Perspectives*. Abingdon: Routledge, 2009.

30. Frampton, Kenneth. *Studies in Tectonic Culture: The Poetics of Construction in Nineteenth and Twentieth Century Architecture*. Cambridge, MA: MIT Press, 1995.

31. See, for example: Harris, Wilson. "History, Fable and Myth in the Caribbean and Guianas." In *Selected Essays of Wilson Harris: The Unfinished Genesis of the Imagination*, edited by A. J. M. Bundy. London: Routledge, 1999. See also Mackey, Nathaniel. *Bass Cathedral*. New York: New Directions, 2008.

32. See, for example: Tymoczko's *The Geometry of Music* (Oxford, 2011), Toussaint's *The Geometry of Musical Rhythm* (MIT Press, 2013), and Cohn's 2016 article, "Graph-Theoretic and Geometric Models of Music," https://www.worldscientific.com/doi/abs/10.1142/9789813140103_0013.

33. The idea of the Black Atlantic cultural sphere as predicated on an ongoing musical conversation is central to Paul Gilroy's chapter "Jewels from Authenticity," in *The Black Atlantic: Modernity and Double Consciousness* (Verso, 1993), and Tsitsi Ella Jaji's *Africa in Stereo: Modernism, Music, and Pan-African Solidarity* (Oxford University Press, 2014).

34. Menkman, Rosa. *The Glitch Momentum*. Network Notebooks 04, 2011. https://networkcultures.org/_uploads/NN%234_RosaMenkman.pdf.

35. Kittler, Friedrich. *Draculas Vermachtnis: Technische Schriften*. Leipzig: Reclam Verlag, 1993, 242.

36. Heylin, Clinton. *Bootlegs: The Secret History of the Other Recording Industry*. New York: St. Martin's Press, 1996, 33.

37. See Bates, Eliot. "Glitches, Bugs, and Hisses: The Degeneration of Musical Recordings and the Contemporary Musical Work." In *Bad Music: The Music We Love to Hate*, edited by Christopher Washburne and Maiken Durno. New York: Routledge, 2004.

38. See Novak, David. "The Sublime Frequencies of New Old Media." In *Punk Ethnography: Artists and Scholars Listen to Sublime Frequencies*, edited by Michael Veal and E. Tammy Kim. Middletown, CT: Wesleyan University Press, 2015. See also Bates, "Glitches, Bugs, and Hisses."

39. Bates, "Glitches, Bugs, and Hisses," 277.

40. Bates "Glitches, Bugs, and Hisses," 280.

41. For an early discussion of the impact of cassettes on music cultures, see Manuel, Peter. *Cassette Culture: Popular Music and Technology in North India*. Chicago: University of Chicago Press, 1993. For a discussion of various bootleg and tape-trading cultures, see the following sources: Sutherland, Ralph, and Harold Sherrick. *A Pig's Tale: The Underground Story of the Legendary Bootleg Label*. Milwaukee: Genius Books, 2022. Rodriguez, Mark A. *After All Is Said and Done: Taping the Grateful Dead, 1965–1995*. New York: Anthology Editions, 2022.

42. Novak "The Sublime Frequencies of New Old Media," 30.

43. Novak "The Sublime Frequencies of New Old Media," 30. Novak borrows the term from the work of Jay David Bolter and Richard Grusin.

44. See Chopra-Gant, Mike. "Pictures or it Didn't Happen: Photo-nostalgia, iPhoneography and the Representation of Everyday Life." *Photography and Culture* 9, no. 2 (2016): 121–33.

45. See the introduction to Pickering, Michael, and Emily Keightley. *Photography, Music and Memory: Pieces of the Past in Everyday Life*. New York: Palgrave/Macmillan, 2015.

46. See the following titles: Eshun, Kodwo, and Anjalika Sagar. *The Ghosts of Songs: The Film Art of the Black Audio Film Collective, 1982–1998*. London: Liverpool University Press, 2007; Jafa, Arthur, with Lærke Rydal Jørgensen and Mathias Ussing Seeberg. *Magnumb*. Louisiana Museum of Modern Art, 2021. See also Jafa, Arthur, with Amira Gad and Joseph Constable. *A Series of Utterly Improbable, Yet Extraordinary Renditions*. London: Serpentine Gallery, 2018.

47. For example, see Buskirk, Matha. *The Contingent Object of Contemporary Art*. Cambridge, MA: MIT Press, 2003.

48. Steyerl, Hito. "In Defense of the Poor Image," *e-flux journal* 10 (November 2009). https://www.e-flux.com.

49. Excellent recent works that engage the concept of archives in relation to Black music and historiography include Brent Hayes-Edwards's *Epistrophies* (Harvard University Press, 2017), Daphne Brooks's *Liner Notes for the Revolution* (Harvard University Press, 2021), and Mark Anthony Neal's *Black Ephemera: The Crisis of the Musical Archive* (NYU Press, 2022).

50. Espinosa, Julio Garcia. "For An Imperfect Cinema." Translated by Julianne Burton. *Jump Cut* 20 (1979): 24–26.

51. This phrase is actually a section heading on page 220 of Novak's 2013 book *Japanoise: Music at the Edge of Circulation* (Duke University Press).

52. Jones evidently made this statement as he was quitting the band in the midst of an engagement at the Jazz Workshop in San Francisco. See his comments as cited in Thomas, J. C. *Chasin' the Trane*. New York: Da Capo, 1975, 207.

53. See *Lenox Avenue: A Journal of Interarts Inquiry*, https://www.jstor.org/journal/lenavenjinte.

54. Hayes-Edwards, Brent. *Epistrophies: Jazz and the Literary Imagination*. Cambridge, MA: Harvard University Press, 2017.

55. See the IICSI website: https://improvisationinstitute.ca.

56. Borgo, David. *Sync or Swarm: Improvising Music in a Complex Age*. London: Bloomsbury, 2005.

57. Alexander, Stephon. *The Jazz of Physics: The Secret Link Between Music and the Structure of the Universe*. New York: Perseus, 2016.

58. For example, see Coleman's essay, "The Sweet Science: Floyd Mayweather and Improvised Modalities of Rhythm," http://m-base.com/essays/the-sweet-science.

59. See Veal, Michael. *Dub: Soundscapes and Shattered Songs in Jamaican Reggae*. Middletown, CT: Wesleyan University Press, 2007.

60. Veal and Kim, eds., *Punk Ethnography*.

61. Ewell, Philip A. "Music Theory and the White Racial Frame." *Music Theory Online* 26, no. 2 (September 2020). https://mtosmt.org/issues/mto.20.26.2/mto.20.26.2.ewell .html.

62. See the chapters "Southern Roots" and "Life Without Father." In *John Coltrane: His Life and Music*, edited by Lewis Porter. Ann Arbor: University of Michigan Press, 1999.

63. See the first chapter of: Davis, Miles, with Quincy Troupe. *Miles: The Autobiography*. New York: Simon and Schuster, 1989.

64. For example, see La Rosa, David. "Jazz Has Become the Least-Popular Music in the U.S." *Jazz Line News*. 2015. https://news.jazzline.com/news/jazz-least-popular-music -genre/. See also Blake, John. "When Jazz Stopped Being Cool." *CNN Online*. https://www .cnn.com/2016/09/25/entertainment/cnnphotos-jim-marshall-jazz/index.html.

65. Saul, Scott. *Freedom Is, Freedom Ain't: Jazz and the Making of the Sixties*. Cambridge, MA: Harvard University Press, 2001. Monson, Ingrid. *Freedom Sounds: Civil Rights Call Out to Jazz and Africa*. London: Oxford University Press, 2007. Kelley, Robin. *Africa Speaks, America Answers: Modern Jazz in Revolutionary Times*. Cambridge, MA: Harvard University Press, 2012. Hayes, Robin J. *Love for Liberation: African Independence, Black Power, and a Diaspora Underground*. Seattle: University of Washington Press, 2021.

66. See Eshun, Kodwo. "Further Considerations on Afro-Futurism." *New Centennial Review* 3, no. 2 (Summer 2003).

67. Pohl and Jack Williamson, *The Reefs of Space*.

68. Borges, Jorge Luis. *Labyrinths: Selected Stories and Other Writings*. Cambridge: New Directions, 1986.

69. Jorge Luis Borges, as quoted in "Borges at NYU." Reprinted in Burgin, Richard. *Jorge Luis Borges: Conversations*. Jackson: University of Mississippi Press, 1998, 123.

ONE

"An Efflorescence of Deconstruction"
Space, Shape, Surface, and the Urban
as Modes of Jazz Consciousness

I tend to be always thinking of time, not space . . . I think that the central
riddle, the central problem of metaphysics—let us call it thinking—is time,
not space. Space is one of many things to be found inside of time.[1]

Jorge Luis Borges

How do we experience the world when we conceptualize it as *rhythm*—or, more
topically, as *a complex of interlocking, repeating rhythms*? If, per Borges, we
consider space an element of time, how do the spatial environments we inhabit
inform our sense of rhythm? Conversely, to what extent do our deeply ingrained
rhythmic dispositions condition our spatial experience of those environments?
What is even the point of attempting to find common ground between fields as
apparently far removed from each other as jazz rhythm and architecture? And
how did the idea even occur to me? These are the questions that guide my narrative of rhythm and space in this chapter: beginning with a historical meditation on the relationship between the two fields, continuing with the semiauto-
biographical theme of the introduction, and moving concentrically outward to
broader meditations on the relationships between jazz, architecture, and urban
space. In the core essays of this book, I will bring these ideas, along with those
in the next two chapters, to bear, in a more subtle manner, on the music of John
Coltrane and Miles Davis.

Besides the interest in architectural forms and concepts that I narrated in the introduction, there was an additional catalyst for my thinking about the relationship between architecture and jazz. Jo Steffens's 2009 book *Unpacking My Library: Architects and Their Books* is an artfully executed photographic chronicle of the libraries of several prominent architectural firms.[2] The format and premise of Steffens's book are simple and straightforward—to document rows of variously colored and sized book spines in order to celebrate the materiality of books, and to demonstrate how freely and promiscuously the discourse of contemporary architecture has drawn on nonarchitectural sources. From the evidence of the shelves Steffens photographed, those sources include (but are not limited to) art history, film studies, feminist theory, philosophy, literature, literary theory, photography, psychoanalytic theory, and—sometimes—works on Western art music, popular music, and experimental music. But what was striking to me was the complete absence of jazz as a conceptual presence in these discussions, despite the fact that many of the concepts these architects are working with have strong corollaries in the work done by well-known jazz musicians since (and in some cases, prior to) World War II. All of the architects cited throughout this book—for example, Zaha Hadid, Peter Eisenman, Greg Lynn, and others—clearly reflect the concept of *improvisation* in their work. Amidst crumbling disciplinary boundaries, the influence of destabilizing philosophical currents such as deconstruction, and the endless reconfigurations of knowledge facilitated by the rise of digital culture and the information age, concepts such *improvisation*, *indeterminacy, flux, transformation, mutability, fluidity*, and *flexibility* have found their way into the language of numerous disciplines and professions, including architecture. But I could not find a single reference to jazz among the hundreds of titles—including the music titles—documented in Steffens's book.

Interpreted in charitable terms, the main reason for the lack of an African American impact on architecture (comparable to our impacts on music, literature, film, and visual arts) is simple and historical. Whereas American architecture developed in centers of advanced learning, secular African American music developed in the crucible of slavery, racial segregation, and later, the "Wild West" atmosphere of the American music industry. In the 1920s, while bluesmen like Robert Johnson, Son House, and Charley Patton were laying the foundation for decades of American music in the tumultuous juke joints and barrelhouses of the Mississippi Delta, American architects were being schooled in the Beaux Arts academies of Europe. In the 1940s, while Charlie Parker and Dizzy Gillespie were creating the revolutionary foundations of jazz modernism in the nightclubs of Harlem and on 52nd Street, American architects were being trained in colleges and universities. But while Western art critics and historians were arguing about whether visual art, film, literature, painting, or architecture was the form that most accurately embodied late modernity, the entire world essentially spent the twentieth century dancing to some musical art form that probably had its roots in the African diaspora—jazz, blues, rock and roll, soul, funk, hip-hop, ska, reggae, dancehall, mambo, salsa, and many other genres. It was the art historian (and my late colleague) Robert Farris Thompson, working across artistic media, who created a model within which twentieth-century black musics heretofore understood as merely "popular" or "vernacular" could be more accurately recast as artistic achievements comparable with the highest and most influential achievements of modernist Western art.[3]

Some of the distance between jazz and architecture also reflects the general reluctance of nonmusically trained listeners to engage with the technical aspects of music. As intriguing as the idea might be, it is probably unrealistic to expect most practitioners and scholars of architecture to engage with ideas such as musical pieces as studies in "structural integrity." But some of the distance between the two fields also undoubtedly reflects the intellectual consequences of America's racial and social divides. A series of recent books have problematized the racialization of architecture as a field, including Victoria Kaplan's *Structural Inequality: Black Architects in the United States* (2006), Melvin Mitchell's *The Crisis of the African-American Architect: Conflicting Cultures of Architecture and Black Power* (2007), and Lesley Lokko's *White Paper, Black Marks: Architecture, Race, and Culture* (2000). Finally, there are specific works that explore the connection between architecture and black music from the architecture side, including portions of Le Corbusier's *When the Cathedrals Were White* (1964),[4] Craig Wilkins's *The Aesthetics of Equity*,[5] portions of Mark Rakatansky's *Tectonic Acts of Desire and Doubt* (2012),[6] Rob Connor's 2006 thesis, "Jazz and Architecture: Intersections of Rhythm, Proportions and Variations,"[7] and David P. Brown's *Noise Orders*, an important forerunner of this book.[8] The 2021 exhibition *Reconstructions: Architecture and Blackness in America*,[9] held at New York City's Museum of Modern Art, does not specifically address the music-architecture discourse, but it does reflect broad (mainstream) institutional acknowledgment of the complexities at the intersection of architecture and race.

Framed by the idea of architecture as a cultural practice, Lesley Lokko's volume brings the apparatus of critical race theory to bear on the field in terms of its discourse and material production. Her introduction, for example, challenges the historical omission of African and Afro-diasporic traditions of building from most surveys of world architecture, and examines the implications of "the mythical identity of the white, male and 'universal' architect."[10] The false set of historical and cultural assumptions underlying all of this is clear: "[B]lacks, either as Africans or as diasporic cultures, have historically had nothing to say about architecture—as a consequence, architecture has had little to say in response."[11] One core argument of this book, by contrast, is that jazz musicians, in their arrangement of musical sounds (I focus largely but not exclusively on qualities of rhythm), have made important contributions to the same spatial understandings and experiences of modernity and postmodernity that we typically associate with architecture. In fact, what I'm doing here might be thought of as bringing together the discourses of rhythm and architecture to help assert something that might be called "critical rhythm studies," another example of which would include Martin Munro's 2010 book *Different Drummers*, in which musical rhythm is explored as a medium through which macromusical considerations of racial identity can be articulated, throughout the Black Atlantic sphere.[12]

————

In the area of Queens, New York, where I grew up, my introduction to music took place in a world shaped and defined by rhythm. My father made his living as a microbiologist but was also a part-time jazz drummer who was fascinated by so-called Latin (i.e., Afro-Caribbean) rhythms, so I was immersed in the sound of drums and percussion from the very beginning of my life. There were also broader, environmental influences. After the rhythmic revolution unleashed by musicians like James Brown and the Meters in the 1960s, the 1970s was an era of funky music in which musicians strove to make their music more self-consciously "black." In terms of instrumental technique, this often implied very percussive ways of playing inspired by imaginings of, or direct encounters with, African musics. To take three examples: the "chicken scratch" guitar style of James Brown's guitarist Jimmy Nolen, the "slapping" style of Sly and the Family Stone bassist Larry Graham, and Stevie Wonder's syncopated phrasing on the electric Clavinet keyboard are all sonic transmutations of the wave of racial pride inspired by the political and cultural liberation spreading throughout the Black Atlantic world as a result of decolonization, Civil Rights, and Black Power. In the Spanish Caribbean areas of New York such as "El Barrio" (Spanish Harlem) and the Bronx, a similar cultural frequency could be felt; the acknowledgment and embrace of the African element of Latinx culture was a strong undertone of the rumba ensembles on street corners, the Latin jazz played in local nightclubs, and the *salsa dura* sound associated with musicians such as Hector Lavoe, Willie Colon, Ismael Rivera, Eddie Palmieri, and the Fania All Stars. It was a reflection of the cultural sensibility of the time that even the "free" piano improvisations of Cecil Taylor—played in free meter and heavily informed by elements of twentieth-century classical composition—were metaphorized by the British jazz writer Valerie Wilmer as "88 tuned drums" and by the Nigerian journalist J. B. Figi as "African Code, Black Methodology," dramatizing the cultural and political imperative of providing an Africanist aura for even the most experimental spheres of Afro-diasporic art.[13] The 1960s and 1970s, then, were decades in which assertions of race and culture were being forcefully articulated through the medium of rhythm, and John Coltrane and Miles Davis were two of many musicians for whom Africa became important (albeit in very different ways) as a source of aesthetic, cultural, and political inspiration.

Between the 1960s and the early 1980s, my area of South Queens was known as a hotbed of music. As I grew older and more aware of my musical environment, it seemed that there was at least one band on every block, and well-known musicians that lived in the area while I was growing up included John Coltrane, James Brown, Count Basie, Roy Haynes, Graham Haynes, Jaki Byard, Roy Eldridge, Milford Graves, Marcus Miller, Omar Hakim, Ronny Drayton, Tom Browne, A Tribe Called Quest, Run DMC, and LL Cool J, among many others. Once I began playing electric guitar as a teenager in the mid-1970s, I stepped directly into a world of jazz (straight-ahead and fusion), funk, soul, rock, R&B, and early hip-hop. Later, in my twenties, I delved deeply into several West African and Afro-Caribbean traditions and spent several years playing in a Balinese gamelan. I also later developed interests in the more experimental forms of jazz, popular, and Western art music. For the most part, however, it was the formative influence of black dance musics that conditioned me to experience music as *a complex of layered, interlocking and repeating parts*. Without reverting to essentialist ideas about African-derived musics as fundamentally *rhythmic*, this is one of the main lenses through which I am approaching the free jazz repertoire discussed in this book—a view of the music as fundamentally oriented around the dance imperative and by a corresponding understanding of *groove* (i.e., the layered, repetitive structures of black dance music) as its conceptual core. In the next chapter, I introduce the idea of "the Africanist Grid" in order to historicize this way of putting sounds together and to contextualize the radical structural propositions of free jazz as a particular manipulation of that structure.

The idea of groove as a conceptual core of jazz might seem unremarkable to most jazz musicians and jazz scholars, who take it for granted that groove is the fire burning at the very heart of the music. But it is not necessarily a typical point of departure for understanding the various approaches typically grouped under the umbrella term "free jazz," which have often been positioned as conceptual (and functional) polar opposites of dance music due to the fact that they are frequently played in free meter, unfolding in time without reference to an underlying, isometric pulse. In the context of jazz, this dichotomy between metered and unmetered music can be understood in different ways, all of which carry different consequences. Some readers, for example, may feel that I am drawing an excessively strict distinction between metered and nonmetered playing. My music theorist colleague Richard Cohn once challenged me to consider the shift from metered to nonmetered music as not a difference of *kind*, but merely a difference of *degree*. This way of thinking through these two rhythmic states is useful in the sense that it helps us understand meter and free meter as points on a continuum, which we might metaphorize as a rubber band: a tight, tense state represents the regimented, isometric rhythms of dance music, while a looser state represents the freer or more "expanded" rhythms of free jazz.

As much truth as this observation holds in abstract terms, however, it is a way of thinking that is not particularly invested in the relationship of culture to music. When we understand rhythm in more socially grounded terms, the distinction between meter and free meter carries a different set of consequences. After all, jazz developed historically from dance music to art music to experimental music within the extremely compressed time frame of sixty years, and understanding the music's structures as rooted in dance is centrally important, with the move into free meter consequently representing a profound paradigm shift. The pianist Paul Bley, for example, belonged to a coterie of jazz musicians in the 1960s that were experimenting with rhythmically and harmonically free playing, and he remembered that "a lot of players managed to handle the absence of chord changes, although for many of them that was traumatic and still is. For myself, when the drummer gave up playing [metered] time, that music sounded totally different . . . But for a lot of musicians, not to mention listeners, the music lost *all* of its meaning."[14] The saxophonist David S. Ware, reflecting on the later music of Coltrane, once remarked, "You can get almost as avant-garde as you want to be, as long as you keep that steady pulse . . . Coltrane lost a lot of people when he broke time, and went into the other world and started messing with that multi-directional time."[15]

From my perspective, the stereotypical dichotomy between metered and free-meter music has had problematic consequences that are different than those with which the music theorists are concerned: it deemphasizes the ideology of groove in free jazz, minimizing the bodily experience of the music and removing it from the well of common understanding assumed of social dance rhythms, while conversely cheapening the profound dimension of social dance rhythms. As Kyra Gaunt has noted, there has been an increasing tendency in musical scholarship to privilege musical sounds without giving equal attention to what those sounds signify in bodily terms.[16] Factoring the body back into free jazz via the ideology of groove allows the music to be understood within the tension-and-release paradigm typically referred to in jazz as "swing," and also, when linked with the book's spatial discourse, evokes the cultural work this music did in the hands of real human beings operating in the real world. Given the centrality of dance in black cultures, then, my own position is that the difference between metered and free-meter music is a difference of degree in *abstract* terms, but a difference of kind in *practical* terms. And I am consequently taking the perspective of musicians like Bley and Ware as fundamental to my explorations in this book, accepting the move into free meter as a profound shift within a socially grounded understanding of jazz rhythm—so profound in fact, that for musicians like Ware, it constituted an entirely new "world."

———

My initial ability to hear and think through free jazz began to consolidate in the early 1980s, largely in relation to the work of musicians who are considered to operate in a universe far removed from social dance music. These musicians such as John Coltrane, Cecil Taylor, Sun Ra, Anthony Braxton (particularly the work of his "classic" quartet of the late 1980s/early 1990s), the "avant-rock" musician Captain Beefheart (Don Van Vliet), and postwar composers like Karlheinz Stockhausen, had worked their various ways from origins in jazz, blues, rock, and art music composition to the experimental fringes of their respective traditions. If the repetitive structures of dance music were my main point of departure, what interested me most in the work of these artists was the various ways that repetitive rhythmic figures and cyclical meter had been "unhinged" from each other or done away with altogether. The rhythmic sensibilities of Coltrane and Cecil Taylor, for example, evolved along very linearized paths over time from metered music to alternately tense and flowing free-meter environments. Sun Ra conformed to this dynamic as well and, along with Beefheart, was a master at juxtaposing rhythmic figures against each other at rhythmically unconventional angles. Braxton often worked in a similarly collagist manner, deploying a variety of metered and unmetered elements against repetitive structures that he referred to as "pulse tracks."[17] Meanwhile Stockhausen, who had partially developed out of the rhythmic language associated with serialism, composed works in which musical time was not always measured in terms of a continuous pulse; it could also be experienced as a succession of sonic "episodes" or "events" dispersed in time and even (as in the case of his pieces *Momente*, *Pole*, and *Sternklang*) in physical space. These are simplified, schematic descriptions of a very diverse range of complex works and ideas, but they do summarize concrete expansions of my own understanding of musical time and structure, expansions that eventually provided part of the foundation of this book.

One of the pieces of music that fascinated me during this period, for example, was "Light Reflected Off the Oceands of the Moon," an instrumental song released in 1982 by Captain Beefheart and the Magic Band that was based on the juxtaposition of riffs in multiple, disjunct meters.[18] I spent a lot of time listening to this track from various angles, trying hard to understand how Beefheart came to use the luminous, aquatic imagery of light, reflections, oceans, and moons to describe a music of such hard angles and lurching rhythms. In time, I would come to understand that the "hard angle" strategies of collage, fragmentation, and juxtaposition have often been used to cultivate states of flow and fluidity, a concept that would reveal itself to me much later as I explored not only the music of Coltrane, Cecil Taylor, and other so-called free jazz musicians, but also several contemporary architects (this is an idea I will return to in the next chapter). In any case, these unconventional rhythmic constructions had already planted several seeds in my mind for what might be thought of as a *spatial* experience of music. As my colleague (and music theorist) Eve Poudrier has noted, the deconstruction of meter actually encourages the listener to expand their spatial awareness of music, as a way of reconciling the tension inherent in simultaneous rhythmic perspectives.[19] Inspired by these musicians, my growing sense of the spatial in music set the stage for an expansion of my musical experience of rhythm into the physical world.

NEW SOUNDS IN THE OLD CITY

Around the same period in the mid-1980s I began to develop an interest in contemporary architecture. Besides the musical catalysts, the groundwork had been laid on one hand by a short but transformative stint I worked in the Art and Architecture Library at the Massachusetts Institute of Technology in the fall of 1985, which was my first exposure to some of the ideas that would ultimately help shape this book. But it had also been laid earlier, by the more simple fact of growing up within the architectural environment of New York City that was typified by variations on the square and rectangle shapes that represented the norms of architectural late modernism. The commercial stretch of Park Avenue to the immediate north of Grand Central Terminal, for example, was defined by modernist architectural styles ranging from Art Deco to the so-called Modern Style of Mies van der Rohe, Louis Sullivan, and others—essentially, rectangles of more or less ornamentation, depending on the stylistic language. But in New York City of the 1970s, these buildings existed in an inescapable dialogue with the shapes and textures of postindustrial decay. Less than a mile west of Park Avenue was the decrepit West Side elevated highway, the crumbling network of Hudson River piers, and the deactivated High Line railroad (more recently rehabilitated into an elevated park). As Tim Edensor has chronicled in his rhapsodic paean to the sensuality of industrial decay, there was a lot to learn from this landscape of structures "burst[ing] out of assigned positions in an efflorescence of deconstruction,"[20] and the works of artists of this period such as Robert Smithson, Nancy Holt, Gordon Matta-Clark, Eva Hesse, and Richard Serra offered varied aesthetic reflections on the forms and energies of the postindustrial city.[21]

Like flowers blooming on a decaying log, the gradual obsolescence of industrial New York created the possibility of new aesthetics and socialities. For example, the rugged textures chronicled in Robert Smithson's works represent not only ironic commentary on the postindustrial landscape but also simultaneously resonate and contrast with the feminist rethinking of the landscape suggested by the "earthworks" projects of the artist Nancy Holt.[22] Alvin Baltrop's photo essay *The Piers* captures the erotic activity in the same postindustrial setting (including some of the exact same abandoned piers) in which Gordon Matta-Clark executed *Days' End*, his "anarchitectural" exploitation of the crumbling Hudson River infrastructure.[23] The "whole car" graffiti murals that graced subways in the 1970s were roundly demonized as the epitome of urban lawlessness, yet they provided color and vibrancy to a grim cityscape in the throes of economic

FIGURE 1.1 Tom Sykes and Jason Ramlugon, *Post-Industrial Transformations*.
Reproduced courtesy of Extended Studio.

crisis and, ironically, established a stylistic template for ostensibly "legitimate" corporations to later advertise with their own "ad-wrap" murals on the city's buses and subways.[24] Meanwhile, the decommissioned industrial lofts of lower Manhattan were being refashioned by jazz musicians such as Ornette Coleman, Sam Rivers, and Rashied Ali as performance spaces for the creation of some of the decade's most innovative improvised music, which also happened to prefigure the later rise of districts such as Soho, Tribeca, and Chelsea as centers of the international art world.[25]

———

I was never particularly invested in comic books or science fiction in my formative years. But after seeing models and photographs of Coop Himmelblau's famous rooftop remodeling project in Vienna (figure 1.2) as part of the Museum of Modern Art's 1988 exhibition *Deconstructivist Architecture*, architecture gradually became my de facto science fiction as an adult—it offered by turns a technical and artistic way of experiencing all of the worlds compacted within the city, and of appreciating its shapes, surfaces, and spaces from the subway to the sky.[26] As Carl Abbott so beautifully documented in his 2016 book *Imagining Urban Futures*, in fact, the city—as a consequence of its highly complex modes

FIGURE 1.2 Coop Himmelblau Architects, *Rooftop Remodeling in Falkestrasse*
(1988). Reproduced courtesy of Duccio Malagamba.

of social and technological organization—has been science fiction's most potent
and consistent interface between Earth and worlds beyond Earth.[27] Captivated
by the resonance I sensed between the cityscape that I knew, the architectural
models and drawings I encountered in books, exhibitions, and lectures, and the
musical soundscape in my ears (as I roamed the city with portable music players), some of the forms I encountered began to strike me as three-dimensional
analogues to what I had sensed in the more experimental spheres of jazz—in
terms of both concepts and actual musical structures. Without formal knowledge
of architecture, design, or urban planning, I followed my path instinctively, and it
consistently led me in two directions. The first path was toward the experimental
architectural currents of the 1960s and 1970s in which some architects, inspired
by the countercultural ethos of the times, challenged established norms of archi-

tectural form and function. The second path was toward the design revolution taking place in the context of what came to be called the "architectural neo-avant-garde" of the 1980s and 1990s, when a subsequent generation of architects began to conduct their own experiments with form as the technical tools of the field evolved from manual drafting to digital rendering and eventually, animation software. In truth, these two moments were not isolated—they exist as very close points on a historical/stylistic continuum spanning a mere four decades. What I found most intriguing within the experimental architectural currents of the 1960s and 1970s was the incredible variety of forms and structures generated in dialogue with broader social and political currents that privileged freedom, mobility, and flexibility. And while the digital architecture of the 1980s and beyond also inspired me to think in terms of varieties of form and structure, its de facto procedures of improvisation also inspired me to think about the types of compositional processes facilitated by digital technology.

I could cite numerous books as catalysts and inspirations, but I will focus here on just two that bookend the trajectory of concepts in this book. *Infinite Polyhedra* was the first to inspire me to explore the connections between jazz and architecture. Published in 1974 by a group of architects affiliated with the Israel Institute of Technology in Haifa, *Infinite Polyhedra* is a photographic compendium of polyhedra models that, in theory, can be infinitely extended ("tiled" or "tessellated") across space.[28] Although a work like this would mainly be of fairly prosaic interest to architects and designers, I was captivated by the formal intricacy and variation of the shapes. Their existence as physical realizations of complex equations reminded me of the densely chromatic, hypermathematical sprawl of John Coltrane's improvisations on pieces such as "Chim Chim Cheree" (1965), with melodic shapes so rigorously sculpted and aggressively transposed that they began to evoke volumes rotating in space. In fact, the use of geometric forms as analogues for harmonic or melodic ideas was a prominent idea in jazz of the 1960s and 1970s, as musicians began to conceive of pitch sequences less in terms of line and more in terms of shape. Coltrane, the multiwoodwind player Yusef Lateef, and the guitarist Pat Martino are three of several musicians who have experimented with geometric visualizations of their harmonic thinking.[29] It is not surprising that these three musicians are all associated, in their various ways, with a tradition of jazz mysticism. Across the various cultural traditions of mathematical thought, there is a long-standing practice of meditating on the formal complexity of polyhedra as a form of mystical contemplation, a history that, as we will see, converges in Coltrane's (and the other aforementioned musicians') manipulations of harmonic shapes and patterns to create a mood of spirituality and mysticism in their music.[30]

In its exhaustive chronicling of symmetric forms and their transformations, *Infinite Polyhedra* reminded me conceptually of a book like Nicolas Slonimsky's *Thesaurus of Scales and Melodic Patterns*,[31] from which Coltrane and other jazz musicians had derived source material for complex chord progressions (such as in "Giant Steps") and melodic ideas (such as the improvisations in "Chim Chim Cheree").[32] But if my fascination with *Infinite Polyhedra* was originally inspired by what I perceived as correspondences with the manipulation of pitch materials in jazz improvisation, I came to realize that the book is equally relevant to rhythmic considerations (as we will see in chapter 5, the Lost Quintet's drummer Jack De-Johnette sometimes conceptualized the group's metrically free passages in terms of shapes). I gradually intuited that one could argue an important and arguably symbiotic relationship between symmetrical pitch relationships that lack tonal gravity, and rhythmic shapes detached from traditional forms of metrical gravity.

Infinite Polyhedra was not exactly a countercultural document, but its emphasis on reconfigurable forms did reflect the experimental currents of the 1960s and 1970s, when values of impermanence, freedom, and mobility were often manifest in modular architectural designs that could be easily assembled, disassembled, reconfigured and transported. These could be found everywhere from various alternative lifestyle communities, to public housing developments, to industrial architecture, to music festivals, and even in outer-space dwellings. As one reviewer of the book observed, in fact, the tessellation of interlocking, symmetric shapes across space was strongly resonant with the modular architecture of outer-space habitats: "[I]t is abundantly evident that . . . the authors have in mind the use of these forms in architecture. The photographs, taken as they are in good lighting on a black background, are very suggestive of habitats for future interplanetary space stations."[33]

At the other end of the historical timeline was Joseph Choma's *Morphing: A Guide to Mathematical Transformations for Architects and Designers*, a 2015 compendium of illustrations in which a series of shapes and surfaces are transformed—in this case, through very complex trigonometric equations.[34] Published almost half a century after *Infinite Polyhedra*, *Morphing* was published in the heart of the digital age, its manipulation of ideas of form in the virtual realm having found concrete expression in the design language of postmodern, deconstructive, and, especially, so-called parametric architecture. This was directly relevant to my project. With regularized meter deconstructed in the wake of the rhythmic innovations of Coltrane, Cecil Taylor, and others, I needed a language to discuss rhythms that now seemed to float freely in metrically untethered space, and I began to sense how beautiful it could be to narrate the structures of free jazz using terms derived from the kinds of forms and gestures analyzed in these books: *Slopes. Splines. Curves. Rotations. Spirals.* Ultimately, my path from John Coltrane to *Infinite Polyhedra* to Cecil Taylor to *Morphing* gradually convinced me that one potential solution to my questions about free meter in jazz might be in partially re-conceptualizing these rhythms in terms of *shapes*, *spaces*, and *surfaces*, with architecture's language of *spatiality* and *design* potentially helping to clarify the varied structural innovations that have been subsumed under the meaningless and misleading umbrella term "free jazz."

In particular, my musical thinking would benefit from the digitally enabled work of architects such as Zaha Hadid and Patrik Schumacher, Greg Lynn, and Peter Eisenman who, in their various ways, sought to transcend an architecture of solid, stable structures by imbuing their projects with sensations of continuous motion, flow, or transformation. Hadid's radical manipulations of perspectival distortion warped her buildings as if they were being viewed through the dis-torted edge of a magnifying glass, while the writings of her chief collaborator Patrik Schumacher theorized her eccentric configurations of space and surface.[35] Greg Lynn was a child of the Space Age whose undulating "spline" surfaces and free-floating architectural "blobs" were simultaneously inspired by the advances of digital technology and the imaginings of science fiction.[36] Some of Peter Eisenman's best-known projects took their shape from the digital juxtaposition of radically dissimilar forms, and his collagist approach to design gave me a way of modeling rhythmic structures generated by the juxtaposition of disjunct metric strata (a process set in motion in jazz by Ornette Coleman's influential 1959 piece "Lonely Woman" and elaborated by John Coltrane in work such as *Meditations* and by Miles Davis in works such as *Bitches Brew*).[37]

In retrospect, it doesn't seem at all random that my initial epiphany took place when it did in the 1980s. Transformations in the world of ideas seem to unfold generationally, and it was also in the 1980s that jazz musicians like Steve Cole-man and Greg Osby were devising novel approaches to the forms of chromatic saturation innovated in the 1960s by musicians like Coltrane, Eric Dolphy, and even Ornette Coleman. In the same way that these musicians were formalizing the angles, slopes, and shapes of pitch sequences detached from established conceptions of tonality, I understand my own spatial musings as a generation-ally parallel exploration of the angles, slopes, and shapes of rhythmic gestures detached from established conceptions of meter.

———

The subject of connections between architecture and music has been well estab-lished within the Western artistic discourse over many centuries, dating back to ancient Greece and Rome. It encompasses figures as diverse as Pythagoras (fifth century BCE), who was mainly concerned with musical sound in relation to ideas of ratio and proportion as expressions of natural laws, and Vitruvius (first century BCE), who was particularly interested in the behavior of sound in space. Much later in the early nineteenth century, we have figures such as the German writer and statesman Johann Wolfgang von Goethe, whose famous comment about music as "liquid architecture" and architecture as "frozen music" has long stood as the emblematic statement for those exploring the connection between the two fields.[38] The modes of correspondence expanded during the twentieth century, explored by several figures associated with the Bauhaus in Germany (particularly the Swiss-German artist Paul Klee), and by experimental composers such as Iannis Xenakis, who collaborated with the French architect Le Corbusier on the famous Phillips Pavilion for Expo '58 in Brussels. In more recent decades, it has been explored by architects who have pursued morphological correspondences between music and architecture, such as Steven Holl, who has built projects inspired by the formal qualities of specific pieces of music.[39] Holl's 1989 "Stretto House" in Dallas, for example, was an attempt to model the formal qualities of Bela Bartok's 1936 piece *Music for Strings, Percussion and Celeste* in architectural form.[40] Meanwhile, experimental composers such as Barry Blesser and Linda-Ruth Salter have drawn on both architecture and acoustics, using concepts such as *echolocation* to musicalize our experience of physical environments.[41]

Almost without exception, however, these figures have used the Western art music tradition (or its experimental offshoots) as the musical point of com-parison. The title of Reyner Banham's canonical text *The Architecture of the Well-Tempered Environment*, a history of environmental engineering, is a clear reference to the Baroque composer Johann Sebastian Bach's series of keyboard pieces, *The Well-Tempered Clavier*.[42] The architect Daniel Libeskind has not only been one of the most creative theorists of architecture's digital turn but has also thought a lot about the relationship between the two media. Two of his books, for example, are titled *Counterpoint* and *Chamber Works*, reflecting the extent to which his architectural practice has been inspired by his love of Western art music.[43] It should be unsurprising, then, that Libeskind's thoughts on the relationship between the two fields are ultimately quite conservative, based on the correspondence between fixed buildings and musical compositions fixed by notation. As he asserted in 1998: "Architecture, the way it's produced and received, is very similar to music. Because music is very precise. Every note is exactly where it has to be. It's extremely structured. Yet its impact is totally emotional."[44]

So, the question becomes: what might the connection between the two fields (and their respective discourses) be if the musical side were strongly based not on notated musical compositions, but on jazz structures generated by improvisation? And which other modes of thought might be generated by this particular intermedial conversation? That is, by definition, a late twentieth-century idea and one that (as we will see) with the exception of the French architect Le Corbusier and the architect-scholar David P. Brown, remains almost completely unexplored. And if Libeskind's conceptual anchor in music is the Western classical tradition, I have been conversely drawn to periods and movements within the history of architecture that I find are particularly resonant with the jazz music explored in this book (more on this shortly). Most directly helpful in this light has been the subset of architects associated with the digital revolution that has taken place since the 1980s, encompassing periods in the work of Lynn, Libeskind, Hadid, Eisenman, and others. Because of their radical formal experimentation, these designers have sometimes been referred to as "theorists of architectural instability,"[45] an idea that is directly relevant to my music-analytical concerns in this book (a recent book-length survey of Libeskind's work is tellingly titled *Edge of Order*, engaging the same order/disorder dichotomy that has been central to the free jazz discourse).[46] Finally, the work of the postwar German architect Frei Otto was profoundly inspiring throughout this project, his "tensile structures" providing particularly valuable analogues for the rhythmic ideas at the heart of my project.[47] Conceived in the midst of the Space Age but modeled after natural structures such as soap bubbles and spider webs, Otto's work and ideas are beautifully relevant to a flexible conception of rhythm that, while a product of the late industrial era, resonates with the complex rhythms of nature as well as the flotation of antigravity environments.

———

Comparisons with architecture not only held implications for formalist thinking, they also provided new ways of understanding physical environments,
institutions, social formations, and forms of political agency. Like the cutting
edge of jazz during the 1960s and 1970s that had been marked by the rise of
artist-controlled performance spaces (such as the jazz lofts of New York City),
artist-run recording labels, and self-sufficient musical collectives (such as the
Association for the Advancement of Creative Musicians in Chicago, the Black
Artists Group in St. Louis, or Horace Tapscott's Pan-Afrikan People's Arkestra
in Los Angeles), the more daring architects and urban planners were creating
work in resonance with the social and political shifts of the time.[48] There were
experiments with ephemeral, modular forms (such as inflatable, "pneumatic" architecture, Buckminster Fuller's geodesic domes, or even entire cities) that could
be assembled, disassembled, transported, and recombined in various ways.[49]
There were the "space frame" forms of French architects like Yona Friedman,
built on stilts that were inherently political in that their see-through aesthetic
simultaneously privileged transparency while their raised foundations empow-
ered ground space as public space.[50] There were architectural collectives such as
Utopie in France or Archigram in England, whose radical interrogation of concepts, structures, and environments challenged the architectural establishment
and whose colorful, self-published pamphlets burst with a youthful energy and
irreverence that was not so different from their later counterparts in punk and
indie rock magazines and pamphlets (jazz, in fact, would benefit greatly from a
'zine culture of its own).[51] Themes of spontaneity, flexibility, and impermanence
were even prominent in works of more mainstream architectural thinkers across
the ideological spectrum.[52]

As helpful as architecture might be as a way of thinking about the context and
aesthetics of jazz, however, contemporary architecture also diverges dramatically
from jazz in certain fundamental respects. Created by the architectural celebrities
of our time, the notorious works of designers like Zaha Hadid have at times been
sharply criticized as embodying several problematic aspects of our neoliberal
economic era. As Douglas Spencer has noted, the blobs, fragments, and curvilinear surfaces of contemporary architecture are often argued by their designers as
inherently progressive, the antithesis of hierarchical forms of organization, and
springing from a democratizing impulse. In fact, as the controversy surrounding
Hadid's Cultural Center in Baku, Azerbaijan, makes clear, the implementation of
these works is sometimes predicated on problematic concentrations of capital,
exploitative labor practices, and the oppressive control of urban space.[53] The

regimes of power and capital underlying some of these projects are diametrically opposed to the contexts within which jazz has historically evolved, and are also arguably reflected in the very racialization of architecture, a field in which, as was discussed earlier, it has been comparatively difficult for people of African descent to place a definitive mark. In this sense, black music has as many potential interventions to make into architecture as architecture does into black music.

THE CITY AS SONG

The connection between jazz and the sounds of the city was
evident to virtually all who listened in. Joel Rogers located the roots
of jazz in African music, but he also acknowledged the influence of
"the American environment," and that environment was filled with noise.
"With its cowbells, auto horns, calliopes, rattles, dinner gongs, kitchen
utensils, cymbals, screams, crashes, clankings and monotonous
rhythm," Rogers remarked in 1925, jazz "bears all the marks
of a nerve-strung, strident, mechanized civilization."[54]

Emily Thompson, from The Soundscape of Modernity

The idea of bringing jazz, architecture, and the city into dialogue might seem new, but as a music that has fundamentally evolved in urban spaces, jazz had been understood as a way of hearing the city from its very beginnings. From the standpoint of architectural history, the French architect Le Corbusier was undoubtedly the central figure in linking the two art forms, his own epiphany occurring after he heard Louis Armstrong perform in New York. Twenty-two years after the Jamaican-American writer Joel A. Rogers offered the more general insights quoted in the epigraph above, Le Corbusier recounted his own impressions in *When the Cathedrals Were White*, a 1947 journal of his reflections compiled during a visit to the US. In Le Corbusier's account:

[Armstrong's] orchestra has not been silent for a second. Its precision is staggering. Nothing in our European experience can be compared to it. That implacable exactitude expresses American taste; I see in it an effect of the machine . . . The men are tireless, like a smoothly running turbine . . . The rhythmic instinct of the virgin African forests has learned the lesson of the machine and in America . . . the rigour of exactitude is a pleasure . . . Manhattan is hot jazz in stone and steel. The contemporary renewal (i.e., of architecture and urbanism) has to attach itself to some point. The Negroes have fixed that point through music.[55]

Although this characterization suffers from typically primitivist ideas of Africa held by Westerners of his generation, Le Corbusier's fundamental observation, in my reading, is that, in the context of late-industrial America, African American sensibilities (in this case, jazz music) often worked to humanize the aesthetics of industry and of the city. His architectural sensitivity to qualities of musical structure, in particular, seems to have enabled him to avoid the traps that so many European auditors of his time fell into—of hearing black music as completely instinctual, unplanned, and unstructured. Furthermore, this view—despite whatever Le Corbusier may or may not have actually understood about African music—enables the values of precision, repetition, and exactitude to be understood as having as many roots in the Africanist aesthetic principles underlying jazz as they did in the mechanical processes of Western industry (more on this in the next chapter). Their connection with dance meant that these values could be understood as capable of generating aesthetic pleasure and community, as opposed to mere alienation and mechanized conformity. The urban environment, by extension, could be experienced as a site of new and dynamic forms, and not only degraded and denatured forms. Taken as a whole, these were very different takes on industry and the urban condition than were extant in Western Europe at the time, where the forward march of industrialization and urbanization were typically experienced as profoundly dehumanizing developments.

From the musical side, jazz has remained in intimate dialogue with architecture in a number of ways including, most immediately, the spaces (for example, areas of cities and musical venues) in which it has typically flourished. Louis Armstrong's *Satchmo: My Life in New Orleans* and Michael Heller's *Loft Jazz* bookend the urban history of the music between 1900 and 1980 and both function as de facto cartographies of their respective environments, mapping out the urban currents through which the music and musicians flowed.[56] This dialogue has also been readily apparent in the traditions of album cover art that situate the music within the urban environments in which it has evolved. The celebrated cover designs and photography of Reid Miles and Francis Wolff for the Blue Note label, for example, typify this sensibility.[57] Thad Jones's *The Magnificent*[58] and Herbie Hancock's *Inventions and Dimensions*[59] situate the jazz musician as a significant presence in the city, their prominent positioning offering thoughtful (Jones) or authoritative (Hancock) commentary on the cityscape around them.

Larry Young's *Into Somethin'* (1965)[60] positions jazz as a mode of global commentary by situating the organist beneath the dramatic curvature of the UNESCO building in Paris, while the similarly dramatic curvature on the cover of Andrew Hill's *Judgment!*[61] suggests an existential weight for the music through a shadow creeping ominously across the underside of a bridge in Central Park. Both covers use the jazz musician to humanize the monumental scale of urban forms, while using details of the forms themselves to suggest parallels with the music.

Some of the most striking covers, on the other hand, tease out more abstract rhythms from the forms and energies of city and industry. For every stereotypical image of Jimmy Smith hanging from the side of a boxcar (e.g., *Midnight Special*)[62] or Freddie Hubbard framed by skyscrapers (e.g., *Goin' Up*)[63], there was also Lee Morgan's *City Lights*[64] and Art Blakey's *At the Jazz Corner of the World*,[65] the covers of which feature surrealist grids of urban imagery juxtaposed on planes suggesting exhilarating, intoxicating motion. Don Cherry's *Symphony for Improvisers*[66] similarly situates the trumpeter against a progression of marble slabs whose rhythms suggest regularity while their surfaces contribute a contrasting range of textural variations. Jackie McLean's *One Step Beyond*[67] positions the saxophonist beneath an irregular network of steel rods and beams that provide an abstract geometry, ordering the infinity of the open sky above him.[68] The striking cover photograph of pianist Mal Waldron's *Mal-1* (shot by Reid Miles but released on the Prestige label) presents what appears to be a wall of rectangular bricks or windows, whose regular spacing and subtle textural variations suggest rhythmic parallels with the music, while hovering between the repetition of minimalist painters like Agnes Martin and the austere sensuality of color field painting typified by painters like Mark Rothko (interestingly, Waldron went on to record a song titled *Tensile Structures*, its title recalling an influential early text by Frei Otto).[69]

———

Of course, music, as a physical (i.e., acoustic) phenomenon, already exists in three dimensions. But, like the artists of the 1960s (such as Eva Hesse and Gego) who devised ways to gradually lift their lines off of the two-dimensional surfaces of painting and drawing and into the three-dimensional spaces of sculpture,[70] I am aspiring throughout this book to "lift" musical sound off of the recorded surface and into a three-dimensional discourse of shapes, spaces, and surfaces. These insights are not necessarily novel. In his biography of Charlie Parker, for example, Stanley Crouch often resorted to the language of sculpture to evoke the way many of the musicians discussed in this book manipulate time and ensemble structure.[71] And in the prologue of *Invisible Man*, Ralph Ellison wrote of an analytical epiphany he experienced while listening to Louis Armstrong under the influence of marijuana, an experience that activated his spatial experience of the music:

> Under the spell of the reefer I discovered a new analytical way of listening to music . . . That night I found myself hearing not only in time, but in space as well. I not only entered the music but descended, like Dante, into its depths. And beneath the swiftness of the hot tempo there was a slower tempo and a cave and I entered it.[72]

As I will discuss in the next chapter, building (or hearing) music in layers of successive rhythmic density (i.e., ensemble stratification) is a core structural principle of West African music that survived the transition into the African diaspora, and which contains obvious resonances with architectural thinking. And as I (and some of the architects I cite) discuss in the John Coltrane essay, mind-altering substances have sometimes played a role in generating new conceptions and experiences of space. But Ellison's "new analytical way of listening to music"—whether he realized it or not—was less reliant on psychoactive agents and more fundamentally reliant on sonic technologies and philosophies that predated the American context, and that had long been a medium for the articulation of social, political, and historical spaces. In fact, it is impossible to discuss the various political transformations of black cultures without discussing the concurrent transformations in black rhythmic technologies. In the 1960s, those technologies would provide the bases for the utopian imaginings of the era and it was through their manipulation of those technologies that John Coltrane and his musicians would find their path to the stars, while Miles Davis and his musicians would imbue the rhythms of city streets with the same cosmic energies.

NOTES

1. From "Borges at NYU." Reprinted in Burgin, Richard. *Jorge Luis Borges: Conversations*. Jackson: University of Mississippi Press, 1998, 123.

2. Steffens, Jo. *Unpacking My Library: Architects and Their Books*. New Haven: Yale University Press, 2009.

3. See Thompson, Robert Farris. *Flash of the Spirit: African and Afro-American Art and*

Philosophy. New York: Knopf/Doubleday, 1983. See also his essay collection: *Aesthetic of the Cool: Afro-Atlantic Art and Music*. New York: Periscope, 2011.

4. Le Corbusier. *When the Cathedrals Were White*. New York: McGraw Hill, 1964.

5. Wilkins, Craig. *The Aesthetics of Equity: Notes on Race, Space, Architecture, and Music*. Minneapolis: University of Minnesota Press, 2007.

6. Rakatansky, Mark. *Tectonic Acts of Desire and Doubt*. London: AA Publications, 2012.

7. Connor, Rob. "Jazz and Architecture: Intersections of Rhythm, Proportions and Variations." Master's Thesis. School of Architecture, University of Cincinnati, 2006.

8. Brown, David P. *Noise Orders: Jazz, Improvisation, and Architecture*. Minneapolis: University of Minnesota Press, 2006.

9. Anderson, Sean, and Mabel Wilson, eds. *Reconstructions: Architecture and Blackness in America*. New York: Museum of Modern Art, 2021.

10. Lokko, Lesley. *White Papers, Black Marks: Architecture, Race, and Culture*. Minneapolis: University of Minnesota Press, 2000, 14.

11. Lokko, *White Papers, Black Marks*, 15.

12. Munro, Martin. *Different Drummers: Rhythm and Race in the Americas*. Berkeley: University of California Press, 2010.

13. See Wilmer, Valerie. *As Serious as Your Life: The Story of the New Jazz*. London: Serpent's Tail, 1977. See also Figi, J. B. "African Code, Black Methodology." *DownBeat* 42, no. 7 (April 10, 1975): 10–14, 31. We might also mention Taylor's own occasional use of Africanist imagery such as his album *Olu Iwa* (Soul Note, 1986) or his poem "Acqueh-R-Oyo" released on *One Too Many Salty Swift and No Goodbye* (Hat Hut TWO 3R02, 1980). Both reference the symbology of the Yoruba-speaking peoples of West Africa.

14. Bley, Paul, and David Lee. *Stopping Time: Paul Bley and the Transformation of Jazz*. Montreal: Vehicule Press, 1999, 90.

15. Ware quoted in Mandel, Howard. "Divine Wind." *The Wire*, July 2002. Portions of the article are reprinted at: https://electriccaves.wordpress.com/2011/03/01/john-coltrane-a-divine-wind-psychedelics-eastern-culture.

16. Gaunt, Kyra. *The Games Black Girls Play: Learning the Ropes from Double-Dutch to Hip-Hop*. New York: New York University Press, 2006, 25.

17. See Locke, Graham. *Forces in Motion: Anthony and the Meta-Reality of Creative Music*. London: Quartet, 1988. The discussion of Braxton's "pulse track" structures begins on page 60.

18. Captain Beefheart and the Magic Band. "Light Reflected Off the Oceands of the Moon." Virgin VS 534-12. Originally released 1982. This is an instrumental version of a song called "Hey Garland, I Dig Your Tweed Coat," which appears on Captain Beefheart's 1982 album *Ice Cream for Crow* (Virgin AET 38274).

19. This was an idea that Eve Poudrier and I generated in a 2011 conversation about free meter.

20. Edensor, Tim. *Industrial Ruins: Space, Aesthetics and Materiality*. Oxford: Berg, 2005, 110.

21. See Steinberg, Rolf. *Dead Tech: A Guide to the Archaeology of Tomorrow*. Los Angeles: Hennessy and Ingalls, 2000.

22. A good survey of this aspect of Smithson's work is Reynolds, Ann. *Robert Smithson: Learning from New Jersey and Elsewhere*. Cambridge, MA: MIT Press, 2004. For a survey of Nancy Holt's work, see Williams, Alena, ed. *Nancy Holt: Sightlines*. Berkeley: University of California Press, 2011.

23. See Weinberg, Jonathan. *Pier Groups: Art and Sex Along the New York Waterfront*. University Park: Pennsylvania State University Press, 2019. See also Reid, James. *Alvin Baltrop: The Piers*. Madrid: TF Editores, 2015.

24. A comprehensive introduction to the history of subway graffiti in New York City is: Miller, Ivor. *Aerosol Kingdom: Subway Painters of New York City*. Bloomington: Indiana University Press, 2002.

25. For the history of the jazz loft scene in New York, see Heller, Michael. *Loft Jazz: Improvising New York in the 1970s*. Berkeley: University of California Press, 2016.

26. See https://www.moma.org/calendar/exhibitions/1813? for a survey of the *Deconstructivist Architecture* exhibition.

27. Abbott, Carl. *Imagining Urban Futures: Cities in Science Fiction and What We Might Learn from Them*. Middletown, CT: Wesleyan University Press, 2016.

28. Wachmann, Avraham, Michael Burt, and Menachem Kleinman. *Infinite Polyhedra*. Haifa: Israel Institute of Technology, 1974. Jay Kappraff defines "infinite" polyhedra as follows: "M. Burt, M. Kleinmann, and A. Wachmann [1974] discovered a large family of infinite regular polyhedral based on nets derived from lattices and point complexes and their duals. Whenever a net defines a space-filling collection of polyhedral with central symmetry, Burt et al define a dual net as follows: place a vertex at the center of symmetry of the polyhedron defined by the net and pair an edge of the dual net with each face of the polyhedron so that the edges connect the center of symmetry of adjacent polyhedral through the centroid of the face. For example, by this definition the dual net of the fcc connects the centers of each tetrahedron to the four surrounding octahedron centers and the centers of the octahedron to the eight surrounding tetrahedron centers." See Kappraff, Jay. *Connections: The Geometric Bridge Between Art and Science*. Singapore: World Scientific, 1991, 362.

29. To cite two examples: John Coltrane's famous "tone circle" is reproduced in Yusef Lateef's *Repository of Scales and Melodic Patterns* (Aebersold Jazz, 1981), and Pat Martino's own geometric scheme is printed in the liner notes of his 2003 album *Think Tank* (Blue Note 7243 5 92009 2 7).

30. The relationship of polyhedra and mysticism is explored in detail in George Fleck

and Marjorie Senechal's 2013 book *Shaping Space: Exploring Polyhedra in Nature, Art, and the Geometrical Imagination* (New York: Springer).

31. Slonimsky, Nicolas. *Thesaurus of Scales and Melodic Patterns.* New York: Hal Leonard, 1947.

32. I am not the only person to have intuited this connection between the shapes of Coltrane's improvisations and the structure of polyhedra. See, for example: Roel Hollander's blog entry "John Coltrane's Music and Geometry" at https://roelhollander.eu/en/blog-saxophone/Coltrane-Geometry/.

33. Wenninger, Magnus J. "Review of *Infinite Polyhedra.*" *Leonardo* 9, no. 2 (Spring 1976): 158.

34. Choma, Joseph. *Morphing: A Guide to Mathematical Transformations for Architects and Designers.* London: Laurence King, 2015.

35. See, for example: Schumacher, Patrik, and Zaha Hadid. *Digital Hadid: Landscapes in Motion.* Zurich: Birkhauser, 2004.

36. See Lynn, Greg. *Animate Form.* Princeton, NJ: Princeton Architectural Press, 1999. See also: Lynn, Greg. *Predator.* Seoul: DAMDI, 2006; Lynn, Greg, Michael Maltzan, and Alessandro Poli. *Other Space Odysseys.* Edited by Giovanna Borasi and Mirko Zardini. Montreal: Canadian Centre for Architecture, 2010.

37. See Davidson, Cynthia, ed. *Tracing Eisenman: Peter Eisenman Complete Works.* London: Thames and Hudson, 2008.

38. This statement by Goethe is accepted to have been made in 1829 and has been most recently published in Eckermann, Peter. *Conversations With Goethe.* London: Penguin, 2022.

39. See Holl's comments in the video "The Architectonics of Music": http://architectonicsofmusic.com.

40. For an overview of Holl's Stretto House project, see https://www.stevenholl.com/projects/stretto-house.

41. See Blesser, Barry, and Linda-Ruth Salter. *Spaces Speak, Are You Listening? Experiencing Aural Architecture.* Cambridge, MA: MIT Press, 2007.

42. Banham, Reyner. *The Architecture of the Well-Tempered Environment.* London: The Architectural Press, 1969.

43. Libeskind, Daniel, and Paul Goldberger. *Counterpoint.* Berlin: De Gruyter, 2008. See also his *Chamber Works: Meditations on Themes from Heraclitus* (Architectural Association, 1983).

44. Libeskind, as quoted in "Counterpoint: Daniel Libeskind in Conversation with Paul Goldberger," *Counterpoint,* 12.

45. For an introduction to these architectural ideas, see Johnson, Philip, and Mark Wigley. *Deconstructivist Architecture.* New York: Museum of Modern Art, 1988.

46. Libeskind, Daniel, and Tim McKeough. *Edge of Order*. New York: Clarkson Potter, 2018.

47. See Nerdinger, Winfried, ed. *Frei Otto, Complete Works: Lightweight Construction, Natural Design*. Berlin: De Gruyter, 2005.

48. See the following works: Lewis, George. *A Power Stronger Than Itself: The AACM and American Experimental Music*. Chicago: University of Chicago Press, 2008. Looker, Benjamin. *The Point from Which Creation Begins: The Black Artists Group of St. Louis*. Columbia: University of Missouri Press, 2004. Isoardi, Steven. *The Dark Tree: Jazz and the Community Arts in Los Angeles*. Berkeley: University of California Press, 2006.

49. For a comprehensive survey of Fuller's work, Hays, K. Michael. *Buckminster Fuller: Starting with the Universe*. New York: Whitney Museum of American Art, 2008.

50. See Larry Busbea's *Topologies: The Urban Utopia in France, 1960–1970* (MIT Press, 2007) for a survey of the French architectural avant-garde of the 1960s.

51. For a survey of this culture of architectural zines, see Colomina, Beatriz, and Craig Buckley, eds. *Clip, Stamp, Fold: The Radical Architecture of Little Magazines, 196x to 197x*. New York and Barcelona: Actar, 2010.

52. Good introductory surveys to this period of architectural experimentation would include: Blauvelt, Andrew, ed. *Hippie Modernism: The Search for Utopia*. Minneapolis: Walker Art Center, 2015. Buckley, Craig. *Graphic Assembly: Montage, Media, and Experimental Architecture in the 1960s*. Minneapolis: University of Minnesota Press, 2019. Busbea, *Topologies*.

53. One journalistic introduction to the Baku controversy is: Wainwright, Oliver. "Wave of Protest over Zaha Hadid's Baku Prizewinner." *Guardian*, June 30, 2014. https://www.theguardian.com/artanddesign/2014/jun/30/zaha-hadid-architecture. For more general discussion of the problematics of contemporary architecture, see: Spencer, Douglas. *The Architecture of Neoliberalism: How Contemporary Architecture Became an Instrument of Control and Compliance*. London: Bloomsbury, 2016.

54. Thompson, Emily. *The Soundscape of Modernity: Architectural Acoustics and the Culture of Listening in America, 1900–1933*. Cambridge, MA: MIT Press, 2002, 130–31.

55. From Le Corbusier, "The Spirit of the Machine, and Negroes in the U.S.A.," in *When the Cathedrals Were White*.

56. Armstrong, Louis. *Satchmo: My Life in New Orleans*. Paris: Hachette, 1952. See also Heller, Michael. *Loft Jazz: Improvising New York in the 1970s*. Berkeley: University of California Press, 2016.

57. For an introduction to the art of the Blue Note label, see: Havers, Richard. *Blue Note: Uncompromising Expression*. London: Thames and Hudson, 2014.

58. Jones, Thad. *The Magnificent Thad Jones*. Blue Note LP 1527. Originally released 1957.

59. Hancock, Herbie. *Inventions and Dimensions*. Blue Note 84147. Originally released 1963.

60. Young, Larry. *Into Somethin'*. Blue Note BST 84187. Originally released 1965.

61. Hill, Andrew. *Judgment!* Blue Note 84159. Originally released 1964.

62. Smith, Jimmy. *Midnight Special*. Blue Note BST 84078. Originally released 1961.

63. Hubbard, Freddie. *Goin' Up*. Blue Note BST 84056. Originally released 1960.

64. Morgan, Lee. *City Lights*. Blue Note 1575. Originally released 1957.

65. Art Blakey and the Jazz Messengers. *At the Jazz Corner of the World*. Blue Note 4015. Originally released 1959.

66. Cherry, Don. *Symphony for Improvisers*. Blue Note 4247. Originally released 1966.

67. McLean, Jackie. *One Step Beyond*. Blue Note LP 4137. Originally released 1963.

68. Background information for many of these covers can be found in Havers, *Blue Note*.

69. Waldron, Mal. *Mal-1*. Prestige 9053. Originally released 1959. Waldron's "Tensile Structures" is included on his 1979 album *Mingus Lives* (Enja 3075). See also Otto, Frei. *Tensile Structures: Basic Concepts and Survey of Tensile Structures*. Cambridge, MA: MIT Press, 1967.

70. See Butler, Cornelia H., and Catherine de Zegher, eds. *On Line: Drawing Through the Twentieth Century*. New York: Museum of Modern Art, 2010.

71. Crouch, Stanley. *Kansas City Lightning: The Rise and Times of Charlie Parker*. New York: Harper Collins, 2013.

72. Ellison, Ralph. *Invisible Man*. New York: Vintage International, 1947, 8.

TWO

Curvilinearity, Swing, and the Spline

The Africanist Grid as a Mode
of Jazz Consciousness

Many people say, "Oh, your architecture is so aggressive. Why do you
slant the pieces? Why do you break it? Why do you twist it?" The simplest
explanation is: if you slant a piece of architecture, then you break the
function so that very interesting spatial effects can be created.[1]

Wolf D. Prix of Coop Himmelblau

A frame or grid only exists within a larger virtual complexity that exceeds it.[2]

John Rajchman, on Peter Eisenman

If African music was an important source of inspiration for African American
jazz musicians working to create a "blacker" music in the context of Civil Rights,
Black Power, and Pan-Africanism, it is also true that many free jazz musicians
and audiences initially functioned under profound misunderstandings of African music, rhythm, and structure. In the United States, one reason for this was
that, while many free jazz musicians were inspired by the idea of African music
as a ritual or ceremonial music, they did not often engage with the idea of it as
danced music—at least, not in any conventional sense of the term. And this is
most likely because, after the paradigm shift from the popular dance music of
the swing era into the listening music of bebop, many American jazz musicians
typically conceived of "modern jazz" in opposition to the world of "commercial"

dance music and, further, had not yet problematized jazz's frequent Eurocentric bias in the criteria of what constituted "serious" art. In Europe, meanwhile, where the memory of colonization and fascism was still fresh, African music (and modern jazz) were typically encountered through conduits established by the political left that conferred on it an aura of an anti-authoritarian, folkloric music.[3] Philosophically, this meant that the music was assumed to exist in opposition to the authoritarian and conformist impulses these listeners felt to be implied by the metronomic pulse of popular dance music. And while they were willing to accept it as dance music (as long as it remained within the conceptual bounds of "folklore"), their philosophical resistance to a consistent pulse prevented them from understanding how the polyrhythmic (and danced) elaboration of an underlying pulse implied a very different social vision than the plodding, monotonous rhythm of the marching military boots that had been such a terrifying element of their soundscape a mere twenty years earlier. Divorced from its danced component, however, many musicians and scholars were unable to properly understand the nature of African (poly)rhythm. Consider the following passage from Philippe Carles's and Jean-Louis Comolli's canonical 1971 text *Free Jazz/Black Power*:

> Because it refers to African polyrhythms, swing cannot be limited by notions such as regularity, uniformity, unity; it is never synonymous with monotony or reducible to a kind of metronomic beat.[4]

This not-uncommon error in hearing polyrhythmic African music results from a failure to distinguish the improvisational freedom of its surface from the rigid, unchanging rhythmic cycles (generally audible but sometimes internalized and inaudible) that provide the foundation of a performance—ironically, the same confusion that makes modern jazz difficult to understand for many listeners. The truth—as any basic-level student of African dance or drumming can attest—is that regardless of how abstract its polyrhythms might sound, the vast majority of traditional music from sub-Saharan Africa is strictly governed by "metronomic" markers such as repeating ostinati and cyclical "timeline" patterns. In both the United States and Europe, then, the political need to project values of "freedom" onto African musics sometimes led to a distorted understanding of their rhythmic structures. At the same time, however, these misunderstandings also sometimes resulted in radically new ways of experiencing, conceptualizing, and executing rhythm. Having acknowledged this, my main priority in this chapter is to reconcile these divergent understandings of Africanist rhythm by historically rooting jazz rhythm and structure within an Africanist sonic sensibility, and then by using architectural ideas to help articulate the way these musical concepts were imagined and transformed by free jazz musicians in the 1960s and 1970s.

THE AFRICANIST GRID

Most traditions of West African–derived dance music can be discussed in architectural terms, built as they are around the practices of *hocketing* (combining simple, repeating individual parts into complex composite structures), *call and response*, and *layering*—all of which, when articulated through the cyclical repetition of patterns, result in the characteristic polyrhythmic quality of West African music. This allows the music to be experienced in hierarchical, spatial terms at times, and at other times as the machinistic matrix of interlocking parts that I will refer to throughout this book using the term "Africanist Grid." I invoke the grid concept to describe an Africanist approach to counterpoint in which hocketing, call and response, and layering are the primary tools in the construction of polyrhythmic complexity. This manner of structuring musical sound can be heard in the traditional and contemporary musical idioms throughout sub-Saharan Africa and, historically, have engendered the West African rhythmic heritage in Afro-diasporic musical traditions. Modern jazz of the type played after World War II does not generally function as dance music, but it is music that developed historically and structurally out of the period of jazz-as-dance-music, a.k.a. the "Jazz Age" or "Swing Era" of the 1920s and 1930s. As a result, Africanist structural concepts of dance music are often embedded within even the most abstract forms of modern jazz.

As Hannah Higgins has written in her comprehensive book on the topic, the grid, as a phenomenon itself and an abstract means of measuring other phenomena, is one of modernity's central organizing concepts. The art historian Rosalind Krauss, meanwhile, has dated the prominence of the grid to the peak of the industrial era in early twentieth-century Europe.[5] In truth, the grid has been a central organizing element across human cultures and historical periods, and this book is based on the presumption that the musical forms of West Africa and the African diaspora constitute some of modernity's most potent and pervasive articulations of the grid concept.

———

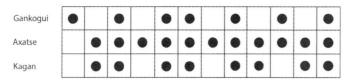

FIGURE 2.1 TUBS reduction of *Agbekor*. Reproduced courtesy of Chloe Smith.

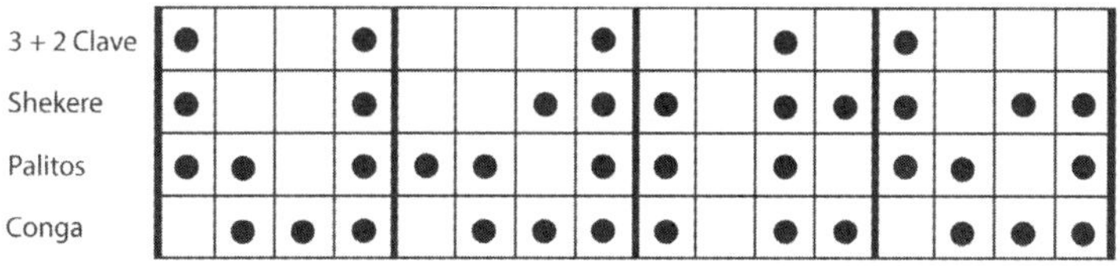

FIGURE 2.2 TUBS reduction of guaguancó rhythm. Reproduced courtesy of Chloe Smith.

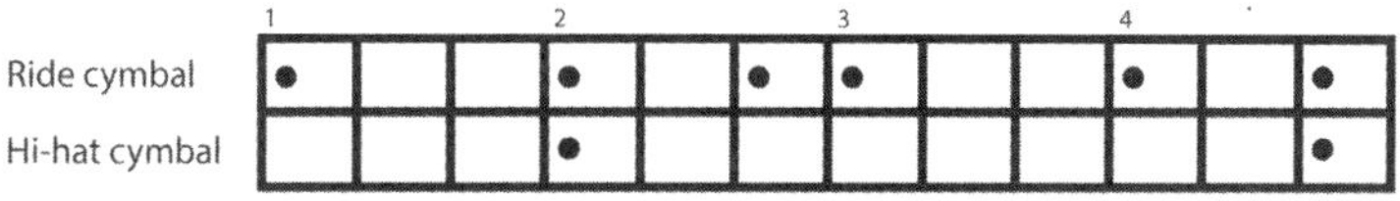

FIGURE 2.3 TUBS illustration of swing drum set rhythm.
Reproduced courtesy of Chloe Smith.

In notational terms, scholars of West African percussion music and its New World derivations have often represented its qualities of repetition and polyrhythmic interlock through the use of grid diagrams. The best-known example of this is probably the TUBS (Time Unit Box System) diagram, originally attributed to ethnomusicologists Philip Harland and James Koetting. This notational system divides a cyclically repeating musical structure into equally spaced parts that can be easily accommodated to Western meters such as 12/8, 6/8, and 4/4. Figure 2.1, for example, is a simplified TUBS notation of a very typical West African rhythm pattern in 12/8. In this case, each graphic unit is equivalent to an eighth-note triplet, with the "timeline" bell pattern on the top line:

Moving into the African diaspora, we can use the TUBS system to distill the Afro-Cuban rumba pattern known as "guaguancó" (figure 2.2). In this case, each graphic unit is equivalent to a sixteenth note, with the entire pattern being equivalent to a measure of 4/4 and the "clave" timeline pattern on the top line:

Similarly, the core timeline (i.e., hi-hat and ride cymbal) pattern of jazz's generic 4/4 drumming pattern can easily be notated using TUBS (figure 2.3).

Curvilinearity, Swing, and the Spline **63**

FIGURE 2.4 Three-dimensional
grid. Reproduced courtesy of
Chloe Smith.

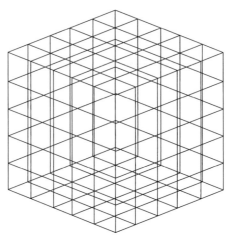

The concepts underlying this type of graphic representation of Africanist rhythm have been artfully expanded by Paul Austerlitz who, drawing on the previous work of art historian Robert Farris Thompson, linked the graphic patterns in grid representations such as TUBS with forms of rhythmicized visual patterning common in West African textile traditions such as Ghanaian *kente* cloth.[6] I would like to subject this Koetting-Thompson-Austerlitz lineage of ideas to a series of three transformations. The first involves expanding the grid representation from two to three dimensions (figure 2.4), which also allows us to move into the de facto sphere of architectural thinking.

Having spatialized the grid into three dimensions, we can now manipulate it. There are, of course, many ways of manipulating a grid. Timothy Samara's 2002 graphic design book *Making and Breaking the Grid*, for example, is a fascinating typology of different ways that grid forms can be manipulated.[7] Even though it generally discusses typographical grids that appear in two dimensions (i.e., on flat surfaces or computer screens), some of the book's language—especially in the section titled "Breaking the Grid"—is very helpful as a way of thinking through the process by which grids, including sonic grids, are broken out of orthogonal, geometric regularity. Samara's operations such as "Modular grid deconstruction," "Nonorthogonal grid deconstruction," and "Hierarchical grid deconstructed into multiple layers" represent techniques that can also be translated into the musical sphere. For the sake of efficiency here, however, I would like to distill the process to two simple operations: *fragmentation* and *juxtaposition*, both of which are fundamental to the rhythmic/structural transformations of free jazz.

We can find three-dimensional corollaries of these operations in contemporary architecture, with two relevant points of correspondence being the stylistic movements of *postmodernism* and *deconstruction*. In the 1980s and 1990s, practitioners of both movements utilized procedures of fragmentation and juxtaposition as a way of addressing a variety of theoretical, aesthetic, and practical issues. Peter Eisenman's Wexner Center for the Arts at Ohio State University (1989), for example, is a good example of both postmodernist and deconstructive tendencies (figure 2.5). Architectural history itself is fragmented in the building's "quotation" of different stylistic periods such as the early twentieth-century armory, the 1960s "space frame" grid, and the 1980s brick and glasswork exterior. Meanwhile, these individual stylistic markers are themselves subjected to formal fracturing, such as in the cleaving of the armory tower into two halves, the system of shifting and colliding grids that the whole structure rests upon, and the dramatic contrasts in building materials.[8]

FIGURE 2.5 Peter Eisenman, Wexner Center for the Visual Arts and
Fine Arts Library, South Entrance Façade, Columbus, Ohio (1983–1989).
Reproduced courtesy of Eisenman Architects.

FIGURE 2.6 Zaha Hadid, Rosenthal Center, Cincinnati, Ohio (2003).
Photograph by Timothy Brown reproduced in black and white, no alterations,
https://www.flickr.com/photos/atelier_flir/4242141117.

Similarly, the basic stylistic element of Zaha Hadid's Rosenthal Center for Contemporary Art in Cincinnati (2003) is the rectangle (figure 2.6). In this case, however, several rectangles are stacked and staggered at different lengths and with different resolutions, such as the disjunct diagonals at their respective ends. Meanwhile the planes are also staggered on the sides of the building, with contrasting materials and coloring used to highlight formal juxtapositions.[9]

Although the jazz musicians discussed in this book were not drawing on the same theoretical or philosophical sources as were architects like Eisenman and Hadid, we can make conceptual and morphological comparisons between these examples and certain instances of jazz performance. A very influential example of collage structuring in jazz, for example, would be the Ornette Coleman Quartet's 1959 piece "Lonely Woman."[10] In this piece, Edward Blackwell's ride cymbal keeps steady, up-tempo time in the standard bebop fashion, while Coleman on alto saxophone and Don Cherry on trumpet float a metrically disjunct, legato melody in unison on top of the structure. Meanwhile, Charlie Haden's bass pivots between these two strata, sometimes playing a drone in conjunction with the ride cymbal, and at other times accenting the disjunct flow of the horn line. Somewhat similarly to Hadid's disjunct rectangles in Cincinnati, Coleman has essentially taken the rhythmic grid of a typical small-band jazz performance and pulled the layers out of metric synchrony with each other to create a type of metric collage that nonetheless achieves a feeling of unity and wholeness. While Coleman's "harmolodic" deconstruction of the harmonic cycles of bebop is widely acknowledged as having influenced composers and improvisers to move beyond the strictures of bebop chord changes, it is crucially important to acknowledge that his collaged juxtaposition of disjunct metric strata was equally influential. Coleman and others in his orbit used "Lonely Woman" as a model for many subsequent compositions, dramatically expanding the experience of space, time, and structure in jazz.[11]

In contrast to Coleman's relatively measured, precomposed disjuncting of metric layers, the opening section (0:00–1:30) of Cecil Taylor's free-meter piece "Idut" (1978) is a more aggressive example of this kind of structural fragmentation.[12] Built from Ramsey Ameen's repeating violin riff that opens the piece, the rest of the ensemble (Taylor on piano, Jimmy Lyons on alto saxophone, Raphe Malik on trumpet, and Sirone [Norris Jones] on acoustic bass) gradually piles on layer after layer of fragmented riffs and melodic gestures until the soundscape reaches a "boiling point" at which the rhythmic environment essentially becomes "liquefied," and a new, composite level of rhythmic organization emerges. As with Coleman's innovations, Taylor's method of generating momentum through the clashing of fragmented riffs was a key contribution to the evolution of jazz structure in the 1960s and 1970s. And, as will become clear later in this book, the methods of both Taylor and Coleman—while often unacknowledged—laid crucial foundations for the innovations of subsequent generations of jazz composers and improvisers.

CURVILINEARITY, SWING, AND THE SPLINE

Whether Coleman's disjuncting of metric layers or Taylor's clashing of fragments, both disruptions of the rhythmic grid can be resolved into a subsequent state I am referring to with the term "curvilinear"—for my purposes, the final transformation of the Africanist Grid concept I have built from the ideas of Koetting, Thompson, and Austerlitz. Merriam-Webster's dictionary defines the term as "consisting of or bounded by curved lines," and "marked by flowing tracery."[13] The term is also associated with the branch of pure mathematics known as *topology*, a field concerned with the ways a geometric object can be deformed— twisted, bent, stretched, etc.—without breaking.[14] In architecture, curvilinearity refers to the ability to design undulating surfaces using the parametric modeling capabilities of digital drafting software and animation technologies. Theoretically, the origins of curvilinearity lie in the 1990s, with its most frequently cited expositions being Greg Lynn's 1999 book *Animate Form* or, in more condensed form, his 2004 essay "Architectural Curvilinearity: The Folded, the Pliant and the Supple."[15] The philosophical foundations of architectural curvilinearity, on the other hand, were ideas of "flowing" and "folding" associated with philosophers such as Gilles Deleuze and Felix Guattari, and articulated in works such as, respectively, *A Thousand Plateaus* and *Le Pli* (The Fold).[16]

Curvilinear architecture was a new design aesthetic that, while embracing the broken shapes and surfaces of postmodernist and deconstructive architecture, also resolved these breakages through a new language of smooth, undulating surfaces that privileged surface continuity over conflict. This fundamentally implied that formal differences could be acknowledged, while ultimately being subsumed within a language that was pliant and flexible. For example, the roof structure of Peter Eisenman's Staten Island Institute for Arts and Sciences (designed 1997, unbuilt) is presented as a graduated succession of fragmented spheres, but one in which the surface rips and tears ultimately resolve into a smoother, curvilinear contour, ultimately providing a greater sense of continuity and flow overall (figure 2.7).

FIGURE 2.7 Peter Eisenman, Staten Island Institute for the Arts and Sciences, Staten Island, New York (1997–2001). Reproduced courtesy of Eisenman Architects.

Similarly, Zaha Hadid's Performing Arts Center in Abu Dhabi (2007) relies on a surface language of torn, fragmented, and juxtaposed planes, which are ultimately harmonized within a much smoother, curvilinear surface contour that provides a sense of formal resolution and a greater experience of flow (figure 2.8).

In architectural designs, curvilinear surfaces have often been graphically modeled using the distorted grid structures called "splines," essentially continuous surfaces based on the averaging of variable slope, elevation, and curvature (figure 2.9). Greg Lynn explains the utility of splines for representing curvilinear surfaces:

> The movement of a point across a landscape becomes the collaboration of the initial direction, speed, elasticity, density, and the friction of the object along with the inflections of the landscape across which it is traveling. The landscape can initiate movements across itself without literally moving. The inflections of a landscape present a context of gradient slopes which are enfolded into its shape.[17]

Referring to the dynamic between Lynn's "point" and the various factors it encounters as it traverses a landscape of depressions, elevations, textural varia-

FIGURE 2.8 Zaha Hadid, Abu Dhabi Performing Arts Center, Saadiyat Island, Abu Dhabi (2007). Reproduced courtesy of Zaha Hadid Architects.

tions, objects, and other phenomena, "collaboration" translates into the sphere of modern jazz as the contour of an improvisation as it is shaped by the ongoing ensemble "conversation." If we situate this improvising ensemble in a metrically free environment, its rhythmic surface becomes inherently curvilinear and the spline surface, representing a distorted grid, provides a model that can visualize changes in ensemble density and metric gravity, as well as the alternating expansion and compression of more traditional metric shapes. Thus, the spline is one model that can help us visualize the fluid abstraction of the Africanist Grid that continues to pulse at the heart of some of the most abstract forms of jazz.[18]

If Lynn's model inspires us to conceptualize metrically free environments as *surfaces*, Patrik Schumacher inspires us to model metrically free environments as *spaces*. His essay on "parametricism" in *Digital Hadid* surveys the manual and, especially, digital techniques that he and Hadid employed to improvise a stage-by-stage expansion of their design language from fragmentation and deformation, through perspectival distortion, and on to the smooth, curvilinear environments of their later projects:

One of Hadid's most audacious moves was to translate the dynamism and fluidity of her calligraphic hand directly into equally fluid tectonic systems. Another incredible move was the move from isometric and perspective projection to literal distortions of space and from the exploded axonometry to the literal explosion of space into fragments, from the superimposition of various fisheye perspectives to the literal bending and meltdown of space.[19]

These distortions, explosions, bendings, or meltings down of gridded space, once established, allow different qualities of space and gravity to be articulated. Similar to Timothy Samara's typology of deconstructed grids, Schumacher is able to delineate the qualities of *magnetic field space, particle space*, and *continuously distorted space*, suggesting that "the inhabitant of such spaces no longer orients by means of prominent figures, axis, edges, and clearly bounded realms. Instead, the distribution of densities, directional bias, scalar grains and gradient vectors of transformation constitute the new ontology defining what it means to be somewhere . . . the significance and ambition of these projects is that they might be seen as manifestos of a new type of space."[20] Meanwhile, as John Rajchman writes, Peter Eisenman approaches from an opposite angle, seeing gridded space as beckoning toward a larger order of organization that transcends the grid: "An architecture of the *informe* is one that exposes its containing grid as 'constraining' or 'framing' something that is always *exceeding* it, surpassing it, or overflowing it."[21]

What is the relevance of this "new type of space" to John Coltrane, Miles Davis, or jazz in general? I believe this concept of curvilinearity to be one of the most important unarticulated rhythmic principles of the music of this period.

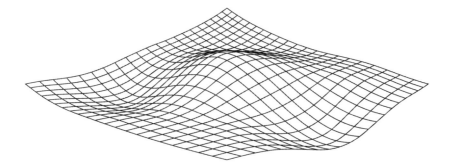

FIGURE 2.9 Spline surface. Licensed from Adobe Stock.

Historical accounts of free jazz have tended to privilege the idea that musicians *fragmented* and/or *fractured* practices of metrical and tonal playing. This is in fact true, but it has led to an overemphasis on the idea that free jazz constituted a *breaking* of some preexisting thing. Applying the curvilinear concept, on the other hand, allows us to hear the music as a *stretching* or *expansion* of preexisting relationships. Whether broken into fragments, stacked in multiple metrically conjunct or disjunct layers, liquefied, or distorted, we can see the apparent breakages and fragments of pieces such as "Lonely Woman" and "Idut" as components of a subsequent and higher order of rhythmic organization, in the same way that we consider the highly chromatic, pan-tonal improvisations of John Coltrane and Eric Dolphy to represent a subsequent order of harmonic organization. In this light, Greg Lynn's idea that "Symmetry breaking is not a loss but an increase in organization within an open, flexible and adaptive system"[22] resonates with the poet and literary scholar Fred Moten's idea of "fragmentation not as a loss, but as *augmentation*" (my italics). Both assert the idea of a higher order of organization, and are useful for thinking through the rhythmic and structural orders that emerged in jazz of the 1960s.[23]

My readings in twentieth-century art history movements such as Cubism and Abstract Expressionism have led me to suspect that this "higher order" might be thought of as an unarticulated "fourth dimension" of rhythmic awareness. In the early twentieth century, the idea of a fourth dimension emerged from the intersection of visual arts (e.g., Cubism) and physics (e.g., Relativity Theory), then gradually expanded into other discursive domains such as mathematics and philosophy. It has also been used, at different times, to interpret the constellation of nontraditional (i.e., non-Euclidean) spatial relationships that emerged in the artistic vanguard of the twentieth century, in relation to aesthetic dialects as distinct as Futurism and Abstract Expressionism.[24]

These visual art corollaries actually provide context for the various attempts to expand the rhythmic vision of jazz that have taken place over the decades. Beginning in the 1980s, for example, saxophonist/composer Steve Coleman and his M-Base compadres would offer their own provocative (and highly influential) reconfiguration, working their own way toward a rhythmic fourth dimension by stacking different time signatures that remained organized around a common pulse and expanding the rhythmic geometries of the Africanist Grid to a more complex state. This approach might be compared to Cubism, i.e., a series of projections and subdivisions based on the established "planes" of the metered rhythmic environment. As I discuss throughout this story, on the other hand, the freer rhythms of late-period John Coltrane, Miles's Lost Quintet, and others are more complex environments that tended to be achieved through intuitive rather than rational means; we certainly do not have a rigorously reasoned rhythmic corollary of the Coltrane "tone circle," for example. This begs the question of the extent to which rational planning is a prerequisite for accessing this higher dimension. The Italian Futurist Umberto Boccioni pondered this in 1914:

> I remember having read that Cubism with its breaking up of the object and unfolding of the parts of the object on the flat surface of the picture approached the fourth dimension . . . Rather, this procedure is . . . the transcription onto the surface of the canvas of the planes of the object that its accidental position prevents us from seeing. It is a *rational procedure* [my italics] which exists in relativity, not in an intuitive absolute . . . we cannot make a *measured and finite* fourth dimension, but rather a continuous projection of forces and forms intuited in their infinite unfolding.[25]

Unifying seemingly disparate (i.e., fragmented) metric gestures into a coherent, continuous surface with varying articulations of rhythmic gravity and ensemble density, curvilinearity is a shorthand way of apprehending the fluid experiences of form, time, and structure generated as a consequence of transposing the Africanist Grid into this "fourth" rhythmic dimension as *intuited* by free jazz musicians.

———

Bringing the languages of jazz and architecture together also engages one of the central artistic issues of twentieth-century culture, which is the wedding of aesthetics and industry. Le Corbusier, after all, was able to intuit the structural synchrony between the gridded Africanist rhythms encoded into jazz and the repetitive rhythms of modern industry. If we accept his observations that African American music provided a humanizing inflection to those industrial rhythms during the early and mid-twentieth century, we must also reciprocally accept that the demands of industry likely accentuated some of the more rigid qualities of the Africanist Grid. These rigidities were deconstructed in the 1960s and 1970s, when the Black Atlantic was a site of open-ended imagination, optimism, and possibility and, more locally, when jazz provided a similarly humanizing inflection for the rhythms of industrial collapse in locales such as New York City. As the soundscapes of John Coltrane and Miles Davis will make clear, those postindustrial rhythmic grids also provided a rhythmic template for Space Age imaginings of worlds beyond Earth. "Clearly," Hannah Higgins writes, "spacetime throws into doubt all of our assumptions about the realism of the perspective screen, the reality of the orthogonal map, and the absolute space enclosed in the manufactured box."[26] Greg Lynn extends this idea into the sphere of architecture, posing the question, "What does it mean in architectural thinking to abandon the ground, or for the ground to cease to exist?"[27] In this context of contested grids and gravities, the spline's utility becomes clear as a tool narrating the continuous transformation of surfaces and spaces, whether rhythmic, terrestrial, or celestial.

———

Sadly, two giants of jazz passed away within days of each other while I was in the final stages of writing this book: the pianist/keyboardist Chick Corea, who figures heavily in the Miles Davis essay, and the drummer Milford Graves, who was one of the most visionary members of the new-school, free jazz drummers that also included John Coltrane's drummer Rashied Ali. Within days of their respective passings, a photo was circulated of them playing together in a New York mambo band sometime around 1960. Corea is seated at the piano, while Graves plays timbales. This photo is telling: these two musicians, who would go on to occupy radically different spheres of the jazz world for over fifty years, emerged at a time when the dominant Afro-diasporic articulations of the Africanist Grid—at least in American popular music—spanned the rhythmic dialects of swing, mambo, and funk. The careers of Corea and Graves would follow very different paths: while Corea viewed free playing as merely one of many styles he played over the course of his career, free playing was more central to Graves, who would in fact transport insights gleaned from his rhythmic experiments into his longer-term studies of the human organism.[28] Nonetheless, both musicians were central participants in the "free meter" transformation that is central to this book.

A similar observation could be made regarding the later music of John Coltrane and the early electric music of Miles Davis. Given that rhythm is this book's primary sonic prism, this particular dialogue allows me to formulate at least a portion of a "unified field theory" of black rhythm encompassing a spectrum from communal dance musics to more rarefied rhythmic dialects that can be alternately experienced as devotional, experimental, and/or linguistic. This stylistic intersection, in turn, symbolizes broader social, cultural, and political visions and alliances that appeal to me as a scholar of the Black Atlantic who happened to be born into the eras of pan-Africanism and the Space Age.

———

Many western students of West African traditional music, when immersed in a field of complex polyrhythm, are frequently heard to ask the question, "Where's the one?"—meaning, the downbeat, the beginning of the cycle, the point of gravitational departure and resolution. Many African teachers, meanwhile, have responded with the idea that there is no "one" in the Western sense, and that the structure is rightfully understood as a *conversation*, with the parts deriving their meaning in relation to each other. To my mind, the question of whether we can swing in free meter is a more structurally complex variant of the same question of gravity, albeit with the same practically and philosophically simple answers: the parts must be understood in relation to each other, with gravity understood more in relation to varying degrees of ensemble density than to any particular gravitational center. And this is where Lynn's "orbital stability" idea and Africanist linguistic traits both become useful, as ways of articulating curvilinear surfaces fashioned from ensemble interaction in a free-meter environment.

As an agent of radical transformation in jazz, free meter has often been mis-understood precisely because of its apparent disassembling of some of the music's core concepts, of which the Africanist Grid is one. History, however, shows that the Africanist Grid has been highly flexible in its articulation. As Hannah Higgins writes, "that which is experienced as chaos could portend an emergent but not yet schematized grid, a decomposing grid, a twisted grid, the interaction of one grid with another, or a truly chaotic circumstance."[29] The potency of curvilinear-ity as an analytical concept in jazz is that it provides a model for understanding the fluidification of jazz rhythm in the 1960s, and for demonstrating that frag-mented surfaces continue to be shaped by the gravitational dynamic of tension and release traditionally known as "swing," as they reconsolidate into splines. Appearing as a magic carpet in the digital reality of screens and software, the spline flows retroactively into the sonic reality of 1960s jazz as a concept that allows us to experience the innovations of free jazz as not only deconstructions of a grand tradition, but also as profound acts of creation, extension, synthesis and regeneration. Continuously undulating in response to sonic and social gravities, its movement provides context for the radical rhythmic surfaces of

Coltrane, Miles, and other musicians of the 1960s who ventured into the "brave new world" of free-meter improvisation.

NOTES

1. Prix, Wolf. D., and Coop Himmelblau. "On the Edge." In *Deconstruction III*, edited by Andreas C. Papadakis, 65. London: Academy, 1990.

2. See Rajchman, John. "Perplications: On the Space and Time of Rebstockpark." In *Blurred Zones: Investigations of the Interstitial*, edited by Eisenman Architects, 154. New York: Monacelli, 2002.

3. See Drott, Eric. "Free Jazz and the French Critic." *Journal of the American Musicological Society* 61, no. 3 (Fall 2008): 541–81.

4. Carles, Philippe, and Jean-Louis Comolli. *Free Jazz/Black Power*. Translated by Gregory Pierrot, 159. Jackson: University Press of Mississippi, 2015.

5. Krauss, Rosalind. "Grids: Format and Image in 20th-Century Art." New York: Pace Gallery, 1978.

6. For a discussion of this tendency, see: Thompson, Robert F. "Round Houses and Rhythmized Textiles." In *Flash of the Spirit: African and Afro-American Art and Philosophy*. New York: Random House, 1984. See also Austerlitz, Paul. "Kente Cloth to Jazz: A Matrix of Sound." In *Jazz Consciousness: Music, Race, and Humanity*. Middletown, CT: Wesleyan University Press, 2005.

7. Samara, Timothy. *Making and Breaking the Grid: A Graphic Design Layout Workshop*. Gloucester, MA: Rockport, 2002.

8. Eisenman's Wexner Center project is discussed in detail in: Davidson, Cynthia, ed. *Tracing Eisenman: Peter Eisenman Complete Works*. New York: Random House, 2006.

9. Hadid's Cincinnati project is discussed in detail in: Dochantschi, Markus, ed. *Zaha Hadid: Space for Art; Contemporary Arts Center, Cincinnati; Lois and Richard Rosenthal Center for Contemporary Art*. Zurich: Lars Müller, 2004.

10. "Lonely Woman" can be found on Ornette Coleman's 1959 album *The Shape of Jazz to Come* (Atlantic 1317).

11. Other "rubato ballads" of this type composed by Coleman would include "Comme Il Faut," "What Reason Could I Give?" and "Broken Shadows," among many others.

12. "Idut" can be found on Cecil Taylor's 1978 album *The Cecil Taylor Unit* (New World NW 201).

13. See *Merriam Webster*, s.v. "curvilinear (adj.)," last modified May 8, 2023, https://www.merriam-webster.com/dictionary/curvilinear.

14. *Wolfram MathWorld* defines topology as "the mathematical study of the properties that are preserved through deformations, twistings, and stretchings of objects. Tearing,

however, is not allowed." *Wolfram MathWorld*, s.v. "Topology," by Eric W. Weisstein, https://mathworld.wolfram.com/Topology.html.

15. Lynn's essay can be found in the volume *Folding in Architecture, Architectural Design* 63 (January–February 1992).

16. Deleuze, Gilles, and Felix Guattari. *A Thousand Plateaus: Capitalism and Schizophrenia*. Minneapolis: University of Minnesota Press, 1997. See also Deleuze, Gilles. *The Fold: Leibniz and the Baroque*. Paris: Editions du Minuit, 1988.

17. Lynn, Greg. *Animate Form*. New York: Princeton Architectural Press, 1999, 29–30.

18. I am not the first person to use the spline to represent unconventional rhythmic surfaces. See also Fowler, Michael. "The Ephemeral Architecture of Stockhausen's *Pole für 2*." *Organised Sound* 15, no. 3 (2010): 185–97. Fowler uses the "non-uniform rational B-spline" to model the spatial elements of Karlheinz Stockhausen's 1970 piece, *Pole*.

19. Schumacher, Patrik. *Digital Hadid: Landscapes in Motion*. Basel: Birkhauser, 2004, 17.

20. Schumacher, *Digital Hadid*, 19.

21. See Rajchman, "Perplications: On the Space and Time of Rebstockpark," *Blurred Zones*, 154.

22. Quote from Lynn, Greg. "The Renewed Novelty of Symmetry." In *Folds, Bodies and Blobs: Collected Essays*. Brussels: La Lettre Voleé, 1998.

23. See Moten's 2010 essay "B3," reprinted at https://www.poetryfoundation.org/harriet -books/2010/02/b-3.

24. For a comprehensive discussion of the fourth-dimension idea in relation to visual art, see: Henderson, Linda Dalrymple. *The Fourth Dimension and Non-Euclidean Geometry in Modern Art* (Revised Edition). Cambridge, MA: MIT Press, 2018.

25. Boccioni, as quoted in Henderson, *Fourth Dimension*, 225.

26. Higgins, Hannah. *The Grid Book*. Cambridge, MA: MIT Press, 2009, 260.

27. See Borasi, Giovanna. "Vantage Points Accessible for the First Time." In *Other Space Odysseys*, authored by Greg Lynn, Michael Maltzman, and Alessandro Poli, edited by Giovanna Borasi and Mirko Zardini. Montreal: Canadian Centre for Architecture/ Lars Müller Publishers, 2010, 15.

28. For a comprehensive profile of Milford Graves, see the documentary *Milford Graves: Full Mantis* (Mantis Films, 2018).

29. Higgins, *The Grid Book*, 257.

THREE

"We No Longer Consider Them Damaged"

Distortion as a Mode of Jazz Consciousness

Their form must be respected in its integrity, embodying a history
that must not be denied. In their damaged state they suggest
new forms of thought and comprehension.[1]

Lebbeus Woods

You do not see less by looking at a field out
of focus through a magnifying glass.[2]

Gerhard Richter

Having spent the previous chapter exploring the theme of spatiality as implied
by the arrangement of musical sounds as well as by jazz's relationship to the
external environment, I will now pursue it through a different spatial medium:
the soundspace—and sonic fidelity—of sound recordings. Whether "official"
recordings of "professional" fidelity released by sanctioned recording companies,
or the "alter-archives" of recorded jazz (unsanctioned recordings of widely varying fidelity, uncertain provenance, and unregulated circulation), the truth is that
sound recordings have played a crucial, if unacknowledged, role in constructions
of jazz knowledge and jazz history. Our current digital era, and especially the
current concern with "digital archives," has radically refracted our understanding
of the kinds of sources that are useful to our thinking as scholars and practitioners. Exploring the analytical, historical, and interpretive potentials of these
sources can challenge our understanding of what jazz sound has been, what it

is, and what it might yet be. Accordingly, this chapter is organized as sections of deliberately decreasing fidelity that I hope correspond to sections of increasing clarity, exploring the issue of the crucial yet complicated importance of sound recordings: as primary tools in the evolution of jazz as a creative tradition, as sources for the construction and interpretation of jazz history, and for the purpose of musical analysis.

———

When Hurricane Katrina tore through New Orleans in 2005, its devastation was as much cultural as it was physical, and the jazz community, long considered the cultural heart of the city, was one of the subcultures that was particularly hard hit. Not only were homes and venues destroyed, but many musicians also perished in the storm and its chaotic aftermath. Around the country and the world, jazz musicians and jazz lovers rallied to the cause of the Crescent City and, in fact, the response to this tragedy helped reassert and reinforce the narrative, resurgent since the 1980s, of New Orleans as the cultural, geographic, and symbolic heart of jazz music.

The best-known post-Katrina jazz document is probably the HBO series *Tremé*, which chronicles the travails of the city's inhabitants as they rebuild their world musically, spiritually, and physically.[3] Lesser known but equally fascinating, however, is the story of the husband-and-wife photography team of Keith Calhoun and Chandra McCormick, the subjects of a 2015 *National Geographic* profile.[4] For over three decades, Calhoun and McCormick had devoted themselves to chronicling the jam sessions, second-line parades, gumbo festivals, jazz funerals, and other aspects of the Crescent City's fabled cultural life. Sadly, thousands of their images were ravaged by Katrina; the photographers returned home to find their entire archive of prints and negatives waterlogged and assumed to be completely destroyed. As chronicled in the *National Geographic* story, the negatives were stored in a freezer, in a last-ditch attempt to salvage what was left of the work by cryogenically arresting the process of decay. Locked away for five years, Calhoun and McCormick finally (and reluctantly) retrieved their images in 2010, after stubbornly avoiding what was almost certainly the complete destruction of several decades' worth of devoted work. The catalyst was a Smithsonian grant that funded the attempted salvage and restoration of several New Orleans art collections affected by the storm. But the salvageability of their archive would not be known until they surveyed the materials inside of the freezer.

FIGURE 3.1 Chandra McCormick, *Jammin' at the Shop in Treme* (1986/2008).
Reproduced courtesy of Chandra McCormick.

The photographers opened their freezer to find partially recognizable images of the city's musical life, permanently transformed by the interaction of photographic emulsion and seawater (figure 3.1). Their original images were now highly abstracted depictions of jazz and community, newly defined by peculiarities of form, texture, and coloration. These new images were as much about a forced dialogue between art and the processes of nature as they were about the putative subject matter of the original images. Despite their initial disillusionment, then, Calhoun and McCormick were ultimately able to find new meaning in nature's forced transformation of their images. As Keith Calhoun wrote: "The mold, cracked film cases, and restoration created abstractions of our initial images . . . the images represent different forms of light that guide and sustain us through trials and tribulations."[5] A subsequent exhibition of their new work, in fact, was titled *We No Longer Consider Them Damaged.*[6]

Of course, these chemically refracted images also suggest that one unintended and arguably *beneficial* by-product of the Katrina tragedy was the rescuing of *imagined* New Orleans from the sanitized narratives of jazz canonization, by forcing these jazz images into a de facto dialogue with experimental trends in contemporary photography. After all, concurrent with New Orleans's post-Katrina recovery, much international attention was devoted to the work of the Czech photographer Miroslav Tichý, a so-called outsider artist known for his eccentric portraits of women in and around his hometown of Kyjov (figure 3.2).[7] Tichý's images, furtively shot with crude, homemade cameras and heavily degraded through intentional abuse and disregard, offer reflections on the landscape and human form that are evocative and formally inventive despite their violation of virtually every tenet of standard photographic technique. Most of his prints have been walked on, ripped, drawn on, chewed by vermin, caked with various foreign substances, and/or developed in ways that would typically be considered highly flawed.

The embrace of Calhoun, McCormick, and Tichý's work from a jazz perspective helps illuminate similarities and differences in the critical and analytical discourses around visual and sonic recording. In the visual sphere, the advent of photography is usually cited as the primary catalyst in the liberation of painting from the burden of representation.[8] Simultaneously with this, photography's actual evolution as an art form can be defined as a series of deliberate and/or fortuitous departures from the idea of itself as a mere documentary medium concerned with the accurate representation of "objective" reality. In fact, it was often the haphazard procedures and accidents that allowed photography to gradually recognize itself as more than a documentary medium and to challenge prevailing modes of reproduction and representation.[9] The reception of the work of artists like Tichý and Calhoun and McCormick, then, implies that the practical, analytical and interpretative discourses around visual art are flexible enough to account for imagery achieved by methodical, haphazard or accidental means.

————

To what extent is this flexibility evident in our understanding of jazz recording? To what extent have jazz musicians asked themselves the questions that visual artists have asked throughout the twentieth century? The truth is that much—if not all—jazz recording is still bound up in the documentary paradigm of "accurately" representing musical events and it has only been comparatively recently, in fact, that we have been able to acknowledge the jazz recording as anything more than a mere artifact of the "real thing" of a live jazz performance. Douglas Kahn's comment, "When compared to the photographic arts, the phonographic arts are retarded," would seem to apply to the auditory culture of verisimilitude that has shaped most jazz recordings.[10]

This is to say that, aside from a handful of isolated articles and several book-length "album studies," the role of recordings in jazz, from the historical, aesthetic, or technological angle, has rarely been critically examined. One notable exception is Jed Rasula's 1995 essay problematizing the status of sound recordings in the construction of jazz history.[11] One of the most valuable insights of Rasula's essay is its framing of that history in terms of an ongoing tension between its grapho-centric (i.e., written) and phono-centric (i.e., sonically recorded) representations. Rasula's redeployment of sound recording as a form of writing *in and of itself*—i.e., as *phonography*—not only brings the graphic and the sonic into parallel as merely *two different types* of writing, but also brings the sonic practice of jazz into historical and conceptual conformity with the Africanist concept of sound (as opposed to writing) as the dominant medium of historical capture and dissemination. This Africanist inflection allows sound recording to be understood as a form of "writing" in the same way that Africanist literary scholars have elsewhere asserted the concept of "oral literature" as a way of reconciling the artistry of West African praise singers, oral historians, and genealogists with the Western grapho-centric concept of literacy.[12] Extending the literary angle a bit further, we can assert that if sound recording represents a form of writing and if every act of writing constitutes some type of narrative, then *every* sound recording has a story to tell us.

The British-Ghanaian writer Kodwo Eshun, emerging from the Cybernetic Culture Research Unit at the University of Warwick in England, coined the phrase "sonic fiction" as a subtitle of *More Brilliant Than the Sun* (1998), his influential collection of music essays.[13] Eshun's intention might be read as Afrofuturist in intent using the interventions of cultural studies, metaphors drawn from cybernetics and the information age, to bring the technological aspects of black dance music and experimental music into resonance with the cinematic and literary narratives of science fiction. But the term "sonic fiction" can also be applied in a more literal sense. Despite the realist conceits of most recorded jazz, both studio and live performances of jazz have been edited, dis- and re-assembled into composite takes, treated with sound processing, overdubbed with applause, re-mixed, and subjected to numerous other post-performance procedures. Whether or not they are always audible or acknowledged, these procedures subvert the assumption of "authenticity" that has been so central to the aesthetics of jazz recording.[14] Regardless of whatever may be done in the process of postproduction to make it appear "authentically" accountable to an original, real-world event, the subsequent sound is by definition different than what it sounded like at the original time and place. Which is to say that, once that sound has been captured by a recording device and transformed into an electronic signal, it becomes by definition a different phenomenon, and *any* recorded sound—regardless of provenance or "fidelity"—is always necessarily a *fiction*.

ALTER-ARCHIVES: SHADOW HISTORIES OF JAZZ RECORDING

> [Columbia] wasn't marketing jazz in the first place. They should
> have really put their money behind marketing it the way that they
> marketed all those [rock] people at that time. So, the bootlegging thing
> is a slap or a slingshot back in their face. And the money that they're crying
> about losing because of bootlegging is just a reflection of themselves,
> upside down. Actually, the companies should have had these bootlegging
> people do their marketing. They should have hired those types of
> minds instead of the usual "go-along-with-business" people.[15]
>
> *Wayne Shorter*

The idea of the jazz recording as a form of "fiction" may be most strongly dramatized by the network of unofficial recordings that circulate among musicians and scholars or, in some instances, are sold commercially as so-called bootlegs. Private and commercial recordings of unauthorized or pirated music have existed since the early decades of the recording industry. Dante Bolletino, for example, is often considered the "father" of jazz bootlegging for his activities in illegally repressing out-of-print material by artists like Louis Armstrong, Bessie Smith, and others during the 1950s.[16] But "pirated" versions of commercial recordings have been the exception rather than the rule. The preferred source material for jazz bootlegs has more typically been live performances, recorded either on-site at performance venues or sourced from radio and television broadcasts. It is obvious why these recordings would tend to be prized among jazz collectors—they help fill in important gaps within the rapid stylistic evolution of both individual artists and the tradition as a whole.[17]

How reliable are *these* documents as historical sources? If commercially released "official" jazz recordings already subvert the fiction of authenticity that they strive to present, unofficial recordings—those unauthorized by the artist or their recording label—are fraught with exponentially more complications due to their nonstandardized modes of production and circulation. Accompanying information is often hazy, incorrect, or nonexistent due to either the haphazard nature of their production or, more frequently, to deliberately falsified information used to disguise unauthorized content.

More immediate than factors of documentation is the issue of fidelity. As a recording is copied over many analog "generations," the fidelity of the audio signal may decrease as it weakens in relation to tape noise. Variations in tape speed result in incorrect identification of pitches and keys, as well as distortion in certain frequency ranges. This process of decaying fidelity can be arrested (or at least slowed) on digital media but, in the case of performances recorded prior to the advent of digital recording, musicians and scholars are obliged to work with analog source recordings that in many cases have already substantially degenerated. Additionally, anomalies produced by digital sound technologies, collectively referred to as "glitches," may further disfigure recorded information.[18]

In general, "soundboard" recordings (made from the sound mixer's desk at live concerts) have been considered preferable to "audience" recordings (made with microphones positioned in the audience), but both have their respective advantages and disadvantages. Soundboard recordings are often excellent ways to hear "the music," since such recordings are taken from the direct signals of the instruments as they pass through the live sound engineer's mixing board without the intrusion of audience noise or ambient sound in the venue. However, what we are hearing on a soundboard recording is based on how the sound engineer balanced the sound at a particular performance, and may not depict the balance as it actually sounded in the venue. The recording engineer Mark Wilder is intimately familiar with these issues:

> The radio engineers recording a performance like that, a lot of times they're not familiar with the band, they're not familiar with the performance, with what the musicians are gonna play. Many times we get tapes and there's not even a list of songs because they don't know them. Here are melodies that are foreign to this engineer. Today he's recording Miles, tomorrow he might be recording the Paris Symphony. So the ability of that engineer to make musical judgments as the performance goes through its arc is challenging at best. And this is why on a lot of those tapes, the balance of the instrumentation is not as if it was studied over in the studio where you have multiple takes and you're in a mix situation. Here you're making flash decisions in a live situation. A lot of time it's flawed in that respect.[19]

The fidelity of audience recordings, on the other hand, can sometimes suffer due to the distance of the recording device from the source (the stage), as well as from ambient and extraneous sound in the venue, and various types of sonic distortion. Sometimes, however, they can present a more accurate representation of what the musicians and audience actually heard in a given venue on a particular occasion.

———

Considering the extent to which sound recordings have accelerated the evolution of the jazz tradition, we must also consider the extremely intimate relationship jazz musicians have with recorded sound. Take, as an example, saxophone teacher (and mouthpiece manufacturer) Jody Espina's web article on how to use the recordings of John Coltrane to cultivate a personal tone on the saxophone:

> *Coltrones* is a word that I invented after working with my students on [the album] *Coltrane Ballads*. *Coltrones* are long tones inspired by Coltrane's sound. David Gross, a fine saxophone teacher in New York City, was the first person to turn me onto playing with recordings of John Coltrane ballads for use mainly as tone studies. I took it a step further with *Coltrones* . . . Your first long tone of the day will be modeled after Coltrane's first long tone on "Soul Eyes" . . . Play the CD, pausing after the fourth note of "Soul Eyes," which is a D concert. Then play that note on your horn and try and get as close as you can to Coltrane's sound . . . Listen again to the fourth note of the CD, then pause it and try and match it. Think about what you have to change about your breath support, your embouchure and your oral cavity to more closely match Coltrane's sound . . . After trying to match the fourth note many times you can move on to the second long note of "Soul Eyes," which is a B concert . . . Don't worry about becoming a Coltrane clone unless you plan on doing this type of work only with Trane's music. You should also do *Hawktones, Webtones, Birdtones* etc. We're just trying to expand your tonal palette so that ultimately your sound comes through and you have the ability to shade it in any way that you want to.[20]

Given this intimacy with recorded sound, it is inconceivable that players who also spend a considerable amount of time transcribing unofficial recordings are not also being influenced by the various lo-fi iterations of a given player's sound. Considering the amount of time and energy the average jazz musician invests in these recordings, shouldn't we hope to recoup more than barely tolerable encounters with barely discernable sound material? Is it really possible that these players haven't had their own instrumental voices subtly modulated by these variously distorted or compressed timbres and eccentric configurations of implied space?

Over the decades, in fact, I had not only become accustomed to tapes of wildly varying fidelity, but had even come to value this alternative sound world, hearing in it an abundance of new narratives about jazz history, technology, and aesthetics, and opening the door to a wide range of listening, creative, analytical, and interpretive possibilities. My experience parallels the experience of composer Pauline Oliveiros, who once wrote of her developing childhood relationship to the radio and the phonograph:

> Sometime during the mid-1930s I used to listen to my grandfather's crystal radio over headphones. I loved the crackling static. The same grandfather used to try to teach me the Morse Code with telegraph keys. I wasn't interested in the messages but I loved the dit da dit dit rhythms . . . I also loved our wind-up Victrola, especially when the mechanism was running down with a record playing. I loved all the negative operant phenomena of systems.[21]

Negative operant phenomena of systems—a reference to technologies performing improperly, of recordings degraded by repeated transposition across time, space, playback formats, or devices. Theorized as "ruins" of the industrial documentation and dissemination of music, the mixed bag of sonic information they present has ensured their consignment to a status of secondary, inferior, or flawed documents. But these unofficial documents simultaneously suggest new possibilities for our understanding of jazz, bringing it into productive dialogue with other artistic discourses. At the same time, however, the alchemical transformation of limitations into advantages arguably anchors these documents more deeply within certain core values of jazz.

Using the glitch aesthetic as a shorthand term for the sonic anomalies of both analog and digital eras of sound recording, I would like to focus on several of those values here, in a discussion of two lesser-known recordings of Charlie Parker that set part of the sonic stage for the microhistories of John Coltrane and Miles Davis that follow in the next chapters.[22] Is there another way we can discuss the recorded traces of Parker, or any other jazz musician, in addition to the usual discourse of scales and chords, while remaining accountable to the sound material and the history? Like the musical revolutions unleashed by experimental music, free jazz, punk, dub, and hip-hop, a recuperation of "noise" as a positive value can help regenerate a stylistic language whose social utility has been compromised by excessive formalization, canonization, and standardization. After all—on any given evening at Jazz at Lincoln Center, one can exult in the sonic splendor of Rose Hall, an architectural space in which the acoustics have been designed to simulate the fidelity of a perfectly mixed and mastered digital recording.[23] Is there another way we can interface with the aesthetics of sound recordings?

———

Portable recording technology was in its infancy when aspiring trombonist Jimmy Knepper hauled his equipment into Charlie Parker's performance at New York's St. Nicholas Arena in February 1950, a recording later released commercially on Charles Mingus's fledgling Jazz Workshop label as *Bird at St. Nick's*. Like many Bird fanatics, Knepper was only interested in Parker's playing and to save disc space, he turned the recorder off whenever Parker wasn't playing. These fragments of performances essentially amount to a sound collage of Charlie Parker that subverts the ideal of the jazz recording as transparent document but which, ironically, belongs to what might be thought of as a subgenre of such recordings. Indeed, one of the most celebrated "archival" jazz releases of the last quarter-century was Mosaic's *The Complete Charlie Parker Recordings of Dean Benedetti*, a similarly conceived collection of seven compact discs of performance fragments, recorded by an equally obsessed Parker fan. Even though it wasn't the conscious intention of the recordists, recordings such as these bring bebop into forced dialogue with musique concrète, remixing, and other genres that depend on tape manipulation as a form of composition.

On the St. Nick's recordings, we find Parker's saxophone voice soaring through a lo-fi but complex soundscape composed of the cavernous hollow of the arena, against a backdrop of barely audible accompanying musicians, and a sea of ambient crowd noise—a radically attenuated mass of conversation, laughter, and exclamation in response to Parker's improvisation. Certainly, there are recordings of better fidelity that document similar settings. Imaginatively, however, the cloudy fidelity serves its purpose as a metaphor for the mists of history through which Parker's voice rings clear despite the passage of time. Recordings such as this, with their lack of sonic "sanitization," can sometimes provide a type of historical portrait lacking in more sanitized recordings, evoking bygone places, times and social formations. *Bird at St. Nick's* depicts an era when jazz musicians, including the reigning high priests of jazz modernism, still sometimes played for social dances in large spaces while enjoying an emotionally intimate relationship with their audiences. Here, then, is one potential benefit of these kinds of recordings: they can help situate a sound historically in a way that also makes a wider range of emotional responses and historical readings available, despite being marked by the very sorts of "extraneous" sounds that jazz musicians, in their ongoing quest to have their art given the respect it deserves, have long complained of.

Bird's Eyes, a series of compilations of live Parker performances issued by the Italian label Philology, offers documents of Parker that are often inferior to even the Knepper and Benedetti recordings. Philology subtitles their discs "Last Unissued"—indicating, in concrete terms, that they provide the buyer with Parker material that no other company would release due to its poor sound quality. This is certainly true in conventional terms; the majority of the recordings seem to have been recorded and/or reproduced under very unfavorable conditions. Most are either distorted or distant-sounding audience recordings, secondary recordings captured from radio broadcasts and marred by a considerable amount of extraneous noise, or transfers from vinyl acetates with considerably degraded playing surfaces. In his online review, Ken Dryden had the following to say about the material contained on the Bird's Eyes series:

> Jazz fanatics feverishly sought to record Charlie Parker whenever possible during radio broadcasts or live appearances, with very mixed results in fidelity . . . Unfortunately, the sound quality ranges from dreadful to barely listenable, simply because the initial recordings failed to capture much more than Parker's alto sax, and even that is often badly distorted . . . this compilation will be of interest primarily to hardcore fans of Charlie Parker.[24]

Volume 13 of Bird's Eyes contains a number of performances recorded at the legendary Pershing Ballroom in Chicago in 1948, when Parker was featured as a guest soloist with the Dizzy Gillespie big band. This particular recording sounds as if it has been transferred from a very distressed playback medium; most listeners would find it unlistenable due to the amount of surface noise. The disc opens with a ballad performance of Thelonious Monk's "Round Midnight," in which the low-density sonic space usually expected of ballads has been filled by a thick patina of surface noise, against which the sound of Parker's alto sax competes for the listener's attention. The beginning of the track also features a skip in the vinyl that lasts for the first thirty seconds of the performance, and which rotates at a disjunct metric relationship to the music at an approximate tempo of quarter note = 84 bpm. If one really wanted to push the issue in music-analytical terms, one could claim the "strong" and "weak" beats of this vinyl skip set up a disjunct "swing" against the tempo of the "actual music." This interpretation might seem a stretch for musicians and music scholars, but in fact the juxtaposition of disjunct tempi has been a standard technique of experimental jazz since at least 1960 or so, typified by pieces such as Ornette Coleman's "Lonely Woman," with its disjunct metric strata that (as I mentioned in chapter 1) expanded the spatial spectrum of small-band jazz. Given that, there is a precedent for hearing the recording in this way.

As with the St. Nick's recordings, the audience is also sonically present, albeit in an extremely abstracted form here, as brief passages of sudden exclamation that periodically erupt from the soundscape in response to the music, nearly indistinguishable in terms of frequency range from the white noise that clouds the song surface. Ditto for Gillespie's horn section which, like the crowd sounds, has been reduced to a wall of intermittent, distorted brass declaration that demarcates climactic moments in the de facto duet between Parker's alto saxophone and the surface noise of the playback medium. The recognition of key, tempo, chord progression, and even the acoustic character of the venue become increasingly abstract and poetic propositions, the sound surface streaked with equal proportions of "musical" and "nonmusical" sound.

What is arguably most profound about recordings like this is revealed when we view them through an expanded understanding of the spatial prism introduced earlier in this book; taken as a whole, they demonstrate the ways in which a given sound (in this case the sound of jazz) registers across the sensorium of jazz as it interfaces with society—for example, within different acoustic spaces, within the virtual spaces of recorded media, on home playback equipment, across broadcast signals, in interaction with other information-in-transit, and as circulated across social space between listeners. In this sense, the recordings constitute a socio-spatial archive in and of themselves.

Unfortunately, jazz has remained largely outside of this sonic discourse, and the reasons for this are obvious: first, many jazz musicians continue to understand themselves as playing an art music that requires and deserves optimum documentation, and second, jazz continues to struggle for the recognition it deserves as America's indigenous art music. Like the exacting preservation of scores and letters, making a case for the importance of the tradition depends on the clear documentation of its achievements. In the case of jazz, sound recordings are the primary documents of its history, making their sonic transparency an utmost priority in the minds of most musicians, listeners, and scholars.

––––––

If history is always an act of interpretation, which kinds of histories, interpretations, and forms of knowledge can we glean from documents that are disfigured? Within the discourses of ethnomusicology and world music, low fidelity has often (and ironically) functioned as an *authenticating* device, in the sense that it sonically marks recordings of non-Western music as products of preindustrial or technologically limited environments.[25] In hip-hop, phenomena such as surface noise and other anomalies of the analog era have essentially served historicizing functions, "time stamping" sampled source materials with the aesthetic and technological context of their creation. But what does it mean to rehear the high priests of jazz modernism through the "phonographic effects" of surface noise and digital glitches?[26] The becomes especially pointed in relation to a musician like Charlie Parker, the towering historical figure who synthesized everything that came before him into a new paradigm to which all subsequent practitioners were compelled to respond, whether by replicating, extending, or deconstructing. To what extent might we consider surface noise a subversion and/or an extension of his innovations?

One answer lies purely in aesthetics; recordings such as these can widen the range of available colors on the listener's palette, their corrosive and ghostly lyricism imparting a painterly dimension to sound recordings as they pass across the sensorium of jazz. Their sonic colors are as rich as the visual colors of an artist like Romare Bearden but, as the degraded products of industry, their textures are corrosive in a way that recalls the postindustrial landscapes surveyed by Robert Smithson, the corrosive, mixed-media surfaces of Anselm Kiefer, or the deliberately corrupted photographic textures of Miroslav Tichý. There is additional aesthetic value here. In a culture of jazz saxophone playing often marked by players constantly changing instruments, reeds, and mouthpieces in an endless quest to refine a signature sound, Charlie Parker is often cited as an embodiment of the truism that a player's true sound is an immutable expression of their inner spirit and, as such, never really changes. Indeed, Parker's sound is remarkably consistent despite his often being forced to play on whatever equipment was at hand, as a result of his legendarily unstable lifestyle. If we substitute sound recordings for musical instruments, we can similarly observe that Parker's sound remains remarkably consistent whether it reaches us via a professionally produced studio recording, or as a variable radio signal pressed onto a distressed playback medium. As focused by the attention of the listener, in fact, Parker's sound acquires a particularly "graphic" weight here, as it cuts through the surface noise as one of the few elements clearly distinguishable as "music."

Artifacts such as those discussed in this chapter could conceivably be recuperated to greater or lesser extent, through complicated processes of audio restoration, into more "accurate" depictions of historical events. But like the sediment that can never be entirely scraped from an ancient tablet without disfiguring the underlying text, the markers of low fidelity are important in the construction of the (in this case, historical) "authenticity" of the recordings—as important as nature sounds have been to the authenticity of ethnographic field recordings and ambient street noise to live news broadcasts. Eventually, their sonic sedimentation becomes not only a verification of age, use, and provenance but also, like the vintage samples heard on hip-hop recordings, a mode of information in itself that helps calibrate our relationship to history and to the history of technology. Listening to these recordings can be compared to reading *Bird Lives*, the notorious biography of Parker by record producer Ross Russell. Russell's biography has been criticized as flawed and occasionally based on fictitious passages, but despite this it remains the biography that most successfully and viscerally conveys not only the human flaws of Parker but also how those flaws were essential to the transcendence of his art.

In fact, the sonic anomalies resulting from the circulation of sound tapes can themselves be heard as radical sonic abstractions of the communal, conversational processes encoded into the very *heart* of the music and this is also where the issue becomes spatial once again; the idea of the improvising ensemble as a "democratic conversation" with its value system of sharing and circulating ideas finds its broader, socio-technological parallel in the variations of sound that emerge as a recorded artifact moves from hand to hand, across the physical spaces of playback devices and trading, broadcast, and commercial networks.[27] This materiality of recorded sound can be as much a component of jazz "analysis" as the more traditionally "musical" parameters of pitch, duration, etc. Beyond its aesthetic attributes, the sound recording survives as a remnant of a historical moment, a technological era, a social formation, an acoustic situation, and a musical structure, our perceptions of which change over time.

This "aestheticization of lo-fi" is an inevitable consequence of musicians' participation in the creation and circulation of sound recordings. The next logical step in this argument is to consider the fidelity of jazz recordings in light of jazz's longstanding valuation of the expressive potential of highly personalized, idiosyncratic instrumental sounds; in the same way that sounds defined by classical musicians as "unconventional" are valued in jazz as unique and highly expressive, sound devalued by recording engineers can be revalued by jazz musicians as de facto extensions of their expressive potential. This essentially applies a jazz philosophy of sound to recording aesthetics.

Jed Rasula lamented in his essay that "the sense of loss, dispossession, opposition, and contradiction that is so much a part of the blues basis of jazz is simply erased" by excessively sanitized constructions of that history.[28] Emily Thompson, meanwhile, has characterized the sonic history of modernity as a battle for control over acoustic space represented by the assertion of ever-increasing "fidelity" as a desired value.[29] Strategically corrupting this value in our listening potentially reactivates the oppositional narrative at the core of jazz history by contesting the idea that better technology and higher fidelity always equate with progress—it literally sounds *back* a level of texture that signifies the past, while its implied experimentalism signifies the future. These complex sonic documents can then be said to reassert the oft-trumpeted "blues impulse" at the heart of jazz—*not* because they support a narrow and nostalgic telescoping into the historical past, but for more profound reasons. The shift from the analog to hearing the analog era with digital ears allows us to view the older format in new ways, allowing us to read not only psychic and emotional states into these distressed aesthetics, but to creatively repurpose them in a way that makes something out of a lack, a philosophy of bricolage that has typified the blues philosophy from the earliest recorded blues to the most rarefied hip-hop sample. Similar to the jazz experimentalism of the 1960s and 1970s, the unintended consequences of tape trading have, in the digital age, provided the foundations for a sonic counternarrative of jazz, and this process is not limited to music. As early as the 1980s, in fact, black filmmakers in Britain and the US such as John Akomfrah and Arthur Jafa were probing the artifacts and media of the analog era for new aesthetic and representational possibilities in the digital age.[30] In the final analysis, these recordings chromaticize the color field in a way that can liberate those jazz musicians who have been indoctrinated to believe that the only color on their palette is *blue*.

———

Toward the end of his life, Miroslav Tichý reflected, "Everything that exists is the world. And when some of it became recognizable, I printed it." His comment implies that the work of art, functioning as a human prosthesis, brings the world into human apprehension. Tichý went on to comment, "The world is anyway, nothing but an appearance, an illusion," implying that the distinction between "representational" and "abstract" art is ultimately unsustainable.[31] We can transport these insights into the practice of jazz phonography. In the same way that over- or underexposure, clouded or foggy prints, blank spots, smudges, streaks, and extraneous materials *facilitate* the narrative qualities of Tichý's images, frequency range distortion, compression, duplication decay, and other degradations of the audio signal have their roles to play in telling the musical story. As much as an embrace of "noise" and "distortion" seems to run counter to the aesthetic values of jazz, these elements can help recuperate the principles of freedom and adventure in the music. And since (per Jacques Attali) "noise" will eventually be recuperated into "music," this embrace of noise is just a way of growing and nourishing the music as it evolves. One day, the ears of jazz may embrace this truth, reconceiving of all jazz recordings as sound objects, and in doing so, jazz will also help *swing* a human listening practice eternally in search of itself.

What the aesthetics of the digital age make clear, possibly more acutely than before, is that these various spheres of sound activity can always be recuperated back into human musical meaning, as they evolve in tandem with our ever-increasing sensory sensitivities and capabilities. Sigfried Giedion, addressing the work of Laszlo Moholy-Nagy, wrote in *telehor* in 1935: "although the various movements in art that are of prime importance for us today may differ in origin, they are nevertheless inspired by a common aim . . . the urge behind all of them is the attempt to give an emotive content to the new sense of reality born of modern science and industry; and thereby restore the basic unity of all human experience."[32] In the relatively recent medium of photography, a significant amount of this emotional and intellectual energy was generated in its early years, when "mistakes" were gradually recognized as openings and possibilities that allowed (or forced) the medium to evolve.[33] And if Moholy-Nagy himself felt that recorded images made with this principle in mind would "prevent the atrophying of our optical organs," an equally strong assertion can be made in the sphere of recorded sound—especially in the case of jazz, a music predicated on devising creative solutions through the process of improvisation.[34] The producer Brian Eno once suggested that musicians "honor [their] mistakes as hidden intentions," bringing to the world of pop experimentation a philosophy already strongly associated with jazz in general and Miles Davis in particular, who notoriously paid his band members not to rehearse so that mistakes and other unplanned developments in live performance could be exploited for their creative potential.[35] This same intentionality can guide the way we hear the anomalies of sound recordings, despite the fact that most of them were not the results of human intention. If, per Siegfried Kracauer, we imagine the intentional and nonintentional sounds of photography to be nature's way of using human beings to catalogue the totality of visual impressions emerging in reality,[36] we can similarly understand the way that these anomalies of sound recordings broaden the spectrum of our auditory awareness. As Miroslav Tichý himself once remarked: "A mistake—that's what makes the poetry."[37] No statement truer to the fundamental spirit of jazz has ever been spoken.

NOTES

1. Woods, Lebbeus. *War and Architecture*. Princeton, NJ: Princeton Architectural Press, 1993, 14.

2. Richter, as quoted in Koch, Gertrud. "The Richter-Scale of Blur." In *October Files: Gerhard Richter*. Edited by Benjamin Buchloh. Cambridge, MA: MIT Press, 2009.

3. *Tremé* (TV series). Eric Ellis Overmeyer and David Simon, producers. 2010–2013. https://www.imdb.com/title/tt1279972/.

4. Harlan, Becky. "Warped and Waterlogged, A Damaged Photo Collection Takes On a New Life." *National Geographic*, October 22, 2015. https://www.nationalgeographic.com/photography/article/warped-and-waterlogged-a-damaged-photo-collection-takes-on-new-life.

5. Keith Calhoun quoted in Harlan, "Warped and Waterlogged."

6. See the exhibition page at St. Olaf's College: https://wp.stolaf.edu/flaten/we-no-longer-consider-them-damaged/.

7. For a book-length profile of Miroslav Tichý, see Tichý, Miroslav, and Harold Szeeman. *Tichý*. London: Thames and Hudson, 2008.

8. See De Font-Réaulx, Dominique. *Painting and Photography, 1839–1914*. New York: Random House, 2012.

9. See Kelsey, Robin. *Photography and the Art of Chance*. Cambridge, MA: Harvard University Press, 2015.

10. Kahn, Douglas. "Audio Art in the Deaf Century." In *Sound by Artists*, edited by Dan Lander and Micah Lexier. Toronto: Art Metropole, 1990.

11. See Rasula's excellent essay, "The Media of Memory: The Seductive Menace of Records in Jazz History." In *Jazz Among the Discourses*, edited by Krin Gabbard. Durham, NC: Duke University Press, 1995.

12. See, for example: Finnegan, Ruth. *Oral Literature in Africa*. Cambridge: Open Book Publishers, 2012. See also: Okpewho, Isaac. *African Oral Literature: Backgrounds, Character, and Continuity*. Bloomington: Indiana University Press, 1992.

13. Eshun, Kodwo. *More Brilliant Than the Sun: Essays in Sonic Fiction*. London: Verso, 1998.

14. This type of documentation was, however, already being undertaken in published discographies of specific artists and recording labels.

15. Wayne Shorter, interview with the author, August 22, 2011.

16. Heylin, Clinton. *Bootleg! The Rise and Fall of the Secret Recording Industry*. New York: St. Martin's Press, 1996, 33–34.

17. In legal terms, not all of these recordings should be considered "bootlegs" by standard definitions. Most of them are more accurately referred to as "protection gap" recordings in which European manufacturers took advantage of discrepancies (i.e., "gaps")

in copyright protection laws between the newly formed European Economic Community and older, nationally based copyright laws. This was particularly the case in Italy, which has traditionally had comparatively loose copyright laws under which, for example, mechanical copyrights expire after a period of twenty years. This is one reason that bootlegs made from performances that took place in the 1960s began to appear in the 1980s—exactly twenty years after they had been recorded across Europe. These releases may have been of questionable legality in the United States and elsewhere, and their release doesn't seem to have been sanctioned by the radio and television networks that had originally broadcast and recorded the concerts. Nevertheless, they eventually began to circulate through the global market from this time.

18. Bates, Eliot. "Glitches, Bugs, and Hisses: The Degeneration of Musical Recordings and the Contemporary Musical Work." In *Bad Music: The Music We Love to Hate*, edited by Christopher J. Washburne and Maiken Derno. New York: Routledge, 2004.

19. Mark Wilder, interview with the author, January 2012.

20. See Espina's article "Have More Fun in the Shed," http://www.saxontheweb.net/Espina/HaveMoreFun.html.

21. Oliveros, Pauline. "Valentine." In *Electronic Music: A Listener's Guide*, edited by Elliott Schwartz, 246. New York: Praeger Publishers, 1975. Thanks to Yale graduate student Andrew Chung for bringing this quote to my attention.

22. My key sources for thinking through glitch aesthetics have been: Menkman, Rosa. *The Glitch Moment(um)*. Amsterdam: Network Notebooks 04, 2011; Bates, "Glitches, Bugs, and Hisses"; Novak, David. "The Sublime Frequencies of New Old Media." In *Punk Ethnography: Artists and Scholars Listen to Sublime Frequencies*, edited by Michael Veal and E. Tammy Kim. Middletown, CT: Wesleyan University Press, 2015.

23. See Wetmore, Thomas Trask. "'Jazz Steel': An Ethnography of Race, Sound, and Technology in Spaces of Live Performance." PhD dissertation. Columbia University, 2022.

24. This passage is excerpted from Ken Dryden's review of Charlie Parker's *Bird's Eyes, Volume 18*, https://www.allmusic.com/album/birds-eyes-vol-18-mw0000435427.

25. For a discussion of this idea, see Novak, "The Sublime Frequencies of New Old Media," 42–45.

26. This idea of "phonographic effects" is introduced on page 6 of Katz, Mark. *Capturing Sound: How Technology Has Changed Music*. Berkeley: University of California Press, 2010.

27. The metaphor of the improvising jazz ensemble as a "conversation" is most often attributed to Albert Murray (see *Murray Talks Music*, 2016), and has also been treated by Ingrid Monson (*Saying Something: Jazz Improvisation and Interaction*, 1998) and Stanley Crouch (*Considering Genius: Writings on Jazz*, 2006).

28. Rasula, "The Media of Memory," 152.

29. See chapter 6 of Thompson's landmark study: "Electro-Acoustics and Modern

Sound." In *The Soundscape of Modernity: Architectural Acoustics and the Culture of Listening in America, 1900–1933*. Cambridge, MA: MIT Press, 2002.

30. See, for example: Sagar, Anjalika, and Kodwo Eshun. *The Ghosts of Songs: The Film Art of the Black Audio Film Collective, 1982–1998*. Liverpool: Liverpool University Press, 2007. See also: Jafa, Arthur. "Black Visual Intonation." In *The Jazz Cadence of American Culture*, edited by Robert O'Meally. New York: Columbia University Press, 1998.

31. These quotes are from the documentary *Miroslav Tichý: Tarzan Retired* (directed by Roman Buxbaum, Zurich: Fondation Tichý Océan, DVD, 35 minutes, 2004).

32. Giedion, as quoted in the foreword to *telehor* 1–2 (1936): 27. This entire issue was devoted to the work of Laszlo Moholy-Nagy.

33. See Kelsey, Robin. *Photography and the Art of Chance*. Cambridge, MA: Harvard University Press, 2015; and Davey, Moyra. "Notes on Photography and Accident." In *Long Life Cool White: Photographs and Essays*. Cambridge, MA: Harvard University Press, 2008.

34. Moholy-Nagy, as quoted in D'Alessandro, Stephanie. "Through the Eye and Hand: Constructing Space, Constructing Vision in the Work of Moholy-Nagy." In *Moholy-Nagy: Future Present*, edited by Matthew Witkovsky, 64. Chicago: Art Institute of Chicago, 2016.

35. Quoted in "Brian Eno Explains the Loss of Humanity in Modern Music." http://www.openculture.com/2016/07/brian-eno-explains-the-loss-of-humanity-in-modern-music.html.

36. This interpretation is inspired by my reading of Siegfried Kracauer's essays on photography. See Kracauer, Siegfried. *The Past's Threshold: Essays on Photography*. Berlin: Diaphanes, 2014.

37. All quotes of Tichý in this paragraph are taken from the film *Tarzan Retired*.

FOUR

Living Space

John Coltrane between Worlds

I: CRESCENT

In those last scenes, as he floats
Above Jupiter's vast canyons and seas,
Over the lava strewn plains and mountains
Packed in ice, that whole time, he doesn't blink.
In his little ship, blind to what he rides, whisked
Across the wide-screen of unparcelled time,
Who knows what blazes through his mind?
Is it still his life he moves through, or does
That end at the end of what he can name?[1]

Tracy K. Smith

In December 1964, after a week of seclusion, John Coltrane entered Rudy Van
Gelder's studio in New Jersey with his quartet to record his four-part suite *A Love
Supreme* (ALS).[2] Essentially a declaration of spiritual faith inspired by his triumph
over personal adversities in the late 1950s, ALS is considered the defining work
of Coltrane's career, as well as one the most-canonized and biggest-selling works
of modern jazz. The story of the album has been recounted in several sources;
suffice to say here that ALS was not only Coltrane's most commercially successful
album, but also the thematic portal to the final two and a half years of his career.[3]
It bundled together the modal jazz he had been playing since he formed his own

quartet in 1960, the intense level of improvisational abstraction that evolved as his technical facility became more and more formidable, and the quartet's remarkably intuitive chemistry, while making explicit a sense of spirituality that had previously been present as a potent—but implicit—undertone in his music.

Blending the earthy sensibility of the country church, the abstract intellectualism of the city, and musical overtones of the decolonizing black and brown worlds, the newly focused spirituality of ALS gave Coltrane's new music a thematic unity, a deeper sense of purpose, a wider range of emotional expressiveness, and more profound political and historical resonances. Charlie Parker and the beboppers had proven in the 1940 and 1950s that jazz could be a virtuosic art music, and Coltrane was now proving that it could be a spiritual music. Here was a musician who, just a few years earlier, had struggled mightily with heroin and alcohol addictions. And although by all accounts, Coltrane had avoided most of the degradations typically associated with that lifestyle, he had nonetheless moved through a nocturnal world of substance abusers, sex workers, hustlers, and criminals, blowing their bluesy soundtrack in bars and nightclubs through his own narcotic haze. Now, having freed himself of his addictions, he was using those same social rhythms and melodies of dance, sex, and the street to confer divinity and nobility upon the same social spaces. *A Love Supreme*, then, was not merely a one-off spiritually themed project for Coltrane but rather a summary of everything he had achieved since turning his life around, and a declaration of his total vision for all of his music that would follow. While the album was really just the latest of several fusions of the secular and sacred that dotted the history of jazz (Duke Ellington's Sacred Concerts, Charles Mingus's "Wednesday Night Prayer Meeting," and much of Alice Coltrane's solo work also come to mind), it also represented a profound new stage.

This vision consolidated at the same time that Coltrane brought long-standing interests in world musics (particularly South Asian and West African traditions) into sharper focus, while entertaining the sonic and structural innovations of the new jazz trends variously referred to as "free jazz," "the New Thing," "the New Music," or the "jazz avant-garde." His friendships with musicians such as the Indian sitarist Ravi Shankar and the Nigerian drummer Babatunde Olatunji are well documented. Meanwhile, the younger generation of saxophonists associated with this new music, such as Archie Shepp, Albert Ayler, and Pharoah Sanders, had brought a new level of emotional expressiveness to the instrument through their experimentation with alternative saxophone techniques. Coltrane sought not only to mentor them but also to play with and learn from them (Shepp is present on an alternate version of ALS, and Sanders would later join Coltrane's working group). This fusion of world music influences, sonic experimentation, and devotional themes was the defining equation in the music Coltrane made during the last two years of his life, a clarion call for a new, politically and spiritually imbued age of jazz. This extended essay encompasses all of these themes, while this opening section lays a music-analytical foundation for the interwoven musical and extramusical observations that follow.

Of *A Love Supreme*'s four sections, the first is set in a mid-tempo Afro-Cuban feel, the middle two feature up-tempo swing feels, while the fourth floats in rubato time. And while all four sections are equally powerful, many people are most familiar with the opening section ("Acknowledgement") built around Jimmy Garrison's famous repeating bass riff, which helps anchor the piece in a bluesy, meditative groove. This four-note riff of "Acknowledgement" was hitched to a mambo pattern that Coltrane's drummer Elvin Jones had previously used for the quartet's 1960 piece "Liberia," and set to minor key, modal harmony. These constituted the album's most accessible element for listeners generally unfamiliar with jazz, and also made Coltrane's best-known work relevant to a younger generation of listeners in the 1960s whose musical sensibilities would be shaped by rhythms from decolonizing Africa and the Caribbean, drones emerging from decolonized South Asia, and various refractions of the guitar blues.[4]

Coltrane's reliance on a repeating riff structure was somewhat ironic at this point in his career, given that the type of modal jazz he was playing was a platform for increasingly abstract and chromatic forms of improvisation. No longer the relatively diatonic excursions that he had played with Miles Davis on *Kind of Blue* nor the regimented ragas of the Indian classical music that inspired him, the modal playing of the Coltrane quartet was particularly dense with chromatic invention. In fact, this type of modal playing is a good place to begin decoding Coltrane's journey into the more complex rhythmic structures he inhabited during the last two years of his career, because we can conceptualize the tonal stasis of the drone or the repeating riff as a "flat" surface that was used as a point of departure for a variety of operations that created increasing amounts of tension. This was a harmonic consideration that eventually had rhythmic consequences. In this essay, I conceptualize Coltrane's post-ALS music as evolving through a series of *curving maneuvers* that arced gradually away from tonal stasis and regularized meter, and I intermittently use architectural imagery to emphasize chapter 2's theme of *curvilinearity* as one of the most significant "unarticulated principles" in his later music. It was these increasingly dramatic "curving maneuvers" that eventually helped morph Coltrane's music into "freer" (in reality, more complex) rhythmic and structural relationships.

While this essay focuses primarily on questions of rhythm and meter, harmonic considerations are important as a point of departure because I believe the "curves" in Coltrane's music first manifested in his handling of pitch material, and were later extended into the sphere of time and ensemble structure. In the early years of the Coltrane quartet, for example, the most frequent types of "curvature" tended to be pitch-based techniques for increasing harmonic tension, such as a) the superimposition of nondiatonic chords and scales (such as tritone substitutions and the technique known as "side slipping"); b) the chromatic transposition of melodic patterns; and, most importantly, c) the "Coltrane changes."[5] "Side slipping" is particularly relevant to my narrative of curvature here, a way of creating harmonic tension by improvising a half-step above or below a given tonality. Operating as lines that slope in dissonant parallel to the given harmony, side slipping momentarily suggests resolution to a different tonal center, in the process giving the impression of "blurring" or "bending" the established tonality. Side slipping is not exclusively associated with Coltrane, but he devised certain novel applications of it.[6] A related technique was to take a melodic motive or pattern and transpose it literally instead of making diatonic adjustments, resulting in a movement of melodic shapes that created varying levels of harmonic tension and color as they cross-cut the underlying tonality. In this, Coltrane was strongly indebted to the innovations of Ornette Coleman who, with his "harmolodic" system, pioneered the free transposition of melodic motives, bypassing the system of intermediate ii-V7 modulations that had typically facilitated movement between unrelated keys in jazz. If side slipping gives the impression of *lines bending* against a straight "surface," these free pattern transpositions can be likened to *shapes spinning* against a straight "surface." Coltrane was unambiguous—almost effusive—in his acknowledgment of Coleman's influence:

> I love him. I'm following his lead. He's done a lot to open my eyes to what can be done . . . Because, actually, when he came along, I was so far into (the chord system of bebop) I didn't know where I was going to go next. I don't know whether I would have thought about just abandoning the chord system or not. I probably wouldn't have thought of that at all. And he came along doing it, and I heard it, I said "Well you know, that—that must be the answer, you know?" And I'm of the opinion that it is.[7]

In this way of thinking, it could be argued that the seeds for many of Coltrane's later, most dramatic innovations had been planted within his 1959 tune "Giant Steps." The bebop-derived "Giant Steps" and the modal music on *A Love Supreme* (and after) are typically considered to be radically different in conception. In fact, there is a crucial link between them that, if seriously considered, forces us to radically reconsider our understanding of the evolution of Coltrane's music. It was "Giant Steps" that introduced his system of chordal movement by major thirds, known as the "Coltrane changes." Coltrane distilled this system from elements of preexisting jazz tunes as well as ideas adapted from exercises contained in Nicolas Slonimsky's *Thesaurus of Scales and Melodic Patterns*, and its application evolved over several stages of his music. In songs like "Giant Steps" and "Countdown," for example, the system was used to split the octave into three equally spaced tonal regions that were then elaborated with their respective ii–V7 progressions. Because of the way it strings together chord sequences from unrelated keys, "Giant Steps" is particularly challenging to improvise over and has long been considered a litmus test for the display of a jazz improviser's mastery of bebop's "obstacle course" approach to harmony.[8]

But the concepts embedded in this composition acquire a very different significance when transported beyond the boundaries of the bebop way of thinking. If we conceptualize its chord progression as a *shape*, "Giant Steps" can be heard as a form of "rotational symmetry," the term being defined in the visual discourse as the property of a shape that is identical when viewed from any angle of rotation (figure 4.1). Like an equilateral triangle that appears exactly the same on every face, the chord sequences of each section of "Giant Steps" are structurally identical. Ultimately, this splitting of the octave into three equal parts encourages a mode of thinking strongly oriented toward symmetric (i.e., whole-tone) scales and harmonies, further away from tonality, and eventually into complete chromaticism.

This is where the link with Coltrane's later music such as *A Love Supreme* becomes relevant. As Paul Bair has documented in his study of the saxophonist's engagement with Slonimsky's book, Coltrane later applied this system of symmetries to generate harmonic tension against the droning tonal centers at the foundation of the modal compositions he favored after forming his own quartet.[9] Most of his improvisations in the modal idiom moved back and forth between tonal harmonies recalling the pentatonic melodies of the blues and so-called Negro spirituals and dissonant scalar and chordal constructions, and on to melodic shapes spun by inversion and chromatic transposition, all juxtaposed against a tonal drone. And although his melodies often spiraled downward toward the

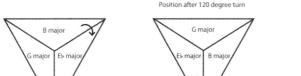
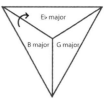

FIGURE 4.1 Key centers in "Giant Steps" as a form of rotational symmetry.
Reproduced courtesy of Chloe Smith.

tonal center (or other consonant pitches) at phrase conclusions, the rotational logic embedded in "Giant Steps" allowed Coltrane to generate increasing levels of tension against the harmonic stasis of the drone. In this, he was drawing on the legacy of other Philadelphia saxophonists such as Jimmy Heath and Bill Barron, who also embraced highly chromatic (and occasionally, serialist) methods to expand bebop harmony.

This was an architectural way of thinking in itself; symmetries such as the augmented triad were for Coltrane what the tetrahedron was for a designer like R. Buckminster Fuller—a symmetric and irreducibly stable element that could be endlessly combined and recombined to build all manner of complex forms. What is important to Coltrane's particular equation of obsessive rigor and passionate abandon is that, as the architectural historian Amber Sadiki has written, such symmetrical lines and harmonies "creat[e] the impression that the structure can be replicated endlessly without sacrificing compositional integrity."[10] At the same time, their lack of tonal gravity also makes the structures feel perpetually on the verge of either levitation or collapse.

———

Trane is Oriental (Eastern) on "Nature Boy." A peace idiom,
and time, placement of himself. When he speaks of God, you realize
it is an Eastern God. Allah, perhaps.[11]
Amiri Baraka

As much as it might be explained by the practices of Western harmony, the dense ornamentation of Coltrane's lines and surfaces also signified structures of feeling beyond the spheres of Western music and culture. Six months prior to his ALS epiphany, the quartet had recorded *Crescent*, an album revered by jazz musicians, although not as well known among the general public.[12] Its five mid-tempo tunes are similar in mood, implying, like ALS, a unity of thematic purpose. Conceived (as legend has it) while Coltrane sketched the moon during an evening in Paris,[13] there is something about the careful and deliberate crafting of the tunes, as well as the overall mood of the album, that—in light of the dramatic direction his music would shortly take—suggests an interregnum of peaceful, nocturnal reflection. Given his musical trajectory of the previous three years, it's also likely that the *Crescent* image contains cultural resonances of Coltrane fixing his gaze to the "east" of Western culture.[14] He had already acknowledged Islam as an inspiring and empowering presence in his social milieu, for example, and a number of the musicians around him had in fact become adherents. Elijah Muhammad's Nation of Islam was a prominent presence in Coltrane's world, and in the 1950s, the Nation typically recruited from the most challenged rungs of the socioeconomic ladder, typically targeting those suffering from substance abuse, sex workers, and the incarcerated. Coltrane himself was from a southern, Christian, working-class background, but as a former heroin user and a long-standing inhabitant of the "floating world" of jazz, he undoubtedly knew many people who had been redeemed by the NOI's ethos of martial self-discipline, and this would have struck a deep chord within him.

Very different from the Nation of Islam's idiosyncratic, African Americo-centric take on the Muslim faith was the Ahmadiyya version of Islam, which was articulated within a very different cultural orientation, set within a network of reference points stretching across the Muslim world from Africa eastward into Southeast Asia. As Robin D. G. Kelley narrates in *Africa Speaks, America Answers*, Ahmadiyya offered a mystical discourse through which jazz musicians' obsession with scales, rhythms, and other musical elements of various non-Western sources could be understood as conveying arcane spiritual truths.[15] But regardless of particular orientations within Islam, these sentiments were the background for comments Coltrane made to August Blume in 1955: "this Muslim thing came up. I got introduced to that. That kinda shook me. A lot of my friends, you know, they went Muslim, you see. So I thought about that, anyway, it took me to something I had never thought about . . . But I never did anything about it."[16]

If Coltrane's words remain vague and if he never actually concretized a religious affiliation, these experiences nonetheless affected him deeply and were reflected in his music. As early as 1961, jazz critic Ira Gitler was using the term "sheets of sound" to describe the way Coltrane crammed the song surface with dizzying sequences of stacked scales and arpeggios.[17] In these moments he was essentially practicing a form of what is called *tessellation* in the visual discourse— a technique of using repeating, interlocking patterns to cover a surface. Now that these symmetries were becoming more pronounced in his improvisations, his music resonated more strongly with the highly ornamented sonic geometries of visual arts from across the Islamic world as they were tessellated across architectural and calligraphic surfaces.

Meanwhile, what might be heard as the heavily "Africanist strain" in Coltrane's quartet reflected not only his own evolving cultural symbols and aesthetic choices, but also the contributions of the other musicians of the quartet, as well as the fact that strong (albeit abstracted) echoes of the mambo era could be heard throughout their body of work. Pianist McCoy Tyner was distinctive because of his characteristic voicings of stacked fourths, as well as his system of contrapuntal comping patterns which, in their style of interlock, were quite similar to structures in West African and Cuban-derived dance musics. Bassist Jimmy Garrison sometimes walked his lines in standard eighth-note fashion but at other moments "broke up" the time with singing, melodic figures (in a manner similar to the bassist Scott LaFaro) that often consolidated into repeating ostinati. In his solo spots (such as in the introduction and conclusion of ALS's second section titled "Resolution"), he frequently strummed the strings of his bass to achieve an effect reminiscent of blues or flamenco guitar styles, or of African lute-type instruments such as the Moroccan *gimbri*, the Senegalese *xalam*, or the Malian *donso ngoni*.

Finally, there was Elvin Jones, Coltrane's hard-swinging drummer of prayer-meeting intensity, among the latest in a progression of modern jazz drummers who manipulated tension by shattering the song surface into innumerable fragments, while never abandoning the underlying meter. Earlier drummers of the swing/big band era such as Papa Jo Jones, Big Sid Catlett, and Cozy Cole usually maintained a steady, "four on the floor" pulse with their bass drums, in order to provide a rhythmic anchor for the large bands and a steady pulse for dancers. Bebop drummers, by contrast, internalized the steady meter while breaking up the "song surface" in their actual playing. Consider the comments of two of the drummers most strongly associated with bebop, Kenny Clarke and Max Roach. Clarke remembered that:

In 1937 I'd gotten tired of playing like Jo Jones. It was time for jazz drummers to move ahead. I took the main beat away from the bass drum and up to the top cymbal . . . The beat had a better flow. It was lighter and tastier. That left me free to use the bass drum, the tom-toms and snare for accents. I was trying to lay new rhythmic patterns over the regular beat. Solo lines were getting longer. Soloists needed more help from the drummer—kicks, accents, cues, all kinds of little things like that.[18]

In Roach's words, meanwhile:

You can say Bird [Charlie Parker] was really responsible, not just because his style called for a particular type of drumming, but because he set tempos so fast, it was impossible to play a straight, Cozy Cole, four style. So we had to work out variations. But it was a logical idea anyway . . . I'd rather use the high hat as a back beat and break up the bass drum rhythm. You get a more definite sound, as though the drums are really contributing something instead of just filling in.[19]

By relocating the steady pulse from the bass drum to a "timeline" pattern shared by the much lighter hi-hat and ride cymbals while using the other limbs to improvise accents and interjections, bebop drummers created a much more abstract rhythmic feel that required musicians and listeners to internalize a metric pulse that, while continuous, was only actually sounded in fragmentary fashion. This move "up" to the cymbals brought the music into conceptual resonance with drumming traditions of West Africa and the African diaspora, in which cyclically repeating timeline patterns (typically played by high-pitched bells, sticks, or other idiophones) often provide a steady reference for highly abstract improvisation by drummers. This abstracting of the rhythmic pulse set the stage for drummers like Elvin Jones, whose displacement and syncopated scattering of rhythmic figures around the various surfaces of the drum set constituted a rhythmic balancing act that provided the perfect accompaniment for Coltrane's increasingly complex improvisations.

From an Africanist perspective, the entire history of African American drum-set playing can be thought of as the increasing mastery of independent coordination to enable a single drummer to fulfill the multiple roles of the African drum orchestra. Jones himself was clear about the inspiration he took from the drum orchestras of sub-Saharan Africa:

I listened to the real authentic African music from the United Nations record store—you can buy ethnic recordings there. And I heard some of the more tribal gatherings, festivals, and things like that. They weren't individual drummers, they were a whole group, maybe three of four hundred people, all using the same tempo, but their rhythms were varied. That contributed to the complexity of what you hear. So I would listen to it as a whole and I would imagine: "What if I could do that?" But you know, it's just something that you feel . . . It's extremely spiritual and extremely emotional.[20]

———

If the "Africanist qualities" in the Coltrane quartet are often understood to intensify the (poly)rhythmic dynamics of swing, the final section of *A Love Supreme* foreshadowed a profound paradigm shift. Titled "Psalm," this section consists of a prayer written by Coltrane, rendered in instrumental form on his tenor saxophone (the text itself appears on the inside of the original gatefold album jacket), while Tyner, Garrison, and Jones provide a dramatic rubato backdrop. *Rubato*—the floating feeling of nonmetered, rhythmic suspension—is in fact a crucially important element in Coltrane's music, and a central analytical point in this essay. Its sources in his work are clearly rooted on one hand in particular moments of the African American Christian liturgy and on the other, in the free-meter *alap* expositions of Indian classical music, which he had deeply investigated. In conjunction with the droning tonal center common to both traditions (whether played by organ pedals or tambouras), rubato works in both traditions to focus the listener's attention in a meditative, devotional space that is sonically distinct from the rhythms of everyday life. And although rubato sections were already a fairly common feature in Coltrane's music, he tended to use them prior to 1965 to offset the intensity of the metered swing sections that comprise the lion's share of the quartet's music (usually bookending them as introductions or conclusions in pieces such as "Alabama," "Spiritual," and "Brazilia"). Throughout 1965, however, they would be gradually transformed from spaces of repose or release into spaces of rhythmic dynamization that increasingly formed the core—not the periphery—of his compositions. "Psalm" represents possibly the first important turning point in this transformation. And, as with many of the African traditions in which instruments are used as "linguistic surrogates" that reproduce the rhythms and melodies of spoken language, it is telling that Coltrane employs free meter when he switches into "speech" mode.[21]

"Psalm" was not actually the first time Coltrane had used his horn to render a spoken text; his 1963 piece "Alabama," for example, has long been understood as an instrumental adaptation of a eulogy the Reverend Martin Luther King Jr. had given for the four children killed in the bombing of the 16th Street Baptist Church in Birmingham, Alabama, on September 15 of that year. But the overtly spiritual outlook that emerged with ALS brought a new rhythmic dimension into Coltrane's playing, for one simple reason: it dictated that whenever he put the horn to his mouth, he was in effect *praying*. In fact, according to biographer C. O. Simpkins, Coltrane confided as much to his first wife Naima, and his rhythms and melodic cadences, as well as the overall rhetorical arc of his solos, do compare closely with those of African American modes of sermonizing.[22] As has often been noted, Coltrane was never exclusively a "time" player as such (which is to say, there was always a lot of rhythmic freedom and flexibility in his phrasing), but the verbal cadences of "Psalm" brought a new and specific rhythmic dimension into his actual playing; it is from this point that his phrasing became increasingly free, encompassing not only ballads and rubato introductions and cadenzas but also, more significantly, the up-tempo, swing-based pieces. This new rhythmic freedom opened up a new realm of imaginative possibility for Coltrane devotees such as multi-instrumentalist Arthur Rhames, who remarked that "the feeling of the line, the phrasing . . . allowed me to understand how Trane was *talking* [my italics] when he played."[23] The comments of guitarist Pete Cosey (best known for his pioneering work in Miles Davis's mid-1970s band) continued this line of interpretation and opened a space for those who heard a poly-African narrative at the heart of Coltrane's music. Cosey told Pat Buzby that the musicians in his Chicago circle believed that Coltrane "had actually transcended music and was actually speaking through his horn. Someone told me that he had tapped into the language which was called *Linguata Dakinda*, the point of departure for the African slaves, where you had different tribes together and one language had been developed, similar to a Swahili, which everyone could understand. He had tapped into that and that's what he was actually playing . . . you can hear the flow of it. It was more than just the melodic lines, he was *speaking* through the horn [my italics]."[24]

Hearing Coltrane's music in terms of these structures of spiritual, intellectual, or cultural feeling has resulted in his prevailing image as a kind of jazz ascetic. But like the ambiguous blend of devotional and erotic longing at the heart of the Indian classical and light classical traditions such as *khyal, thumri,* and *dhrupad*—not to mention the highly passionate music of the African American sacred traditions—some also sensed an erotic energy pulsing within the cultural and spiritual frequencies of his music. Producer Michael Cuscuna, for example, has vivid memories of the quartet in performance:

Over the course of 50 years of hearing plenty of live music, nothing I've experienced has surpassed the many occasions on which I was lucky enough to hear the John Coltrane Quartet at Birdland or the Half Note. Often Coltrane would start off playing the brief melody of one of the triple-meter pieces he favored and leave the stage as McCoy Tyner, Jimmy Garrison and Elvin Jones built the intensity gradually with chorus after chorus until Elvin's thunderous quarter-note triplets on the bass drum would announce Coltrane's soaring return. For the next hour or more, these men would take us to a place that was as deep in spirituality as it was charged with sexual energy. For me, nothing has come close to what they achieved nightly.[25]

———

Embodying the liberation and experimentation that defined the 1960s, these passionate performances by the Coltrane quartet projected the new articulations of spirituality, power, and freedom that were consolidating among African Americans at that time. While *Crescent*'s reflective mood, loose thematic unity, and implied cultural breadth can be heard as the perfect prelude to *A Love Supreme*, the two records can also be heard as a dyad, with the celestial motif of the former and the spiritual motif of the latter complementing each other to suggest that the classic Coltrane quartet had ascended to an exalted space in late 1964—a space that set the stage for the explosion that would take place in their music during 1965. Juxtaposing the simultaneously fluid and rigid bebop gestures of "Giant Steps" against the stasis of tonal drones, the quartet built maximal tension as ballast to leverage their gradual curve into freer domains—harmonic, rhythmic, cultural, and eventually, cosmic.

II: CHURCH

We're all human beings. Our spirituality can express itself any way
and any where; you can get religion in a bar or jazz club
as much as you can in a church.[26]
Elvin Jones

It's unsurprising that, half a century later, Coltrane's fevered sets at the Half Note continue to loom large in Cuscuna's memory. A small club and Italian restaurant on Hudson Street in lower Manhattan, the Half Note operated from 1957 and presented a diverse array of jazz until it closed in 1972. It's well known that Coltrane preferred the intimacy of clubs to larger concert halls and, with a capacity of about 120 people and the ability to perform uninterrupted sets of music, the quartet often used the Half Note's stage to experiment with new or less frequently performed material. By early 1965, the club had become the setting for some of their most lengthy and dramatic excursions.

In Burrill Crohn's 1985 film *The Coltrane Legacy*, Elvin Jones remembers with incredulity occasional club dates when Coltrane would call one tune that the quartet would end up playing for an entire forty-five-minute set.[27] Jones may well have been recalling the Half Note gigs, several of which were broadcast by WABC-FM as part of a series called "Portraits in Jazz" hosted by the announcer Alan Grant. Grant himself can be heard laughing as he concludes the broadcasts, presumably exhilarated and astonished at the intensity of the quartet's performances.

The existing recordings of Coltrane's Half Note performances are drawn from several sources; some are professionally recorded tapes found in Coltrane's personal collection, and a few are audience recordings. But the bulk of them are home recordings of radio broadcasts captured by a New York-based archivist named Boris Rose (1918–2000). For several decades, Rose amassed an enormous collection of jazz recordings, primarily by taping radio broadcasts of live performances, many of which he later pressed into bootleg LPs. And although his recordings of musicians such as Coltrane, Miles Davis, Charlie Parker, and others remain crucially important documents of modern jazz, the writer Will Friedwald has characterized Rose as an "inveterate prankster" who delighted in confounding jazz collectors and discographers. Indeed, Rose's releases abound with whimsical titles and deliberately falsified information, issued on nonexistent labels with names such as Session Disc and Ozone (figure 4.2).[28] And since his releases were already beyond the bounds of regulation, other shadow companies have freely copied and recirculated the material in ways that create further complications of both sound quality and annotation. In the end, however, Boris Rose did the jazz world a tremendous service; regardless of their compromised sound quality and questionable provenance, the Half Note recordings remain among the most potent documents of Coltrane's music, allowing listeners to enjoy one of the greatest working bands in the history of jazz at the height of its powers, as its music evolved over several months. By now, several generations of jazz musicians and listeners have benefitted mightily from Rose's efforts.[29]

While Coltrane's catalog of studio recordings is fairly diverse given his brief

FIGURE 4.2 Album covers, Boris Rose. Photograph by author.

career, the majority of live recordings of his original quartet find them plying their way through their repertoire with relatively little variation from night to night. The seven-disc *Live Trane* box set, for example, chronicles nine European concerts given between 1961 and 1963 and contains six versions of "My Favorite Things," five versions each of "Impressions" and "Mr. P.C.," and four versions of "Naima." Rose's Half Note captures differ significantly in this regard, given that there are several tunes among them that are not found in the same form anywhere else in Coltrane's recorded oeuvre.[30]

The Half Note recordings also demonstrate the challenges that materials of uncertain provenance can pose for musical scholarship. How do we construct music history accurately when primary source documents are misidentified? Given that many fly-by-night recording companies in many countries, with little or no apparent knowledge of Coltrane's music, have dipped their hands into the Half Note trough over the years, several tunes scattered throughout these recordings have either been mistitled or given generic titles (by Rose and others) such as "Untitled Instrumental." For example, the song listed as "Brazilia" on an album of the same name issued by the label Blue Parrot (which may or may not have been one of Rose's fake labels) is simply a duplicate version of "Song of Praise" from the same show, mastered at a different speed (I will discuss this performance later in this section).[31] But the best-known example of this is the quartet's legendary, twenty-seven-minute tear through "One Down, One

Up" recorded on March 26, which did not actually appear on any of the many bootleg releases that list it as a title; presumably the mistitlings were deliberate, since Rose and the other bootleggers probably knew "O.D.O.U." to be the Half Note track most desired by listeners.

Coltrane's son Ravi eventually discovered a professional-quality recording of the performance and, along with other Half Note material, it was finally given an official release in 2005.[32] But as a bootleg recording, "O.D.O.U." had circulated for years among Coltrane devotees such as Michael Brecker, Dave Liebman, Steve Grossman, Arthur Rhames, and innumerable other musicians. Coltrane had actually documented several versions of "O.D.O.U." during the spring and summer of 1965, but of all these recordings, the Half Note version was most prized for decades, despite the low fidelity of the versions that circulated prior to its official release.[33] At first glance, the tune's simple construction (a five-note motive transposed across two alternating, adjacent augmented dominant seventh chords) would seem to belie its significance. But the brilliance in this performance lies in its elaboration; over twenty-seven fevered minutes, Coltrane wrings every bit of musical and emotional substance out of the musical materials. In addition, Tyner and Garrison drop out at 10:50 and 13:15, respectively, leaving Jones alone to accompany Coltrane for sixteen and a half minutes as they explore the quartet's white-hot interior space. In moments like these, Coltrane and Jones would often work themselves into a mode of such convoluted phrasing that the music would seem to swirl as if it were being played at the center of a cyclone. These were moments when they often transcended the rhythmic language of "swing" as traditionally understood, with Jones supporting or responding to every tempestuous rhythmic or melodic gesture that Coltrane hurled across the soundscape. Together, they would gradually open a portal, as we will see, into a new rhythmic reality.

Pharmacologically speaking, it is probably not entirely irrelevant that back in his own days of heroin addiction, Jones and Coltrane were dope buddies. As Martin Torgoff relates in his memoir of jazz and addiction, long before the quartet was formed, Coltrane and Jones would spend hours, days, weeks, and months together in the numbed-out zone of the heroin high. Now they were in a different but equally intense zone together, and it is not unreasonable to suspect that their earlier journeys through the synaptic spaces of opiate consciousness somehow prepared them for their later musical journeys through consciousness altered by sound.[34]

Some of the Half Note performances, such as the quartet's twenty-minute revamping of Richard and Robert Sherman's show tune "Chim Chim Cheree" (from the 1964 Walt Disney musical motion picture *Mary Poppins*) are complex, impassioned versions of material that would be recorded in the studio later that spring in more condensed form.[35] Other recordings feature themes that had already been recorded but remained unreleased. For example, one of the songs often identified as "Untitled Instrumental" was recorded on April 2 and is sometimes also known by the title "Creation," a low-fidelity recording released on a Blue Parrot album of the same name (figure 4.3).[36] Given that this performance rivals "O.D.O.U." in inventiveness, intensity, and duration, the main reason it is not equally revered is probably its unofficial status, which has constrained its circulation. "Creation" is built from a chromatically ascending, seven-note motive—as much pure gesture as melody—that is obsessively manipulated over the course of twenty-three minutes, and which also includes a sax-drum break-down in the manner of "O.D.O.U." McCoy Tyner and Jimmy Garrison generally imply a drone pitch of D on the bottom, but the highly chromatic construction of Coltrane's theme and his improvisation departs from the modal harmonies he had typically favored:

This motive might be heard as a sped-up, but otherwise almost identical, version of a theme Coltrane would record in August under the title "Ascent (figure 4.4)."[37] In the August recording, he has slowed the tempo while adding a sequence of pickup notes to give the main motive more of a hard-bop feel and altered the pitch sequence to give bluesier, Mixolydian inflection.

"Creation"/"Untitled Instrumental" says a lot about the direction in which Coltrane's music was moving and the new approach to improvising that he

FIGURE 4.3 "Creation" (April 2, 1965). Transcription by author.

FIGURE 4.4 "Ascent" (August 26, 1965). Transcription by author.

inspired; there is almost a serial aspect to the way he builds his improvisation through obsessive transformation of motivic material. Most interesting here is the shape of that motive and its relationship to the pulse maintained by the rhythm section. From the outset of the performance, he develops the theme in a deliberately uneasy tension with the underlying meter of the rhythm section. Its sharp drop-off at the end (alternating between a diminished fifth and a major second) creates an asymmetry that impresses the listener as a stock phrase in swung eighth notes, the end of which has been clipped off, and which Coltrane then displaces in various ways. Like a child's spinning top, he spins the theme in conjunction with the underlying rhythm at times, and wobbles it against it at others, with the clipped ending providing a perpetually "off-kilter" effect. Coltrane hyperventilates his solo for over eleven minutes, pushing the metric disjunctions more and more aggressively, shortening the motive into disjunct fragments that fly freely in every metrical direction, and eventually moving into purely expressionistic playing. Tyner's piano solo follows, and at its conclusion around 16:30, Garrison begins to play bass shapes that detach metrically from Jones's underlying pulse, with the ensemble shapes they create together providing part of the structural blueprint for the next stage in the quartet's evolution.

The particular way Coltrane fragmented those rhythms can be conceptualized in terms of the architectural concept of "folding," a design strategy in which formal complexity is generated through various processes of truncation.[38] An interesting example of architectural folding is Peter Eisenman's Alteka Office Building project in Tokyo, Japan (1991).[39] Eisenman's schematic drawings depict a process of gradual deformation: an L-shaped form comprising two rectangles juxtaposed at a ninety-degree angle is gradually deformed as corners at the base of the structure are sheared away, causing the vertical section of the structure to "collapse" upon the horizontal section (figure 4.5). This collapsing, in turn, produces creases and folds that ultimately result in a much more complex form than the original.

Architects and architectural theorists such as Eisenman and Greg Lynn embraced folding as a procedure because it enabled them to impart a sense of motion and transformation to stable, built forms. The very structure of a project such as Alteka, for example, encourages the viewer to experience the form as if in the midst of an ongoing collapse. Furthermore, to the extent that the form of the building mirrors the stylistic contradictions and conflicts of its context (i.e., buildings of many different styles and conditions in the same environment), the building's "motion" could be seen as extending beyond its own discrete form into a dialogue with the complex and varied forms of the general environment.

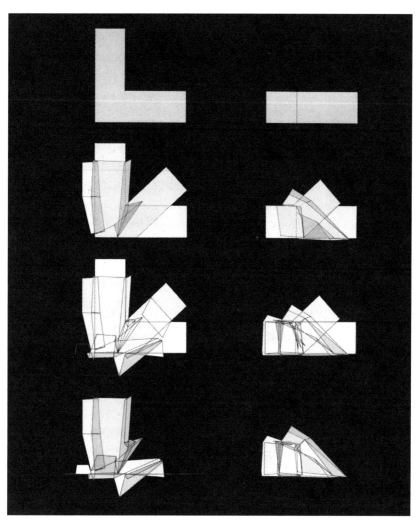

FIGURE 4.5 Peter Eisenman, Alteka Office Building, Folding Diagrams, Tokyo, Japan (1991). Reproduced courtesy of Eisenman Architects.

Coltrane's own process of deforming the motive could easily be referred to using more traditionally musical terms such as *foreshortening, elongation, metric displacement,* and *chromatic ornamentation.* I have chosen to reference "folding" here in order to dramatize a sense of the musical motive as *shape* by giving it a three-dimensional component. Further, Coltrane's manipulation of the main motive of "Creation" renders it inherently unstable in rhythmic terms so, like Eisenman's Alteka project, the concept of folding also helps dramatize the idea of a particular conception of rhythm in a state of gradual collapse. Like the relationship between Eisenman's building and the broader built environment, Coltrane's way of playing has implications for the broader ensemble environment given that the increasingly fragmented superstructure of his improvisation flows in juxtaposition against the densely syncopated underlying meter maintained by the rhythm section. Greg Lynn's seminal essay "Architectural Curvilinearity: The Folded, the Pliant and the Supple" presents folding as setting into motion a process of collapse that will ultimately resolve into a state of curvilinearity, and in a few months' time the bifurcation between rhythmically free foreground soloist and metered rhythm section in the Coltrane band would eventually collapse or "fold in" upon itself as the musicians brought the two layers into closer conformity.[40]

The concept of folding—understood in terms of pitch relationships here as "collapsing *away from*" or "collapsing *within*" a given tonality—can be applied in a different way to "Song of Praise," another dramatic performance from the Half Note that illustrates the huge amount of structural tension being generated by the quintet. In its studio take recorded on May 17, "Song of Praise" was performed entirely in rubato by the quartet, an extension of Coltrane's earlier adaptations of Negro spirituals such as "Spiritual" and recitation pieces such as "Alabama" and "Psalm." As performed at the Half Note on May 7, however, the piece has been remodeled—it begins with the same rubato exposition but around 1:50, the band falls into mid-tempo, metered swing. In this sense, the rubato section allowed Coltrane the space to explore the minor mode before the band falls into meter and the main body of the song begins. An obvious point of comparison here, in terms of form, is the *alap* section of a piece of Indian classical music, an expository section in which the soloist explores the pitches and themes of the *rag* (scale) in free time before switching to a predetermined rhythm cycle (*tal*) that supports the statement of the main theme (*bandish*).[41] After all, it is well known that Coltrane had an abiding fascination with Indian classical music and it's obvious why this tradition would be a reference point for a scale-obsessed musician like himself; the function of the *alap* is to build emotional tension and to prepare both performer and listener for the more detailed exploration of the rag that takes place once the tal enters and the piece shifts into a metered rhythmic space.

But here the similarities between the two traditions end; in the case of "Song of Praise," Coltrane spends two minutes patiently constructing a D minor environment in rubato time, only to deconstruct the established tonality by shifting into highly chromatic side slipping and pattern transposition as soon as the rhythm section shifts into time, his freely verbal phrasing building every kind of harmonic and rhythmic tension against that foundation. This sudden destabilizing of the tonality, with Coltrane's melodic lines spinning off like whirlpools to different tonal centers, would never take place in the Indian classical context in which improvisers are restricted to the pitches of the rag. The overall effect here is similar to what a person might experience when entering an amusement park funhouse—ascending to the top of an evenly spaced set of stairs, only to have the floor begin to sway diagonally back and forth once they step off the stairway and into the hallway. The juxtaposition of this "harmonic vertigo" with a hard-swinging rhythm underneath was enough to throw any nervous system into an altered state and, in fact, the level of harmonic abstraction found in Coltrane's music could be argued as a means of using pitch relationships to achieve the same psycho-emotional effect that is achieved, in West African musics meant to stimulate altered states of awareness, via extreme levels of polyrhythmic tension.

Other elements of "Song of Praise" also highlight Coltrane's techniques for stimulating an altered state of consciousness in himself and his listeners. As much as he is recognized as a master of alternate fingerings, for example, the naturalist discourse of jazz sound has obscured the extent to which he was also a master of microphone technique as a means of manipulating the textual and spatial qualities of distortion in his playing. The famous recording of "Chasin' the Trane" recorded at the Village Vanguard in 1961 is often used as a study of alternate fingerings. This is a way of playing the instrument that allows the same pitch to sound dramatically different when it is fingered differently. The microtonal inflections that result can be compared to a person uttering the same word out of different sides of their mouth—the same pitch can sound full bodied, thin, airy, nasal, etc., depending on how it is fingered. Add to this technique varying degrees of proximity to a microphone and, similarly to the Chicago blues harmonica player Little Walter, Coltrane's alternate fingerings result in a myriad of distortion effects.

The narrative of altered consciousness is made concrete on another performance captured by Boris Rose (in this case, from the Symphony Sid radio show broadcast from the Birdland club), which runs around fourteen minutes and is built from the harmonically ambiguous modal theme.

This piece has generally been titled on releases as either "Untitled Original" or "One Up, One Down" (not to be confused with the piece "One Down, One Up"), and a 1963 studio recording of the same piece (titled "One Up, One Down") was given an official release by Impulse in 2018.[42] Its central phrase, reharmonized to the Dorian mode, is actually quite similar to a theme Coltrane would record on June 10, 1965 (with a concluding phrase added), as "Transition."

At over fourteen minutes, this is another intense Half Note performance, and while the powerful impression given by Coltrane's Half Note recordings is a result of the performances themselves, it is also ironically buttressed by the generally low fidelity of the Rose captures. Rose's recording techniques remain unclear; at times he smuggled recording devices into live performances, while the sound of other recordings suggests that he sometimes positioned a microphone directly in front of his home radio speaker(s) instead of recording through a direct line. As with his earlier (and widely circulated) captures of Charlie Parker broadcasts, the resulting distortion and highly compressed frequency range give the overall impression of a hothouse atmosphere, the venue sometimes seeming to collapse in on the band. At other times, the cloudy quality of the recording (as a result of serial duplication and transfer from mono to stereo), in conjunction with the polymetric feel of the band's playing and the substantial saturation of Jones' ride cymbal (in the 8–10kHz range), obscures metric markers and intensifies the apparent "free" qualities of the performance. What is striking beyond the musical content, however, is what the recording itself (apparently made with a microphone placed very close to the audience and in turn, by Boris Rose recording from his home radio) reveals about the circumstances of the performance. Reminiscent of prayer meetings or the 1950s rhythm-and-blues shows with their requisite tenor sax solos of orgiastic intensity (Bob Willoughby's iconic 1951 photo of Big Jay McNeely comes to mind),[43] audience members can be heard screaming and yelling in response to Coltrane's solo. At a certain point, so many notes blown at such velocity take on the verbal quality of not only recitation (as in "Psalm"), but the more aggressive quality of sermonizing. Like a band of Pentecostal preachers, the quartet's improvisational testimony transported their audience into states of

FIGURE 4.6 "One Up, One Down" (March 6, 1963). Transcription by author.

FIGURE 4.7 "Transition" (June 10, 1965). Transcription by author,
modified from sheet music copyright Jowcol, Hal Leonard.

de facto trance and/or possession by intensifying, and ultimately abstracting, core African and Western European principles of musical tension and release. And in their multiple sonic (in)fidelities, the variously sourced recordings of the Half Note sets document these experiences with varying degrees of sonic accuracy but unerring emotional impact. The irony is that, when heard through the prisms of distortion resulting from a sound signal serially degraded through generations of duplication, a coloristic and textural component emerges that intensifies the psycho-emotional impact of these recordings. And so the Half Note recordings live on to give listeners a powerfully visceral experience of the quartet's combination of church and classroom, despite intervening factors of technical fallibility.

III: ESCAPE VELOCITY

What is it?
I'm trying really to remember
The clock has stopped
Now I can never know
Where the edge of my world can be
If I could only enter that old calendar
That opens to an old, old July
And learn what unknowing things know . . .[44]

Romare Bearden

The intensity of the Half Note performances suggested that the amount of tension being channeled through the harmonic and metric grids of the Coltrane quartet would *demand* outlets; the grids would have to shatter, or at least distort. Harmonically, in fact, the music had already exploded into a haze of chromaticism, albeit chromaticism tethered to an underlying drone. Rhythmically, the beat was being subdivided every night into a maze of polyrhythmic abstraction although the quartet was still tethered to the underlying beat. What the Half Note gigs suggested was that Coltrane's increasing grafting of "speech" rhythms onto the quartet's metered swing would gradually force a reconceptualization of the rhythm section. As the spring of 1965 gave way to summer, this increasingly implied a metrically free environment for the band as a whole. But this was a contentious issue among the members of the quartet and was said to be a particular problem for Jones.[45] The drummer's reticence about free-meter playing was understandable—after all, his groove was one of the strongest jazz had ever known precisely because his extremely syncopated, polyrhythmic shattering of the song surface actually reinforced the underlying meter. The irony, of course, was that Jones's *unaccompanied* drum solos during this period on recent tracks such as "Pursuance" (from *A Love Supreme*) and "Vigil" (recorded on June 16) were played entirely in free meter. But to do away with meter *during ensemble playing* was a different proposition that would remove the primary generator of dynamic tension from the quartet's music—or would it?

There are many moments during the quartet's spring 1965 recordings that might be heard as "launching pads" into metrically free playing. But the studio take of "Brazilia" (recorded on May 17 and released on *The John Coltrane Quartet Plays*) offers a particularly interesting example.[46] Given the tensions within the quartet, perhaps it was more than coincidental that this "launch" seems to have happened by accident. "Brazilia" begins, like many of Coltrane's tunes, with a rubato, minor-key exposition that, like "Alabama" and "Spiritual," forms the first part of an ABA form, the two rubato statements of the head bracketing an E♭ minor vamp that provides the basis for solos. Most interesting, however, is what happens toward the tune's end. Around 9:50, Coltrane concludes his solo and seems to cue a return to the rubato opening; the dramatic pause before his phrase almost allows us to visualize him lifting his horn in the air to cue the change. However, there is a bit of "flux and flutter" in the ensemble at that moment, as if the rhythm section, in the intensity of their playing, might have missed his cue. Coltrane and Garrison return to the free-meter space of the rubato introduction, while Jones and Tyner continue to swing in meter. As a result of the confusion, the ensemble texture lightens momentarily, and Coltrane seems to play a bit busily to cover the discrepancy. He repeats the opening theme again around 10:35, again with no clear resolution into either metered or rubato time. Was this a miscommunication between the members of the quartet? Or, were they deliberately experimenting with the kinds of disjunct metric strata typified by pieces such as Ornette Coleman's "Lonely Woman?" In any case, the apparent confusion is resolved at 11:05, when the band follows Coltrane's third cue and clearly returns to the rubato section. Instead of returning to the spacious, balladic feel of the introduction, however, they launch directly into a high-density, free-meter space with Coltrane improvising much more aggressively than he typically would in his rubato introductions/conclusions. Surfing through metrically free space for the remainder of the tune, the moments of apparent confusion have been leveraged into an exploration of a new type of rhythmic field. The fact that, whatever the circumstances, Coltrane ultimately included it on the album (instead of rejecting it as a flawed take) might indicate that he recognized it as an important step forward.

To my knowledge, this is the first example of the Coltrane quartet exploring what might be called a "fast free-meter space" on its own terms. Let me clarify what I mean by "fast free meter." To my ears, there are two different articulations of rubato time in Coltrane's music. The first and most common can be heard in songs such as "Spiritual" or "Alabama," which feature ABA forms; the rubato introduction builds tension in a way that (like the Hindustani *alap*) resolves into metered playing, while the rubato conclusion provides a space of release or "exhalation" from the intensity of the metered section of the tune. Both of these free-meter sections tend to be balladic in feel and, as such, inherently "slow" in affect since they are typically marked by low ensemble density.

"Fast free meter," on the other hand, is a rubato environment that extends out of the density and intensity of a metered, up-tempo piece. This free-meter space is no longer a balladic space of release and repose but a space in which the ensemble energy/density is lifted even higher than it was in the metered section—as if the energy could no longer be contained within meter, and the energetic abstraction of metered material led naturally to figures that transcended the boundaries of metered time. Admittedly, this is a preliminary distinction since, as the quartet moved more definitively into free-meter space, Coltrane and his musicians would articulate that space in more complex ways than my simple binary distinction suggests, the salient distinction being between levels of ensemble density. Nonetheless, the contrasting densities do successfully imply momentum and velocity as they unfold in time and, as such, the terms "fast" and "slow" help clarify this important transitional moment.

———

During the late spring/early summer of 1965—arguably the most intensively transformative period in the quartet's four-year existence—this freedom gradually became more clearly manifest. A case in point is "Transition," recorded on June 10, and one of their most celebrated recorded performances. "Transition" is a medium-up groove in D minor that builds in intensity minute by minute and perfectly sums up the quartet's powerful brand of swing. So powerful was their groove on this day, in fact, that it seemed as if the quartet might blow apart at the seams. Of course, most listeners would not hear "Transition" as a transformative moment so much as a moment of culmination; it not only makes a case for the quartet's commitment to swing, but it also suggests that their swing had never been more powerful. But like the duet breakdown section of "One Down, One Up" from the Half Note, there are several passages during the unbelievably intense, fifteen-minute performance (for example, between 1:25 and 1:32) when Coltrane plays passages of whirling, double-timed triplets that pull Elvin Jones into a swirling rhythmic vortex. And while metric perturbations such as these remained momentarily tethered as articulations of the underlying pulse, it was logical to assume that in these passages, they were in fact generating the momentum that would soon enable them to fly beyond the bounds of meter. The June 10 session concluded with "Suite," a five-part work similar to *A Love Supreme* in theme, conception, and overall construction, which alternates between movements of metered and rhythmically free playing.

There were no documented gigs in the interim, but when the quartet returned to Van Gelder's studio on June 16, something seems to have definitively shifted. With the exception of "Dusk Dawn," which was similar to a number of the quartet's performances of that year, each of the other three pieces recorded that day represent clear departures from their usual way of putting songs together. "Vigil," for example, begins with a drum solo by Jones, before settling into a medium uptempo duet for drums and tenor sax that was clearly a formalization of the sax-drum breakdowns he and Coltrane had been performing in concert. In "Living Space," Coltrane double-tracked his soprano sax into an eerie unison, rendering a rubato theme that recalled the old Negro spirituals and field hollers. When the rhythm drops in, he turns in one of his most expressionistic solos on the instrument (it was in fact his last studio recording using the soprano saxophone). After a solo by Tyner and a concluding solo by Coltrane, the band returns to the rubato theme, before swirling away on a hypnotically repeating tag, the otherworldly quality of which presaged the rhapsodic heights Alice Coltrane would later scale in her own works such as *Universal Consciousness* (1971). According to Coltrane scholar David Wild, the saxophonist initially derived the song's melody from a pattern he observed while studying the rug on his living room floor.[47] The recording that resulted was thus provisionally titled "The Living Room Rug" and later retitled "Living Space"—itself a thematic reference apparently inspired by a 1956 Isaac Asimov short story of the same title that Coltrane had recently read.[48] Even this retitling was in accordance with Coltrane's cosmological bent, given that Asimov's story concerned an Earth whose problems of severe overpopulation were solved by the discovery of "dimensional portals" that provided access to an infinite number of parallel worlds that could be settled.[49]

———

The world of the open can be inhabited precisely because, wherever life is going on, the interfacial separation of earth and sky gives way to mutual permeability and binding . . . earth and sky, far from being confined to their mutual domains by the hard surface of the ground, continually infiltrate one another. Thus the ground is not, in truth, a coherent surface at all but a zone in which the air and moisture of the sky combine with substances whose source lies in the earth in an ongoing constitution and dissolution of living things.[50]

James Ingold

Although "Living Space" is notable (along with earlier pieces like "Countdown," "Fifth House," and "Satellite") as one of the first explicitly cosmological references in Coltrane's work, Isaac Asimov's idea of "dimensional portals" has more than mere thematic resonance with the music the quartet recorded on June 16. To conclude the session, they dove confidently into the choppy waters of an untitled free-meter piece (numbered 90320 on the Impulse session log) that, while rarely mentioned in studies of Coltrane's music, is equal in intensity to the previous week's impassioned performances of "Transition" and "Suite" while simultaneously representing a definitive turning point.[51] "Untitled (90320)" is significant as the quartet's first documented attempt at a "fast free-rhythm" performance and one that also demonstrates, by its passionate performance, that the quartet is now in the proverbial "zone."

Similarly to "Prayer and Meditation" from the previous week's session and "One Down, One Up," the melodic point of departure here might be heard as a major 7 augmented motive (Gb–Ab–D–F), which Coltrane elaborates into a complex, chromatic improvisation as he accelerates and decelerates his lines and shapes, pulling the entire ensemble through regions of varying density while swinging back and forth across tonic and altered V7 sonorities, the floating sensation of the chromatic and symmetric harmonies finally spiraling outward to transform the entire ensemble's rhythmic structure. Considering that the rubato sections had generally been used in Coltrane's music to introduce and conclude tunes, we might say that "Untitled (90320)" turns the tune "inside out," so to speak—the rubato "exterior" has been remade as the "interior," then elaborated with an intensity that ultimately makes the very distinction meaningless.

At the beginning of Coltrane's opening solo, we can hear the players tentatively feeling each other out, while a clear centrifugal force can be felt binding them together by the solo's climax (about 3:48–4:09). A reflection of his expansive harmonic imagination and staggering technique, it is Coltrane's bebop-derived ability to spray alternately continuous and fragmented streams of lines, shapes, and patterns that unites the different levels of activity and provides the "binding element" within the free-meter environment. Meanwhile, modes of expanded, free-meter counterpoint can be heard within the interwoven punctuations of Tyner and Garrison. Like pylons evenly spaced across the open sea, Tyner's percussive punctuations, many passages of which are rhythmically regular and almost metered, simultaneously create tension against the free-meter environment while giving form and shape to it. Garrison, meanwhile, "strolls" through his own line, which like Tyner contains a substantial amount of rhythmic regularity at times but is also variable in rate and almost completely displaced from the other instrumentalists' rhythmic trajectories.

The theme of "dimensional portals" becomes particularly relevant in relation to Elvin Jones, who has finally moved into a free-meter space, of a kind. Here, he orchestrates a collagist succession of tempo fragments, abruptly alternating between fragments of fast, medium, and slow swing, each of which can be considered a portal to a different experience of musical velocity. These fragments can also be likened to slopes of varying inclinations or gradients that create varying degrees of resistance for the other musicians to improvise against. Jones's reluctance to completely embrace free-meter playing at this juncture—a stubborn compromise between the old and the new—makes it easier to hear his playing as a collage of *deformed* swing rhythms. For his part, Coltrane is working against the shifting slopes of Jones's "tempo fragments" like a surfer against the waves or a boxer working the edge of a continually tilting ring, using dense, speech-like cadences to simultaneously push back against and embroider the edges of the fragmented rhythmic planes Jones throws at him. Fred Scharmen, discussing the experimental architecture of Claude Parent and Paul Virilio, speculated on the effect of tilted surfaces for our experience of space in his essay "Folding Space":

> [A]rchitectural work between 1963 and 1969 . . . demonstrated that offering tilted surfaces for human use and existence opened up new possibilities for the relationships between bodies and space. This move linked spaces that were otherwise disconnected, but it also hinted that people could occupy, however uneasily, the changing surface of difference itself.[52]

Scharmen's piece was included in a volume of architectural writings on outer-space habitats and, as such, "the changing surface of difference" is a poetic evocation of the utility of tilted surfaces in expanding the scale of our spatial awareness. Artists such as Ornette Coleman, Cecil Taylor, Albert Ayler, Sun Ra, Steve Lacy, and Paul Bley were working their various ways out of meter but "Untitled (90320)" suggests that in the case of the Coltrane quartet, it was the dynamic tension generated by the leader's desire for complete rhythmic freedom and Jones's desire to remain within the framework of metered playing that was leveraging their move into free-meter playing.

The ethnomusicologists Richard Widdess and Ritwik Sanyal have pondered the applicability of the concept of "pulse" to the nonmetered *alap* sections of Hindustani classical and light classical genres such as *khyal*, *dhrupad*, and *thumri*.[53] "Pulse" in this context is something that typically manifests in two ways:

it is on one hand a continuous point of rhythmic reference, albeit one that can be accelerated or decelerated at will by the improvising vocalist or instrumentalist. "Pulse" can also refer to momentarily stable points of rhythmic reference that underlie cadential passages of singing or improvisation and that demarcate the overall song form. In both cases, the concept is flexible, malleable, and momentary, and can be elegantly applied to both Coltrane's streams of evenly spaced eighth and sixteenth notes, Tyner's and Garrison's layers of disjunct punctuation, and Jones's "tempo fragments."

With meter deformed/deconstructed in this way, the experience of time in "90320" gives the impression of "accelerating" and "decelerating" in relation to passages of greater and lesser ensemble density/complexity. This new rhythmic geometry—which had previously been a mere fluid superstructure within the quartet's environment of metered swing—has now erupted to constitute a rhythmic order of its own. "Untitled (90320)," then, is an example of these musicians not only *filling* space but also continually *reshaping* space. Ultimately, of course, the structure of "Untitled (90320)" is nothing more than a free-meter elaboration of the conversational dynamic that has shaped jazz improvisation from its earliest days. On a more profound level, however, it is a radical distortion/fragmentation/expansion of the Africanist Grid and a profound turning point in the evolution of Coltrane's music.

We might also telescope out to get a different perspective on the quartet's inner working. The architect Greg Lynn uses the term "orbital stability" to describe the way a group of elements can hold each other in dynamic balance despite the absence of an "unchanging constant force of a ground point," "ground point" translating into jazz rhythm as any cyclical meter with clearly stated strong and weak beats:

Since the time of Sir Isaac Newton, gravity has been accepted as the mutual relative attraction of masses in space. Given a constant mass, stability is achieved through orbits rather than stasis. This distinction between stasis and orbital or dynamic stability is important. In the case of a single, simple gravity, stasis is the ordering system through the unchanging constant force of a ground point. In the case of a more complex concept of gravity, mutual attraction generates motion; stability is the ordering of motion into rhythmic phases. In the simple static model of gravity, motion is eliminated at the beginning. In the complex, stable model of gravity, motion is an ordering principle.[54]

Lynn's distinction between "stasis" and "stability" helps illuminate the way musicians hang together in metrically free space in a state of ensemble equilibrium, with Fred Scharmen's "changing surface of difference" imbuing that space with a feeling of gravitational tension and release (i.e., "swing"). With their leader probing continuously morphing configurations of space through lyrical and mathematical gestures, the Coltrane quartet arguably achieved "escape velocity" on "Untitled (90320)."

———

If we consider 1965 a year of transformative artistic breakthroughs for Coltrane, this period of his work can be compared with the work of another artist whose breakthrough was virtually simultaneous. Like Coltrane, the painter Romare Bearden (1911–1988) was a North Carolina native. Over the course of a career that took him from Pittsburgh to New York to Paris and back to New York, from figuration to abstraction to abstract figuration, and from painting to drawing to collage, Bearden's artistic vision had been shaped by the earthy sensibility of the South, the sensuality of Paris, the metallic hues of industrial Pennsylvania, the jazz energy of midcentury Harlem, various trends in twentieth-century art, the multiple imaginings of Africa that proliferated throughout the African diaspora in the 1960s, and the unavoidably intense political energy of that decade.

As with Coltrane, this political energy eventually caused Bearden's own (visual) surfaces to shatter into freaky, kaleidoscopic refractions of African and Afro-diasporic themes. After decades of painstaking work (both abstract and figurative) mainly executed in the medium of canvas painting, Bearden changed course in 1964 and unveiled his first set of "photomontage projections," a series of photographically enlarged collages (figure 4.8).[55] Formally, these early collages are almost all built from fragmented or distorted grids, while thematically they are formed of radically juxtaposed emotional and cultural intensities. Like work of mid-twentieth-century Russian/Soviet collagists such as Alexandr Rodchenko, Varvara Stepanova, Vasily Elkin, Piotr Galadhev, and Valentina Kulagina, the work is essentially representational but its fragmented re-composition of the picture surface gives a freakish spin on observed reality.[56] In Bearden's photomontages, African masks carved for ritual purposes are juxtaposed with exaggerated faces from Harlem, Watts, and Mississippi that give simultaneous voice to the urban and the rural, the terrifying and the sublime, the sacred and the profane, the local and the trans-African. Similar to the Russian collages, faces of ordinary people are distorted and juxtaposed in Bearden's work in a way that makes them seem no longer merely human, but rather like energies or archetypes—spirit beings forced by extraordinary circumstances into dramatic political, cultural, and spiritual testimony. Rachel Delue makes a similar point, from a slightly different angle, in her 2012 essay "Conjure and Collapse in the Art of Romare Bearden," which interprets the accumulation and fragmentation of Bearden's surfaces as in the service of states of altered consciousness and the conjuring of new realities.[57] Structurally, Bearden's collages read like a hybrid of Picasso, Matisse, and the Constructivists, filtered through an Africanist philosophy of perspectival distortion and surface accumulation, cast in industrial hues, and forced into formal fragmentation by an ethos of modernist experimentation on one hand, and by the intensely pressured political climate on which it commented, on the other. In addition to these factors, Bearden himself was clear about another catalyst that has rarely been mentioned in relation to his work:

> Since men envision the world in many ways, they have concomitantly devised many spatial structures. Spatial structures are the architecture for describing the visible world . . . For example, we can now comprehend some of the problems of journeying through outer space, and soon man will be landing on the moon. This will affect the way painters, in their particular time, translate their perceptions of space . . . The shrinking concept of Earth in which it is possible for a man on one side of the world to encounter another on the opposite side, in a matter of hours, has inspired artists to enlarge their spatial visions.[58]

We can assume that a cosmic frame of reference would allow a viewer to discern formal unity in patterns that seemed chaotic and disorganized from a mere terrestrial perspective. Similar to the "orbital stability" of the Coltrane quartet in "Untitled (90320)," Bearden's use of a cosmic point of reference provided a unity to pictorial spaces shattered from a single perspective into a keening juxtaposition of colliding planes, and it was his own deep internalization of the Africanist Grid that allowed the fragmented surfaces and distorted perspectives of his collages to hang together in contrapuntal unity. That their work in different media would come to signify a very similar set of cultural and political sentiments demonstrated that the intertwined cosmological and Africanist turns in the work of both Coltrane and Bearden were not only thematic but also deeply cultural and powerfully political.

FIGURE 4.8   Romare Bearden, *The Prevalence of Ritual: Baptism* (1964).
Copyright Romare Bearden Foundation/VAGA, 2022. Reproduced courtesy
of Artists Rights Society (ARS), New York.

Since Coltrane had begun applying the chromatic, rotational symmetries of "Giant Steps" to modal drones, his music had seemed to pull increasingly "upward," and this implied a new articulation of space. After all, Romare Bearden had studied Chinese calligraphy, in which one strongly emphasized value was the use of empty space that allowed the canvas to "breathe." But Coltrane's own playing was the opposite of this—he improvised densely and obsessively, filling most of the sonic space. And as his improvisations became even denser during 1965, his most immediate option for the creation of additional headroom probably became the explosion of the rhythm beyond the restrictive bounds of meter. Resonating with the ideas of Lynn, Parent and Virilio, and Bearden, the idea of meter as a passive conceptual backdrop for measuring the passage of musical time was now being replaced by the idea that time itself (like the ground) is a musical element to be continuously molded and reshaped. Now that the quartet was bringing the rhythm entirely into conformity with the freely chromatic harmonies, the "upward" feeling became even stronger, and the music merely awaited the cosmological imagery of the Space Age to provide thematic context. In the coming months, in fact, the idea of "orbital stability" would become as thematically significant to Coltrane as it was structurally. Thus, June 16, 1965, was probably the most transformative recording session in the quartet's five-year history. That they could span the distance from "Transition" to "Untitled (90320)" in the space of a single week suggests that, like Romare Bearden during the same period, extremely potent energies were driving their evolution. And whatever those energies were, more would be unleashed before summer's end.

IV: STARGAZERS

we should go to the moon
astronauts in outer   interspersed images of colorful garb
b&w in time inter-
spersed   sense of the evolution
of their costumes have remained
the same you are welcomed   to be citizens
of the omniverse . . . [59]

Anais Duplan

[Coltrane] had a pair of binoculars and, back in San Francisco, during the intermission from his playing at the Jazz Workshop, we'd walk ten blocks to a field down by the freeway, and he'd start looking at the stars. He knew where the Milky Way was, and everything . . . Coltrane looked at the sky, the stars, scrutinizing the night for a long moment of infinity as if to discover the secrets of the universe, a universe that appeared to trouble him with its complexity, its power and its unknown dimensions . . . After a while, we climbed back up, slowly and always in silence, the slope to Broadway, I to recover my corner and continue to listen feverishly; Coltrane to anxiously reclaim his saxophones and his work of research, his mysterious quest.[60]

Louis-Victor Mialy

If the cosmological imagination of Coltrane's generation of jazz musicians was ignited by the expanded technologies of the Space Age and to a lesser extent, the ancient symbolism of Western astrology, it was equally inspired by the cosmologies that emerged from Africa and other spheres of the decolonizing world. While

African Americans were involved in NASA from its earliest years, the euphoria of African independence inspired many jazz musicians to look beyond the Apollos and Sputniks to the indigenous cosmologies of Africa, in order to give the Space Age a black inflection.[61] Against this backdrop of extraterrestrial phenomena deployed as factors in terrestrial struggles, the jazz musician who most strongly Africanized the Space Age was Sun Ra (figure 4.9).

There are many reasons for Sun Ra's importance to modern jazz: he was a respected and credible link to the big band era who had worked under the great Fletcher Henderson and who, like Duke Ellington, had managed to keep his own big band going for decades, through many economic and stylistic phases of jazz, with a remarkably stable core personnel.[62] He was an important pioneer in the use of electric and electronic instruments in jazz, experimenting with a variety of keyboard instruments, tape-manipulation techniques, and sound-processing devices. By the 1960s, as he adapted his music to the new innovations of Ornette Coleman and other avant-gardists, he was leading what was probably the first and best-known free jazz big band, which was functioning as a de facto university of the "new music" through which many influential musicians passed, including tenor saxophonist Ferrell Sanders (whom Sun Ra famously renamed—and respelled—"Pharoah"), and drummer Rashied Ali, both of whom would go on to play with Coltrane.[63] His body of recorded work, issued on his own Saturn label as well as many other labels, is among of the most voluminous in jazz, encompassing literally hundreds of titles. Retroactively hailed as an icon of Afrofuturism, his albums such as *Interstellar Low-Ways*, *Astro Black*, *Space Is the Place*, and *Strange Celestial Worlds* helped Africanize the iconography of the Space Age.[64]

Despite all of these achievements, Sun Ra was for many years dismissed as a charlatan because of his eccentric demeanor, outlandish stage costumes, and pronouncements such as those referring to his own origins on the planet Saturn. But all of these apparently contradictory angles on Sun Ra—his verifiable contributions to jazz and his eccentric profile as a provocateur and myth spinner of the Space Age—can be reconciled within what I believe is his most important and fundamental contribution to jazz. Sun Ra ultimately emerged as an important architect of the new music in the 1960s because he was, in his own way, a charismatic and poetic heir to a Chicago-based tradition of black mysticism that enabled him to musicalize his thematic pre-occupation with "outer space" in a powerful and influential way. Along with composers like Ellington and Tadd Dameron, he had been a pioneer of "jazz exotica" and, as the Space Age unfolded, he instinctively and ingeniously transposed his evocations of non-Western cultures to various off-planet locales. The human cosmological imagination in the 1960s had been greatly expanded by the space race and its imagery: space stations, interstellar vessels escaping earthly gravity, heavenly bodies spinning at odd and oblique angles to each other, rocket launches and landings, comets and asteroids, galaxies, star clusters, ringed planets, vast stretches of apparent emptiness, and the possibility of extraterrestrial beings. Sun Ra evoked all of this through his musical manipulations of meter, texture, musical structure, and instrumentation. In doing so, he greatly expanded the repertoire of structural devices available to musicians in the 1960s, as well as—more profoundly—the ways in which jazz could be understood as a form of spatial and cosmological commentary.

Although his career spanned six decades, the cluster of albums he recorded in the late 1950s and early 1960s form the core of his body of work, each containing tracks that, through a combination of song titles, instrumentation, and musical techniques, orchestrate his characteristically exotic and/or otherworldly musical mood.[65] "The Others in Their World" (1960) uses modal harmony in a way that recalls Miles Davis's *Kind of Blue*, while its unusually placed accents and subtle hints of polytonality impart a searching, otherworldly quality to the music. The themes of "Saturn" and "Future" (both 1956) create a feeling of disorientation through dense chromaticism and dramatic interval leaps that destabilize a sense of tonal gravity. "Overtones of China" (1956) juxtaposes polytonal harmonies with pentatonic clichés meant to evoke the "Orient," with additional exotic texture added by Chinese gongs and the clipped, percussive tones of Sun Ra's electric piano. "Music from the World Tomorrow" (1960), "Interplanetary Music" (1960), and the entire album *Strange Strings* (1967) create exotic soundscapes by combining insistent rhythmic riffing with freely improvised pitch relationships played on unusual instruments; the rhythmic bounce on the former track is thickened by the reverberating textures of Ra's electric organ. The theme of "Lights on a Satellite" (1960) juxtaposes a searching, muted trumpet melody against a chromatically shifting saxophone background, before drawing the listener up and out on the wings of a plaintive, legato riff.

Sun Ra's profile began to rise in the mid-1960s, as his idiosyncratic music began to be favorably received at the intersection of the new jazz, the resurgence of astrology, the exploration of outer space, and the psychedelic exploration of inner space. He would expand his toolkit as a composer several times during these years, first recasting the Arkestra's repertoire through the prism of free improvisation on albums such as *The Heliocentric Worlds of Sun Ra* (1965) and *The Magic City* (1966). His music would take another dramatic turn around the time that he appeared on the cover of *Rolling Stone* in early 1969, when he acquired a prototype model of the newly invented Moog synthesizer (Ra was introduced to Robert Moog by the Nigerian journalist Tam Fiofori, who would later bring the Arkestra to Lagos for the 1977 Festival of Arts and Culture).[66] But the core musical elements that allowed him to portray other worlds with such evocative power were already well established in his music by 1960.

———

I remember as a kid learning that gravity was a concept describing
the attraction of masses, and that gravity was what drew things
to the Earth, but it was also what made things orbit in curves . . .
a conventional thing like gravity thought of in a different scale
or in a different context gets really interesting . . . you could suddenly
think of all kinds of structures just by changing the frame of how you
look at it. I think the space age did that for a lot of people.[67]

Greg Lynn

If we wanted to choose any composition as a "mission statement" of Sun Ra's music because of the way its thematic and structural elements combine to evoke a sense of the cosmic, we might point to a 1970 performance of his composition "The Shadow World" (table 4.1). This piece was originally recorded in 1965 in the loft of the Nigerian drummer Babatunde Olatunji, released the following year on the album *The Magic City*, and given a definitive concert performance five years later in Saint Paul-de-Vence, France in 1970, which was released on the album *Nuits de la Fondation Maeght, Volume 1*.[68] If songs such as "We Travel the Spaceways" and "Space is the Place" can be considered anthemic Arkestra performances because of their lyrical themes, this live performance of "The Shadow World" is a vivid study of the ways that orbiting celestial bodies and cosmic energies can be evoked via musical structures. A staple of the Arkestra's concerts throughout the late 1960s and 1970s, "The Shadow World" was remodeled many times but was arguably given its most iconic documented performance at Saint Paul-de-Vence.

The core element in this piece is an interlocking ostinato, introduced by Sun Ra on the piano and then taken up for the duration of the performance by baritone saxophonist Pat Patrick and tenor saxophonist John Gilmore. The theatrical aspect becomes important and literally "orbital" here, as Gilmore and Patrick repeat this ostinato while physically strolling around the interior of the performance space. As such, this ostinato takes on the framing character of a rotating sphere or network of rings, as Gilmore and Patrick move in, out, and across the listener's sphere of audibility while being sonically cross-cut by the various sonic events taking place on the stage: a frantically played, bebop-inflected horn theme, a section of free-meter drumming, a succession of individual and collective horn solos, and a bombastic synthesizer solo by Sun Ra intercut with flourishes of medieval organ. The most potent moments occur when Sun Ra interjects counter bass lines on his Minimoog (for example, around 2:40), orbiting cycles against the basic horn ostinato at disjunct angles. Like Ornette Coleman's "Lonely Woman," but expanded to cinematic proportions (and audible despite the poor fidelity of the recording), this performance of "The Shadow World" is dramatically structured as a stack of rhythmic orbits spinning in and out of conjunction with each other.

To take a bit of analytical license with the term I introduced in relation to "Giant Steps," performances like the concert version of "The Shadow World" portray Sun Ra as a master of what might be called rotational *asymmetry*—creating tension through rhythmic cycles juxtaposed and thrown off-kilter that, like the innovations of Ornette, eventually helped liberate musicians like Coltrane from the strictures of bebop rhythm and ensemble structure. Like Ornette's, Sun Ra's structural innovations were also derided by many jazz musicians as illogical and incompetent. Of course, not all of his work was so provocative. During the late 1960s, in fact, he had recorded an album of straight-ahead organ blues titled *Universe in Blue* and another of reworked standards titled *Some Blues, But Not the Kind That's Blue*.[69] But it might be a phrase in Gerald Zugmann's 2002 book *Blue Universe*, surveying the model-building work of the Vienna-based architectural firm Coop Himmelblau (in this case, with all of the models cast in a blue haze by moody backlighting), that best evokes Sun Ra's most visionary work: "Spaces are distorted as if gravity were suspended, the gravity of thinking included."[70]

———

Playing with Sun Ra was often more than a mere musical gig. He ran his band like a combination of an army and a monastery, with restrictions on sex, drugs, drink, and diet, even exercising control over the colors of musicians' clothes and rooms at times.[71] Rumors abounded of his psychic abilities, and it was even claimed that his music had recuperative powers that had helped heal ailing musicians. So deep were his musical discoveries that several of his greatest musicians

TABLE 4.1 Sun Ra and His Intergalactic Arkestra: "The Shadow World"
Fondation Maeght, St. Paul-de-Vence, France (August 3, 1970)

PERSONNEL

Sun Ra: piano, keyboards, synthesizer

Gloristeena Knight: vocals

June Tyson: vocals

Verta Grosvenor: vocals

Kwame Hadi: trumpet

Akh Tal Ebah: trumpet, cornet

Marshall Allen: alto saxophone, flute, piccolo flute, oboe

Danny Davis: alto saxophone, flute

John Gilmore: tenor saxophone, drums, vocals

Pat Patrick: baritone saxophone, bass clarinet, alto saxophone, tenor saxophone, flute, clarinet, percussion

Absholom Ben Shlomo: clarinet, flute, alto saxophone

James Jacson: clarinet, flute, oboe, percussion

Robert Cummings: bass clarinet, drums

Alan Silva: bass, cello, violin

Rashied Salim IV: vibraphone, drums

Lex Humphries: drums, percussion

Nimrod Hunt: drums

John Goldsmith: drums, tympani

TIMING	EVENT
REGION 1:	*Introduction*
0:00	Piece begins with piano ostinato, loosely outlining E♭ minor, with freely improvised percussion. Bass plays a disjunct counterostinato, also in E♭ minor.
0:10	Tenor and baritone saxophones take up ostinato pattern along w/piano (this ostinato continues intermittently throughout).
REGION 2:	*Theme*
0:20	Saxophones play main theme in disjunct time against sax/piano ostinato, with support from percussion.
REGION 3:	*Transition*
0:50	Free rhythm-section improvisation, with conga drums prominent.
1:30	Percussion recedes, saxophone ostinato assumes foreground.
REGION 4:	*Solos*
2:00	Sun Ra improvises low-register solo on Moog synthesizer.
2:40	Sun Ra plays low-register counterostinato, against sax ostinato.
2:56	Rhythm section reenters, along with John Gilmore's tenor saxophone solo. Sun Ra's counterostinato continues.
5:00	Gilmore and rhythm section continue, Sun Ra drops out.
5:30	Sun Ra reenters on organ.
6:15	Rhythm section drops out, saxophone solo continues unaccompanied.
7:00	Drums and percussion reenter to brief applause.
7:15	Tenor/baritone saxophone ostinato reenters.
7:40	Sun Ra improvises on synthesizer, sax ostinato continues, percussion accompaniment.
8:10	Other instruments drop out, Sun Ra synthesizer solo continues largely unaccompanied.
8:30	Tenor/baritone sax ostinato reenters intermittently.
10:25	Entire ensemble reenters with free collective improvisation.

TABLE 4.1 *continued*

REGION 5:	*Ending*
11:37	Brief pause, Sun Ra briefly plays original ostinato on organ.
11:55	Organ improvisation (harmonically fairly free, but begins in F minor and concludes in D minor).
13:25	End of piece.

stayed with him for decades. One of these was the influential tenor saxophonist John Gilmore, for whom Ra's genius was confirmed by the chromatic intro to his 1956 piece "Saturn," which Gilmore heard as a brilliant extension of Thelonious Monk's method of composing with unusual intervals.[72] Gilmore was Coltrane's primary link with the Arkestra. Coltrane's association with Sun Ra and Gilmore apparently dates to 1956 and continued, according to Gilmore, until Coltrane's passing in 1967, but has not been widely discussed.[73] In addition to references in C. O. Simpkins's 1975 Coltrane biography and John Szwed's 1997 biography of Sun Ra, the relationship between the two tenor men is most extensively chronicled in Valerie Wilmer's 1985 profile "A Quiet Screamer from Mississippi," published in the *Wire*. One reason this article is so valuable is that it privileges a different aspect of jazz history than contemporary constructions based almost exclusively on the progression of musical styles; it chronicles the personalities, human stories, and belief systems that were evolving in the 1960s and shows how the "floating world" of jazz was a breeding ground for new and sometimes highly esoteric formulations of sonic, spiritual, and scientific thought and practice.

Coltrane was drawn to the Arkestra for two main reasons: he was fascinated by Gilmore's system of false fingerings that enabled the saxophone to be played with a more vocalized sound (the most frequently cited example of Gilmore's influence is Coltrane's 1961 recording of "Chasin' the Trane"), and he had apparently had several enlightening conversations with Sun Ra encompassing musical and spiritual themes.[74] But Gilmore also credits Sun Ra with helping Coltrane break his addictions around the time of the latter's first stint with Miles Davis. As he explained to Wilmer:

> Trane was kind of out of it. He was having his drink and drug problems and actually would be searching for a lot of things that he couldn't make on his horn. He had the sketch of what he wanted to do then but he'd be missing a lot of times . . . it was really that Trane was searching and he was so untogether in

FIGURE 4.9 Jan Persson, *Sun Ra*. Reproduced courtesy of Jan Persson/CTSImages.

his personal thing . . . Sun Ra played some of his tapes to Trane over the phone and [Arkestra baritone saxophonist] Pat [Patrick] gave Trane some records and some of Sun Ra's philosophy. At that time he used to print little pamphlets and papers instructing people on Biblical interpretations and things that they had never thought of . . . [Coltrane] gave up all his vices and came out playing like a champ! He was cooking like he really wasn't the same cat. And from that point on he was aware of [the Arkestra] and he kept track of its movements.[75]

Musically, what Coltrane got from Sun Ra and Gilmore was, most immediately, a refining of his saxophone sound. But he also internalized deeper ideas about musical structure that took longer to manifest. *Ascension* would be the first of Coltrane's works that directly addressed cosmological themes, but many others would soon follow: *Sun Ship, Cosmic Music, Interstellar Space, Stellar Regions*. As Coltrane himself began to use radical revisions of meter and structure to convey his own cosmological musings, Sun Ra's "pathways to unknown worlds" likely provided the most durable and reliable point of comparison.[76] But while Coltrane acknowledged Ornette Coleman's influence (in the form of payments he sent to

Ornette for lessons as well as in several supportive public statements), he never seems to have done the same for Sun Ra, who was acknowledged as a genius by many of his contemporaries but shunned by an equal number of them due to his eccentricities and the extreme demands of his gig. It may not have seemed strategic to be associated with Sun Ra in a high-profile way in the 1960s, but the musical evidence suggests that Coltrane benefitted greatly from his exposure to the bandleader's concepts. This is reflected in the cohesion that Coltrane brought to his most focused experiments, a cohesion that was also rooted in his mastery of bebop and that arguably separated him from the proverbial pack of mostly younger "new thing" musicians. As Gilmore explained to J. C. Thomas, Coltrane "really wanted to play more avant-garde music, but he didn't get the foundation until he listened to Sun Ra a lot. I think we helped him get his Oriental and African music together, too. I'll tell you this—whenever I saw him after he'd studied with Sun Ra—he was *smoking*."[77]

V: ASCENT

Black Noise. What must be voices bob up, then drop, like metal shavings
In molasses. So much for us. So much for the flags we bored.
Into planets as dry as chalk, for the tin cans we filled with fire
And rode like cowboys into all we tried to tame.[78]
Tracy K. Smith

"Free Jazz," "the Avant-Garde," "Energy Music," "the New Thing"—all terms used more or less indiscriminately to describe the new forms and structures that were being created by jazz musicians in the 1960s. Each was essentially a marketing or journalistic term, each a necessarily partial descriptor of the complex new forms that could be loosely tethered to one sphere of the new music or the other. For example, the term "free jazz" (which had also been the title of Ornette Coleman's landmark double-quartet album of 1960) implied the liberating of boundaries associated with the existing tradition, and worked reasonably well as a description of Ornette's music, which was essentially a folk-inflected loosening of bebop's formal and harmonic strictures.[79] Similarly, the French military term "avant-garde," which implied a more gradual advancing of the boundaries of the existing tradition, made sense in terms of musicians like Coltrane (in the later period of his career discussed in this essay) and Sun Ra, who had progressed methodically from blues through swing, bebop, hard bop, Monk, modal, and into the new structures of the day. "Energy Music" was a vague but fair enough evocation of the performance styles of artists like Coltrane and Cecil Taylor, whose marathons of improvisation sometimes seemed like feats of endurance. The vaguest descriptor was "New Thing," but even that made a certain amount of sense in relation to younger, more experimental players like Albert Ayler and Pharoah Sanders, whose radical conceptions sometimes seemed to detach completely from anything that had been previously associated with the term "jazz." But if there was one recording in which these various streams coalesced into a reasonably representative mission statement of the new music, it was arguably Coltrane's *Ascension*, recorded on June 28, 1965—a mere two weeks after the landmark session of June 16—but not commercially released until the following February.[80] Like Ornette Coleman's *Free Jazz* (1960) or Sun Ra's *The Magic City* (1965), *Ascension* is best heard as a stand-alone concept album. And if *A Love Supreme* had been the thematic portal to the final stage of Coltrane's career, *Ascension* was the sonic portal.

The album's cover is a bit misleading in the sense that photographer Chuck Stewart portrays a seated Coltrane cradling his soprano saxophone (which he never actually plays on the album), in a moment of apparent contemplation that is belied by the music itself: a dense and fairly frenzied collective improvisation for an ensemble of eleven musicians that included Freddie Hubbard and Dewey Johnson (trumpets), Pharoah Sanders and Archie Shepp (tenor saxophones), John Tchicai and Marion Brown (alto saxophones), plus Garrison, Tyner, and Jones along with second bassist Art Davis. At its core *Ascension* is a reassertion of group improvisation that hearkens back to the collectivities of New Orleans, the black church, work songs, and the Negro spirituals, while being shaped by the experimental aesthetic values of the late 1960s. But what is typically heard as its wild, unbridled sound obscures the fact that the piece actually unfolds via a fairly transparent set of precomposed parameters. *Ascension* is, in the end, a tonally conceived piece that moves across several tonal centers, to which the players are at liberty to conform or not. Like much of Coltrane's modal music until this point—but within a much wider sonic arena—the result is a highly chromatic and gestural foreground with a strongly implied tonal underpinning. The main thematic material here is a riff, similar in structure to the one that forms the basis of "Acknowledgement" from *A Love Supreme*, that could easily have been adapted from a Delta blues song, field holler, or old Negro spiritual (Cecil Taylor would later adapt and slightly tweak this riff on his 1985 song "Taht").[81] The horn solos display a wide range of approaches: some players improvise with a level of harmonic complexity reflecting roots in bebop (arpeggiated chords, high level of chromaticization), others emphasize scalar thinking that reflects an orientation toward modal playing, while the rest play in a language shaped primarily by gesture and texture, reflecting free improvisation as a primary reference point. The piece alternates between solos supported by the rhythm section playing largely in time, and sections of collective improvisation with the entire ensemble playing largely in free meter. Structurally speaking, this alternation may be the most provocative element of this work, providing novel articulations of energy and velocity, and of expansion and contraction.

Some have imported the evolutionary scheme of Western art music in order to interpret this music as a pinnacle of jazz abstraction and avant-gardism. Wynton Marsalis, for example, wrote, "The Coltrane of *Ascension* was a modernist ripping away the shackles of tradition some sixty years after Europeans had freed themselves."[82] Even Archie Shepp, in the album's liner notes, compared the density of *Ascension*'s melodic figuration to the streaked surfaces of "action" painters like Jackson Pollock. But Coltrane could just as convincingly be heard as an artist ripping away the pretensions of modernist art in order to immerse himself in what was actually, in its primal sonic and emotional intensity, a very traditional sound environment of the African/Afro-diasporic continuum. One historical point of sonic reference, for example, might be the ceremonial drum, trumpet, and *alghaita* orchestras that accompany royal processions across the West African savannah, clearing the processional space with a cacophony of sound (more on this in the final chapter). But the more immediate reference point is the African American church. If all of Coltrane's improvisations after "Psalm" can be heard as acts of prayer, *Ascension* collectivizes this endeavor, its battery of horns resonating most strongly with the intense portions of a prayer meeting in the Baptist or Pentecostal traditions, with congregants singing, shouting, speaking in tongues, and testifying.[83] Regardless of how the point is argued, the observation must be made that in the space of a single year, Coltrane's music had evolved from the calm clarity of *Crescent* to the turbulent group shout of *Ascension*. The pace of change was becoming dizzying and, for some, disorienting. This included the members of the original quartet, struggling to find their places within this new music.

———

> Magicians and practitioners of the occult use amulets and talismans as tools to capture the powers of the stars in order to protect their clients from the negative sway of the planetary daemons.[84]
>
> *Matilde Battistini*

> Drake had thought long and hard about what an alien civilization might sound like to the giant telescope at Green Bank. Planet Earth had itself only just developed technologies that made interstellar communication theoretically possible . . . He believed it was self-evident that any cosmic civilization would want to reach out to other intelligent species on other planets.[85]
>
> *Trevor Paglen*

Despite these tensions, Coltrane continued to aggressively explore the structures of the "New Thing" based around free meter, gesture, and texture. Having temporarily shattered the bounds of traditional meter with "Untitled (90320)," "Sun Ship" (recorded on August 26) used a more jagged rhythmic theme to exert a blunt force, so to speak, "breaking" the metric space into sharper fragments than the generally "smoother" surfaces of "Untitled (90320)." The theme of "Sun Ship" amounts to a series of repetitions and slight variations of a four-note motif, played in free meter (figure 4.10). Coltrane composed several melodies of this type in the latter part of his career. They are very simple melodic cells, scalar fragments, or melodic gestures obsessively repeated, transformed through processes of permutation, and gradually extended into emotionally charged playing. Charlie Parker was famous for *signifying* in his improvisations, tossing in fragmented, coded references to all kinds of sources, from excerpts of the Woody Woodpecker theme to bits of Igor Stravinsky's *Firebird Suite*. At times he might use a particular melody to flirt with a female acquaintance in the audience, while at others he might send a message to a drug dealer. Coltrane's melodies like "Sun Ship" might be heard as belonging to that tradition of signifying; they similarly strike the ear as coded messages of some kind, but in this case, directed toward much more remote, inscrutable, and, in all likelihood, less worldly auditors. At different times, they resemble Morse code, numerological sequences, talismanic invocations, abstract pitch formulae, or satellite transmissions of some kind.

With a slight bit of rhythmic realignment, the theme of "Sun Ship" could easily be quantized to fit into 4/4 swing. Instead, Coltrane, Garrison, and Jones orbit

FIGURE 4.10 "Sun Ship" (August 28, 1965). Transcription by author, modified from sheet music copyright Jowcol, Hal Leonard.

around each other on three metrically disjunct planes, with Jones supporting Coltrane's line with metrically disjunct rolls and "bomb" accents while Garrison plays a series of contrasting accents between them. Meanwhile, the solo section of "Sun Ship" gives a clear indication of where Coltrane was heading, and also of the musical tensions that may have contributed to the break-up of his quartet. For example, although Jones does a lot of shortening, elongation, and fracturing of the time, he ultimately reverts to a fast 4/4 swing under McCoy Tyner's solo (around 0:50), although when Coltrane returns for his own solo, he uses a rapid "rifling" figure to pull Jones and the rest of the band forcibly out of meter. While it is certainly one of the examples in which Jones sounded most willing to follow Coltrane into free-meter territory, it is simultaneously a stubborn resistance to the same. Similarly to "Untitled (90320)," we can hear his performance here as more of a fragmented collage of different tempi than an embrace of truly free rhythmic movement.

In case anyone assumed *Ascension* to be a mere one-off experiment, "Sun Ship" doubled down on Coltrane's intent to explore the structures of the "New Thing." But the music itself wasn't released until 1971, graced with a cover that, in its graphic script and fevered image of Coltrane projecting his soprano saxophone into the foreground, clearly aimed the album at audiences aligned with the Fillmore crowd. Musicians such as the Grateful Dead's Jerry Garcia and The Doors's Ray Manzarek had frequently acknowledged the modal adventurism of works like *My Favorite Things* and *A Love Supreme* as seminal influences on their long-form, psychedelic improvisations.[86] But performances like "Sun Ship" were much more challenging propositions. After all, it is one thing to channel the sensations of psychedelic experience by using atmospheric sound processing over a steady beat and conventional chord progression (as many popular musicians were doing), supplying a "supplementary" level of complexity that ultimately does not destabilize the familiar devices of meter or tonality. It's another to do away with meter entirely, exploding the interlocking, "conversational" dynamic of the small jazz band into an exponentially more complex state.

If the titles of his pieces around this time are any indication, Coltrane might have felt as if he was blowing stars or other cosmic matter from his horn, channeling cosmic energies to Earth, or as if the horn itself was powering a departing space vessel. Was he hearing a new and revolutionary structural code, or was he becoming a medium for higher forces? The titles of *Ascension* and "Sun Ship" both suggest that, whatever extramusical resonances they may have had for him, Coltrane was now trying to break definitively free of "earthly" gravity, and his experiments with free meter helped move his music into a much freer, more fluid and more exalted temporal space.

Fueled by the antigravity technologies of Sun Ra, the experimentation of the younger players, and his own restless need to evolve, Coltrane was now leaving the modal paradigm behind and wholeheartedly entering a new musical space with startling and sometimes controversial results. The immersive group shout of *Ascension* and the impassioned fragmentation of "Sun Ship" have often been misunderstood in simplistic terms as sonic assaults. But their emergence at the crossroads of black spirituality and the Space Age also fundamentally seemed to assert that rocket ships and telescopes were not necessarily the only means of accessing the wider universe; the wider universe could also be accessed through the ancient, Afro-inflected cauldrons of prayer and possession, practices powered by strategic manipulations of the Africanist Grid that were calculated to generate the escape velocity that would catalyze these expansions of consciousness.

VI: "WITH THE FORCE OF A CYCLONE"

Ascension would hit the jazz world like a bomb but would not be released until February 1966. In the meantime, there were live dates to fulfill. Between June and August 1965, the quartet soldiered through a string of summer festival dates and a brief, four-date European tour that included two festival concerts at Antibes, France, on July 26 and 27, one at the Salle Pleyel in Paris on July 28, and another festival at Comblain-La-Tour in Belgium on August 1. With the quartet expressing ideas and feelings that had grown exponentially in scope from what they had been even a few months earlier (and especially since their last European tour, in 1963), the performances on this tour channeled new energies into the more established song forms of the quartet's established repertoire. Presenting a mix of old and new material, their summer run of astonishing musical peaks momentarily outshone the internal tensions that were pushing the group toward its end. Of all the European concerts Coltrane gave in the summer of 1965, Antibes in particular amounted to a mission statement of his new music, and given the weight of the occasion, we can assume that he intentionally programmed the concerts with this in mind.

Away from the usual grind of gigs, the quartet's set list opened up and became as adventurous as the late nights at the Half Note, the music also being played with a grandeur that acknowledged the significance of the high-profile festival gigs. Vehicles of long standing like "My Favorite Things," "Naima," "Afro Blue," and "Impressions" were augmented by newer pieces such as "Ascension," "Vigil," and, in Antibes, one of the few live performances ever given of the complete *A Love Supreme* suite.[87] It's unfortunate that these European concerts could not have been included as part of Pablo's *Live Trane: The European Tours* box set, because their inclusion would have provided the perfect conclusion to the recorded evolution of the quartet in concert; some of what was played on this tour was among the most intense and powerful music the quartet ever documented.[88]

These concerts contained strong clues of the elements that would shape Coltrane's music for the next two years. According to Lewis Porter, Coltrane warmed up for his Antibes sets by playing for hours along with a live recording of Albert Ayler, and in fact there is a well-known photo taken by Jean-Pierre Leloir of him in his hotel room at Antibes, practicing in front of a tape recorder.[89] Ayler's influence is particularly pronounced throughout these European concerts, inspiring Coltrane to expand the pitch component of his playing into a more expressionist, "pure sound" conception. Writing about the huge tone of tenor saxophonist Coleman Hawkins, Ben Ratliff once observed that "instead of using a thin-nibbed pen to trace out melodies, [Hawkins] used a paint roller."[90] In a similar line of thinking, the expressiveness of Coltrane's tenor saxophone tone in 1965 can be likened to the thick impasto textures created with a palette knife. The palette knife was a central implement for the Abstract Expressionists like Franz Kline and Willem De Kooning, who used it to reconceive the canvas as a landscape across which they moved huge swaths of paint. And, in fact, Coltrane's rhythm section increasingly functioned during these concerts as a kind of "canvas" against which he moved swaths of saxophone tone distorted into thick texture by multiphonics, overblowing, and alternate fingerings. As much as he had selectively relied on these devices in the past, this was a new way of playing for Coltrane.[91]

The heavy texturing and intense emotion of these performances meant that even recently recorded material was dramatically recast. *A Love Supreme*, for example, had barely been available for six months but was given a reading at Antibes that surpassed the original recording in depth, complexity, and intensity of emotion. The quartet's performance of the "Acknowledgement" segment of the suite is particularly fascinating—an epic performance in which Coltrane moves back and forth between playing discernible pitches and playing pure texture and gesture, draping the groove with gradations of tone color and edging his way across multiple modes of distortion and coloration while the rhythm section spatializes the core riff by moving fluidly back and forth between sections of clearly metered time and sections of metric ambiguity. In fact, looseness and spatiality are keys to the musical drama that unfolds within "Acknowledgement." Coltrane had remarked on a number of occasions that he did not particularly like playing open-air concerts, because the sound was too diffuse and it was consequently difficult to achieve ensemble coherence and flow. As he explained to Michel DeRuyter, "I don't prefer 'em, because usually the acoustics are kind of horrible . . . Some places as soon as you hit the first note it goes all over the place and you can't feel the flow of the thing . . . I've found the smaller places, the more compact they are . . . our sound is held together. We can hear and feel each other better, the smaller the place is."[92] This problem was presumably exacerbated with a piece like "Acknowledgement," based not on a driving swing rhythm that would unite the band around a strongly stated common pulse, but on a more complex Afro-Cuban rhythmic grid interwoven between Garrison's bass ostinato and a bell pattern played by Jones on his ride cymbal.

Obviously, the members of the Coltrane quartet had no difficulty playing with each other. But at points in "Acknowledgement" it sounds as if the band might have been struggling in the diffuse acoustic space to adjust themselves around the interwoven anchors of Jones and Garrison, an anchor that starts to shred about a minute after its introduction as Garrison opens up and fragments the line, and Jones subdivides the time in increasingly complex ways. Dynamic tension is generated by moments of apparent metric dissolution and reconsolidation, with the performance ultimately achieving transcendence through the band's ongoing efforts to mold the acoustic space around them. It also demonstrates the rhythmic (and emotional) courage involved in simply playing through moments when the bottom seems to open up, drop out, or slip away. Several times during this and other pieces, in fact, Coltrane himself seems intent on pulling the band into a state of rhythmic free fall.

During the tour, Coltrane confided to the writer and photographer Randi Hultin that, "I'm really afraid of losing Elvin, he's really special . . . there's nobody like him."[93] Having developed his drumming style in the midst of bebop, America's mambo craze of the 1950s, and the "Cubop" experiments of Charlie Parker, Dizzy Gillespie, Machito, and Chano Pozo, Jones was one of the jazz drummers who had internalized the concepts of Afro-Latin drumming. He explained his mixture of timeline-based groove and abstraction to Ashley Kahn in a way that speaks directly to the Antibes performance of "Acknowledgement": "Some parts of Latin music are very rigid, as are some aspects of African rhythms. The flexibility comes from the number of people that are playing the rhythm. It is not always synchronized, so that gives it a certain movement that makes it more fluid. When I applied it, I opted for the fluidity rather than the static portion of the rhythms . . . [But] I always try to maintain some kind of continuity with the cymbal."[94] There is an inherently spatializing element to Jones's emphasis on polyrhythm. The saxophonist Pat LaBarbera, who played with him over several decades, once observed that "Elvin brought a form of relaxation to the music . . . When I worked with Buddy Rich, everything had that real heavy swing feel, which I enjoy playing with sometimes. But Elvin really loosened up the time, and when I played with him, the music felt so open."[95] Trying to play with a highly polyrhythmic and abstract drummer like Jones could be unbearably frustrating if a player lacked a deeply internalized sense of time. If a player could keep the groove inside of them, however, it could be a transcendent and rhythmically liberating experience. And although LaBarbera's comments refer to Jones's polyrhythmic drumming within the paradigm of meter, his idea of rhythmic intensification as creating a feeling of "relaxation" or "looseness" would become centrally important to Coltrane's music from the summer of 1965 on. Hearing free-meter music as an elaboration of intensely polyrhythmic meter, LaBarbera's comments allow us to appreciate the stark experiential difference between players and listeners who experience pleasure through the security of heavily emphasized meter, and those who can relax into the multiple rhythmic perspectives suggested by free-meter music, experiencing the latter as an expansion—not dissolution—of swing.

———

While a substantial amount of attention has been devoted to the first Antibes show as the only live performance of *A Love Supreme*, virtually none has been devoted to the second night (and the following night in Paris), which feature the only documented live performances of "Ascension."[96] Part of the reason for this might be that, similarly to some of the Half Note material, the recordings were mistitled on several decades' worth of semi-official releases as "Blue Valse."[97] Unless these pieces were deliberately mistitled, their incorrect titling is another reflection of the poor documentation of the jazz avant-garde. The "Blue Valse" mistitling in particular is unfortunate because it helped obscure the thematic unity of much of the new music played in Europe. Besides the fact that neither performance resembles a waltz in any way, the opening notes are clearly those of "Ascension" and the structure of both performances embodies the "Ascension" theme.

If the studio takes of "Ascension" would soon throw down a gauntlet for collective free improvisation, these "miniaturized" quartet versions are valuable in the manner of a painter's sketchbook, rendering the basic structure of the piece much more transparent. One striking observation that can be made, for example, is that for canonical pieces of "free improvisation," the rubato introductions to the two live versions of "Ascension" are remarkably similar in design: the approximate difference in timing between them is a mere thirty seconds (table 4.2).

Although the entire introductory section is in rubato, the passages featuring the cascading figure referred to as "Theme C" above show the quartet articulating different qualities of space within the overall rubato feeling. Built around Coltrane's cascading trichords and underpinned by the harp-like glissandi of Tyner's piano, "Theme C" articulates a different kind of "flotation space" that is offset from the general rubato structure. Given that this theme precedes the climax of the introduction, it can also be likened to a momentary "fugue" state of disorientation that precedes the onset of a state of altered consciousness with the actual possession represented in this case by the transition into fast metered swing. Rather than showing a stereotypical free jazz free-for-all, in fact, the surviving Antibes footage clearly shows the musicians working together to dynamize the free-meter space into an explosive climax that—in this case—resolves into meter.[98]

This is to say that they reflect Coltrane's internalization of some of the structural lessons of Sun Ra and his mastery of the sensation of "lift-off," the sonic equivalent of blasting off into outer space. These are the possession dynamics inherited from West Africa, channeled through an African American (Chris-

TABLE 4.2 John Coltrane Quartet
Opening of "Ascension," Antibes version (July 27, 1965)

PERSONNEL

John Coltrane: tenor saxophone
McCoy Tyner: piano
Jimmy Garrison: acoustic bass
Elvin Jones: drums

TIMING	EVENT
0:00	Theme A (primary theme).
0:16	Theme B (secondary theme).
0:22	Theme A.
0:34	Theme C (cascading figure, secondary flotation space).
0:41	Theme A.
0:46	Improvised transpositions of themes A, B, and C.
1:34	Return to themes A and B, played straight.
1:45	Emotional climax and transition to Theme D.
1:57	Theme D (into fast swing).

TABLE 4.3 John Coltrane Quartet
Opening of "Ascension," Paris version (July 28, 1965)

PERSONNEL

Same as July 26, 1965

TIMING	EVENT
0:00	Theme A.
0:17	Theme B.
0:22	Theme A.
0:28	Theme C (cascading figure, secondary flotation space).
0:55	Improvised transpositions of themes A, B, and C.
1:25	Return to theme A and emotional climax.
1:42	Theme D (into fast swing).

tian) religious orientation and thematically recast within the Space Age. Like the exalted moments when meter is suspended and a congregation bursts into ecstatic praise, the sensation of lift-off was a result of tension being channeled into moments of high ensemble density in rubato time, resulting in a sudden feeling of levitation or suspension. In the southern religious culture of Coltrane's upbringing, these moments would be experienced as the arrival of the Holy Spirit, or the ascension of the human spirit to a state of divinity. But in the Space Age, with the heavens brought closer to Earth through the advances of science and technology, and with popular culture abounding with images of outer space exploration, they could as easily signify the ascension of a space vessel or, conversely, the dramatic moment when an extraterrestrial vessel descends out of the clouds to Earth. In the age of psychedelic agents and Eastern spirituality, they could signify a sudden, epiphanal expansion of consciousness. Either way, the sensation suggested ecstatic levitation, divine revelation, and/or otherworldly visitation, a meeting of human and suprahuman energies. Some musicians prize this as a particular skill, such as the saxophonist Steve Lacy, who remarked on his time spent playing with Thelonious Monk: "When I used to work with Monk, he used to say 'Let's lift the bandstand.' That's magic, man, when the bandstand levitates. I didn't know how to do it—but I knew what he was talking about."[99]

These concerts also presented intensely impassioned and expressionist readings of Coltrane's standard repertoire. Comparing any of the early live recordings of "Naima" with the Antibes version, for example, is akin to comparing "The Star-Spangled Banner" as sung at a sporting event to the same anthem as performed by Jimi Hendrix at Woodstock. Unlike the radical deconstructions of this tune that Coltrane would document during 1966, the song's form remains recognizably intact here. But it is stretched to every other possible sonic and emotional extreme. In terms of emotional expressiveness and technical command, this version of "Naima" is arguably one of Coltrane's greatest documented live performances, a much more substantial reading of the tune than the one he would give just a few nights later in Comblain-La-Tour. Like the great Bay Area school of painters (including Richard Diebenkorn, David Park, Manuel Neri, Nathan Oliveira, Elmer Bischoff, and Joan Brown) who combined the textural advances of Abstract Expressionism with rigorous representational painting, it reveals the emotional depth that the textural, "New Thing" saxophone techniques could facilitate when wedded to technical command, more traditional notions of form and genre, and a deep understanding of harmony and the ways it can extend into purely textural thinking.[100]

An inverse observation can be made of Coltrane's customary vehicles for the soprano saxophone, "My Favorite Things" and "Afro Blue." As he increasingly used the tenor to venture further and further into pure sound territory, the soprano became more narrowly cast as the vehicle for Coltrane's mathematical obsessions. Rarely, if ever, did he explore the extended sonic capabilities of the instrument as thoroughly as he had the tenor. In this, he differed from players like Steve Lacy, Evan Parker, Roscoe Mitchell, Anthony Braxton, or Sam Newsome, who have investigated and extended the sonic potential of the soprano in comprehensive ways that Coltrane himself seemed to reserve for the tenor. The straight horn became Coltrane's de facto "note machine," and his improvisations on the tour's versions of "Afro Blue" and "My Favorite Things" offer an unbelievably profuse spray of scales, arpeggios, and chromatic patterns executed with extreme technical precision and crystalline mathematical clarity, while sacrificing none of the emotional impact of his best work.

———

At his European concerts Coltrane seemed to be playing ever more passionately at a crossroads of sorts, waiting for the next path to reveal itself by exposing himself to as many new ideas as possible. Arrigo Polillo wrote of the Antibes concerts, "You really had to be there . . . Like a furious hurricane, Trane grabbed the crowd with the force of a cyclone, traversing a long series of choruses that I can only describe as stupefying."[101] The French jazz journalist Michel Delorme remembered that at the first night's conclusion, "A third of the audience was yelling because they wanted more . . . Another third was yelling because they didn't like it, and the last third was yelling because they loved it."[102] The commercially available video of the Comblain-La-Tour date similarly shows most of the audience responding with sustained applause, undercut by a substratum of booing. As far back as 1963, reviewer Michael James had observed (following the quartet's appearance in Amsterdam) that "Coltrane and his men carry their music to the very brink of disorder, yet somehow never quite transgress the boundary which separates intricacy from chaos."[103] Now they appeared to be pushing the music across yet another boundary, and it was left up to listeners to perceive either chaos or a new level of complexity. The issue would remain unresolved and bitterly contested for the next eighteen months or so, arguably finding a kind of clarification before his work was completed. One thing is certain, however—after the summer of 1965, the music of John Coltrane would never be the same.

FIGURE 4.11 Michael Ochs, *Alice Coltrane*. Reproduced courtesy
of Michael Ochs Archives, Getty Images.

VII: CHRYSALIS

Coltrane returned from his European tour to a major life event; his wife Alice
gave birth to their second son, Ravi, on August 6. This would be their second of
three children; John Jr. had been born in 1964 and their third son, Oran, would
be born in 1967. He and Alice would legally marry in 1966, but they had been
a couple since mid-1963. With two children of their own, another on the way,
plus Alice's daughter by a previous marriage, John was now deeply enmeshed in
family life. He was also now half of a profound musical partnership. Although
perpetually misunderstood (and often maligned) by the jazz press during her
active years, Alice Coltrane (figure 4.11) was much more than merely the wife
of John Coltrane. She was a highly accomplished musician—a world-class jazz
pianist and keyboardist, as well as a prolific composer and imaginative concep-
tualist who, by the end of the year, would also be a central collaborator with her
husband, and who would later go on to create one of the most compelling bodies
of work in the history of modern jazz.[104]

There is existing footage of Alice in her pre-Coltrane incarnation, dressed conservatively and comping (and soloing) dutifully behind saxophonist Lucky Thompson in full bebop mode.[105] Between her demeanor and her playing, it's almost impossible to imagine her chrysalis-like transformation into an avant-garde visionary. But the expansive, experimental mood of the times, along with her partnership with her husband, took her life and music down a radical and presumably unexpected path. Among the things they shared were a sense of spirituality deep enough to encompass musical spheres from the devotional to the experimental, and a conceptual imagination wide-ranging enough to encompass the sublimities both sought to express in their art.

Like Yoko Ono, Betty Davis, Lee Krasner, Elaine de Kooning, Shirley Scott, or other wives of male artistic legends, the reasons Alice Coltrane is not as well known as she should be is due to a combination of gender bias in her profession, general misunderstanding of her artistic vision, as well as the simple fact of having been overshadowed by her husband's titanic reputation. These dynamics not only do a disservice to her career but also minimize her role in her husband's career. The eleven-year difference in their respective ages might seem to imply a mentor-student dynamic, but the benefit of having a sympathetic partner and sounding board should not be underestimated for John during this period, when he faced increasingly hostile responses to his new music. In fact, Alice's radical reconceptualization of jazz performance as a devotional activity was a vision that, while developed in tandem with her husband, only she would survive to pursue to its full realization.[106] Alice Coltrane enables us, among other things, to rethink free jazz and its implications. Was it just a music of racial rage, sonic histrionics, and unbridled experimentalism, as it has been long stereotyped? Or was it something that could be understood as having been generated out of love, romance, and companionship, something not only fighting worldly battles but at least partially celebrating domestic triumphs?

Although Alice was still a few months away from joining her husband's band in September 1965, it may well be an aura of personal fulfillment that suffuses the final recorded work of the original John Coltrane Quartet, an aura that Elvin Jones traced as far back as *A Love Supreme*: "[W]hat I think is that it began to materialize when he started having children. [I]t had everything to do with the spirituality that was there and how he's thanking God for this gift."[107] Jones's sentiments might be applied equally to the five-part suite recorded in early September and issued in 1977 as *First Meditations* (to distinguish it from a later rerecording of the same suite). Of the five individual sections ("Love," "Compassion," "Joy," "Consequences," and "Serenity"), three are set in the type of rubato drawn from the African American sacred tradition, while harmonically, all five represent an elaboration of the freedoms that Coltrane integrated from Ornette Coleman. Like his playing on "Acknowledgement" from *A Love Supreme*, most of the sections involve him stoking the ensemble energy by manipulating fairly basic diatonic motives, underpinned by the flowing, harp-like textures of McCoy Tyner's piano and the free counterpoint between Garrison's bass and Jones's drums. And like their playing on the Antibes rendition of "Naima," these are all highly emotional performances with a fullness of feeling overflowing, by turns, into passages of passion and turbulence.

If the performance dynamic of the classic quartet could be likened, as Michael Cuscuna suggested, to the building of erotic energy through the polyrhythmic tension of swing, Coltrane was now beginning to articulate a different mode of sensuality, via a more immersive sound environment less predicated on building polyrhythmic tension within a metered rhythmic field, and more on the continuous sensations of flowing and floating. His ballad playing had always been marked by very free, vocalized phrasing. The difference in the fall of 1965 was that his rhythm section now floated and flowed with him in increasingly liquified rubato time. Overall, *First Meditations* was a fitting capstone to the four-year run of the original Coltrane quartet. The tragedy for jazz was that, like "Untitled (90320)" and the European festival performances, their mastery of controlled liberation gave every indication that they could easily have continued to move masterfully into the deeper waters of the avant-garde. Even the idea that Elvin Jones's resistance was the main source of tension is contradicted by his own later series of collaborations with Cecil Taylor, who remembered that "playing with Mr. Jones . . . was a great musical experience . . . When I played with him the most unifying musical characteristic was that we played as if we were one person. He understands the music that I construct, all the dynamics, the aspects of form."[108] The evidence suggests that the Coltrane quartet could have gone on to develop a similar chemistry, had other factors not intervened. For the moment, Coltrane seemed to be in a very good place in his life and music. But his search remained a restless one.

VIII: BAPTISM

In order to get . . . to a place, you have to . . . blow it apart . . .
you have to look inside it and find the seeds of the new.[109]

Tadao Ando

There may have been love in the air, but "love" is not what most listeners experienced in Coltrane's music in the fall of 1965. And although they sought explanations, none were immediately forthcoming. This isn't surprising. There are times, when the winds of change blow through a life, that a person may not know exactly how to proceed, or even understand the destination toward which the winds are blowing. In this case, if they remain committed to moving forward, the only immediate option is to proceed on raw instinct with the hope that time and vigilance will clarify the destination. It is not unreasonable to suspect that John Coltrane might have been in such a situation with his music in late 1965, a period in which he seemed to be playing—more passionately than ever—a music that he himself did not yet fully understand. What the first half of 1965 had made abundantly clear was that the quartet's music had evolved to a point where it simply had to take a dramatic step forward. And while that music had been increasingly radical in its design, it could still be heard as an extension (or deconstruction) of the quartet's longstanding repertoire, of the structural dynamics of swing, and of more generalized norms of jazz performance. But while the path ahead was clearly moving further away from those points of reference, the actual goal seemed to remain obscured within uncharted territory. In time, a coherent concept would consolidate within Coltrane's new music, but, for now, he seemed to have only the visceral certitude of pure action to guide him forward.

Despite the ambiguities, Coltrane remained committed and methodical as the quartet (now augmented with Pharoah Sanders plus other assorted musicians in different cities) embarked on a tour of the West Coast. If the summer had been a period of intense transition, September seemed to portend a season of irrevocable change as the balance between intellect and emotion in his own playing began to swing much more strongly toward the latter. Even as he had gradually transformed the rhythmic design of his pieces earlier in the summer, his lines had remained doggedly rigorous in their construction, complex patterns that, in their complexity, effectively stitched together the players' various rhythmic perspectives as they moved further into free meter. But as summer gave way to fall, Coltrane's thickly textured lines increasingly resolved in screams and cries that simultaneously subverted and transcended the traditional logics of pitches, scales, and harmonies. At different moments, his solos might sound like bebop warped by extraterrestrial tongues and residual memories of African languages, like bugle calls or military salutes, like a terrified soul screaming into the existential void, like a mathematician obsessing over every conceivable solution to an equation, or like a Baptist preacher at the peak of their sermon.

That Coltrane was operating primarily on instinct became gradually clear in his appearances from the fall of 1965, when he essentially began using the studio take of "Ascension" as a template for live performance, communalizing the band's operations by opening it up to players of all skill levels including, in the estimation of some, virtual beginners. The earliest documented occasions of Coltrane letting relatively untested players sit in would probably be the Half Note sessions of spring 1965, which is evidently how the drummer Rashied Ali came to register on his radar, although Ali remembers encountering Coltrane during their earlier years in Philadelphia (Ali would join Coltrane's band later in 1965).[110] But by late fall he seemed to operate a virtual open-door policy, allowing players of any skill level to sit in with the band, much to the chagrin of the virtuosi of the original quartet. Communalizing the band's performances in this way seemed to disregard the criteria of jazz mastery that had accumulated over the previous six decades, ultimately undermining the very notion of what constituted a credible performance. For some, this was a highly unsettling notion coming from a musician who was considered the reigning virtuoso of his generation. For others, it was a brave and generous way to democratize the music by rendering it open to musicians with radically different levels of preparation, the performance now considered less a display of virtuosity and increasingly, more an inclusive, communal ritual of spiritual devotion.

By doing this on public stages, Coltrane was exposing himself to harsh and sometimes fierce criticism. But he was no stranger to negative reactions. Onstage in Paris with Miles Davis in 1960, he had been booed and even had objects thrown at him by audiences who found his improvising garrulous and long-winded.[111] And soon after forming his own band, he and Eric Dolphy had endured John Tynan's famous diatribe in *DownBeat* in 1961, in which they were publicly forced to defend themselves against accusations of playing "anti-jazz."[112] In time, most of his critics had been rendered mute as his mastery became inarguable, and his artistic advances almost universally lauded. Nevertheless, the tide began to turn back against Coltrane during the final months of 1965. What was actually happening in his music? And what would inspire the world's reigning saxophone virtuoso—a man who, by all accounts, never stopped practicing—to remodel his music in such a drastic manner?

————

Coltrane periodically needed other horn players as sparring partners, to spur his own explorations of new musical areas. Back in the early days of the original quartet, Eric Dolphy joined as a fifth member for several months in 1961, adding a voice that was at once rigorous in logic and expressionist in color. And although many people felt that the quartet was a powerfully self-contained unit that did not need a second horn, Coltrane and Dolphy's exploration of arcane scale systems and gestural playing helped both players work their ways definitively out of the vestiges of the bebop system, while also opening up the modal approach in more adventurous and experimental ways than Coltrane had been able to pursue with Miles. Dolphy died tragically in Berlin in the spring of 1964 following a tour with Charles Mingus, and by 1965, Coltrane was moving into yet freer territory with a younger crop of saxophonists providing him with the inspiration for further exploration. Several of them such as Sanders, Marion Brown, Archie Shepp, and John Tchicai had turned up as part of the expanded ensemble he convened for *Ascension*. Also involved was the saxophonist Albert Ayler, who had arrived in New York in 1963 after a stint in the US Army and a sojourn through Scandinavia. Ayler never formally recorded with Coltrane but is documented as having guested on several of Coltrane's gigs during 1965 and 1966. With Coltrane's support and encouragement, a number of these players would establish themselves as important voices within the "New Thing," recording for new labels such as Impulse and ESP-Disk. Of all of these musicians, Coltrane was probably closest to Sanders, who had arrived in New York City from his native Arkansas in 1961 (his nickname was "Little Rock") and scuffled for a bit before subbing briefly for John Gilmore when the latter took a sabbatical from the Sun Ra Arkestra. Sanders would join Coltrane's band later in 1965.

While Coltrane has often been depicted as the "Pied Piper" of the jazz avant-garde, he should be equally understood as a student of the movement. In addition to his expressed admiration for the primary architects of the new music such as Ornette Coleman and Cecil Taylor, he was particularly intrigued by the sonic innovations of the younger saxophonists such as Sanders, Ayler, and Shepp who focused less on pitch-based harmonic thinking at this point in their careers, and more on pure sound, texture, and gesture. These players inspired, challenged, and learned from Coltrane as they passionately and systematically explored overtones, overblowing, alternate fingerings, and other extended saxophone techniques that expanded the expressive vocabulary of the saxophone. Of course, these techniques were not at all unfamiliar to Coltrane (many were things he had learned from John Gilmore or picked up earlier, during his days as a rhythm-and-blues sideman), but their way of using them helped expand Coltrane's sonic palette and emotional range. Inventing a new language for the saxophone as social change swirled turbulently around them, it must have been as exciting a time for these younger players as it had been for the Abstract Expressionists a decade earlier. Painters like Willem de Kooning, Jackson Pollock, and Franz Kline had all begun their careers as representational artists, but by the late 1940s/early 1950s their landscapes, still lifes, and portraits were giving way to explorations of color, geometry, light, energy, and exultations in the textured sensuality of pure paint. And while they initially seemed to be completely turning their backs on the observed world, they were actually revolutionizing the way the world could be observed. It was the same with the saxophonists who, while not necessarily crafting hummable, toe-tapping melodies, were using their instruments to fashion their own revolutionary musical codes and envision new worlds. But the influence of these younger players extended beyond music. Members of the Baby Boomer generation, they were generally freer in their attitudes than the older players who had come up through the ranks of bebop. Revolution and experimentation were the guiding principles in their music, worldviews, and lifestyles. And since psychedelic drugs were part of the experience of some of them, these became an element of their interaction with Coltrane.

––––

It is unclear exactly when Coltrane began experimenting with LSD, but its influence is usually claimed to be apparent in concerts and recording sessions of the last two years of his life. The most we can currently say about the issue is that it is generally assumed that his album *Om*, recorded in Seattle in September 1965, was recorded under the influence of LSD (it is worth mentioning that another recording made during the band's run of Seattle gigs, "Evolution," features thirty minutes of collective vocal groaning, free improvisation, and droning, meditative long tones).[113] Various other authors have mentioned and/or alluded to this issue over the years including, most notably, jazz writer Howard Mandel. Various blogs and websites also ponder the radical changes in Coltrane's late music as a consequence of his LSD use.[114] In biographical terms, Mandel's 2002 article "Divine Wind" addresses the topic most directly but his article, strictly speaking, is not concerned with music-analytical observations.[115] Like all of the writings that broach this topic, it is also somewhat hampered by the fact that while several of Coltrane's associates were willing to speak about his LSD use, none were willing to be identified. This is why, a half-century later, the topic is still a matter of rumor, speculation, and conjecture.

The circumspection of these musicians is understandable. As much as mind-altering substances were a part of the jazz subculture and the counterculture of the 1960s, the idea of them as mediums for personal or political liberation was never going to be accepted by any significant number of African Americans. The reasons for this are obvious. First, a major political struggle was being waged, and intoxication was not considered conducive to the clear thinking necessary for political activism. Second, that struggle was largely defined and orchestrated, at least in Coltrane's time, by political leaders who had emerged from religious organizations (Christian or Muslim) that were fundamentally conservative and hostile to what they legitimately considered to be destructive influences within the African American community—many of them deliberately planted by forces opposed to African American self-determination. After all, a serious heroin epidemic had decimated urban areas since the 1940s (it had accelerated during the period of America's military engagement in the heroin-producing region of southeast Asia) and in light of this social devastation, mind-altering substances were "drugs"—mediums of degraded self-destruction—and were to be avoided at all costs. Few people were willing to make the distinction often heard within the counterculture between substances used for "enlightenment" versus those used for "escape."

It could also be more cynically argued that in Coltrane's time, the image of the psychedelically liberated jazzman was not nearly as archetypal as the image of the heroin-addicted jazzman. More pertinent, however, is the fact that the "psyche-delic Coltrane" has been downplayed because of the significance that his personal transformation held for jazz as a cultural and political force in the 1960s. Similar to Malcolm X, he was viewed as an icon who overcame a lifestyle of dissipation and self-destruction in order to consolidate his energies and emerge as one of the most powerful and transformative voices of his generation. In doing so, he counteracted the image of the jazz musician as junkie—still a reality for many musicians of his own generation who continued to struggle with the heroin-addiction-as-rite-of-passage cult of which Charlie Parker is typically considered patron saint. In the rock music associated with the counterculture, mind-altering substances, while sometimes demonized as a destroyer of minds and lives, were as often heralded as a liberator of minds and especially, of artistic creativity. But the narrative of Coltrane's redemption, crucially necessary to the broader priorities of the 1960s, carried much more weight than could any narrative of the liberatory potential of psychedelic drugs. Despite these cultural sentiments and the reticence of musicians to speak publicly on the matter, psychedelics were as important a catalyst in the stylistic transformations of jazz in the 1960s as they were in other forms of music. Even a canonized figure such as Sonny Rollins has acknowledged the role that his psychedelic experimentation played in the freer type of jazz he was creating in the mid-1960s, when he aligned himself with musicians from Ornette Coleman's orbit such as Don Cherry, Henry Grimes, and Billy Higgins.[116] In the case of Coltrane, the very fact that the performances of "Transition" and "Untitled (90320)" were separated by a mere week while only two weeks separated "Untitled (90320)" from *Ascension*, implied an unusually accelerated evolutionary curve. To the extent that the turbulent catalyst of LSD did in fact sweep through Coltrane's music, then, it is important to distinguish between music shaped by emotional or spiritual priorities, versus music shaped by intellectual or conceptual priorities. This distinction can help navigate the difference between those thinkers who completely minimize the influence of psychedelics on Coltrane, and those who overemphasize the psychedelic interpretation as a convenient means of either championing or dismissing all of the saxophonist's post-summer 1965 music.

———

Given the paucity of precise factual information, it makes the most sense to build a case from the musical evidence. Of course, even this presents a challenge since virtually all of the transformations that took place in Coltrane's music made perfect *musical* sense in the context of the transformations that had preceded them. Still, a comparison with the effects of psychedelics in other musical genres make it clear that most of the markers of sonic-psychedelic culture are abundantly present in Coltrane's late music, albeit refracted through the hyperintellectualized materials of modern jazz.

In studying the sounds and structures of the psychedelic popular music that was contemporaneous with Coltrane, we can hear at least four prominent tendencies that tend to repeat themselves from case to case. First is a preference for swirling soundscapes that a) mimic the perceptual distortions of the hallucinogenic experience, and/or b) fashion the music as an "immersion experience." In this period of rapidly evolving music technology, one cutting edge was in the development of multichannel sound-projection systems that could immerse the listener in sounds from multiple directions simultaneously. Psychedelics had sometimes played a role in this, such as when the famed LSD chemist Owsley Stanley and electronics engineer Ron Wickersham founded the pioneering electronics company Alembic as a direct result of the early "acid tests" for which the Grateful Dead provided the music. Owsley would later develop the legendary "Wall of Sound" for the Grateful Dead, a system that used massive and highly sophisticated stage amplification to saturate performance spaces without the aid of a conventional PA system or external signal processing. In this trajectory, LSD was a catalyst for the expansion of the sound world of 1960s popular music, perfectly timed to take advantage of the decade's explosion in transistor technology. The idea here is that psychedelics can intensify a listener's spatial awareness, hence the emphasis on spatializing effects such as stereo panning, channel separation, echo, and reverberation in the music of that era. This in turn makes it easier to experience the music in three-dimensional, immersive terms.

If we listen to them as potential examples of psychedelic music, Coltrane's studio recordings at this time were not nearly as technically sophisticated as canonized psychedelic rock albums such as the Beatles's *Sgt. Pepper's Lonely Hearts Club Band* or the Jimi Hendrix Experience's *Are You Experienced*, both of which were released in 1967.[117] With the exception of those at the very top of the music industry economic ladder (and even then, in limited amounts), jazz musicians did not typically have access to (or, in most cases, interest in) the same studio production resources as did popular musicians (records, including those that made use of editing, were typically presented as documents of real-time performances), and neither did their live performances benefit from sound systems comparable with what the rock musicians had at their disposal.[118]

Within the more traditional implements of the jazz language, however, similarly immersive effects could be achieved by design elements such as free meter, with the kaleidoscopic multiplicity of rhythmic perspectives implicitly dynamizing the listener's spatial experience of the music. On one hand, free meter can be liberating in that it relieves the strain of orienting toward specific points of (metric) tension and release for some listeners, while other listeners experience greater tension as they struggle to reconcile the competing metric gravities. Either way, the tension between these two rhythmic orientations forces the listener to expand their spatial awareness of the music. Immersion in the metric multiplicity of pieces such as *Ascension* then becomes a formidable sonic analogue for the pulsating, visual and rhythmic environments associated with psychedelic music, even without the benefits of multimedia accoutrements such as light shows. We could by extension make the case that psychedelics contributed to a transformation of the spatial relationships implied by jazz structure. Thus, it is unsurprising that even architects were conducting their own experiments with psychedelics (it's very interesting that, unlike jazz musicians, they could address this issue openly), some of which were chronicled in a surprisingly evenhanded 1966 profile in *Progressive Architecture* titled "LSD as Design Tool?" Although written in a fairly clinical tone, it contains a number of spatial insights by architects that resonate with what could be heard in the music:

> Architects report that the relevance of psychedelic drugs should be apparent: a substance that enables man to increase his visual awareness, that heightens his ability to visualize three-dimensionally, might have serious and far-reaching applications to the practice of architecture, especially as buildings become more complex . . . for the visually sensitive person, the effects of mescaline and LSD include an increased ability to visualize three-dimensionally, to see images visually—in general, a heightened sense of spatial relations.[119]

A second common effect of psychedelics upon music is the active dissolution of established formal boundaries and the transformation from finite forms to open-ended, adventurous improvisations. The removal of standard formal markers parallels the idea of the psychedelic trip as an exploration, and of the song as a *process* as opposed to a *product*. The legendary performances of the Grateful Dead's long-form improvisational vehicle "Dark Star," for example, regularly featured free-meter breakdowns that allowed the band to move into sections in which the song's tonality is left far behind, and to conduct elaborate explorations of texture and spatiality.[120] "Dark Star" could go literally anywhere; some versions are light and pastoral, while others are dense and electric. Some swing like jazz while others unfold gently, with the lilt of folk music. Some manipulate fairly traditional melodic materials, while others are much more focused on manipulations of electronic textures.[121] In a general sense, this mirrors Coltrane's trajectory from *A Love Supreme* to *Ascension*, in which pitch relationships are gradually chromaticized, meter is gradually abandoned, and rigorous pitch sequences expand into detailed explorations of pure texture.

This dissolution of boundaries is often accompanied by a heightened *synesthesia*—the interrelationship between different sensory faculties, reflected in an awareness of the correspondences between different artistic media—which is itself a localized version of the "interrelationship between all things" often mentioned by psychedelic users. For example, Coltrane's supposed derivation of a melodic sequence from a pattern in a rug ("Living Space"), his correlation of pitch sequences with color charts (see the discussion of "Leo" in section ix), and his use of geometric forms to map pitch relationships (e.g., the so-called Coltrane pitch circle) resonate with other instances of lysergic synesthesia.

Finally, such changes in musical structure are often accompanied by what we might call a thematic change—a profound shift in the musician's understanding of their role in society. For example, there are numerous examples of musicians suddenly reimagining themselves as avatars of peace and universal understanding, and reimagining their secular music as a religious or spiritual music, following psychedelic experiences.[122] The 1964 recording of *A Love Supreme*, when the thematic focus of Coltrane's music became more explicitly spiritual, undoubtedly helped consolidate his vision within a higher devotional purpose. But even if spirituality had always been a shaping influence on his music, the dramatic recasting of his music as devotional activity, the reconceptualizing of his improvisations as prayers, and the inclusion of a rhapsodic, devotional poem all have the hallmarks of a fairly sudden "conversion" experience, coming from a musician who, for all his emotionalism, had until that point been equally hyperrational in his playing and thinking. (There is a website that ponders, in extensive detail, the possibility that *A Love Supreme* was inspired by a psychedelic experience.)[123] Assuming the context of these comments is not misunderstood, this might provide at least partial context for the change in Coltrane's comments about himself and his art. In 1962, he summed up his artistic vision to Valerie Wilmer: "I know that I want to produce beautiful music, music that does things to people that they need. Music that will uplift, and make them happy—those are the qualities I'd like to produce."[124] By 1966, he remarked to Ennosuke Saito that, "In music, or—as a person . . . I would like to be a saint."[125] And it may be telling that the two musicians closest to Coltrane in his later period, Pharoah Sanders and Alice Coltrane, continued to conceive of their own music in a similarly devotional manner after Coltrane's passing.

———

The spirit of Coltrane suffuses Kasper Collin's 2007 documentary *My Name Is Albert Ayler*, which does a lot to clarify the role psychedelics played in the work of some of the younger, "New Thing" players during this period.[126] One of Coltrane's guiding inspirations as he moved into freer territory, Ayler came to believe that he was on a musical mission to spread love, peace, and brotherhood and many of his songs were (or were modeled after) Christian hymns, anthems, or marches, refracted through the sensibility of free jazz. Almost all were played in rubato time, aimed at the heavens with a musical mood associated with the most emotional moments of the Afro-Protestant (especially Baptist and Pentecostal) liturgies. The titles on the 1967 concert recording *Albert Ayler Live in Greenwich Village* make this abundantly clear: "Holy Ghost," "The Truth Is Marching In," "Our Prayer," "Divine Peacemaker," and tellingly, "For John Coltrane."[127] Collin's narrative implies that many of the triumphs and tragedies of Ayler's life and career were connected to his LSD use, including his breakthrough to a radically new conception of improvisational music, but also to the eventual psychological breakdown of his trumpeter brother Donald, as well as Albert's own apparently guilt-fueled demise.

Like Ayler's, Coltrane's music and pronouncements increasingly took on a messianic tone, the titles of his pieces referencing astrological, cosmological, or spiritual concerns. They came in quick succession over the next two years (although several were not released until years later, sometimes with titles posthumously supplied by Alice Coltrane): *Ascension*, "Sun Ship," "Leo," "Mars," "Cosmos," *Stellar Regions, Interstellar Space*, "Peace on Earth," "Ascent," "Amen," and many others. As for "Sun Ship" itself, the title may or may not be connected with the fact (as depicted in Collin's film) that the Ayler brothers were at one point involved in a dangerous practice of "sun worship" in which they claimed to regenerate their energy by gazing directly into the sun for extended periods (a track from Ayler's 1968 album *New Grass* is titled "Sun Watchers").[128]

––––––

While Ayler had obviously exerted a transformative influence on Coltrane's saxophone playing, Pharoah Sanders was the central catalyst in the changing sound of Coltrane's live performances. In his post-Coltrane career, Sanders would record a series of powerfully moving albums for Impulse and other labels such as *Karma, Tauhid, Thembi*, and *Live at the East*.[129] The music on these albums was much more stylistically diverse than the work he did with Coltrane, juxtaposing his gospel/R&B/free jazz–inflected tenor (and sometimes sopranino) saxophone style with spiritual themes, all of which unfolded upon a foundation of pan-Africanist rhythm grooves. In the Coltrane group, however, those more traditional modes of Sanders's melodicism were rarely heard. Most of his solos are built almost exclusively with the extended saxophone techniques of the New Thing—multiphonics, overtones, and false fingerings—delivered at fortissimo level with very little dynamic variation. The result was, for some, a fairly harrowing emotional experience, and on the other hand a catalyst for Coltrane to push his own playing into new sonic and emotional dimensions.

Sanders joined Coltrane's working band in time for fall dates in San Francisco (September 14–26), Seattle (September 27–October 2), and Los Angeles (October 7–17) (a tour documented on *Live in Seattle*, a recently unearthed live version of *A Love Supreme* recorded the same week in Seattle and the studio session released as *Om*).[130] Interfacing with the psychedelic currents that LSD proselytizers like Owsley, Alfred Hubbard, and others were spreading up and down the West Coast, the tour appears to mark a definitive turning point in Coltrane's evolution.[131] This was most dramatically evident on *Om*, a studio recording made on October 1 during a run of gigs at Seattle's Penthouse club, by a Coltrane allegedly tripping on LSD.[132] This music, with its swirling vectors of wild, expressionistic sound, is certainly no less psychedelic than anything coming out of Haight-Ashbury, London, or Greenwich Village. The recording begins with an abstract bit of African thumb piano, and continues with a fevered recitation of an excerpt from the *Bhagavad Gita*, before exploding into almost thirty minutes of extremely intense, frenzied collective improvisation. Coltrane's playing remains rigorous and at an extremely high level of execution but the overall sensation, heightened by the reverberant production, is of a churning maelstrom of sound. Those who, in retrospect, sought a psychedelic explanation for the drastic changes in Coltrane's music (the album would not be released until 1968) could cite *Om* as a prime example of the extreme transformations that LSD was unleashing across the arts—transformations that were unleashing heightened creativity and chaos in equal measure.

Despite the fact that Coltrane felt he was genuinely pursuing a new type of music (the question of whether or not it should be called "jazz" was becoming increasingly complicated), this music had as yet no clearly articulated rules or criteria of evaluation, and the sheer intensity of the band's sound was one of the main factors obscuring the structural concepts he was striving to articulate. This was compounded by Coltrane's own apparent unwillingness, as a man of few words, to explain exactly what he was trying to do. In fact, he tended by this point to explain his music via recourse to spiritual or philosophical ideas and in any case, he was very rarely asked the types of questions that would elicit musically specific explanations. As his music became increasingly intense and listeners struggled to find a context for the sound, most of the questions directed at Coltrane centered on racial or political themes. At times, in fact, the discourse swirling around the music—which pitted African American writers such as LeRoi Jones (Amiri Baraka) against the largely white, mainstream jazz critical establishment—detracted attention from the musical sound and placed the emphasis on more racially and socially grounded interpretations of the music, often making it seem that what was at stake was more the issue of who was going to control the discourse, rather than the music itself.

In the end, however, the debates among writers, journalists, and scholars were in many ways peripheral to the cultural transformations this music was catalyzing; entire spiritual and political orientations were literally being generated out of Coltrane's new sound. The St. John Will-I-Am Coltrane African Orthodox Church (popularly known as "The Coltrane Church") was the manifestation of a vision that its founders Franzo and Marina King had of Coltrane as a saint, while the saxophonist was performing at San Francisco's Jazz Workshop. The date of the concert they attended, September 18, 1965, continues to be commemorated annually by the church as the "Sound Baptism," the epiphanal moment in which the founders dedicated themselves to founding the church.[133] Meanwhile, the activist Assata Shakur proclaimed that "[Coltrane] and his disciples open the metaphysical doors of sound and vibrations like musical shamans, [bringing] forth an approach to science and sound that was long lost to us . . . When I tell people we can save our people and redeem our god-mind with music they think I'm insane . . . !" Shakur concluded with the admonition, "Dig deeper into some of Coltrane's later work, for this is where he starts to dig deep[ly] into the spirit world."[134]

———

While Coltrane himself kept his own distance from these polemics, he was engaged in his own balancing act, trying to maintain the core of his original quartet even as he added new musicians and took the music deeper into New Thing territory. It wasn't the musicians in his band that he had grown distant from; rather, it was the way they had made music over the previous four years. In November 1965 the quartet, now augmented by both Sanders and Rashied Ali, returned to Van Gelder's studio in to record a revised version of the *Meditations* suite that refined many of the explorations of the West Coast tour, and which was released in September 1966 as *Meditations*.[135] Amidst the growing bewilderment and discontent of his audience, the revised *Meditations* is arguably one of the most conceptually coherent documents of what Coltrane was reaching for in his last two years, although it has rarely been discussed in these terms.

Compared to the material later released as *First Meditations*, the new *Meditations* presents a much more complex vision of ensemble structure; whereas the songs on the original version alternate between metered swing and free meter, every track of the later version juxtaposes Jones's swing feel with Ali's free meter, resulting in a much more complex composite. Jones's drums are more resonant and percussive in the mix, while Ali's provide more of a constant rolling texture. With this texture as a foundation, Coltrane works himself from sequences of melodic transposition into an emotional fire of multiphonic growling and screaming. Sanders's role is different. At several moments (especially on the opening track "The Father, the Son and the Holy Ghost"),[136] he plays counterlines under and against Coltrane's Ornette-ish transposition of diatonic motives, serving simultaneously rhythmic and textural roles. While the open-ended and woolly free-for-all feeling here is quite different from the controlled turbulence of the earlier version, the revised *Meditations* clearly reflects a deeper level of thinking about ensemble structure. Its most visionary quality is that it renders fluid, sonically and conceptually, the axes across which modern jazz was stretched into free jazz. Along the pitch/noise axis, it creates fluidity by juxtaposing pitch-based and even tonal playing with pure sound playing, while along the rhythm/time axis, it creates fluidity by juxtaposing metered time with free meter. At the conceptual center of this balancing act are Tyner and Garrison, who flesh out the implications of Ornette's system of free transposition to result in a fully chromaticized texture, and the two drummers, who in their juxtaposition complement each other at the point where the freest implications of Elvin's metered polyrhythms blend with Rashied's textured free meter. Coltrane was essentially using ensemble layering to juxtapose two distinct feels and, in doing so, to arrive at a complex composite that simultaneously implied freedom and structure, abandon and control. This might be heard as a far-reaching elaboration of the detachment of foreground and background structure proposed by Ornette Coleman in pieces like "Lonely Woman."

Conceptually, the structure of the revised *Meditations* can be compared to what the architect Peter Eisenman orchestrated in his Church of the Year 2000 project (figure 4.12):

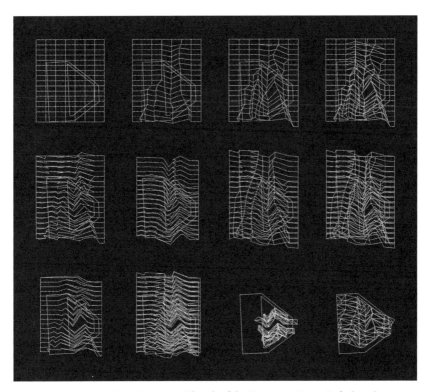

FIGURE 4.12 Peter Eisenman, Church of the Year 2000, Rome, Italy (1996).
Reproduced courtesy of Eisenman Architects.

The extraction of the figural was attempted by imposing an external diagram of a liquid crystal onto a diagram of program and site . . . The liquid crystal itself is a condition of between, a state of suspension between a static crystalline form and a flowing liquid state . . . The overlay of the two diagrams attempted to produce a form that would embody neither the first nor the second diagram. Instead, this overlay reproduces the gradual distortion of the original liquid crystal phase to a between state of flux. In the form of the church, the multiple layers of the overlays of the diagrams become deformations of the former solid/void, figure/ground relationship of the container . . . In this sense, the church is literally formed out of a ground of the molecular order of the liquid crystal.[137]

This peculiar form of poetry, common throughout Eisenman's writings, marbles technological and elemental imagery within digital-age architectural theory, and is in fact a fitting narration of a process whereby a dynamic, *com-*

posite form is derived from a process of juxtaposing stable (the building site) and unstable (the continuously morphing form of a liquid crystal) elements, transforming the structure of both original forms. Ultimately, however, such a collage strategy should be seen as a transitional step en route to a more stable and organic sensibility. And in fact, the end result of Eisenman's collage strategies (detailed in books like *Diagram Diaries*)[138] was the unique and identifiable design language of several of his best-known projects. As such, *Church* supplies a spatial/structural analogue for Coltrane's juxtaposition of two drummers (one metered, one playing in free meter) on *Meditations*.

Meditations was an important turning point in Coltrane's evolution as a composer; while he continued to play pieces from his old repertoire, he would remodel several of those older pieces to be played in free meter. But this particular configuration of Coltrane's band was not to last, due apparently to personality conflicts between Jones and Ali, the other members' ongoing dissatisfaction with the increasing lack of ensemble dynamics, and Coltrane's open-door policy on gigs, which they all felt was compromising both professionalism and musical quality. It must have been a bewildering time for Tyner and Jones, who increasingly found themselves inhabiting a radically reconceptualized version of the very sound they had helped create. The frustrations of the previous months finally boiled over with the departure of Jones in late 1965 and Tyner in early 1966, bringing the classic Coltrane quartet to its end. Jones's departing comments were tinged with a note of bitterness:

> I didn't want to leave Coltrane, but the personnel had changed. He added another drummer, and I couldn't hear what I was doing any longer. There was too much going on, and it was getting ridiculous as far as I was concerned . . . I think Coltrane was upset, and I know in those last weeks I had a constant migraine headache.[139]

Although Jimmy Garrison would continue to play intermittently with Coltrane, Ali was now alone in the drum chair, while Tyner was replaced by Alice Coltrane. The changing personnel also left the reception of *Meditations* (which was eventually released in September 1966) suspended in the critical limbo created by the months of growing confusion over Coltrane's work. Its significance would arguably be overshadowed by the release of *Ascension* in February 1966 and Coltrane's own comments carry a hint of disappointment. As he lamented to Frank Kofsky in 1966: "I was trying to do something . . . I figured I could do two things. I could have a band that played like the way we used to play, and a band that was going in the direction that the one I have now is going in—[I thought I] could combine these two, with these two concepts going . . . it could have been done."[140]

IX: FLOTATION

"Separate things," "forms," "objects," "shapes," etc., with beginnings
and endings are mere convenient fictions: there is only an uncertain
disintegrating order that transcends the limits of rational separations.[141]

Robert Smithson, 1968

Our architecture has no physical ground plan, but a psychic one.[142]

Coop Himmelblau, 1968

In *The Inflatable Moment*, Marc Dessauce chronicles the late-1960s period among experimental architects in Paris in which the bubble figured as a prominent design motif (figure 4.13). Inflatable furniture, rooms, and buildings were championed—most immediately, as solutions to the weightiness, permanence, costliness, and immobility of traditional architecture and, more broadly, to a post–World War II urban culture in which congestion, alienation, and environmental pollution resulted in a heavy cloud of mass disenchantment. Undoubtedly these innovations were also given context by the atmosphere surrounding the 1968 student protests in Paris (and elsewhere in the Western world), which had dramatic consequences for the emergent generation of architects.[143] In the United States, meanwhile, Buckminster Fuller was proposing projects like Cloud Nine—enclosed, airborne dwellings that would float in the sky because the air inside of them was warmer than the ambient temperature outside.[144]

In the natural world, bubbles float when the air inside of them is lighter than the air outside. In the case of Coltrane and his musicians, the "air" inside of their bubble was their ongoing experiments in free-meter levitation. The heavier external air, upon which their musical bubble floated toward a new bodily experience of freedom was, as in Europe, the incredibly pressurized environment of society in the 1960s. But whether in experimental architecture or free jazz, flotation was clearly a particularly desired and liberating sensation in the tense, turbulent environment of the 1960s. And one interpretation of Coltrane's music during this period is that although he was neither architect nor engineer, his eyes

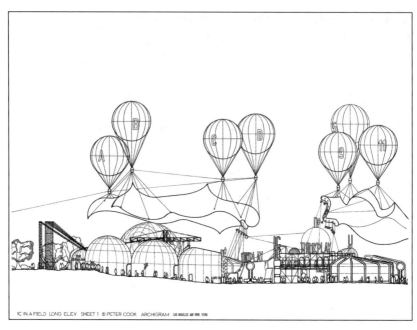

FIGURE 4.13 Peter Cook, *Instant City in a Field, Part Elevation of Typical Set-Up* (1969). Reproduced courtesy of Archigram Archives.

were focused on the heavens, and he was thus, in his free-meter music, proposing his own model of flotation.

But Coltrane's new music was not only a music of flotation; it was equally one of excoriation. Having exhausted the mechanics and mathematics of bebop and modal jazz, and with his psychedelic indulgences having gradually eroded his jazz-based insistence on decorum and respectability at all costs, he and his musicians now began to plumb the emotional legacy of the last 400 years of black history. Perhaps this is one reason that Coltrane leaned strongly toward live recording during 1966; the performance ritual was a potent site for the urgent form of testimony that his music had evolved into. Virtually all of the 1966 recordings issued under his name were live performances, and these recordings lie at the heart of the divided and contentious reception of his later work.[145] The most controversial works in his oeuvre, they are also generally thought of as among the most inscrutable jazz recordings of the 1960s. These would include commercially issued recordings sourced from performances at the Village Vanguard in New York City (May 1966), Tokyo, Japan (July 1966), Philadelphia (November

1966), and New York City (April 1967), and unofficial recordings sourced from performances in Newport, Rhode Island, and Kobe, Japan (both July 1966).[146] All of these recordings articulate the tension between the two priorities implied in Coltrane's new music—the celestial, spiritual priority of achieving flotation/levitation and the earthbound, political priority of slash-and-burn testimony—which shaped his music for the rest of his career. In music-analytical terms, what his 1966 music forces us to consider is form understood not in abstract terms but form as a by-product of ritual and its states of altered consciousness. And from the perspective of its recorded representation, whether Coltrane's ritual felt like flotation or excoriation depended not only on the configuration of the ensemble and the way the music was played but also on the physical space in which it was played and the way it was recorded.

———

The two best-known recordings released during this period are *Ascension* and *Live at the Village Vanguard Again*. And while one is a studio recording and the other a concert recording, both present relatively "dry" or "flat" soundscapes that lack a substantial amount of room sound or synthetic reverberation and that consequently do not necessarily articulate the spatial dimensions of the music being played. This in itself is not surprising, since *Ascension* was recorded and mixed in a way that was consistent with other recordings on the Impulse label at that time, while the live recording was made in the small and (relatively) acoustically dry basement space of the Village Vanguard. Nonetheless, the way that recordings of free jazz were produced in the early years of its development had important consequences for how transparent its structures sounded to listeners.

Artificial reverberation is typically used for two purposes in recordings: to provide depth and fullness to the sound, or to simulate traditional spatial environments such as cathedrals or concert halls. But reverberation, whether natural or synthetic, can also provide an acoustic depth that helps clarify complex or unconventional musical structures by dramatizing the way musical parts are moving in relation to each other in sonic space. For example, Ornette Coleman's status as an innovator rests primarily on his early recordings for the Atlantic label. But these (relatively) acoustically dry recordings produced according to the aesthetics of late-1950s rhythm and blues are arguably less successful at representing the intricacies of his "harmolodic" system than later recordings such as *Ornette at Town Hall* (1965)[147] with its luxuriant room sound, or even recordings with his electric Prime Time band such as *In All Languages* (1985),[148] which bathe the music in a degree of synthetic reverberation that give Coleman's structural ideas greater spatial definition. And this is why Coleman's status as an innovator rests primarily on his system of pitch manipulations (i.e., "harmolodics") as opposed to his structural innovations (e.g., as heard on compositions like "Lonely Woman," "What Reason Could I Give," "Broken Shadows," "Sound Museum," and similar compositions).

———

The new John Coltrane quintet had not even existed for a full year when the Tokyo and Philadelphia concerts were recorded, but there are moments of these performances when Coltrane's new musical concept begins to come into focus. In Tokyo, for example, the concert opens with the band floating the rhapsodic strains of "Peace on Earth" over a wave of rapturous audience applause while Coltrane (especially in his second solo) methodically stretches the melody into a dense and dizzying cloud of chromatic invention. His opening solo on "Naima" from Philadelphia is similarly executed. Like the solo piano performances of Art Tatum (but more radical in conception), these solos are built from a provocative juxtaposition of a rigor that vigilantly references the form's structural integrity, and a radical improvisational freedom that warps the form in and out of regularity.[149] In practical terms this meant that, while Coltrane's solo does in fact conform to the chord changes of "Naima," the length of time that each chord is played is highly flexible, and this in turn opens a space for extremely dense chromatic ornamentation. The most expansive moments of the documented 1966 concerts, in fact, are ballad performances such as these, probably because the (implied) slower tempi of those pieces afford the players greater rhythmic flexibility to expand and contract the time, form, and harmony. Coltrane's solos in Tokyo and Philadelphia derive their dynamic tension from the pliability with which he moves back and forth between contrasting states: languid diatonic playing versus tight chromaticism, or the rhythmic looseness of rubato juxtaposed with the obsessive linearity of his harmonic logic. This dynamic of loosening and tightening gives the music its qualities of flotation, an effect buttressed by the manner of recording that seems to combine direct signals with the expansive room sound of the respective Tokyo and Philadelphia auditoriums. Taken together, these strategies really do convey the sense that Coltrane's expansion of his earlier ballads is an attempt to reconfigure the heavens.

Besides Coltrane's playing, his wife Alice was also a powerful—if occasionally understated—presence in this new music. Early on, the couple bonded over, among other musical interests, their shared passion for the harp, with the saxophonist not only buying a harp for their new home but also encouraging Alice to play the piano in harp-like fashion in her performances with the band. After her husband's passing, the harp would continue to be an iconic feature of her music; despite her prodigious talents as a multi-instrumentalist, for example, photographs of her playing the harp seem to outnumber those of her playing keyboard instruments. The instrument was a powerful symbol of the musical mission she shared with John, and the celestial sensibility with which both sought to infuse their music. Alice told Dolores Brandon in 1987: "He ordered that harp—a beautiful concert grand golden crown. It took us a year to get it because they are practically handmade . . . He was really responsible for that being part of my life. I still have that harp today."[150]

Alice Coltrane was not the first musician to play jazz on the harp—a distinction that belongs to Dorothy Ashby—but, like the harp's influence on her husband's "sheets of sound" approach to the saxophone, she was unique in the way she transplanted the instrument's cascading sequences of notes to the keyboard instruments. In fact, it was the sensibility of the harp, transposed to the piano, that enabled her to adopt McCoy Tyner's style of tightly syncopated punctuations into the more elastic spaces of the new quintet's free-meter playing. Rippling and cascading across the metrically free soundscape while maintaining the conversational interaction central to small-band jazz, the rhythmic web she created was a crucial component of the new experiences of rhythmic gravity that the band was working together to articulate.

Their elastic, expansive sense of musical time was especially evident when they played as a quartet. Jack Bernstein reviewed Coltrane's Boston concert at the Massachusetts Institute of Technology in October 1966, and his nuanced description of its atmospheric and dynamic variety differs markedly from most of the reviews of the saxophonist's music—live *or* recorded—from this period:

John Coltrane treated a near capacity crowd at Kresge Auditorium Friday night to an extraordinary example of what contemporary music (The New Jazz) should sound like . . . Coltrane, his wife Alice on piano, James Garrison, bass, and Rashied Ali on drums literally shook the audience with a music that was as peaceful and quiet as a Debussy Prelude and as frenetic and exciting as the climax of a Ravi Shankar raga . . . To my knowledge, this was the first time since

Newport of 1965 that Trane has performed with a quartet, or to put it another way, as the only horn; this gave us an unusual opportunity to appreciate how far Coltrane has developed.[151]

———

But this music sounded earthbound realities as often as it did celestial longings. "Alabama," recorded by the original Coltrane quartet in 1963, had been Coltrane's first overtly political reference, a eulogy composed in memory of the child victims of the 16th Street Baptist Church bombing in Birmingham on September 15 of that year. And although very few of his subsequent song titles referenced political themes in any overt way, the music of the last four years of his career was nevertheless given unavoidable context by the dramatic racial and political events of the time.

With the exception of his comments praising a speech of Malcolm X that he attended, Coltrane generally refrained from public commentary on political issues.[152] Nonetheless, it was against this backdrop of the era's dramatic events that *Ascension* exploded onto the jazz world in February 1966. Suddenly, everyone—not just those who attended his live performances—was aware of how dramatically Coltrane's music had changed. And as with the big-picture political events, the album's impact was such that listeners were forced to take positions on the music. Writing in *Music Journal*, the jazz journalist Stanley Dance lamented that "*Ascension* mark[ed] [Coltrane's] descent to the screaming regions of 'The New Thing,'"[153] while the British journalist Ronald Atkins derided the album as

> a cacophonous barrage. The soloists blaze indiscriminately [with] only John Tchicai showing the intelligence to use the background of grunts and squawks to offset his own lines. Coltrane's rhythm section is all wrong for this type of music and, if the LP is not without its moments, the central idea must be judged a failure.[154]

Bill Mathieu, on the other hand, felt the album's resonance with its political moment:

> This revolution, this black one, has a vested interest in "now" as opposed to "then." The forces that spawned it are wasting no love on old things. The old order was "then." It passeth to "now." No one alive today can remember a more

concerted cry for a new social being. *Ascension* (among other things) is at the center of this cry.[155]

Several reviewers found a degree of clarification in Archie Shepp's more conceptual comments in the album's liner notes: "The idea is similar to what the action painters do, in that it creates various surfaces of color that push into each other, creating tensions and counter-tensions and various fields of energy."[156] The difference was whether or not these auditors heard the surfaces as supportive or precarious, the color contrasts as blended or bracing, and the tensions as resolved or unresolved.

Since its recording in the summer of 1965, the ritualized feel of *Ascension* had provided the template for Coltrane's live appearances, a connection strengthened by the addition of Pharoah Sanders to the working group in the fall of that year. Coltrane's live performances had always been marked by a very high level of emotional intensity, but Sanders's style of playing raised the emotional stakes substantially and gave the band's performances their often excoriating quality. The saxophonist clearly inspired Coltrane's own continued exploration of the instrument, with Coltrane following Sanders deeply into the territory of extended techniques. Recordings made during 1966–67 find the two saxophonists spurring each other on to greater and greater heights of frenzied improvisation. Their most frequent vehicle for this type of playing was "Leo," which features on several recordings from this period. With a harsh, incantatory theme reminiscent of the peal of several prayer bells, it is conceptually similar to "Sun Ship," and an argument might be made that "Leo" was to this band what a tune like "Impressions" was to Coltrane's original quartet—their flagship up-tempo (in a manner of speaking) piece, a "burnout" tune that allowed them to stretch out, flex their collective muscles, and journey deep into the improvisational zone. And although "Leo," unlike "Impressions," is not a metered composition, its percussive, pointillist melody and high level of ensemble density articulate a fast free-meter space. "Leo" was recorded in the studio by Coltrane and Rashied Ali in February 1967, part of the series of duets that were later released as *Interstellar Space*. But the only surviving recordings of the piece being performed by the full quintet are live recordings (and fragmentary footage) from Newport, Tokyo, and Kobe (all July 1966), and Philadelphia (November 1966). And despite the varying sonic character of these official and unofficial recordings, they collectively articulate the different priorities embedded in "Leo."

Like the French and Belgian festival concerts of the previous summer, the main stage of Newport faced an open-air seating area for the audience. But the surviving recording is apparently a direct "line" recording that captures little of the acoustic quality of the performance venue. The result is a dry, one-dimensional quality to the sound, with the saxophonists' lines existing more like markings on a chalkboard than lines in three-dimensional space. Surviving footage of "Leo" from the Newport festival in July shows Coltrane and Sanders digging deep physically, rocking back and forth and gesticulating wildly, sometimes sinking almost to their knees to summon the sounds they desired.[157] But in general, Coltrane was too mathematical an improviser to give himself over completely to the emotional side of music. When Alice Coltrane introduced her own rendition of "Leo" in 1978 (the introduction is actually titled "Krishnaya"), she implied that the tune had a particular conceptual significance for John. Over the hushed, solemn tones of her organ, she tells the audience of a chart the saxophonist devised for "Leo" that was "about the basic energy of people who have [the astrological sign] Leo . . . and he saw a vibration which was energy."[158] The form and whereabouts of this color chart are currently unknown (it doesn't seem to be the well-known "tone circle" image reproduced in Yusef Lateef's *Repository of Scales and Melodic Patterns*) but the piece clearly resonated deeply for Alice because the trio (including bassist Reggie Workman and drummer Roy Haynes) suddenly explode into their own blistering version of "Leo." As a fire sign, the qualities most typically associated with the sign of Leo include passion, expression, creativity, and courage, and the trio's performance is the very definition of a "burnout" piece, with the keyboardist using the ribbon controller of her Wurlitzer electric organ to blend the microtones of Indian classical music with passionate cries and the aggressive, highly chromatic type of improvisation pioneered by her husband.

In Kobe, Japan, the band's performance, the acoustics of the venue, and the various anomalies of the surviving audience recording combine to create a very different but compelling picture of "Leo." The incantatory theme is now played by the two tenor saxophonists in an interwoven, antiphonal manner, but factors resulting from the low-quality recording device—variations in tape speed ("warble"), a severely truncated frequency range, the distance of the recorder from the stage, and the recorder's distorted representation of the acoustics of the performance space—all combine to give the saxophones the droning sonority of foghorns. Meanwhile, the decayed recording signal (a result of generations of duplication) and resultant tape hiss create the impression of aural distance, as if the saxophonists are guiding the listener through levels of consciousness, an effect intensified by variations in tape speed that create a de facto microtonal effect that can almost be heard as a mechanical variation on the "side slip" effect. In fact, the sound of the room, distorted through the tight compression of the aural space of the recording, makes the horns sound like two Tibetan *dung-chen* musicians playing a call to meditation which, all things considered, was probably close to the psycho-emotional effect that Coltrane and Sanders were going for in the first place. In Coltrane's case, however, this peculiar interweaving of distorted industrial aesthetics with the Asianist technologies of mantra and drone were subject to the emotional prism of the African American experience, as witnessed around the same time by a confounded Ravi Shankar—one of the musicians most responsible for turning Coltrane's ears and heart eastward:

> I was much disturbed by his music. Here was a creative person who had become a vegetarian, who was studying yoga and reading the Bhagavad-Gita, yet in whose music I still heard so much turmoil. I could not understand it.[159]

Music like this had a strongly visceral effect on the normally reserved Japanese audience. If the audience in Tokyo greeted the band's opening number "Peace on Earth" with the type of respectful, reverent applause that Japanese concert audiences typically confer on visiting jazz musicians, forty-five minutes of the incantatory "Leo" whipped them into a near riotous frenzy that can be clearly heard in the applause at the piece's conclusion.

The Japanese tour of July 1966 looms large as one of the high points—some would say *the* high point—of John Coltrane's career as a bandleader.[160] From the moment the band stepped off of the plane in Tokyo, where they were greeted by cheering crowds, a red carpet, and life-size, cardboard cutout photographs of each band member, they were embraced by the Japanese jazz audience in the most reverential manner. Besides playing lengthy concerts at every stop on the tour, they sat for extensive interviews with fans, journalists, and even student activists who questioned them about the state of jazz, Black Power politics, the nuclear arms race, and other topics. They sat in with local musicians, and were offered sponsorships by local instrument manufacturers. And although Coltrane was by all accounts a humble man, he and the other band members were deeply moved by their reception which, unlike in the US, was commensurate with their paradigm-shifting achievements. But as much as this tour has been glorified as a peak moment for Coltrane, it was also a turning point. Rashied Ali took a number of photos of Coltrane during the trip, several of which show the saxophonist clutching his stomach area in apparent discomfort. It would be several months before Coltrane understood the source of the pain he was experiencing. In the meantime, he would continue to immerse himself in denser and more complex sound worlds.

X: OTHER REALMS OF FOUR

> He always played off the drums. He told me the drums freed him, he didn't
> have to worry about chord changes. He got the freedom to play what he
> wanted from working directly off the drums.[161]
>
> *Rashied Ali*

What arguably united the quintet's dual priorities of flotation and excoriation was the flow of Rashied Ali's drumming. With Ali now manning the drum set alone, the time was no longer stretched back and forth between his free meter and Jones's metered swing (as on *Meditations*), and the music moved definitively into free-meter territory as 1966 unfolded. Along with Coltrane's harmonic loosening and tightening and Alice Coltrane's harp-like sensibility, Ali's approach to free-meter drumming helped give the music its feeling of levity, while also stoking the group's ceremonial fire when it was time to burn.

Ali's early inspirations were Max Roach, Art Blakey, and Philly Joe Jones, while he credited his fellow Philadelphia native Sunny Murray as the chief catalyst for the freer style of drumming that developed in the 1960s. He remembered to drummer Bob Moses that: "At that time it was Sunny Murray, of course . . . it was beautiful because Sunny really moved us in a whole other direction."[162] But while Ali was one of the chief architects of the new style, he maintained throughout his career that his drumming was fundamentally meter-based, even claiming on one occasion that his style was actually conceptualized "in 4/4, but the other realms of 4/4 that we don't usually hear."[163] He also explained the thinking behind his playing in more detail to Moses:

> I wanted to play anything except "ding-ding-da-ding . . . " I had to find something else to play. The music called for that. The music was moving on . . . I heard stuff that Philly Joe Jones would play where he would extend the phrase. He would do it for just a short time. But I was thinking, "What if he could keep extending it and keep it out there like that, but keep in mind where everything else is [and] keep stretching it out . . . ? So I started practicing hard, playing with everybody, trying to get this kind of a sound together."

The group's full-on embrace of free-meter playing was difficult for many listeners, including some of Coltrane's most devoted followers, for whom the feeling of "swing" was as sacred as scripture. But Ali and other emerging drummers such as Milford Graves, Andrew Cyrille, and Sunny Murray had different ideas, and with Murray as the central figure, all four were at the forefront of these new articulations of time. Many credit Murray as being the first to transmute the intensity of up-tempo swing by abstracting its system of syncopations beyond the constraints of bar lines, varying the tempo and dynamics in a way that ultimately forced "tempo" to be experienced as a matter of density as much as of regularity. The rhythmic field he orchestrated with artists such as Albert Ayler and Cecil Taylor could be heard in several ways. From the standpoint of the cymbals, it could be likened to the movement of a spinning wheel that wobbles from side to side while never toppling over. From the standpoint of the drums, he often played sequences of pulsating rhythms that almost recall the constant pulses of some Native American drumming traditions, while his manner of advancing to and retreating from the forefront of the soundscape almost mimics an echo effect. The bassist Alan Silva (who worked alongside Murray with Ayler, Taylor, and Ornette Coleman) offered insightful comments about Murray's innovations, conceptualizing his playing in terms of velocity and "drone": Silva heard Murray's drumming as "[A] whole new approach . . . Acceleration and deceleration of time. Sunny's vibrating cymbal idea eliminated beats and the bass [drum] became a drone, a hum. It was the end of swing as we know it—it became so fast it became *slow*: Sunny Murray is the first drummer who ever played the Theory of Relativity."[164] Jack DeJohnette (who would sit in with Coltrane in Chicago in 1966 and would help bring free-meter playing into Miles Davis's "Lost Quintet" two years later), on the other hand, cites other drummers.

> The guys who really did that clearly were Rashied, Andrew Cyrille, Milford Graves and even Paul Motian. You hear Rashied do that really clearly with Coltrane, his "multi-directional" rhythm—it's kind of a motion. And Andrew could also do that. Paul Motian who was another guy who doesn't get mentioned as much but Paul was just great *period*—he was a great colorist and drummer. That's a very difficult way to play, especially what Rashied was doing. Energetically and stamina-wise, it takes a lot because there are a lot of subtleties to it.[165]

In contrast to Sunny Murray's spooky, shamanistic pulsations, Rashied Ali took a different approach, sculpting a rhythmscape with less dynamic variation but more internal complexity and close attention to melodic aspects of drumming. His playing gave the impression of different meters, tempi, and melodies simultaneously stacked, deconstructed and extended—hence Coltrane's oft-repeated description of Ali's style as "multidirectional." Ali could conform to the rhythmic contours of melodic themes in the "phrase length" manner of Ornette Coleman's drummers, could play combatively in a way that gave Coltrane an adversary to play against in the manner of Cecil Taylor's drummers, or, most often, could provide a continuous textural commentary in the manner of Sunny Murray. In synthesizing these approaches in order to extend the ideas of the two most important drummers that Coltrane had played with (Philly Joe Jones and Elvin Jones), Ali seemed the ideal drummer for Coltrane at this point. His drumming was in many ways a perfect complement to the saxophonist, whose playing at this point was similarly "multidirectional," ranging freely across a soundscape of stacked and implied scales, keys, tonal centers, and chords. If the Coltrane/Jones duets of 1965 contained passages that beckoned beyond the rhythmic language of metered swing, these duets take the most rhythmically provocative moments of those performances as a point of departure. As Ali himself explained to Bob Moses in 2003: "Elvin Jones and Trane blew my mind because they started [playing] in a way where it was elastic . . . And when I heard that, I was thinking, 'I wonder how far you could stretch that out?'"[166]

When all of these directions are considered, what becomes most striking is the fact that—with fast becoming slow and slow becoming fast—Ali's free meter essentially reconceptualized jazz rhythm, transforming the drum set into an ambient drone that unified the variously implied meters and tempi within a continuum of sound. We can hear in these streams of metrically untethered pulses the sensation that some musicians characterize as "pulse without time." What is particularly provocative in Silva's comments is the conceptual transformation of the drone concept from something passive and nontemporal (as it exists in the Indian classical traditions, for example), into something that incorporates dynamic and temporal components. In many of Coltrane's later recordings, then, the drum set replaces the tamboura as the provider of a drone, and Leonard Feather's image of Coltrane "rotating unpredictably on a base reminiscent of the Indian sitar players" evokes the structural reality that, with the role of the drum set transformed, the saxophonist was now playing over a *constellation* of juxtaposed and competing drones.[167]

As a wind player who was directing his music from the top, did Coltrane necessarily have conceptual clarity regarding the workings of the rhythm section? It's unclear how clear (or interested) he was at conceptualizing and articulating exactly what he wanted his drummers to do in this new music. In fact, he expressed doubts about this on several occasions throughout his career, such as when he confided to Don De Micheal that, "I want to be more flexible where rhythm is concerned. I feel I have to study rhythm some more. I haven't experimented too much with time; most of my experimenting has been in a harmonic form. I put time and rhythm to one side, in the past."[168] And as the spring/summer of 1965 made clear, Coltrane only moved into free-meter playing after he had completely exhausted the possibilities of metered swing. Nonetheless, as Rashied Ali remembered, Coltrane "was in a drummer thing" during this period, and many of the group's performances from 1966 on featured additional percussionists.[169] Taking Ali at his word, it might make sense to look more closely at the drums to get clues about what Coltrane was hearing during this period when he had moved so far away from conventional jazz concepts of rhythm and drumming.

———

The additional percussionists Coltrane most frequently employed during 1966–67 were players of the *bata*, a trio of double-headed drums historically associated with the Yoruba people of Nigeria and Benin Republic, where they were typically used in the liturgy for *Ṣango*, the *orisha* (divinity) of thunder. This tradition had survived the cultural disruptions of the trans-Atlantic slave trade to flourish in Cuba, where it provided the liturgy for a tradition variously referred to as *Santeria* or *Lucumi*, a syncretic fusion of the Yoruba religion and Catholicism. The bata ensemble's subsequent conduits to the United States were multiple; they came with the Cuban *bataleros* who emigrated to the US just before and after the Cuban Revolution, and who played congas and bongos in secular dance bands and bata in religious settings. They came via African Americans who traveled to Nigeria in the 1960s to investigate ancestral roots, and they also came, at least indirectly, via Nigerian drummers and percussionists who emigrated to the US in the 1950s and 1960s, such as Babatunde Olatunji and Solomon Ilori (neither Olatunji or Ilori were bata drummers, but their presence contributed to a general awareness of Yoruba cultural practices in the US). What we might think of as the "drum circle" around Coltrane reflected all of these currents. Elvin Jones, for example, had emerged as a jazz drummer during the mambo era, and developed his uniquely polyrhythmic approach to the drum set in partial dialogue with Afro-Cuban drummers such as Candido Camero, and the abstracted Cuban bell pattern he plays on "Acknowledgement" contributed to the Africanist feel of *A*

Love Supreme. The bata drummers such as Algie DeWitt were African Americans (referred to Coltrane by Ali) who were coming from the cultural-nationalist angle. Meanwhile, Coltrane had befriended Olatunji, and the two would talk intermittently about collaborating and traveling to Nigeria.[170]

Similar to Coltrane's grafting of freely chromatic playing over drones conceived in the Indian classical context as accompaniment for highly regimented ragas, his integration of these drums was a radical redeployment of his West African source materials. Referencing this book's consistent use of the "Africanist Grid" idea, West African and Afro-Cuban drums such as the bata were typically played in complex, strictly metered structures hocketed into polyrhythmic grids of tightly interwoven, cyclically repeating parts. Free meter was almost never employed, except in introductory or concluding flourishes or, sometimes, during passages when musical instruments functioned as linguistic surrogates in "speech" mode.[171] But Coltrane was integrating these drummers and their music into a resolutely free-meter environment, and the examples of him playing over African drumming accompaniment certainly do not find him reining in his composing or improvising to conform to any metric structure.[172] What was he reaching for, in terms of a rhythm-section concept? Was he employing additional percussionists in order to extend the drum set's polyrhythmic thunder? Or was he simply seeking to immerse himself in as much raw percussive sound as possible? The issue is not clarified by any of the currently extant recordings, most of which either privilege Ali's drum set in the mix at the expense of the percussionists, or are so poorly recorded that they render the entire percussion section as a distorted, indistinct mass.

It is most logical to assume that, with his addition of percussionists, Coltrane was envisioning a more complex articulation of the same meter/free-meter juxtaposition that was at the core of the revised *Meditations* suite. And the fact that he was seeking to immerse himself within such a constellation of spectacularly conflicting metric fields strongly suggests that his music during this period was fundamentally oriented toward stimulating states of altered consciousness—states of possession, trance, and ecstasy of an intensity beyond that typically stimulated by jazz music. This is where we might return, structurally and philosophically, to the bata drums and their symbolic association with not only thunder, but also with spirit possession. In their traditional African and Afro-Caribbean contexts, the bata are used to create an environment in which devotees are possessed by orishas, divine spirits who embody archetypal energies of the spiritual and natural worlds (and which in some cases are also apotheosized representations of figures from Yoruba history).[173] The sonic technology that facilitates these possessions is what I referred to above as the "polyrhythmic grid of tightly interwoven, cyclically repeating parts," elaborated through a system of increasingly staggered, clashing phrasing that induces possession by throwing the listener's nervous system into a momentary state of disorientation. But with American culture as a whole already reasonably entrained into the complexities of African-derived rhythm via its historical sublimation into African American music and the more recent influence of Cuban dance music, it arguably follows that a music of more complex rhythmic construction would be necessary to facilitate the states of altered consciousness that Coltrane sought. Hence the necessity for more complex, "multidirectional" rhythms. Although they might not be explicitly aligned with a particular religious or spiritual tradition, Coltrane's 1966 recordings and performances navigate the most psycho-emotionally charged regions of Afro-diasporic traditions of spiritual possession, their alchemical agent a system of fractured and radically reconstructed Africanist rhythmic grids.

Of course, the states of altered consciousness that these drums catalyze mean different things to people in different cultures. In the Yoruba culture, whether in West Africa or the Caribbean, spirit possession is first and foremost an occasion for a devotee to be "mounted" by an orisha who then offers advice, admonitions, and prognostications to the assembled. In the African American Baptist or Pentecostal traditions, the same psycho-emotional space of possession is stimulated not by drums, but by pianos, organs, and other instruments of the Western tradition, and expressed through the religious vision of Christianity. Given that Coltrane was a very religious man making his art in a period when an African cultural consciousness had been reawakened in African American culture, the entire Black Atlantic continuum of religious practice was present in his music. But it was also taking place in a moment when centuries of repressed black beauty, rage, and genius were being explosively expressed. In the end, then, the complex of free-meter juxtapositions made perfect sense because Coltrane, who had always been a very verbal player, was himself now operating entirely in speech mode. The music had evolved into a form of testimony giving voice to 400 years of traumatic black history while helping to forge the psychic conditions for a different kind of levitation—the broader social, cultural, and political transformations of the 1960s. It is no wonder, as Alice Coltrane related in a 1984 interview, that people were essentially becoming possessed, cleansed, and transformed at Coltrane's later concerts:

I've seen listeners do all kinds of things. Sometimes, as soon as the music started, someone in the audience would stand up, their arms upreaching, and they would be like that for an hour or more. Their clothing would be soaked with perspiration, and when they finally sat down, they practically fell down. The music just took people out of the whole material world; it lifted them up.[174]

XI: CURVED SPACE

Our ship was funneled directly through the center of the sun—
and *out* the other side . . . But the instruments recorded our path.
We had gone straight through the nova.[175]

Samuel Delany

He carried me away in the spirit to a great and high mountain,
and showed me that great city, the Holy Jerusalem,
descending out of heaven from God.

The Holy Bible, *Revelation 21:10*

If Rashied Ali had introduced the concept of "multidirectional" rhythm into Coltrane's music, his concept is also a fitting thematic lens through which to view Coltrane's reality at the beginning of 1967. The previous year had arguably been his most contentious ever as a bandleader. Hailed as the avatar of a revolutionary new music and received abroad in a manner reserved for the world's greatest artists, he was simultaneously having his appearances at home terminated by club owners and audiences who found his new music intolerable.[176] On the other hand, a close listening to the studio recordings he made during February and March (eventually released as *Stellar Regions*, *Interstellar Space*, and *Expression*) reveals refinements in his music that give lie to the Coltrane-went-into-free-jazz-and-lost-all-perspective narrative. In the big picture, however, his overall level of activity was rapidly decreasing; he was accepting fewer gigs and increasingly avoiding the public eye as the symptoms of what would eventually be diagnosed as liver cancer sapped his strength and vitality. Between January and July, he is documented as having performed only three concerts, and he was only in the studio for four recording sessions.[177] And although it is a bit too convenient to make such interpretations in retrospect, the elegiac tone of many of these final pieces has often been taken as a sign that Coltrane was already contemplating his mortality.[178]

The decrease in activity does not imply a decrease in musical development; Coltrane's recordings of early 1967 arguably comprise a period of consolidation that resolved the transformative growth spurt of spring 1965. If the live recordings of 1966 can essentially be heard as ritual documents, the 1967 studio sessions were much more transparent presentations of Coltrane's design thinking at the time. Taken as a whole, they suggest emotional focus, conceptual clarity, and a sense of calm after the proverbial storm of the previous year. Essentially, it was on these recordings that the saxophonist's time spent staring at the stars seemed to pay its most obvious dividends: definitively liberated from the constraints of meter and the restrictive harmonic cycles of bebop, his final music might be heard as not only an act of devotion or testimony, but also as a spiritually charged inquiry into the nature of space.

Part of this is likely attributable to the fact that the ensemble has been scaled down to the core quartet for these sessions. There are no additional drummers or percussionists present and, for the most part, Pharoah Sanders does not participate on these sessions despite the fact that he remained a regular member of Coltrane's working group (the one piece that includes Sanders features him on flute).[179] This is not to cast Sanders's playing in a negative light but only to suggest (as Jack Bernstein did in his review of the 1966 MIT concert) that Coltrane's groups played differently as quartets. After he joined the band in late 1965, Sanders seemed to serve two roles. He inspired Coltrane's investigation of the extended techniques that the former had previously explored alongside John Gilmore, Eric Dolphy, and Albert Ayler. In terms of the live ritual, on the other hand, the extra intensity that Sanders added helped set the band on fire, allowing them to attain states of trance and possession while burning away musical structures that had outlived their usefulness. Coltrane himself also admitted to Frank Kofsky in 1966 that he sometimes relied on Sanders's energy in the group's live performances: "I like to have somebody there in case I just don't, can't get that strength. I like to have that strength in the band, you know, from someone. And Pharoah is very strong in spirit."[180] In the studio sessions of 1967, by contrast, it seemed that Coltrane was most interested in refining the raw energy of the band's live performances into new types of formal structures. Hence the necessity of turning down the proverbial "heat" a bit in order to distill salient aspects of form, structure, and atmosphere, a process that may have been aided by scaling down the ensemble. And herein lies the main difference between the ritual documents of 1966 and the monastic meditations of 1967.

These studio recordings provide the clearest analytical insights into the new musical language birthed in the cauldron of the previous year. *Stellar Regions* comprises eight pieces (including three alternate takes) recorded on February 15 and considered lost for several decades until they were rediscovered by Alice Coltrane in 1994, and commercially released the following year. The album's reception benefitted from almost three decades of retrospective thinking about Coltrane's music and it is unfortunate that they couldn't have been heard at the time they were recorded, as they would have gone a long way toward clarifying many of the misunderstandings surrounding Coltrane's later music.

With moods alternating between the meditative, the shamanic, and the elegiac, *Stellar Regions* can be compared to *Crescent* in its overall musical and thematic unity, while the titles continue the post-*Ascension* trend of referencing cosmological themes—as does Chuck Stewart's cover photo, which depicts Coltrane in devotional pose with horn in hand and eyes lifted upward toward the heavens. But if the saxophonist's eyes seem focused on the heavens, his head is not lost in the clouds here. For someone whose recent compositions seemed so strongly defined by marathons of improvisation, he devotes considerable attention to formal design on this session, moving between quartet, trio, and duet settings with a collection of relatively short, finely wrought themes. Almost all of them unfold in metrically free space while, in terms of pitch materials, they are constructed from a variety of elements including floating modal ballads ("Seraphic Light"), simple, folkish melodics ("Stellar Regions," "Jimmy's Mode"), and gestural fragments or abstract formulae ("Sun Star," "Configuration," and "Tranesonic," the last of which Coltrane plays on alto saxophone).[181]

The clarity of the studio setting does particular justice to the internal structure of this music, replacing the clutter, distortion, and/or dynamic flatness of the live recordings with a more revealing portrait of the new group's inner workings. Besides highlighting Alice Coltrane's strengths as a soloist and accompanist, they also reveal the subtleties of Rashied Ali's touch, the textural variations he was able to coax out of the drum set, and how central his "multidirectional" rhythms were to the flowing contours of this music. It also renders more transparent the crucial role of Jimmy Garrison, whose improvised countermelodies provide structural counterpoint between Ali and Alice Coltrane, crucial to the horizontal flow of the music.

C. O. Simpkins's biography of Coltrane reproduces a chart (which had evidently been in the possession of Rashied Ali) of synchronized saxophone-drum patterns written out by Coltrane.[182] This chart notates the following sequence:

1-2	1-2	1-2	1-2-3
1-2	1-2	1-2	1-2-3
1-2	1-2	1-2	1-2-3
1-2	1-2	1-2	1-2-3
1-2-3-4	1-2-3-4-5-6-7		1-2-3-4-5
			(last group played 3x)
1-2-3-4	1-2-3	1-2	1
1-2-3-4	1-2	1-2-3-4	

With a couple of minor discrepancies (such as repetitions within the form, two opening figures that are apparently missing from the chart, and two closing figures that are also missing), this sequence conforms exactly to the thematic sections of "Tranesonic," with the track timings as follows:

THEME 1 (0:00–0:02, MISSING FROM CHART) (PLAYED 2X)

1-2-3-4	1-2

REPETITION OF THEME 1 (0:14–0:17, MISSING FROM CHART) (PLAYED 2X)

1-2-3-4	1-2

THEME 2 (2:06–2:23) (PLAYED 2X)

1-2	1-2	1-2	1-2-3
1-2	1-2	1-2	1-2-3
1-2	1-2	1-2	1-2-3
1-2-3	1-2-3	1-2-3	

THEME 3 (3:57–4:17) (PLAYED 2X)

1-2-3-4	1-2-3-4-5-6-7	
1-2-3-4-5	1-2-3-4-5	1-2-3-4-5
1-2-3-4	1-2-3-4-5-6-7	
1-2-3-4-5	1-2-3-4-5	1-2-3-4-5
1-2-3-4	1-2-3	
	(missing from chart)	
1	1	
	(missing from chart)	

Playing alto saxophone and blowing the sequence in rhythmic synchrony with Ali, it's telling that, at this point, Coltrane seems less interested in precise pitch formula than in the overall rhythmic motive; the pitches are generally consistent but it's clear that he is more interested in gesture and melodic shape than in actual "melody" as such (although the switch to alto sax might have presented embouchure-adjustment issues that compromised his articulation at some points). Nor was this the first time that Coltrane used an alternate system of notation for his music, according to Elvin Jones, who, with a background in symphonic percussion, was a proficient reader of music:

> I never saw a sheet of music the whole time I was in that group. I think John had a notebook in which he used a system of dots—it looked like an address book. I'd see him with it sometimes and get a glimpse of it every now and then, and it was just full of dots, like braille. I guess that was his music notation code.[183]

The mode of composing Coltrane uses on "Tranesonic" is sonically and conceptually reminiscent of pieces like "Sun Ship" and "Leo," and presents a particular way of organizing free-meter time, in this case, as a progression of finite, asymmetrical phrases. In fact, pieces like this are a defining feature of Coltrane's late music, a feature that Ali himself would continue into the 1970s on recordings such as *Swift Are the Winds of Life*, a series of similarly structured duets with Association for the Advancement of Creative Musicians (AACM) violinist Leroy Jenkins.[184]

Like "Sun Ship" and "Leo," the head of "Tranesonic" has the feel of an incantation, and it would seem that only in the hands of a musician like John Coltrane could this kind of musical thinking take flight as something more than dry, abstract formula. And that is because, as dry as the thematic material might be, it is rendered with a shamanic intensity and emotional urgency that transcends the literality of the musical materials. After all, Coltrane once told Jean Clouzet and Michel Delorme that he would like to make a music that could induce happiness, rain, and wealth.[185] And clearly, the chemistry between Coltrane and Ali was essential to the powers at the quartet's command.

———

One of the most interesting pieces on *Stellar Regions* is "Configuration," in which passages of solo drums and passages of quartet alternate with passages of intense saxophone-drum duet playing. Coltrane elevates his "sheets of sound" approach to a new plane here, sequencing chromatic runs, multiphonic shapes, and melodic motives so rapidly that, as with some of his playing in the saxophone-drum breakdowns with Elvin Jones back in 1965, they seem to represent pure velocities and slabs of sound more than they represent melodies in any traditional sense of pitch sequence. And it was evidently this way of thinking that generated the most forward momentum from the February 15 session, since Coltrane and Ali returned alone to Van Gelder's studio a week later on February 22 to record a series of saxophone-drum duets later released collectively under the title *Interstellar Space*. As with *Stellar Regions*, all the pieces bear (or have been given) astrological or cosmological titles. The session's format was apparently a surprise to Ali, who apparently arrived at the studio expecting to play with the entire band.

The fact that each track at this session was introduced by the shaking of temple bells lends the music a solemn, devotional aura, as does the recording quality, which is relatively dry and austere. Ironically, however, this austere quality allows the complexity of the music to stand out in stark relief. Virtually every scholar of Coltrane's music has asserted that, as free and emotional as his improvisations became over time, they never lost their fundamental rigor and meticulous construction. *Interstellar Space*, recorded in the midst of what most consider Coltrane's most inscrutable period, bears this out this assertion. The absence of any chordal instrument, for example, would seem to have released Coltrane from the necessity of thinking in harmonic terms. Certainly, his stylistic compatriots such as Sanders and Albert Ayler were carving out distinctive spaces within the new music with styles of saxophone playing that deemphasized harmonic thinking in favor of melodic, rhythmic, and textural development. But Coltrane, who had sat at the feet of Charlie Parker during the halcyon days of bebop, was by nature an obsessively mathematical player. Lewis Porter's analysis of "Venus," for example, demonstrates that even as he navigates the soundscape without any harmonic underpinning, Coltrane's improvisations remain strongly shaped by recognizable scales, arpeggios, and melodic patterns.[186] At many moments, in fact, the playing on *Interstellar Space* is more controlled, less abandoned, and more shaped by harmonic thinking than much of his playing during 1966.

———

If one of the fundamental assertions of this book has been that "swing" can manifest in metrically free rhythmic spaces, recordings like *Interstellar Space* help illuminate the mechanics through which musicians like Coltrane and Ali accomplish this. Ali's concept of "stretching," after all, could not exist without an acute sensitivity to tension and release, and it is the deft manipulation of this quality—via the ongoing interplay of melodic theme and variation on one hand versus ensemble density and sparseness on the other—that allows Coltrane and Ali to contour metrically free space so effectively. So while it is difficult to make a definitive statement on Coltrane's thematic intentions for these pieces, the "interstellar" imagery nonetheless resonates with the various ways Coltrane and Ali manipulate musical gravity.[187] Those gravities are the internalized assumptions of meter and tonality that, while only intermittently sounded here, still provide a conceptual core for them to play against. This is to say that significant portions of Coltrane's saxophone improvisation reveal fragments of standard scale and chord patterns, while Ali's drumming also reveals fragments and deformations of standard jazz metric shapes. In the same way that we can hear the core thematic motif of "Jupiter (Variation)" (one of the duets recorded on February 22) as built from a melody very typical of Coltrane in 1965, we can similarly accept Ali's aforementioned claim that his playing references "other realms of 4/4." In this sense many of Coltrane's late works were commentaries on gravity, regardless of their titling, that questioned how far one could push the music while remaining tethered to the melodic, harmonic, and rhythmic elements that had traditionally defined "jazz." For most of the performance of "Jupiter (Variation)," for example, Ali provides a complex temporal fabric for Coltrane to play over—a latticework of accelerating and decelerating rhythmic slopes, swirling rhythmic vortices, varying degrees of textural density, and a cornucopia of elongated, fractured, and staggered phrases. As the performance intensifies, they alternate modes of dialogue—synchronized, gestural passages of the "Tranesonic" variety, passages when they battle each other in an antiphonal, responsive fashion, and passages when they simultaneously explode into full-on "energy" playing.

———

This sense of fluidity and elasticity lay at the heart of the 1967 quartet recordings. That Coltrane and Ali were trying to orchestrate the energy of *Interstellar Space* for a larger ensemble format seems evident in the music released as *Expression*, recorded on March 7, 1967, and currently assumed to be Coltrane's final recording session.[188] "Offering," for example, starts out as a typical late-period Coltrane rubato ballad floating through a cycle of chord changes punctuated by passages of pointillistic gestures, before suddenly launching (around 3:30) into an impassioned, *Interstellar Space*–styled saxophone-drums duet. Thematically, the breakaway feel of this formal change could be heard as evoking an actual offering of some kind, in the sense that a devotional feel gives way to a literal "lifting up," as if an offering is being made to the heavens. Despite this and the full quartet's return for a final restatement of the theme, however, the duet section has the abrupt, inelegant feel of a non sequitur. The formal transitions are much more smoothly executed on the opening "Ogunde" and especially on "Number One," a track that wasn't part of the original album but which was recorded at the same session and which has been included on more recent compact disc reissues.

"Ogunde" is an instrumental reading of Bidu Sayao's 1947 recording of "Ogunde Varere," an Afro-Brazilian religious song that, like the bata drums, is historically rooted in the Yoruba culture of West Africa.[189] Sung in praise of the orisha (divinity) Ogun, the enduring power of this religious song despite centuries of African cultural dispersal is reflected in the fact that a version of it was documented in 1957 by Lydia Cabrera and Josefina Tarafa in Cuba, where it was being sung as part of the *Oru Cantado* portion of the Santeria liturgy (i.e., songs sung in veneration of the various orishas).[190] Coltrane's rendition is striking, not only because it extends the rubato feeling of Sayao's version but also because, like his improvising on the introduction of the Antibes version of "Ascension," of the way he articulates different qualities of flotation by seesawing back and forth between passages of tonal and symmetric harmonies.

This idea of rubato as charged flotation space is also vividly articulated by "Number One," a quartet track recorded on March 7 that can be heard as a revisiting of "Sun Ship" and a standout example of the new musical space the quartet was navigating. Like the earlier "Untitled (90320)," this important recording is not particularly well known because it remained unissued for so long—in this case until 1978, when it was finally released as part of the compilation *Jupiter Variation* with the nondescript title "Number One" (because the piece was the first piece recorded at the session and remained untitled at the time of Coltrane's passing).[191] Despite the generic title, the piece contains several explicit iterations of the same melodic motif on which "Sun Ship" was based. This motif is distinctly recognizable beginning around 2:38, and more emphatically from 5:12 to 5:20, from 7:15 to 7:23, from 7:41 to 8:00, and from 8:50 to 9:12. The most obvious difference between "Sun Ship" and "Number One" is that in the earlier version, Coltrane begins the piece by stating the theme whereas in the later version, he begins the piece by improvising and gradually works his way around to it.

The more significant difference between the two versions, however, is in the drumming accompaniment and its implications for the overall soundscape. Here, we might adapt Greg Lynn's idea of "hard" and "soft" geometries—the first, a deformation of well-established rhythmic shapes, and the second, a more pliable, fluid language that ultimately emerged from that deformation.[192] Whereas Elvin Jones had sounded stiffly resistant to the freer rhythmic implications of Coltrane's playing on songs like "Untitled (90320)" and "Sun Ship," Rashied Ali provides a fluid, flexible accompaniment that seems more organically integrated and less like a preliminary foray into new territory. With Ali, Alice Coltrane, and Garrison maintaining the kind of free rhythmic flow that Coltrane had already achieved harmonically with the benefit of the chromatic slippages of bebop and Nicolas Slonimsky's octave-splitting harmonic patterns, it can be argued that Coltrane went a level further in 1967, refining these ensemble structures in a way that blended fast and slow, dense and spare into an elastic form of ensemble playing and a new, curvilinear articulation of "swing" for which the spline surface is a fitting visual analogue.

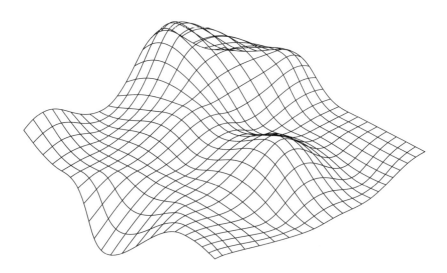

FIGURE 4.14 Spline surface. Licensed by Adobe Stock.

While turbulence and lack of regularity can sometimes be threatening and unsettling, a number of ideas have been developed that help us understand the complex—and often elegant—orders within what initially appears to be chaos: chaos theory and fractal theory, fluid mechanics, and swarm theory. But beyond mathematical and scientific ideas, there are the elemental, everyday sensations of nature. And regardless of whether we perceive them as defined by a lack of regularity or more complex regularities, phenomena such as wind patterns, wind-blown leaves, cloud formations, flocks of birds, and schools of fish generally provide us with sensory comfort despite their apparent lack of regularity. After all, no loving couple complains about chaos as they stroll hand in hand through the park on a wind-blown afternoon with piles of dried leaves blowing randomly to and fro.

This is topical; the music on *Stellar Regions* and *Expression* suggests that "smoothness" factors into Coltrane's late music in another way that has been rarely discussed. Although many have been quick to stereotype this music as either a) an embodiment of race, rage, and turbulence, or b) as Coltrane's tortured farewell note, few seem to have heard the qualities of tenderness, romance, and sensuality that can also be felt flowing within its curvilinear contours. If this is a turbulent music, it is nevertheless, like the original quartet's version of the *Meditations* suite, imbued with passion, suggesting most immediately the musical and personal synergy enjoyed by John and Alice. Certainly, much of Alice's post-1967 music, which shares many characteristics with this music, sounds like an ongoing love letter to her late husband. It is quite possible that one reason Coltrane's late music has not received its proper accounting is because a discourse of sensualism has been written out of it, leaving us with the austere image of a group of ascetic sonic intellectuals working toward greater and greater degrees of abstraction, or, alternately, an image of enraged sonic activists using symbols of Africa and "the East" to channel their black American rage into musical sound. In truth the musical and romantic partnership between John and Alice exploded multiple stereotypes, producing not only soothing or meditative music, but also turbulent, challenging music that dramatized the synergy within and between states of love and politics.

But the masculinist, spiritualist, and political discourses around the history of the music have generally obscured discussion of the raw sensuality of its curvilinear rhythms, which might also be heard as resonant with another vector of liberation: the sexual revolution of the 1960s and its explosion of erotic energy into the public sphere. Consequently, the powerful erotic energy that Michael

Cuscuna had observed during the original Coltrane quartet's Half Note gigs in 1964–65 had now become much more prismatic and multidimensional, as flagrantly and elementally sensual in its own way as the nude bathers on the margins of the Woodstock Festival.

As such, there is ample space for hearing his late soundscapes as suffused with romance and sensuality. How much of this music—or indeed, much of the music Coltrane had produced since the first take of *Meditations*—was Coltrane's coded love letter to his inspiring muse/partner/collaborator? John and Alice's mutual immersion in the passionate, free-floating rubato environments of the African American Christian liturgy and the Hindustani *alap* inspired them to radically remodel the rhythmic language of jazz not only as a proclamation of freedom, but also to articulate their experiences of floating and flying through love.

But such an interpretation would have required a Herculean effort for anyone who heard the full band in concert at this time. In 1966, saxophonist Dave Liebman had attended the legendary "Titans of the Tenor" concert at New York's Philharmonic Hall, and described the set as "disturbing, but fascinating—like a bunch of maniacs just screaming at the top of their lungs . . . It was hard to believe it was Coltrane . . . at least half the audience got up and left."[193] And if Coltrane was slowing down in early 1967, no one attending the band's April performance at Babatunde Olatunji's Cultural Center on 125th Street in Harlem would ever have guessed it. Aside from the unusual fact that he played sitting down, the band (augmented on this occasion by an unidentified number of percussionists) is in full-on excoriation mode with Coltrane playing with his usual passion and Sanders in particularly intense form. For those who could only understand free jazz performance as an enactment of racial rage, Sanders's extended solo on the group's radical remodeling of "My Favorite Things"—which has to stand as not only one of the most rigorous, but also one of the most emotionally harrowing examples of free improvisation ever recorded—provides all the apparent evidence they ever needed. Over ten minutes, he methodically sculpts a solo of the utmost emotional intensity, wringing every possible shriek, scream, cry, and stutter out of his instrument. J. B. Figi provided the most visceral account of what the band's concerts were like at this time:

[The band] sounded as though giant hands were breaking open the earth, great sounds and chunks of things coming loose. John was blowing against a wall which tottered but wouldn't fall, then backing off into the stomach-lurching roller coaster of his more familiar style . . . the most urgent voice of the night was Pharoah Sanders, toes plugged into some personal wall-socket, screaming squealing honking . . . Pharoah was a mad wind screeching through the root-cellars of Hell . . . How do you review a cataclysm? Evaluate an earthquake? An apocalyptic juggernaut that rolled across an allusion to "My Favorite Things" into a soundtrack from an old Sabu movie—jungle-fire, animals rampaging in panic, trumpeting of bull elephants . . . ? Like a convulsion they had induced but no longer seemed able to control, it ground on and on, beyond expected limits of endurance, past two hours, past closing time, until the management intervened and closed it down.[194]

The impact of Sanders's solo at the Harlem show was considerably amplified by the extreme distortion of the surviving recording. According to the liner notes, Coltrane arranged to have the music recorded by a (presumably) amateur recordist named Bernard Drayton. Completely saturated, the listener encounters a thunderous wall of distorted sound that is unquestionably much more intense than what the listeners actually heard in the venue. The closest point of comparison to this recording would probably be the "noise" music of Japanese musicians such as the electric guitarist Otomo Yoshihide, in which music of a similar emotional intensity is achieved through more reliance on electronic circuitry.[195] Regardless of which particular technique of distortion we use as a portal, recordings such as this made Coltrane's music, which had always struck a powerful balance between intellectual and emotional priorities, suddenly seem overdetermined by the most extreme of emotions. This is a key reason that the jazz establishment remains divided about Coltrane's later music almost fifty years after its creation; it would be extremely difficult to find a place for Sanders's playing of this period within the increasingly sanitized jazz sounds, histories, and narratives that have been aggressively promulgated since the 1980s.

———

Of course, such a position can only be maintained by refusing to acknowledge the increasing prominence of distortion and texture within the sonic culture at large, from the honking tenor saxophones of 1950s rhythm and blues, to the electronic distortion devices created out of the advances in transistor technology, sound processing, and amplification in the 1960s and 1970s, to the digital "glitch" culture of the 1980s and beyond. And while it might be somewhat difficult to imagine Coltrane participating in a movement like jazz-rock fusion (which in any case was dominated and defined by rhythm-section players), it is equally difficult to imagine him failing to make a contribution to the thickening soundscape of the late 1960s. After all, the extended saxophone techniques that he had mastered were already producing thickly textured sounds that were comparable to the increasingly sophisticated distortion devices that were being mass marketed to players of electric instruments. Spending more time at home during the spring of 1967, he had even begun experimenting with a prototype model of the Varitone electric saxophone (later made famous by Eddie Harris on albums such as *The Electrifying Eddie Harris*).[196]

Some of these experiments were duet sessions with Larry Young, the Newark, New Jersey-based organist who had cut a series of organ jazz albums for Blue Note featuring Elvin Jones, guitarist Grant Green, and other hard-bop luminaries (Young appears in C. O. Simpkins's biography as simply "Khalid," the name he was given when he converted to Islam).[197] Young had sometimes been called the "Coltrane of the organ" because of his unusual harmonies and the way he colored his improvisations with explosive "sheets of sound" flurries of chromatic coloration. Around the same time that he began to cite Coltrane, Cecil Taylor, and Elijah Muhammad as primary influences, in fact, he began to use the legato capabilities of the organ to melt the organ jazz repertoire into languid modal harmonies, free-meter spaces, and more explicitly electric textures. Shortly after recording his final album (*Mother Ship*) for Blue Note in early 1969, Young would record with the rock guitarist Jimi Hendrix, would become the third member of Tony Williams's pioneering jazz-rock fusion trio Lifetime, would make substantive contributions to Miles Davis's landmark album *Bitches Brew*, and by 1971 would participate in one of the most remarkable fusions of free jazz and hard rock as one-third of Nicholas and Gallivan's *Love Cry Want* trio.[198]

———

The mathematician Rene Thom is known for his contributions to the branch of pure mathematics known as *topology* that (as mentioned in the "Africanist Grid" chapter) models the ways that geometric objects can be stretched and twisted without breaking. As such, Thom is a central figure in the discourse of curvilinearity, articulating his ideas more precisely through another branch of mathematics that he founded known as "catastrophe theory." Derived from the final turning point in Greek tragedies, Thom uses the term "catastrophe" to describe the amount of pressure a curved line can withstand before it cracks. His "Seven Elementary Catastrophes"—*fold, cusp, swallowtail, butterfly, elliptic umbilic, hyperbolic umbilic, parabolic umbilic*—are considered the "alphabet" of curvilinearity, applicable to all manner of curved phenomena including blobs, the human body, and the space-time fabric of the universe.[199]

The resonance of this way of thinking with the music of John Coltrane is clear. Did he and his musicians break jazz, or did they merely twist it? That is the question I have pursued throughout this extended essay. But however his late music is heard, the imagery of curves, cracks, and catastrophes are thematically relevant to the Coltrane of early 1967 who, having spent the previous two years forcibly bending jazz rhythm into a state of curvilinearity, now found himself encircled by the dire consequences of his earlier lifestyle. While he seemed poised to cross yet another musical frontier with his Varitone experiments, the fire that seemed to burn with such intensity as recently as the Olatunji concert in April began to flicker by late spring. With his energy and morale declining, he apparently entered a period of doubt about his new music and cancelled all of his scheduled appearances. Meanwhile, according to John Gilmore, a frustrated Coltrane confided to Sun Ra that:

> [T]he ideas he had been getting from the cosmos weren't coming anymore . . . Sun Ra told him "Well Trane, if you lose your ideas, all the young fellas are going to outplay you. The best thing for you to do . . . is to come over and rehearse with [the Arkestra] and record with us. It'd be good for you spiritually and it would help the group namewise and financially, too, from the prestige of having Coltrane record with us." But he went right out and donated the money to Olatunji instead and he never did come to rehearsal. And he died about a week or two later . . . There have been members in this band who have been *out of it* and they've completely recuperated . . . It could have worked the same way with Trane. His whole history could have been changed if he had done what he said he was going to do. Coming over to Sun Ra would have energized him to the point where he could have recuperated from whatever ailment he had.[200]

Whatever we may make of Gilmore's claims for the restorative powers of Sun Ra's music, Coltrane was already gravely ill at this point. Impulse Records producer Bob Thiele was alarmed when he encountered an ailing Coltrane in the Impulse offices in mid-July, and echoed the suspicions of several people that the saxophonist's earlier heroin and alcohol addictions had ultimately damaged his system beyond repair:

> I don't know about the drugs he was using in the early days. He confided that he went cold turkey . . . But I think the damage had been done over so many years that even though he stopped over the next ten years he was going downhill all the time. When he visited my office three days before he died, I went to the sales manager of the company, who was in the next office, and I said "I hate to tell you this, but he's going to die."[201]

In reality, Thiele was one of very few of Coltrane's associates who had known anything was wrong at all when the saxophonist passed away of liver cancer on July 17. Even as close an associate as Rashied Ali remembered that:

> I had no idea he was sick. I knew he was drinking juices and stuff. But he was not the kind of person that complained . . . The way he played on the stage and as much power he used to play the saxophone, I had no idea that he was sick. But I have pictures of him where he had his hands on his liver at times, he was getting pains there. And he complained sometimes about being tired, you know, being not as energetic as he usually was. But that was about the only complaint that I ever got. I was totally in shock when I heard that he had died that morning, July 17 . . . I had no idea.[202]

Curiously, Miles Davis later remarked to Eric Nisenson that "Coltrane died from taking too much LSD."[203] The substance is not typically known to have lasting physical effects but, as Lewis Porter has speculated, it's possible that Coltrane's use of LSD may have distracted him from realizing the seriousness of his illness until it was too late.[204]

We might speculate something similar of Coltrane's later music. Considering where the original quartet was in mid-1965, it is entirely conceivable that they could have continued their journey and taken a more disciplined, less chaotic path into the structures of the avant-garde. But from the standpoint of his musical intentions, it's also likely that without traversing the turbulent, transformative space of 1966, Coltrane may not have arrived at the consolidations of 1967. Either way, his passing represented a serious blow to the aspirations of the first-wave jazz avant-garde. And even though his close associates—Alice, Pharoah, Rashied—as well as other luminaries of the new music—Ornette, Cecil, Ayler, and Sun Ra—continued to explore the paths they had collectively blown open, there was undeniably a sense that something fundamental to the movement had died along with its leading figure. In this sense, a substantial region of space definitively collapsed in the summer of 1967.

———

Viewed through one prism of analysis, John Coltrane's career as a bandleader followed a clear trajectory from the hyperchromaticized pitch preoccupations of late modernism through a Space Age preoccupation with the cosmos. Were there ever to be an exhibition of his material artifacts, in fact, it would be great to display those that fired his creative imagination: telescopes, rugs, astrological charts, star maps, works of music theory, spiritual and religious treatises, non-Western musical instruments, star charts, and other tools. Maybe one day, future scholars in some branch of astronomical science will hear in the sonic-cosmological imaginings of John Coltrane salient insights into the universe in which human beings dwell.

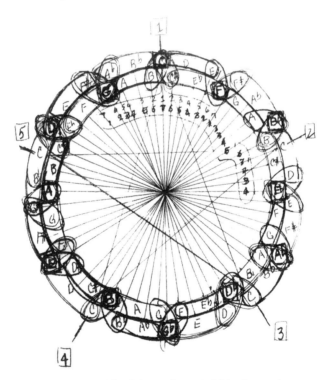

FIGURE 4.15 John Coltrane, "tone circle" (early 1960s).
Copyright John Coltrane Estate.

Much has been made of a chart that Coltrane drew in 1960 and gifted to the saxophonist Yusef Lateef, which most people have probably encountered through its reproduction in Lateef's 1981 book *Repository of Scales and Melodic Patterns*.[205] Often referred to as "the Coltrane tone circle" (figure 4.15), the chart has been the subject of many analyses, speculations, interpretations, and even alterations, some of which are narrowly relevant to the world of jazz theory (or music theory more broadly), and some of which are more mystical or esoteric in tone.[206] Ultimately, it is the blend of the theoretical and the mystical that makes this chart the key to uniting the music of Coltrane's entire solo career, from "Giant Steps" to his final recordings.

The outer two concentric rings comprise twelve equally spaced regions that detail the two adjacent whole-tone scales, their tones interwoven by an interlocking system of chromatic neighboring tones that wrap around each scale degree. The inner rings, which appear incomplete, are more difficult to decipher. Meanwhile all of the chart's C pitches are united by a pentagram. The correlation of a five-pointed shape with the chart's twelve basic divisions probably indicates that Coltrane was particularly interested in the symbolism of the pentagram shape and was trying to reconcile it with his harmonic thinking here. Thus, the chart cannot be read literally; it must be read as symbolizing Coltrane's blended music-theoretical and cosmological concerns. Considering his parallel obsessions with harmony, astronomy, cosmology, geometry, and numerology, in fact, it's difficult to avoid making a connection between this dodecaphonic division of the circle and the twelve houses of the zodiac. In this reading, it is tempting to speculate that Coltrane fused the symmetric whole-tone scales' lack of tonal gravity with the symbolism of the twelve houses of the zodiac, to create an astrologically inflected equation for levitation.

———

Viewed through a more terrestrial prism, Coltrane's career essentially conformed to the two stages of a very traditional African American Baptist or Pentecostal liturgy. The first stage, with his "classic" quartet, found him and his musicians fostering a state of maximal tension and excitability via a style of music that juxtaposed the rhythmic/harmonic technologies of the vamp with highly chromatic improvisation. The second stage, with his final quintet, was essentially him and his musicians in a state of altered consciousness, speaking in tongues and "testifying" according to the unfettered free rhythms of speech. Throughout, his creative sensibility was interpolated by an obsessively mathematical sensibility, by the cosmological concerns of the Space Age, and by a postcolonial fascination with the sonic and spiritual technologies of cultural others, including India, Africa, even the ancient Greek melodic modes—Dorian, Lydian, Mixolydian, Aeolian, Phrygian, etc.—upon which much of his music depended on for much of its evocative, mystical sensibility.

A listen to a more complete version of the recorded evidence, then, supports a different interpretation of Coltrane's later music than the one that has prevailed for the past four decades. By early 1967, he and his musicians had definitely arrived at a new conception of ensemble playing, and this simultaneously held harmonic, metric, and structural implications. If we agree with trumpeter Don Ellis's assertion that Coltrane was not, for the bulk of his career, a purely "time" player,[207] his longest-term goal might then be considered to find a rhythmically sympathetic ensemble setting for his very free sense of phrasing. Given that he had spent the first five or so years of his solo career working toward a certain kind of melodic freedom, it makes sense that his post-1965 frontier lay in finding a rhythmic parallel to this freedom—in other words, a cohesive conception of ensemble playing within a nonmetered environment, which would parallel the pantonality of his own improvising, and which would complement his free, speech rhythm-derived way of playing. However else other personal and social events may have impacted him, the recordings indicate that this was the main musical task to which he had devoted himself during 1966 and 1967. And the recorded evidence indicates that he and his musicians had solved their various creative equations, breaking through to a new conception of both improvising and ensemble playing by the time of Coltrane's passing. Harmonically pantonal and rendered in free rhythm, "Number One" and other compositions from the spring of 1967 make a persuasive case that, rather than being two years of chaos and confusion, Coltrane's final years were defined by a purposeful and productive search through uncharted musical territory. "Limits have incited revolutions," wrote the astrophysicist Janna Levin in her book *Black Hole Blues and Other Songs from Outer Space,* and, certainly, Coltrane's gazing at the stars while pondering the limits of jazz rhythm and harmony led to extraordinary and transformative breakthroughs.[208] And as he took leave of this human plane, a revolutionary, utopian, and profoundly traditional configuration of Black Atlantic rhythm remained in his stead.

NOTES

1. From Smith, Tracy K. "My God, It's Full of Stars." In *Life on Mars*. Minneapolis: Graywolf Press, 2011.

2. Recently, a recording has surfaced of Coltrane playing one section of the piece, "Resolution," in September 1964 at Pep's club in Philadelphia. This obviously suggests that at least part of the suite was composed by Coltrane prior to the December epiphany of legend. For a recording of this performance, see https://www.youtube.com/results?search_query =coltrane+resolution+pesps.

3. See Kahn, Ashley. *A Love Supreme: The Story of John Coltrane's Signature Album*. New York: Penguin, 2003.

4. There were other instances of riff figures in Trane's music around this time (such as on "Nature Boy"), much of which had to do with Jimmy Garrison's increasing prominence in the band concept. Extended interludes of solo bass would soon become a feature of the quartet's live sets.

5. For an explanation of the "Coltrane Changes," see "Coltrane Changes Explained," at https://www.thejazzpianosite.com/jazz-piano-lessons/jazz-chord-progressions/coltrane -changes/.

6. For an explanation of "side slipping," see "Side-Slipping and Bitonality," at https:// www.thejazzpianosite.com/jazz-piano-lessons/jazz-improvisation/side-slipping/.

7. Coltrane, as quoted in Quersin, Benoit. "Interview with John Coltrane." In *Coltrane on Coltrane*, edited by Chris DeVito. Chicago: Chicago Review Press, 2010.

8. For more comprehensive discussion of "Giant Steps" and the concepts behind it, see: Weiskopf, Walt, and Ramon Ricker. *Giant Steps: A Player's Guide to Coltrane's Harmony for All Instruments*. New Albany, IN: Jamey Aebersold Jazz, 1991.

9. Bair, Paul. "Cyclic Patterns in John Coltrane's Melodic Vocabulary as Influenced by Nicolas Slonimsky's Thesaurus of Scales and Melodic Patterns: An Analysis of Selected Improvisations." PhD dissertation. University of North Texas, 2003.

10. Sadiki was commenting on the geodesic domes that were part of the design of Andrija Mutnjaković's National and University Library of Kosovo (built 1971–82). See Stierli, Martino, and Vladimir Kulić. *Toward a Concrete Utopia: Architecture in Yugoslavia, 1948–1980*. New York: Museum of Modern Art, 2018, 168.

11. Jones, Leroy (Amiri Baraka), from the liner notes to *New Wave in Jazz*. Impulse AS-90. Originally released 1966.

12. John Coltrane Quartet. *Crescent*. Impulse A-66. Originally released 1964.

13. This story is related in Simpkins, Cuthbert O. *Coltrane: A Biography*. Baltimore: Black Classic Press, 1975, 172.

14. In fact, the modern version of the star-and-crescent symbol itself is ultimately

traceable not to the Muslim religion but to the Ottoman Empire, on whose flag it flew and in which it was known as *al-yildiz* (Turkish for "star-crescent").

15. Kelley's chapter on bassist Ahmed Abdul-Malik from his book *Africa Speaks, America Answers* (Harvard University Press, 2012) provides a richly detailed introduction to the topic of the Islamic influence on modern jazz musicians. For other book-length treatments of this topic, see: Turner, Richard Brent. *Soundtrack to A Movement: African-American Islam, Jazz, and Black Internationalism*. New York: NYU Press, 2021; Monson, Ingrid. *Freedom Sounds: Civil Rights Call Out to Jazz and Africa*. Oxford: Oxford University Press, 2007.

16. Coltrane quoted in Blume, August. "Interview with John Coltrane." In *Coltrane on Coltrane* edited by Chris DeVito. Chicago: Chicago Review Press, 2010.

17. Gitler first coined this term in his October 16, 1958 *DownBeat* interview with Coltrane. "Trane on the Track." In *Coltrane on Coltrane*, edited by Chris DeVito. Chicago: Chicago Review Press, 2010.

18. Kenny Clarke, as quoted in Russell, Ross. *Bird Lives: The High Life and Hard Times of Charlie (Yardbird) Parker*. New York: Da Capo, 1973, 133.

19. Max Roach, as quoted in Reisner, Robert. *Bird: The Legend of Charlie Parker*. New York: Da Capo, 1962, 194.

20. See Chinen, Nate. "Keeping Up with the Jones," interview with Elvin Jones. *My City Paper*, October 16–23, 1997. https://mycitypaper.com/articles/101797/music.jones1.shtml.

21. Several articles on the theme of linguistic surrogates in African music can be found on the website "Surrogate Languages and the Grammar of Language-Based Music," https://www.frontiersin.org/research-topics/14801/surrogate-languages-and-the -grammar-of-language-based-music.

22. Coltrane's first wife Naima told biographer C. O. Simpkins that "after *Love Supreme*, ninety percent of his playing was actually prayer!" (179). See also Gerhard Putschögl's excellent essay: "John Coltrane und die afroamerikanische Oraltradition." *Jazzforschung/ Jazz Research* 25 (1993). https://jazzresearch.org/en/jazz-research/jazzforschung-25-1993/.

23. See Rhames's comments, as quoted at http://en.wikipedia.org/wiki/Arthur_Rhames #Quote_By_Arthur_Rhames_On_Improvisation.

24. Pete Cosey quoted in Buzby, Pat. "Time on His Side" (interview). *Signal to Noise*, 34 (Summer 2004): 30.

25. Cuscuna, as quoted on the Mosaic Records webpage, "Jazz Icons DVD Box Set," http://www.mosaicrecords.com/prodinfo.asp?number=6001. Accessed April 15, 2012.

26. Elvin Jones, as quoted in the foreword to Kahn, Ashley. *A Love Supreme: The Story of John Coltrane's Signature Album*. New York: Penguin, 2002, x.

27. Crohn, Burrill, dir. *John Coltrane: The Coltrane Legacy*. Video, 60:00. New York: Video Artists International, 1985.

28. For a profile of Boris Rose, see: Friedwald, Will. "Recording History as It Was Made," *Wall Street Journal*, December 4, 2010. https://www.wsj.com/articles/SB1000142 4052748704354704575651483072044218.

29. The Half Note material was officially released by Impulse as *One Down, One Up: Live at the Half Note* (Impulse B0002380-01, 2006). Releases of Half Note material connected with Boris Rose would include *J for Jazz Presents John Coltrane* (JFJ800, date unclear), *John Coltrane* (Ozone 21, date unclear), and possibly *Creation* (Blue Parrot AR700, date unclear) and *Brazilia* (Blue Parrot AR 705, 1978).

30. See Coltrane's *Live Trane: The European Tours* (Pablo 7PACD-4433-2, 2001). I have written "several" here because the sources and annotations of several of the recordings on this box set have been disputed. See Tegnell, David. "John Coltrane (Pablo: *Live Trane: European Tours*)." All about Jazz, December 1, 2001. https://www.allaboutjazz.com/live -trane-european-tours-john-coltrane-fantasy-jazz-review-by-david-tegnell.php.

31. A higher-fidelity recording of the same performance was eventually released by Impulse in 2005 as *Live at the Half Note: One Down, One Up* (Impulse 9862143).

32. See Coltrane's *Live at the Half Note: One Down, One Up*.

33. Other versions of "One Down, One Up" released by Impulse include a version taken from a March 28 benefit for the Black Arts Repertory Theater held at the Village Gate, where it was paired in a continuous medley with "Nature Boy" (released in 2002 on *John Coltrane: Legacy*, Impulse 5892952). A studio take from May 26 with Roy Haynes substituting for Jones was released in 1977 on *To the Beat of a Different Drum* (Impulse 9346). A July 2 performance from the Newport Jazz Festival was released in 1966 on Coltrane and Archie Shepp's *New Thing at Newport* (Impulse AS-94).

34. See chapter 23 (especially pages 238–45) of Torgoff, Martin. *Bop Apocalypse: Jazz, Race, the Beats, and Drugs*. New York: Da Capo, 2016.

35. The studio take of "Chim Chim Cheree" was recorded on May 17 and released on *The John Coltrane Quartet Plays* (Impulse A-85, 1965).

36. Coltrane, John. *Creation*. Blue Parrot AR 700. Year unknown.

37. "Ascent" was released on the album *Sun Ship*. Impulse 9211. Originally released 1971.

38. For a comprehensive volume devoted to the theme of architectural folding, see: Lynn, Greg, ed. *Folding in Architecture*. London: Architectural Design, 1993.

39. See a description of the project at https://eisenmanarchitects.com/Alteka-Office -Building-1991.

40. See Lynn, Greg. "Architectural Curvilinearity: The Folded, the Pliant and the Supple." In *Folding in Architecture*.

41. I am using the terminology associated with the Hindustani tradition here; in the Carnatic tradition, they would be rendered as *raga*, *alapana*, and *kriti*, respectively.

42. See the John Coltrane album *Both Directions at Once*. Impulse B0028228-02. Originally released 2018. The live version from Birdland was apparently recorded on

February 23, 1963, captured (and subsequently bootlegged) by Boris Rose on the album *John Coltrane* (Ozone 21, date unclear).

43. See Willoughby's photo at https://www.artsy.net/artwork/bob-willoughby-big -jay-mcneely-drives-the-crowd-wild-at-the-olympic-auditorium-downtown-los-angeles.

44. This untitled poem by Bearden is reprinted in: Gelburd, Gail, and Thelma Golden. *Romare Bearden in Black-and-White: Photomontage Projections 1964*. New York: Whitney Museum of American Art, 1997, 63.

45. See, for example: Porter, Lewis. *John Coltrane: His Life and Music*. Ann Arbor: University of Michigan Press, 1999, 266.

46. "Brazilia." *The John Coltrane Quartet Plays*. Impulse A-85. Originally released 1965.

47. In an interesting parallel, the composer Morton Feldman would later derive inspiration for elements of his compositions from the weave patterns of Oriental rugs. See Javadi, A. A., and M. Fujieda. "A Study on the Rug Patterns and Morton Feldman's Approach." *International Journal of Music Science, Technology and Art* 2, no. 1 (2020). http://www .ijmsta.com/Vol_2_1_Papers/IJMSTA_Paper_7.pdf.

48. See David Wild's liner notes to Coltrane's album *Living Space* (Impulse IMPD-246, 1998). The "Living Space" short story was published in: Asimov, Isaac. *Earth Is Room Enough*. New York: Doubleday, 1957. The "Living Space" concept was apparently Asimov's reinflection of the Nazi resettlement policy of *Lebensraum*.

49. "Living Space" and "Dusk Dawn," released on *Living Space*. "Vigil," released on *Kulu Se Mama* (Impulse A-9106, 1967).

50. Ingold, paraphrasing psychologist James Gibson in the essay: "Bringing Things to Life: Material Flux and Creative Entanglements." In *State of Flux: Aesthetics of Fluid Materials*, edited by Marcel Finke and Friedrich Weltzien. Berlin: Reimer, 2017.

51. "Untitled (90320)," *Living Space*.

52. Scharmen, Fred. "Folding Space." In *Space Settlements*, 270–71. New York: Columbia University Press, 2019.

53. Widdess, Richard. "Involving the Performers in Transcription and Analysis: A Collaborative Approach to Dhrupad," *Ethnomusicology* 38, no. 1 (Winter 1994): 59–79.

54. Lynn, Greg. *Animate Form*. New York: Princeton Architectural Press, 1999, 14–15.

55. See Gelburd and Golden, *Romare Bearden in Black-And-White*.

56. For a reference on these artists, see: *Russian and Soviet Collages, 1920s–1990s*. St. Petersburg: The State Russian Museum, 2005.

57. Delue, Rachel. "Conjure and Collapse in the Art of Romare Bearden." In *The Romare Bearden Reader*, edited by Robert G. O'Meally. Durham, NC: Duke University Press, 2019.

58. Bearden, Romare, and Carl Holty. *The Painter's Mind: A Study of the Relations of Structure and Space in Painting*. New York: Crown, 1969, 87.

59. Duplan, Anais. "Ephraim Asili, *Points on a Space Age*, 2007, 32:42." In *Blackspace: On the Poetics of an Afrofuture*, 32. Boston: Black Ocean, 2020.

60. Louis Victor-Mialy, as quoted in "Interstellar Space." *Jazz Hot* (July–August 1992). Reprinted and translated from the French in Porter, *John Coltrane: His Life and Music*.

61. As far as individual source cultures are concerned, most prominent would probably be the Dogon people of central Mali, who first came to the attention of Westerners through the art establishment's recognition of their unique sculptural and architectural traditions, as well as through the ethnographic work of the French cultural anthropologist Marcel Griaule, who documented their cosmology. The imagery and symbolism of Dogon cosmology, as detailed in Griaule's 1948 book *Conversations with Ogotemmeli: An Introduction to Dogon Religious Ideas* (International African Institute, 1948) found its way into the jazz imaginary in the 1970s to the extent that we might even assert "Dogon jazz" as a thematic subgenre of post-1960s jazz. This trend is reflected in the works of saxophonist/composer Julius Hemphill's *Dogon A. D.* (Mbari, 1972), portions of Joseph Jarman and Don Moye's *Egwu-Anwu* (India Navigation, 1978), Steve Coleman's "Dogon" (from *Def Trance Beat*, RCA/Novus, 1995), and Evan Parker's "Those Doggone Dogon" (from *Time Lapse*, Tzadik, 2006). Dewey Redman's *Look for the Black Star* (Fontana, 1966) provides an earlier, more oblique reference. For a survey of indigenous African cosmologies, a good starting point is: Kreamer, Christine, Erin Haney, Katharine Monsted, Karel Nell, and Randall Bird. *African Cosmos*. New York: Monacelli Press, 2012.

62. The best book-length studies of Sun Ra include: Szwed, John. *Space Is the Place: The Lives and Times of Sun Ra*. New York, Knopf, 2012; and Youngquist, Paul. *A Pure Solar World: Sun Ra and the Birth of Afrofuturism*. Austin: University of Texas Press, 2016.

63. See Szwed, *Space Is the Place*, 196–97.

64. Numerous works discuss Sun Ra in relation to Afrofuturism. A good place to begin is Youngquist, *A Pure Solar World*.

65. See, for example, the Sun Ra albums *Sound of Joy* (Delmark DSS-414, 1968), *Fate in a Pleasant Mood* (Saturn LPSR99562B, 1968), *Angels and Demons at Play* (Saturn 407, 1967), *Supersonic Jazz* (Saturn H7OP0216, 1957), *Interstellar Lo-Ways* (Saturn LP-203, 1967), and *Jazz in Silhouette* (El Saturn K7OP-3590, 1959).

66. Sun Ra appeared on the cover of the April 19, 1969 issue of *Rolling Stone*.

67. Lynn, Greg, Michael Maltzan, and Alessandro Poli. "Greg Lynn and Giovanna Borasi Meet in Venice, Los Angeles, in the Fall of 2009." In *Other Space Odysseys*, edited by Giovanna Borasi and Mirko Zardini. Montreal: Canadian Centre for Architecture/Lars Müller Publishers, 2010.

68. Sun Ra. *Nuits de la Fondation Maeght, Vol. 1*. Universe UV 080. Originally released 1970, reissued 2003.

69. Sun Ra and his Blue Universe Arkestra. *Universe in Blue*. El Saturn 200. Originally Released late 1960s. Sun Ra. *Some Blues, But Not the Kind That's Blue*. Atavistic ALP265CD. Originally Released late 1960s.

70. Reder, Christian. "Transforming Models into Pictures Before Building." In *Blue Universe*, edited by Gerald Zugmann. Vienna: MAK, 2002.

71. See Szwed, *Space Is the Place*, 173.

72. Wilmer, Valerie. "John Gilmore: A Quiet Screamer from Mississippi." *Wire* 17 (July 1985): 14–19.

73. See Szwed, *Space Is the Place*, 148.

74. The best-known version of "Chasin' the Trane" was released on *Live at the Village Vanguard* (Impulse AS-10, 1962).

75. Gilmore quoted in Wilmer, "John Gilmore," 16. Arkestra baritone saxophonist Pat Patrick claims that Sun Ra also played some of his music for Coltrane in person, during one of the latter's visits to Chicago in the late 1950s. See Szwed, *Space Is the Place*, 176.

76. *Pathways to Unknown Worlds* is the name of a 1975 album by Sun Ra.

77. Gilmore, as quoted in Thomas, J. C. *Chasin' the Trane*. New York: Da Capo, 1975, 182.

78. Smith, Tracy K. "The Universe: Original Motion Picture Soundtrack." In *Life on Mars*. Minneapolis: Graywolf Press, 2011.

79. Coleman, Ornette. *Free Jazz*. Atlantic SD 1361. Originally released 1961.

80. Coltrane, John. *Ascension*. Impulse AS 95. Originally released 1965.

81. Taylor, Cecil. "Taht." *Winged Serpent (Sliding Quadrants)*. Soul Note 1089. Originally released 1985.

82. Marsalis, Wynton, and Geoffrey C. Ward. *Moving to Higher Ground: How Jazz Can Change Your Life*. New York: Random House, 2006, 126.

83. For more writing along this line of interpretation, see: Weinstein, Norman. "John Coltrane: Sounding the African Cry for Paradise." In *A Night in Tunisia: Imaginings of Africa in Jazz*. New York: Limelight, 1992. See also: Howison, Jamie. *God's Mind in That Music: Theological Explorations through the Music of John Coltrane*. Eugene, OR: Cascade, 2012.

84. Battistini, Matilde. *Astrology, Magic, and Alchemy in Art*. Los Angeles: J. Paul Getty Museum, 2007, 196.

85. Paglen, Trevor. "Listening to the Moons." In *Astro Noise: A Survival Guide*, edited by Laura Poitras, 105–6. New York: Whitney Museum of American Art/Yale University Press, 2016.

86. For example, see: Malvinni, David. *Grateful Dead and the Art of Rock Improvisation*. Lanham, MD: Scarecrow Press, 2013, 88. See also Manzarek's comments in: Weidman, Rich. *The Doors FAQ: All You Need to Know about the Kings of Acid Rock*. New York: Backbeat Books, 2011, 72.

87. The live version of *A Love Supreme* from Antibes is available on the deluxe edition of the album (Impulse 589 945-2, 2002). The second Antibes concert and the concert in Paris are available as *John Coltrane Quartet: Live in France, July 27/28, 1965* (Gambit 69317, 2009).

88. Coltrane, John. *Live Trane: The European Tours*. Pablo 7PACD-4433-2. Originally released 2001.

89. Porter, *John Coltrane: His Life and Music*, 264; and Kahn, *A Love Supreme*, 172.

90. Ratliff, Ben. *Coltrane: The Story of a Sound*. New York: Farrar, Strauss, and Giroux, 2007, 8–9.

91. For an interesting music-analytical/interpretive discussion of this way of approaching the saxophone, see: Wallmark, Zachary. "The Most Powerful Human Sound Ever Created: Theorizing the Saxophonic Scream in Free Jazz." In *Nothing But Noise: Timbre and Musical Meaning at the Edge*. London: Oxford University Press, 2022.

92. See Coltrane's 1965 comments in: DeRuyter, Michiel. "Interview with John Coltrane." In *Coltrane on Coltrane*, edited by Chris DeVito. Chicago: Chicago Review Press, 2010.

93. DeVito, *Coltrane on Coltrane*, 257.

94. Jones, as quoted in Kahn, *A Love Supreme*, 101.

95. LaBarbera, quoted in Mattingly, Rick. "Hall of Fame: Elvin Jones." Percussive Arts Society, n.d. https://www.pas.org/about/hall-of-fame/elvin-jones.

96. The *Ascension* theme can be heard on the quartet's August 15 performance at Chicago's Soldier Field.

97. Several sources report that Coltrane's comments to the recording engineers were misunderstood, leading to the incorrect title. See DeVito, Chris, Yasuhiro Fujioka, Wolf Schmaler, and David Wild. *The John Coltrane Reference*, edited by Lewis Porter, 735. New York: Routledge, 2008.

98. For a brief definition of the fugue state, see: *Encyclopaedia Britannica Online*, s.v. "Fugue State," by Karen Sottosanti, last modified May 5, 2023, https://www.britannica.com/science/fugue-state.

99. Lacy, as quoted in Weiss, Jason. *Steve Lacy: Conversations*. Durham, NC: Duke University Press, 2006, 86.

100. See Shields, Scott. *Richard Diebenkorn: Beginnings, 1942–1955*. Portland, OR: Pomegranate, 2017; Selz, Peter, Susan Landauer, and Joann Moser. *Nathan Oliveira*. Berkeley: University of California Press, 2002; Bishop, Janet, Sarah Wessen Chang, Lee Hallman, Corey Keller, and Tara McDowell. *David Park: A Retrospective*. Berkeley: University of California Press, 2019; Reynolds, Jock. *Manuel Neri: The Human Figure on Plaster and on Paper*. New Haven: Yale University Press, 2018.

101. Arrigo Polillo. "Successo a Juan-Les-Pins." *Musica Jazz* (October 1965), reprinted in Kahn, *A Love Supreme*.

102. Delorme, as quoted in Kahn, *A Love Supreme*, 169.

103. James, Michael. "In Person: The John Coltrane Quartet in Amsterdam." *Jazz Monthly* (December 1963): 16–17.

104. For a biography of Alice Coltrane, see: Berkman, Franya. *Monument Eternal: The Music of Alice Coltrane*. Middletown, CT: Wesleyan University Press, 2010.

105. One clip of Alice Coltrane with Thompson is available at https://www.youtube .com/watch?v=-dYIPhkoJ6U.

106. This is a prominent theme in Berkman, *Monument Eternal*.

107. Elvin Jones, interview with Anthony Brown and Ken Kimery, 2003. Archives Center, National Museum of American History, Washington, DC. https://jazzday.com /media/AC0808_Jones_Elvin_Transcript.pdf.

108. Taylor, interview with Jason Gross. https://www.furious.com/perfect/ceciltaylor .html.

109. Tadao Ando, as quoted in: Rajchman, John. "Perplications: On the Space and Time of Rebstockpark." In *Blurred Zones: Investigations of the Interstitial*, edited by Eisenman Architects, 153. New York: Monacelli, 2002, 153.

110. See Ali's comments in "Rashied Ali (1935–2009), Multi-Directional Drummer, Speaks," https://www.artsjournal.com/jazzbeyondjazz/2009/08/rashied_ali_1935_-_2009 _multi.html.

111. See *Miles Davis and John Coltrane: The Final Tour (The Bootleg Series, Vol. 6)*. Sony 88985448392. Originally released 2018.

112. See Tynan, John. "Take Five." *DownBeat* 28, no. 24 (November 23, 1961): 40.

113. See Porter, *John Coltrane: His Life and Music*, 265. "Evolution" can be found on *Live in Seattle* (Impulse 9202-2, 1971).

114. See, for example: moodyp2. "Coltrane on Acid: How the Jazz Legend Mixed LSD and the Book of the Dead." *Destroy.All.Hipsters* (blog), September 24, 2012. https://pat moodywrites.wordpress.com/2012/09/24/coltrane-on-acid-how-the-jazz-legend-mixed -lsd-and-the-book-of-the-dead/.

115. Mandel, Howard. "Divine Wind." *Wire*, July 2002. Portions of the article are re- printed at https://electriccaves.wordpress.com/2011/03/01/john-coltrane-a-divine-wind -psychedelics-eastern-culture/.

116. See Rollins's comments in: Nisenson, Eric. *Open Sky: Sonny Rollins and his World of Improvisation*. New York: St. Martin's Press, 1995, 172. For musical examples of Rollins during this period, see: Rollins, Sonny. *The Complete 1963 Stuttgart Concert*. RLR Records 88645. Originally released 2009.

117. The Beatles. *Sergeant Pepper's Lonely Hearts Club Band*. Parlophone PMC 7027. Originally released 1967. The Jimi Hendrix Experience. *Are You Experienced*. Reprise 6261. Originally released 1967.

118. This isn't to claim that considerations of studio craft were entirely absent from the recording of avant-garde jazz. One interesting article in this light is: Silverstein, Steve. "Recording History: The AACM and the Chicago Avant-Garde Jazz Scene of the Mid-

Sixties." In *Tape Op: The Book about Creative Music Recording*, Vol. 2., edited by Larry Crane, 18–20. Sacramento, CA: Singlefin, 2007.

119. Author uncredited. "LSD: A Design Tool?" *Progressive Architecture* (August 1996): 147–53.

120. These sections of textural, free-meter exploration were later formalized in the "space" sections of the Grateful Dead's concerts.

121. See Malvinni, "'Dark Star' as Cosmic Expansion" and "'Dark Star': Theorizing Improvisation," *Grateful Dead and the Art of Rock Improvisation*.

122. This is an intermittent theme throughout Lee, Martin A., and Bruce Shlain. *Acid Dreams: The Complete Social History of LSD: The CIA, The Sixties and Beyond*. New York: Grove, 1985.

123. See "John Coltrane as a Catalyst for Spiritual Revelation in Focused Psychedelic Experiences," http://www.miqel.com/jazz_music_heart/coltrane/coltrane_lsd.html. Accessed July 10, 2014.

124. Coltrane, as quoted in Wilmer, Valerie. "Conversation with Coltrane." *Jazz Journal* (January 1962). Reprinted in DeVito, *Coltrane on Coltrane*, 118.

125. Coltrane quoted in 1966 interview with Ennosuke Saito. Reprinted in DeVito, *Coltrane on Coltrane*.

126. *My Name Is Albert Ayler*, produced by Kasper Collin, Sweden, 2007. Although it has been publicly screened, Collin's film is currently unavailable commercially. See https://www.imdb.com/title/tt0963778/.

127. Albert Ayler. *Live in Greenwich Village: The Complete Impulse Recordings*. Impulse IMPD-2-273. Originally released 1998.

128. Albert Ayler. *New Grass*. Impulse AS-9175. Originally released 1969.

129. See Sanders's albums *Tauhid* (Impulse 9138, 1967), *Karma* (Impulse AS-9181, 1969), *Thembi* (Impulse 9206, 1971), and *Live at the East* (Impulse 9227, 1972).

130. See *Live in Seattle, Featuring Pharoah Sanders*. Impulse AS-9202-2. Originally released 1971; and *A Love Supreme, Live in Seattle*. Impulse B0034291-01. Originally released 2021.

131. For biographies of Owsley Stanley and Alfred Hubbard, see: Greenfield, Robert. *Bear: The Life and Times of Augustus Owsley Stanley III*. New York: St. Martin's, 2017. See also Holden, Dan. *Seattle Mystic Alfred M. Hubbard: Inventor, Bootlegger and Psychedelic Pioneer*. Cheltenham, UK: History Press, 2021.

132. *Om*. Impulse AS-9140. Originally released 1967.

133. For background on the John Coltrane Church, see: Baham, Nicholas Louis III. *The Coltrane Church: Apostles of Sound, Agents of Social Justice*. Jefferson, NC: McFarland, 2015.

134. See Shakur's comments at http://www.assatashakur.org/forum/shoulders-our-freedom-fighters/24640-happy-earthday-orisha-johncoltrane.html. Accessed September 2012.

135. *Meditations*. Impulse 9110. Originally released 1966.

136. "The Father, the Son, and the Holy Ghost" is the only part of the revised *Meditations* suite that was not part of the original version.

137. Eisenman, *Blurred Zones*, 260.

138. Eisenman, Peter. *Design Diaries*. New York: Rizzoli, 1999.

139. Jones, as quoted in Balliett, Whitney. "Elvin Jones: A Walk to the Park." *New Yorker*, May 10, 1968: 46.

140. From Kofsky, Frank. "Interview with John Coltrane," 1966. Reprinted in DeVito, *Coltrane on Coltrane*.

141. Smithson, Robert. "A Sedimentation of the Mind: Earth Projects." *Artforum* 7, no. 1 (September 1968): 44–50.

142. See http://www.coop-himmelblau.at/architecture/philosophy/our-architecture-has-no-physical-ground-plan.

143. For histories of experimental currents in French architecture at this time, see Dessauce, Marc. *The Inflatable Moment: Pneumatics and Protest in '68*. Princeton, NJ: Princeton Architectural Press, 1999; Buckley, Craig, Jean-Louis Violeau, and Jean-Marie Clarke. *Utopie: Texts and Projects*. Cambridge, MA: MIT Press, 2011; Busbea, Larry. *Topologies: The Urban Utopia in France, 1960–1970*. Cambridge, MA: MIT Press, 2007.

144. Fuller's Cloud Nine ideas are discussed on pages 408–9 of Seiden, Lloyd. *Buckminster Fuller's Universe*. New York: Basic Books, 1989.

145. The exceptions include a studio session on February 2 that provided material for the 1968 release *Cosmic Music* (Impulse 19141), and two more sessions of which the tapes have apparently been lost (April 21 and April 28), according to David Wild's discography: http://www.wildmusic-jazz.com/jcdisc_index_chrono.htm.

146. For the official releases, see *Live at the Village Vanguard Again!* (Impulse AS-9124, 1966), *Live in Japan* (GRD/Impulse GRD-4-102, 1991), *Offering: Live at Temple University* (Impulse B0019632-02, 2014), and *The Olatunji Concert: The Last Live Recording* (Impulse 314 589 120-2, 2001).

147. Ornette Coleman. *Town Hall 1962*. ESP Disk ESP 1006. Originally released 1965.

148. *In All Languages*. Caravan of Dreams Productions. CDP CDP85008. Originally released 1987.

149. Art Tatum. *The Complete Capitol Recordings of Art Tatum*. Capitol CDP 521325. Originally released 1997.

150. Alice Coltrane, as quoted in Brandon, Dolores. "The Evolution of Alice Coltrane." 1987. http://doloresbrandon.com/interviews/the-evolution-of-alice-coltrane-1987/.

151. Bernstein, Jack. "Coltrane's New Jazz Enthralls Listeners." *Tech* (MIT student paper), October 11, 1966. Reprinted in DeVito, et al., *The John Coltrane Reference*, 352–53.

152. Coltrane's comments about Malcolm X were voiced during a November 1966

interview with Frank Kofsky, which can be found at https://soundcloud.com/pacifica radioarchives/bc1266-an-interview-with-john-coltrane-by-frank-kofsky. The date that Coltrane attended the Malcolm X speech is unclear.

153. Dance, Stanley. "Jazz." *Music Journal* 24, no. 3 (March 1, 1966): 140.

154. Atkins, Ronald. "Coltrane and Disciples." *Tribune* (UK), (September 2, 1966): 30, 35.

155. Mathieu, Bill. "Reviews." *DownBeat* 33, no. 9 (May 5, 1966): 25.

156. See Shepp's comments in the liner notes to *Ascension*. Impulse AS-95. Originally released 1965.

157. The Newport footage is available at https://www.youtube.com/watch?v=as1r TILOZDQ.

158. Alice Coltrane. *Transfiguration*. Warner Bros. WB 3218. Originally released 1978.

159. Ravi Shankar, as quoted in Thomas, *Chasin' the Trane*, 199.

160. For a chronicle of Coltrane's Japan tour, see: Whatley, Katherine. "Tracing a Giant Step: John Coltrane in Japan." *Point of Departure*, 2201, https://www.pointofdeparture .org/PoD57/PoD57Coltrane.html.

161. Rashied Ali quoted in Thomas, *Chasin' the Trane*, 202.

162. Ali, Rashied. "Rashied Ali: Mastery and Mystery: A Conversation with Rakalam Bob Moses." *Modern Drummer* 27, no. 1 (January 2003): 90–104.

163. Stanley Crouch, as quoted in Grimes, William. "Rashied Ali, Free Jazz Drummer, Dies at 76." *New York Times*, August 14, 2009.

164. Alan Silva, interview with Dan Warburton, http://www.paristransatlantic.com /magazine/interviews/silva.html.

165. Jack DeJohnette, interview with the author, Woodstock, NY, November 2009.

166. Ali, "Mystery and Mastery," 94.

167. Feather, Leonard. "Coltrane: Does It Now Mean a Thing, If It Ain't Got That Swing?" *Melody Maker* 41, no. 11 (April 16, 1966): 4.

168. Coltrane, as quoted in Coltrane, John, and Don DeMicheal. "Coltrane on Coltrane." *DownBeat* (August 1960). Reprinted in DeVito, *Coltrane on Coltrane*.

169. Rashied Ali, as quoted in Porter, *John Coltrane: His Life and Music*, 269. The original source is a 1990 interview conducted by Howard Mandel for the film *The World According to John Coltrane*.

170. Coltrane's 1962 song "Tunji" was dedicated to Olatunji (release on the album *Coltrane*, Impulse A-21). Olatunji was to Coltrane's interest in West African music what Ravi Shankar was to his interest in Indian classical music. Which is to say he was Coltrane's primary conduit for information about West African music. For more information on Olatunji, see Olatunji, Michael Babatunde. *The Beat of My Drum: An Autobiography*. Philadelphia: Temple University Press, 2005.

171. A number of scholars have discussed the distinction between "musical mode" and "speech mode" in Yoruba drumming. See Villepastour, Amanda. *Ancient Text Messages*

of the Yoruba Bata Drum: Cracking the Code. New York: Taylor and Francis, 2016; Euba, Akin. *Yoruba Drumming: The Dundun Tradition*. Bayreuth: Iwalewa Haus, 1990; Waterman, Christopher. *Juju: A Social History and Ethnography of an African Popular Music*. Chicago: University of Chicago Press, 1990.

172. Some examples of the Coltrane group augmented with African or Afro-Caribbean percussion would include the *Olatunji Concert: The Last Live Recording* (Impulse 314 589 120-2, 2001), *Offering: Live at Temple University* (Impulse B0019632-02, 2014), and *Kulu Se Mama* (Impulse A-9106, 1967).

173. See Sanabria, Felix, and Susan Richardson-Sanabria. *Ilu-Ana: Handbook for Orisha Practitioners*. Miami: Eleda, 2021. See also Idowu, E. Bolaji. *Olodumare: God in Yoruba Belief*. New York: Original Publications, 1994.

174. Coltrane quoted in Palmer, Robert. "Alice Coltrane's First Concerts Here in Seven Years." *New York Times*, September 21, 1984.

175. Delany, Samuel. *Nova*. London: Victor Gollancz, 1970, 120.

176. One such incident, which took place at Newark's Front Room club, is vividly narrated by C. O. Simpkins. See Simpkins, *Coltrane: A Biography*, 211.

177. See in Porter, et al., "Chronology: 1967," *The John Coltrane Reference*.

178. Coltrane, John. *Stellar Regions*. Impulse IMP 169. Originally released 1995; Coltrane, John. *Expression*. Impulse AS-9120. Originally released 1967; Coltrane, John. *Interstellar Space*. Impulse ASD-9277. Originally released 1974.

179. Sanders plays flute on the track "To Be" from *Expression*.

180. This interview has been reprinted in several places. I am quoting from Kofsky, "Interview with John Coltrane."

181. *Stellar Regions*. On the first printing of this CD, Coltrane is erroneously listed as also playing soprano saxophone whereas on a later printing, he is erroneously listed as only playing tenor saxophone.

182. This reproduction is included in the photo gallery of Simpkins, *Coltrane: A Biography*.

183. Jones, as quoted in Howland, Harold. "Elvin Jones." *Modern Drummer* 3, no. 4 (September 1979). Accessed July 19, 2019. https://www.moderndrummer.com/article /august-september-1979-elvin-jones/.

184. *Swift Are the Winds of Life*. Survival Records 112. Originally released 1976.

185. Clouzet, Jean, and Michel Delorme. "Interview with John Coltrane." *Les Cahiers du Jazz* 8 (1963). Reprinted in DeVito, *Coltrane on Coltrane*, 182.

186. See Porter, "The Final Years: 1965–1967," in *John Coltrane: His Life and Music*.

187. Apparently, two of these titles were retitled by Alice Coltrane as they were being prepared for release: "Mars" was originally titled "C Major" on the ABC/Paramount session sheets, and "Venus" was originally titled "Dream Chant." See Porter, et al., *The John Coltrane Reference*, 764.

188. The Impulse studio log lists subsequent recording sessions on February 27, March 29, and May 17, but these sessions remain unreleased.

189. Bidu Sayao. "Ogunde Varere." *Canta Bidu Sayao.* Columbia Masterworks 5231. Originally released 1958.

190. See Cabrera, Lydia, and Josefina Tarafa. *Havana, Cuba ca. 1957: Rhythms and Songs for the Orishas.* Smithsonian SFW CD 40489. Originally released 2001.

191. *The Mastery of John Coltrane, Volume 3: Jupiter Variation.* "Number One" has subsequently been included on the CD reissues of *Expression* (Impulse GRD-131, 1993).

192. See Lynn, Greg. *Form.* New York: Random House, 2008. See also Lynn's essay "Architectural Curvilinearity."

193. Liebman, as quoted in Kahn, *A Love Supreme*, 180–81.

194. Figi, Jerry. "Coltrane and Co. at the Plugged Nickel." *Change* 2 (Summer 1966): 55–56.

195. See Novak, David. *Japanoise: Music at the Edge of Circulation.* Durham, NC: Duke University Press, 2013.

196. Harris, Eddie. *The Electrifying Eddie Harris.* Atlantic 1495. Originally released 1968.

197. For a comprehensive profile of Larry Young, see: Grundy, David. "Unity: Larry Young and Black Music, from Soul Jazz to Free to Fusion." *Point of Departure*, 2021. https://www.pointofdeparture.org/PoD75/PoD75Young.html.

198. Nicholas and Gallivan with Larry Young. *Love Cry Want.* New Jazz NJC-001. Originally released 1997.

199. For a preliminary portrait of Rene Thom, see the introduction of: McRobie, Allan. *The Seduction of Curves: The Lines of Beauty That Connect Mathematics, Art, and the Nude.* Princeton, NJ: Princeton University Press, 2017.

200. Gilmore quoted in Wilmer, "John Gilmore," 17–19.

201. Bob Thiele quoted in Kahn, Ashley. *The House That Trane Built: The Story of Impulse Records.* London: Granta, 2006.

202. Ali, as quoted in "Rashied Ali (1935–2009), Multi-Directional Drummer, Speaks."

203. Nisenson, Eric. *Round about Midnight: A Portrait of Miles Davis.* Paris: Hachette, 1996, 166.

204. Porter, *John Coltrane: His Life and Music*, 266.

205. Lateef, Yusef. *Repository of Scales and Melodic Patterns.* New Albany, IN: Jamey Aebersold Jazz, 1981.

206. There is actually a fair amount of commentary on Coltrane's "tone circle," including two undated online articles by Roel Hollander: "John Coltrane's Tone Circle," https://roelhollander.eu/en/blog-saxophone/Coltrane-Tone-Circle/ and "The Geometry of John Coltrane's Music," https://roelhollander.eu/en/blog-saxophone/Coltrane-Geometry/. See also Jones, Josh. "John Coltrane Draws a Picture Illustrating the Mathematics of Music." 2017. http://www.openculture.com/2017/04/the-tone-circle-john-coltrane-drew-to

-illustrate-the-theory-behind-his-most-famous-compositions-1967.html; Gonze, Lucas. "Coltrane Pitch Diagrams." 2018. https://medium.com/@lucas_gonze/coltrane-pitch-diagrams-e25b7d9f5093.

207. See Ellis, as quoted in Ratliff, *Coltrane: The Story of a Sound*, 163.

208. Levin, Janna. *Black Hole Blues and Other Songs from Outer Space*. New York: Knopf, 2016, 5.

FIVE

Electricity Was Just Another Color

Miles Davis between Worlds

I: REBIRTH

It was a very exciting period in Miles's life.[1]

Dave Liebman

Miles changed every five years, whenever he got a new girlfriend.[2]

Teo Macero

Sometime in early 1969, the British guitarist John McLaughlin invited Miles Davis to a screening of *Monterey Pop*, D. A. Pennebaker's new documentary about the 1967 Monterey Pop Festival. The trumpeter had been cautiously integrating the electric guitar into his own music since 1967, and McLaughlin suspected that Miles would be impressed by the young blues-rock guitarist Jimi Hendrix (figure 5.1), who had blazed a trail across England and Europe during 1966–67 before arriving at Monterey for his American debut, a debut immortalized in Pennebaker's film. In England, McLaughlin himself had been associated with a jazz scene that was progressive and expressive but also fairly purist in orientation at times and relatively insulated from popular music. He had come to the United States to participate in drummer Tony Williams's Lifetime project but was also contributing to some of Miles's recording sessions and occasionally sitting in with his band for concerts. Despite being aligned with Miles at the center of the jazz world, McLaughlin was one of many younger jazz musicians who were intrigued and inspired by Hendrix's Space Age refractions of blues guitar, sensing the potential its blend of virtuoso improvisation and electronic ingenuity held for jazz improvisation.

The popular music soundscape was exploding in the mid-to-late 1960s, and at the technological heart of this explosion was a series of developments in electronic circuitry that had manifested most dramatically in advances in the manufacture of electric and electronic instruments, an explosion of sound processing devices, and the rapidly expanding capabilities of the recording studio. But while these changes were transforming popular music, they were affecting jazz much more slowly. The historical irony, of course, is that even when all of its instruments were acoustic, jazz had always been a de facto electric music. The very idea of "jazz" as a genre had been fundamentally predicated on the recording age ever since its sounds were first captured and converted into electronic signals via sound recording in 1917.[3] Vocalists had used microphones since the very beginning of the music, and electric guitars (associated with players such

FIGURE 5.1 Jan Persson, *Jimi Hendrix*. Reproduced courtesy of Jan Persson/ CTSImages.

as Charlie Christian, Floyd Smith, and Leonard Ware) and electric basses (associated with players such as Monk Montgomery) had made their entry into the music in the 1930s and 1940s. Pianists like Sun Ra had pioneered the use of electric keyboards as early as the 1950s.

But few older jazz musicians were willing to accept this latest and more dramatic wave of electrification as the basis of any kind of comprehensive remaking. The symbolic figureheads of jazz in the 1960s were still mostly horn players, and most remained in the thrall of the harmonic revolution unleashed by Charlie Parker, Dizzy Gillespie, and their bebop compatriots in the 1940s, while the more adventurous musicians were still busy digesting the innovations of free jazz visionaries such as John Coltrane, Ornette Coleman, and Cecil Taylor. Despite the fact that the songs and improvisations of musicians such as Hendrix were, like so much jazz, fundamentally based in the language of the blues (and sometimes even directly inspired by concurrent developments in jazz), most jazz musicians derided rock music as a technically inferior, commercial intrusion of gimmickry and artifice and resented its severe downsizing of jazz's listening audience, which had rendered the latter a virtual footnote in the commercial music market of the 1960s. If the death of jazz, at least from the standpoint of the commercial music world, seems to be predicted every ten years, the late 1960s certainly gave the impression that the music was on its last legs.

The reality was much more complex, however. Viewed from a different perspective, the late sixties and early seventies were actually incredibly fertile, creative periods for jazz, with this latest "death" more accurately understood as a radical rebirth. Miles, who had participated in or presided over several previous stylistic shifts in jazz, was once again taking note. The song from Hendrix's Monterey set that was included in Pennebaker's film was his cover of the Troggs's 1965 rock and roll hit "Wild Thing," a mid-tempo dance tune with coy, come-on lyrics and a primal, raunchy beat that Hendrix slowed to a sexy, distorted, guttural drag prefaced with an electronic sound sculpting that was every bit as experimental as Sun Ra's synthesizer interludes or the music being produced by experimental composers.[4] To create this "sound painting" (as he sometimes called them), Hendrix manipulated amplifier feedback by swinging his Fender Stratocaster through the air to modulate the signal, bumping it against his body to produce a thunderous sound, raising and lowering his tremolo bar to create heavily textured glissandi while waving his other hand as if he were controlling a theremin, and aiming the head toward the sky as if it were an antenna picking up signals from outer space. With every dramatic gesticulation, the electric guitar and its new modes of distorted coloration came a step closer to challenging the primacy of horn instruments in popular music—and potentially, it seemed, in jazz—as the instruments of choice to conjure the new worlds implied by the Space Age and beyond.

There is a brief, almost poignant, moment at the end of this sound painting (approximately 1:13–1:16), after Hendrix adjusts his tuning and before he attacks the opening chords of the song, when a descending wisp of amplifier feedback whistles across the soundscape. That moment of gentle demarcation between the "noise" and the "song" seems to subtly signify the recalculating boundary between pitch and pure sound that was one of the sonic revolutions of the 1960s and which, as heard in the sound worlds of John Coltrane, Albert Ayler, and Sun Ra, had already profoundly affected jazz. Hendrix's triumph at Monterey (June 18, 1967) came exactly one month before Coltrane's passing (July 17, 1967), and if the latter event symbolically signaled the end of the first phase of jazz's radical remaking in the 1960s, Hendrix's ascent arguably signaled the embrace of electricity and the infusion of new rhythmic and textural vocabularies as the two crucial implements of a second phase of this remaking.

The actual song "Wild Thing" was bookended by this introduction and a free-meter, sacrificial conclusion that has gone down in history as one of the legendary episodes of rock and roll theater, during which Hendrix destroyed his guitar by setting it on fire, the flaming instrument emitting a coarser version of the same unearthly sounds that Hendrix had coaxed from it with his hands just a few minutes earlier. It might seem surprising that Miles, whose understated lyricism and taciturn demeanor was considered the embodiment of jazz cool, would respond so enthusiastically to such an outrageous and calculated act of entertainment. But McLaughlin's instincts proved correct; the guitarist reported that Miles was incredulous after seeing Pennebaker's footage of Hendrix at Monterey.[5] Clearly Miles, like McLaughlin and several jazz musicians of the time, was able to listen beyond the histrionics to hear the true nature of Hendrix's genius, and, in fact, the inspiration he took from Hendrix accelerated a process that had been taking place in his music since 1967, when he had occasionally augmented his quintet with straight-ahead electric guitarists such as Joe Beck, Bucky Pizzarelli, and George Benson.

———

He had just gotten married again and he was celebrating his happiness.
When you're happy in a relationship you want to do things.[6]

Wayne Shorter

McLaughlin wasn't Miles's only portal into the new sounds of the late 1960s. Exactly concurrently with the 1968–1970 period of the Lost Quintet, Miles's marriage to model and singer/songwriter Betty Mabry (1944–2022) (figure 5.2) irrevocably transformed his creative life. As abstract and unbridled as his music was about to become, Betty was the muse who inspired the earthy, funky elements that would ground Miles's foray into free jazz. The two had met in New York City in 1967, and Miles remembered this time fondly in his 1989 autobiography:

> Betty was a big influence on my personal life as well as my musical life. She was really into new, avant-garde pop music. She introduced me to the music of Jimi Hendrix—and to Jimi Hendrix himself—and other black rock music and musicians. She knew Sly Stone and all those guys and she was great herself . . . The marriage only lasted about a year, but that year was full of new things and surprises and helped point the way I was to go, both in my music and in some ways, in my lifestyle.[7]

Like Alice Coltrane (albeit from a radically different perspective), Betty Mabry was a talented creative artist in her own right who had already placed a song ("Uptown") on the Chambers Brothers hit 1967 album *The Time Has Come*[8] and who went on to release several innovative and influential albums of brash, sexually audacious funk-rock during the 1970s.[9] Like Alice Coltrane, her long-misunderstood body of work has been reappraised in recent years, inspiring reissues of her albums, articles and essays, and a full-length film documentary.[10]

Betty Mabry grew up outside of Pittsburgh, Pennsylvania, but spent her first fourteen years in Durham, North Carolina. Over the years, she has tended to depict herself as a "country girl" at heart, and, like the old country bluesmen and blueswomen, images of transport were formative elements in her musical imagination. In a 2007 radio interview with Jesse Thorn, she related her earliest musical influences as blues musicians like Muddy Waters, B. B. King, Koko Taylor, Big Mama Thornton, and John Lee Hooker, while specifically citing Jimmy Reed's "Going to New York" and Lightnin' Hopkins's "Automobile Blues" as seminal influences.[11] A blend of rural grittiness and urban flair defined her sensibility—in her interview with Thorn, she recalls slopping hogs as a teenager in North Carolina, but at the time she met Miles, she was working in New York

FIGURE 5.2 Robert Brenner, *Betty Davis*. Reproduced courtesy of Emily Brenner.

City as a model, represented by the prestigious Wilhelmina Agency. This blend of the earthy and the urbane was paralleled in Betty's musical tastes and probably helped open a musical channel for Miles's appreciation of the blues-based innovations of musicians like Hendrix. After all, it was musicians like Hendrix that made the "country blues" of musicians like Waters and Robert Johnson seem hip and cutting edge to jazz musicians who would have otherwise shunned a music they typically considered raw and untutored, by blending them with innovative electronics and virtuoso improvisation.

Mabry's influence on Miles was not merely musical. For example, she also inspired him to revamp his wardrobe, by introducing him to the downtown world of upscale hippie fashions in the chic clothing boutiques that were sprouting up around Greenwich Village. And if Miles's music was, for this brief period, balancing the worlds of jazz and electricity so deftly, this balance was paralleled in his dressing. Several of the most iconic photos of him come from this interregnum, such as those taken at the 1969 Newport Jazz Festival (July 5) by David Redfern, or those taken at the 1969 Salle Pleyel concert in Paris (November 3) by Guy Le Querrec. In these portraits the defining figure of jazz cool, formerly clad in Italian suits, had suddenly metamorphosed into an avatar of electric jazz sporting snakeskin pants, denim ensembles, North African fabrics, fringed leather, and wrap-around sunglasses. Betty recalled to Jeff Chang, "I loved him in suits, [but] he would go with me when I would shop for my clothes, and he would pick him some things, and that's how his look changed."[12]

Murray Lerner's 2004 documentary *Miles Electric* devotes an entire section to Betty, in which the musicians around Miles vividly recall her impact on both the man and the music. In Herbie Hancock's words: "Here was this young beautiful black woman with this fire and spirit and freshness that kind of opened Miles's eyes up . . . She introduced Miles to the music of Jimi Hendrix and it kind of opened that avenue up for Miles and got him interested in rock and roll—but the hard core rock stuff."[13] Carlos Santana portrayed Mabry as "the first Madonna, but Madonna is more like Donny Osmond compared to Betty Davis! Betty Davis

FIGURE 5.3
Don Hunstein,
Miles Davis (1969).
Copyright Don
Hunstein Estate.

was a real ferocious Black Panther woman and I could see why Miles was very attracted to her . . . She was indomitable; you couldn't tame Betty Davis. Musically, philosophically and physically, she was extreme and attractive. So I could see why Miles changed so drastically. The next time we saw him, everything [had] changed. It all happened in a period of three to six months" (figure 5.3).[14]

Betty also supposedly inspired Miles to clean up his lifestyle, at least temporarily. During this period, he abstained from drugs, alcohol, and meat, and exercised obsessively. Betty clarified her connection with the zeitgeist of the sixties: "My connection with the sixties was just really a *musical* connection . . . I didn't get high at all. I didn't feel that I needed to. When everybody started to get high, I'd leave."[15] The clean living held dramatic consequences for Miles's music, especially for his technique on the physically demanding trumpet. Drummer Jack DeJohnette, who would become a member of the Davis quintet in early 1969, remembered, "By this time Miles had stopped using drugs and he was eating macrobiotic. We were all kind of health conscious in that band, and Miles kind of got into that. And through that period he was playing so aggressive, so amazing. Miles is at the height of his playing around that point, around '69–'70."[16] The inside of the gatefold cover of *Bitches Brew* would even contain a sunny outdoor photo of a smiling, shirtless Miles, implying a period of rebirth, cleansing, naturalness, and emotional transparency.

Facing one of the most challenging periods of his professional career, Miles was crucially inspired by his new wife, a woman almost twenty years his junior who made her own innovative music with some of the leading musicians of the day, and who turned him on to the cutting-edge sounds and fashions of the late 1960s. Though he was no longer necessarily considered the sole defining icon of the jazz world (the free camp had taken that over, and the rhythm-section players of the fusion camp—for which he was ironically the main catalyst—would take it from them shortly), Betty was one of the most important influences enabling him to define *one* of its most provocative cutting edges. What she helped inspire was certainly a form of "jazz" by then-current definitions but one that brimmed with the exciting promise of a new and fluid electric era. Over the next year and a half, Miles would record a reworking of a Jimi Hendrix ballad, add the electric guitar to his sound, and playfully boast to *Rolling Stone* that he could put together a better band than Hendrix.[17] By the mid-1970s, he was leading a larger band that featured a screaming battalion of Hendrix-influenced electric guitarists. Most immediately, however, he would form a new quintet in 1969 that channeled the electric excitement of the new rock, soul, and funk music into a new kind of jazz that also drew freely on the advances set in motion by Coltrane, Cecil Taylor, Ornette Coleman, Albert Ayler, and others.

If these musicians had loosened the rhythmic moorings of jazz during the early 1960s, Miles would now use the recently invented Fender Rhodes piano to help electrify and colorize those free-meter spaces, while catapulting himself into a highly abstract orbit around a world dominated by the likes of Jimi Hendrix, Sly Stone, James Brown, Carlos Santana, and their ilk. His new band retained all of the complexity of jazz as it had evolved in the mid-1960s but featured a new palette: a melodic and harmonic foreground that extended the abstractions of his previous quintet, a bottom that was simultaneously funky and abstract, and a newly electric resurfacing provided by the electric piano. Unlike his famed "First Great Quintet" and "Second Great Quintet," Miles would never make a formal studio recording with this band that barely existed for a year, and because of this, it is often referred to as the "Lost Quintet."[18] Despite its semi-fugitive status in jazz history, however, the band's sound would be permanently etched into the memories of those who heard it. But it is impossible to fully understand their innovations without understanding the ways they functioned as an extension of the legendary quintet that preceded them.

II: "LIQUID DOT-DASH"

With Miles, we were spelling out the details of how
the world was changing around us.[19]

Wayne Shorter

While assembling *The Complete Columbia Recordings of Miles Davis and John Coltrane* box set (featuring the work of the First Great Quintet), reissue producer Bob Belden chose to complement his liner notes with the images of the New York photographer Louis Stettner (1922–2016). Stettner, born in Brooklyn, made his name with moody, black-and-white dreamscapes depicting the street life of postwar Paris and New York (figure 5.4). As a chronicler of urban life, his subject matter was not merely the city but, more specifically, its elusive energies and abstract qualities—light, smoke, shadows, and other ephemeral phenomena that exist in stark contrast to the right angles, stark surfaces, and hard materials typically associated with the urban environment. In the context of his times, Stettner would be viewed in the company of other photographic chroniclers of the urban such as Ray Metzker, Willy Ronis, and Henri Cartier-Bresson, who

FIGURE 5.4 Louis Stettner, *Woman with Hand on Chin, Pennsylvania Station* (1958). Reproduced courtesy of Janet Stettner.

not only captured their respective cities' raw allure, but who also humanized it by portraying the dignity of everyday people and their activities. Seen with early twenty-first century eyes, Stettner's own images chronicle a New York City that no longer seems to exist in the same way, a metropolis in which the ever-present drudgery of work and commuting was offset by seductive corridors of art, romance, mystery, and intrigue. In this light, Belden's decision made perfect sense; the images form a perfect complement to the sound of Miles's "First Great Quintet," a sound that was on one hand hard-hitting and intellectual and on the other, bluesy, impressionistic, exotic, and romantic, and which, in its own sonic imagery, also presented the city as a form of poetry.

Several of the images chosen for the Davis/Coltrane box set are taken from Stettner's *Penn Station* series. These are generally fleeting portraits taken through windows of passenger trains in New York's old Pennsylvania Station, depicting commuters in various states of contemplation or conversation.[20] Shot in hazy black and white, most of the images cast the station's platform area in a dark, atmospheric ambience, with subterranean images that are moody, somewhat melancholic, and ultimately similar to the ambiance of a late-1950s jazz club. Stettner's heroizing of figures suspended in a sea of subterranean darkness resonates strongly, for example, with Leigh Weiner's legendary photo of Miles that appeared on the front cover of two volumes of the trumpeter's *In Person: Friday and Saturday Nights at the Blackhawk*, from 1963.[21] His overcoat draped over his shoulders like a cape, Miles lights a cigarette in the dark shadows of stage left while his wife, the dancer Frances Taylor Davis, looks on from the opposite side of the frame, equally shrouded in darkness, her face a mask of muted uncertainty.

In a 2001 essay, the historian Robin Kelley discussed this image—among the most iconic images of Miles and one of the most striking jazz album covers of the 1960s—as cloaking the trumpeter in the dark aura of a pimp: a complex, solitary, brooding purveyor of intrigue and mystery who led his partners at times to the heights of romance and at other times, to the depths of violence.[22] But while the Miles-as-pimp theme is well-worn territory at this point, Kelley introduces another compelling motif later in the essay. The charismatic Miles, in Kelley's words, "knew how to stand, how to move, how to compose himself in space so that the world revolved around him."[23] Kelley's image is a beautiful psycho-spatial construction that gives space itself qualities of emotion and velocity, while conferring gravity on Miles as a protagonist in the midst of his musical collaborators and the world at large. This idea of "composing space" is, in addition to its obvious architectural overtones, also a fundamentally *photographic* concept given that photography is a form of motion capture that allows an acute understanding of how a particular space can be articulated differently depending on the perspective of the photographer as well as the action taking place within it.

So it was with Miles, whose positioning within his own musical soundscape had long been defined by qualities of the oblique, the understated, and, as his sixties music evolved, the sonic sleight of hand. And if the trumpeter had been a player of *songs* during the years of the First Quintet, the members of his Second Quintet (with saxophonist Wayne Shorter, pianist Herbie Hancock, bassist Ron Carter, and drummer Tony Williams) would present themselves as players of *moods*—fashioning songs that emerged, dissolved, reconstituted, and/or morphed into other songs. And so, the theme of the *snapshot*—of the song as a series of fleeting musical gestures requiring self-recognition through improvisation and capture through the recording process—is one potent tool for apprehending the recorded archives of Miles's "Second Great Quintet" as they skirted the outer regions of the jazz mainstream, transmuting Davis's elusive persona into the increasingly abstract, ephemeral form of jazz they played between 1965 and 1968. In the same way that the field of photography came to recognize itself through a history of experimentation, improvisation, and darkroom accidents, the Second Quintet came to recognize itself by improvising their way through both song form and the recording process.

This Second Davis Quintet—along with the original Coltrane quartet, Sonny Rollins's work with members of Ornette Coleman's band, the Charles Mingus sextet of 1964, as well as the work of musicians such as Andrew Hill and Sam Rivers—came to represent some of the most visionary possibilities of so-called post-bop jazz in the 1960s. All of these bands were led by players who had come of age during the bebop era, all of them following a strategy of pushing the boundaries of the mainstream by drawing on the discoveries of the jazz avant-garde. Given Miles's own well-known, contentious relationship with the jazz avant-garde, the quintet's rapprochement between the mainstream and avant-garde was in many cases hard-won.[24] But the recorded evidence clearly demonstrated that while Miles was openly dismissive of the avant-garde in print, he was in practice quite willing to selectively integrate its advances into his music. Jack DeJohnette, for example, remembered that "Ornette influenced Miles, because Miles wanted to get that Ornette freedom, but with more discipline. He loved Don Cherry, he thought Don Cherry had great ideas."[25] And overall, the quintet's flexibility of form, structure, and interpretation shows that Miles was in fact willing and able to entertain the innovations of the avant-garde, as long as the music was played by musicians he respected. Wayne Shorter even recounted occasions in which Miles would openly acknowledge the free influence on his own playing. As he told Michelle Mercier "More than once, [Miles] came backstage after a set and bragged 'I was really getting into some Don Cherry shit there, wasn't I?'"[26]

The goal of this section is not a definitive accounting of the Second Quintet; such accounts have already been given (in full or part) in excellent works by authors Todd Coolman, Jeremy Yudkin, Keith Waters, and others.[27] Rather, my goal is to briefly discuss a handful of recorded performances that demonstrate how the band's manipulation of fragmentary gestures, harmonic colors, and sonic atmospheres drew on the innovations of the avant-garde to help remake the languages of jazz composition, improvisation, and performance, in turn setting the stage for the innovations of the Lost Quintet.

———

With Miles, I felt like a cello. I felt viola, I felt liquid,
dot-dash and colors really started coming.[28]

Wayne Shorter

A fair amount of ink has been devoted to the studio recordings of the Second
Quintet. Surprisingly, however, comparatively little has been written about their
body of live recordings. This is unfortunate, since the live recordings in many
cases reveal the studio takes to be mere preliminary sketches and/or blueprints,
their form and content reimagined by the passion and sense of adventure that
the quintet brought to live performance. Several performances of Miles's tune
"Agitation" are vivid examples of this. The original studio recording was made
on January 22, 1965, and begins with a drum solo by Tony Williams—probably Miles's way of announcing the presence of the young prodigy who would
revolutionize the sonic and imaginative possibilities of the jazz drum set. As
Miles himself remarked in his 1989 autobiography: "Tony Williams was such a
progressive drummer . . . I can tell you this: there ain't but one Tony Williams
when it comes to playing the drums. There was nobody like him before or since."[29]

Set at a very fast 4/4 swing at an approximate tempo of 266 bpm, "Agitation" is
an open-ended, highly chromaticized vamp in C minor that alternates with two
contrasting sections: a pedal section on G altered dominant (that serves as an
introduction and also as a transition between solos), and a turnaround section
with a floating, half-time feel (during which the bass emphasizes the pitches D♭
and A♭).[30] It is important to note that these sections are not organized into a strict
formal pattern, such as a cyclical chorus structure. Rather, the quintet changes
between sections according to the whim and cue of the improvising soloist. At
the moments of greatest levity, the two sections even seem superimposed upon
each other. Thus, the formal structure of "Agitation" is mutable rather than strict
and as much layered as it is linearized. The song's head, a chromatically descending figure played by Miles on muted trumpet (and lightly shadowed by Shorter
on tenor), was possibly his most abstract and minimalist theme to date, giving
the impression of a carelessly off-handed gesture—a melodic shape, in fact, of a
type that could have easily been composed by Don Cherry.

As a composition, then, the raw materials of "Agitation" are fairly simple; the
song is brought to life by the quintet's imaginative performance. What interests
me most here is a particular structural trait embedded within this original version
and elaborated subsequently, in live performances. For my purposes, I will refer
to this trait as a "warp." Dictionary.com defines the term "warp" as both a noun

("a bend, twist, or variation from a straight or flat form in something") and a verb ("to bend or twist out of shape, especially from a straight or flat form").[31] Applying this idea of a *deformation* to issues of rhythm and meter, I use the term "warp" in this essay to indicate a particular type of tempo modulation—specifically, a momentary deceleration, acceleration, or fluctuation of tempo.[32] "Agitation" is particularly useful as it was, like "Footprints" and "Masqualero," one of the few songs recorded by the Second Quintet to be actually added to the group's live repertoire (it was also one of the songs recorded by the Second Quintet that was retained in the repertoire of the Lost Quintet). This "warp" gesture was gradually adopted as a consistent structural feature of the tune, and I will compare the way it manifests in several different live performances of "Agitation." Like the surface turbulences of Coltrane's "Transition," this gesture would have profound consequences for Miles's evolution over the next three years.

In the original studio take of "Agitation," the warp gesture is introduced during Miles's opening trumpet solo, and is fairly simple in execution: the band begins in full time, and switches abruptly to half-time about two minutes into Miles's solo (or just under four minutes into the total timing of the tune). Presumably, this type of deceleration was originally developed under Miles's solos to let him downshift into the mid-tempo swing at which he was most comfortable. In fact, this exact same gesture can be heard more dramatically executed on commercially released performances of "Agitation" recorded in Stockholm, Sweden, and Karlsruhe, Germany in 1967.[33]

A version of "Agitation" recorded during the second set of the quintet's appearance on December 22, 1965, at Chicago's Plugged Nickel club, by contrast, is characterized by a much higher level of chance taking and overall adventurousness (table 5.1).[34] Miles had been out of action for several months due to a bout with pneumonia, and he remembered that the band was eager to rebound on the Plugged Nickel gigs. "I have always believed that not playing with each other for a while is good for a band if they are good musicians and like playing with each other. It just makes the music fresher, and that's what happened at the Plugged Nickel . . . it seemed like everyone was playing out. It had really taken root."[35] Shorter, meanwhile, remembered that, "At the Plugged Nickel we were raising so much hell musically that when we came off, we couldn't say nothing to each other. We were lethargic in a princely way."[36]

As Miles was recovering from his illness, his playing was fairly rough during the Plugged Nickel engagement. But it was a shining moment for Shorter and the rhythm section, whose improvisational daring demonstrates all the ways that

TABLE 5.1 Miles Davis Quintet, "Agitation"
Plugged Nickel Club, Chicago, Illinois (December 22, 1965)

PERSONNEL

Miles Davis: trumpet
Wayne Shorter: tenor saxophone
Herbie Hancock: piano
Ron Carter: acoustic bass
Tony Willams: drums

TIMING	EVENT
0:00 (3:13 of entire track)	The ensemble floats in a metered but diffuse transitional space between Davis's and Shorter's solos (i.e., metered swing at quarter note = 304, obscured by Hancock's rhythmically free comping and Williams's coloristic accents).
	Carter emphasizing scale degree 5 in preparation of Shorter's entrance.
	Shorter enters playing around with G altered dominant sonorities.
	Davis ends his solo with a brief fragment of the "Agitation" motif.
0:22	Ensemble texture "flattens out," with Carter settling into walking eighth notes at quarter note = 304.
	Shorter improvises a series of loosely connected phrases, leading to his so-called "egg scrambling" phrases (i.e., rapid, frenzied chromatic patterns), beginning around 1:18.
	WARP #1: Williams toys with a variety of tempi and coloristic effects.
	Hancock inserts sporadic harmonic colors.
0:49	Shorter quotes a fragment of the "Agitation" theme.
1:32	Williams eases into a fast swing at quarter note = 288.
	WARP #2: Carter decelerates to half-time in relation to Williams (i.e., to quarter note = 144), then decelerates further (eventually to quarter note ≈116).
	Shorter continues "egg scrambling" phrasing through 2:40.
	The ensemble moves through free harmonic space toward first climax, reestablishes C minor environment around 2:26.
2:21	Increasingly agitated phrases by Shorter, punctuated by vocalized cries.
2:40	CLIMAX #1: Thematic fragments of "Agitation" from Shorter.

2:50	WARP #3: The ensemble thins out in density; both Williams and Carter decelerate, alternately toying with fast and slow tempi. Shorter improvises with sparse accompaniment from ensemble.
3:11	Shorter improvises around G altered dominant, using the theme from his composition "Chaos" to work his way back to the "Agitation" theme.
3:44	Strong thematic section: various statements of the "Agitation" theme by Shorter leading to more "egg scrambling."
3:49	Metered ensemble swing is restored at quarter note = 304.
4:28	WARP #4: The ensemble momentarily diffuses meter (via implied deceleration) in preparation of final climax.
4:31	Back into metered swing at quarter note = 304, Shorter's final restatement of theme, with a non sequitur ending at 4:42.

"Agitation" could be reinvented, reenvisioned, and remodeled. Carter alternates between improvising a series of inventive figures based on a central motif, and playing sustained pedal tones (both diatonic and nondiatonic) that sometimes have the effect of transforming Hancock's chords into clouds of pure color. This was sometimes extended into the "Time No Changes" approach—passages clearly influenced by Ornette Coleman's operating procedures, during which the quintet spiraled out into completely free harmony with predetermined chord changes momentarily abandoned, and the song form expanded or contracted at will.[37] Williams created a groove that was, in the main, powerful and propulsive but that, at times, could switch up to function more as coloration or dramatic disruption, using his snare drum rolls to create eddies and whirlpools within the time and his ride cymbal to impart a pronounced atmospheric dimension to the music.

The manipulations of tempo by the ensemble during Shorter's tenor saxophone solo (approximately 3:10–7:55 of the track's timing) are much more complex than in the previous examples. Breaking this passage down into a series of formal "snapshots" demonstrates how "warping" can be elaborated into something more than a simple, unidirectional (i.e., always decelerating) gesture. Here, it has been expanded into a kind of "cat-and-mouse" game in which the members of the rhythm section alternately "chase" each other across a soundscape of conjunct and disjunct tempi, while simultaneously performing various accelerations and decelerations:

Listening to the ensemble's accompaniment of Shorter's solo, it is as if a surface has been carved into separately curving roads, with each indicating different speeds for motorists. The motorists agree to drive together intermittently, before diverging back onto separate paths. This process of convergence and divergence repeats itself cyclically underneath Shorter's solo, a dynamic of metric weaving that imparts a dynamic of tension and release to the performance. Another component of tension and release is contributed by Tony Williams, who uses a more expanded version of the same strategy that Elvin Jones used on John Coltrane's "Untitled (90320)": a collagist fragmenting of the time into fast, medium, and slow tempo levels.

In 2010, the architects Ferda Kolatan and Jenny Sabin published a volume of projects titled *Meander*, in which the architectural design process is presented as, among other things, the weaving together of structural lines, strands, and loops. The resulting projects are discussed as analogues to other objects that result from the weaving of lines: baskets, braids, tapestries, and the like. At the core of these projects, as usual, is the ability of parametric design to transform ostensibly "solid" *structures* into dynamic *processes*, and to model incredibly complex geometries. "This is astonishing to someone wandering in the old domains of architecture looking at buildings as formal objects made of inanimate material," writes Cecil Balmond in the book's introduction. "Out of the jumping shifting moments arises a product that is so subtle, so that the literal and the metaphor are woven one in the other."[38]

An architect such as Zaha Hadid, meanwhile, might employ a language of surfaces to describe this, with "ribbons"—independent strips cut from a continuous, common surface—staggered, juxtaposed against, or woven around each other. This is a prominent feature of several of her works such as the Heydar Aliyev Center (Baku, Azerbaijan, 2007) (figure 5.5) and the Rublyovo-Arkhangelskoye project (Moscow, Russia, in planning). The language of divergent and deformed pathways and temporalities is most relevant here. And if what is being deformed in the case of Hadid is the uniformity of a level physical surface, the quintet is intermittently deforming their collective conformity to a common, unified tempo. When this "formerly continuous surface" is cut into "ribbons" that are then pulled out of metric synchrony with each other, ensemble tension and release is orchestrated in the movement between moments of simultaneity and correspondence on one hand, and of ensemble diffusion, on the other. The words of Hadid's structural engineer Patrik Schumacher are relevant here, as he narrates the modes of complexity that result from the juxtaposition of surfaces in some of the firm's projects:

The introduction of gradients and of simultaneous interpenetrating orders of reference with overlapping domains. Intensive networks of cross-reference can be spatialized and articulated . . . there is a potential for an absolute continuum, a continuous movement . . . through different zones that flow and blend into each other. The movement never stops . . . There are . . . moments of vertical connections that deliver a sense of simultaneity [along] with deep vistas crossing the multiple levels . . . where many elements come together in a deep, layered, and multidirectional simultaneity. That's the idea.[39]

Borrowing a term from visual arts discourse, the performance can also be understood in "Cubist" terms, similar to treatments of portraits and still lifes in the work of painters such as Pablo Picasso, Georges Braque, and others; the rhythmscape of this version of "Agitation" is defined by a series of disjunct "tempo trajectories" derived from the rhythmic grammar of swing, and distorted in juxtaposition with each other by simultaneous accelerations or decelerations of tempo. In 2000, in fact, Shorter, used a metaphor of a fragmented human face to describe the operating procedures of the Second Quintet, and that metaphor applies here:

As I look back—we were actually tampering with [the] DNA in a song. Each song has its DNA. So you just do the DNA and not the whole song. You do the characteristics. You say "Okay, I will do the ear of the face, I will do the left side of the face. You do the right side of the face."[40]

If only the imagery of Shorter, Kolatan, Sabin, Balmond, Hadid, and Schumacher had been available to the jazz writers of the 1960s, who were trying to find a language with which to narrate the way that Miles, Wayne Herbie, Ron, and Tony wove their musical visions around each other to create the dreamscapes of the Second Quintet. The colors, shapes, and spaces they created may not have been quite as dramatic as those being created in the heart of the avant-garde, but they were remarkably vivid and varied within the region of 1960s jazz that was still invested in chord changes and precomposed song forms—residual elements of jazz modernism that they were frequently willing to abandon on the spur of the moment. The tragedy is that, since Miles was vigilant about retaining his audience by mainly offering them his well-known repertoire, relatively little of the quintet's original material was ever elaborated in live performance.

———

FIGURE 5.5 Zaha Hadid, Heydar Aliyev Center, Baku,
Azerbaijan (2012). Licensed by Adobe Stock.

Unlike the Davis-Coltrane box set, there are no photos in *The Miles Davis Quintet, 1965–'68*, save the portraits of the musicians themselves on stage or in the studio.[41] And the packaging of the original albums—with covers sporting blurry portraits, photomontages, and faux-psychedelic imagery—was only provisionally resonant with the music itself. While they do evoke a sense of the surreal, a more Afrocentric twist on the dreamscapes of an illustrator like Roger Dean (best known for his covers for the progressive rock band Yes) or a photographer like Ming Smith (discussed later in this book) might have given listeners a more accurate sense of the musical adventure awaiting them.[42] Nonetheless, several images come to mind as resonant with the qualities of their music in the same way that Louis Stettner's images resonated with the music of the First Davis Quintet.

An image taken by Henri Cartier-Bresson in 1932 in the French city of Hyères presents a blurred bicyclist speeding out of the left side of the picture frame, beneath the snaking, repetitive geometry of a spiral staircase in the foreground (figure 5.6).[43] The overall mood is one of fugitivity and velocity juxtaposed against a backdrop of repetition, of a subject who can only be briefly apprehended before moving out of the viewer's arena of vision. The curator Clément Chéroux used the notion of "fixed-explosive" to narrate this photograph: a composition defined by the juxtaposition of fixed and dramatically motive elements.[44] Similarly to Stettner's Penn Station photos but with a different cultural sensibility, this work also captures the phantom energies of the city; Cartier-Bresson's cyclist could as easily have been one of Stettner's wisps of steam escaping from a sidewalk grating. Many of the Second Quintet's melodies were presented in this way, in fact—a juxtaposition of phantom themes zipping in and out of the listener's clear perception, against the hypnotic geometry of Tony Williams's ride cymbal patterns, resulting in an atmosphere of suspense marked off by episodes of ensemble explosion. The sound of Williams's thick marching-band sticks on his heavy, cracked twenty-two-inch Zildjian ride cymbal cast the entire band in an airy, metallic glow, his masterful, manual control of shading and dynamics imparting a pronounced atmospheric dimension to the music. And while specific details of the mixing decisions of producer Teo Macero remain unclear, a compelling

FIGURE 5.6 Henri Cartier-Bresson, *The Var Department, Hyères, France* (1932).
Reproduced courtesy of Henri Cartier-Bresson/Magnum Photos.

argument could be made for Williams's ride cymbal as equally important to the history of recorded jazz as, for example, the reverberant bathrooms at Memphis's Sun Studios or Detroit's Motown Studios were to the history of recorded rock and soul music, respectively.

Framed by the thick sonority of Williams's ride cymbal, the textures of the quintet's recordings often recall the early decades of photography when factors such as limited resolution, over- or underexposure, or atmospheric conditions virtually guaranteed an evocative, moody take on the observed world. These haphazardly achieved aesthetic traits would gradually become part and parcel of photography's language.[45] Between 1940 and 1976, for example, the Czech photographer Josef Sudek took a series of atmospheric photos later collectively published as *The Window of My Studio* (figure 5.7).[46] Given that Sudek, a veteran of World War I who had lost an arm in combat, became increasingly reclusive over the course of his career, he preferred to document the external world through his studio window and consequently, the typical genres through which photographers represent the observed world—portraits, objects, and landscapes—are refracted in his work through the variations of his window surface—frost, rain, humidity, light saturation, and other conditions. These have the effect of rendering apprehension of the people, objects, and landscapes in Sudek's work highly ethereal, with each image a meteorological elegy to the conditions in and around his studio. Picking up (per Wayne Shorter's earlier comments) on the exoticism of *Kind of Blue*, the quintet's music remains similarly atmospheric, driven through a progression of psychic and emotional "climates" by the ambient haze of Williams's ride cymbal.

———

Recently unearthed footage shows the Second Quintet onstage in Milano, Italy, in 1964, on their first European tour.[47] Dressed in designer suits, the band looks sharp, fresh, and brimming with confidence. They had good reason to be confident: over the next four years, they would create an oeuvre that would eventually be adopted at the core of the modern jazz canon, with Shorter in particular hailed as perhaps the preeminent jazz composer of his generation. Today, songs like "Nefertiti" and "Footprints" are taught in schools and conservatories, and played everywhere from high school auditoriums to international jazz festivals. But a half-century later, in fact, jazz musicians are still struggling to decode the mysteries of the quintet's working procedures. What most fail to realize is that those procedures can't be taught or learned; much of what made the quintet so

FIGURE 5.7 Josef Sudek, *The Window of My Studio* (1940–1954).
Reproduced courtesy of I&G Fárová Heirs.

magical was simply a matter of emboldened imagination and the willingness to take unplanned leaps in the moment of performance.

Although it is mainly Sun Ra who is associated with the cosmic imaginary of 1960s jazz, Miles's Second Quintet, with its ephemeral musical sketches, seems to channel the same energies in a more oblique and cerebral way. Listening to much of their music seems like thumbing through an artist's sketchbook, as opposed to viewing finished works hung neatly on display. Rendered in smudged pastels, charcoal, and watercolors, they are full of phantom gestures and erasure, with form being defined as much by manipulations of light as by the counting of measures. In fact, these vignettes don't seem as if they were conceived to impress the listener as finished works; rather, they stimulate the imagination as questions, dreams, and mirages. While the Second Quintet is not typically cited in discussions of Afrofuturist music, much of their work could be heard on the terms of science fiction due to the way their music suggests worlds slipping in and out of existence, summoned into being through musical sound. Even without the cosmological imagery of Ra and Coltrane, they remain potent ways of composing jazz's place within the sixties and the Space Age.

The quintet itself began to slip out of existence at the beginning of 1968, inaugurating the beguiling period of transition in Miles's music that roughly spanned 1968 through 1972, as the members gradually went their various ways (only Shorter stayed on) while expanding their horizons in tune with the adventurous ethos of the late 1960s. Shorter himself, for example, recorded his final three albums for the Blue Note label (*Super Nova*, *Odyssey of Iska*, and *Moto Grosso Feio*), on which he (like Ornette Coleman) sometimes put musicians on unfamiliar instruments to achieve novel results, while basing the dramatic sweep of his new compositions on novels (Cyprian Ekwensi's *Iska*, Charles Kingsley's *Water Babies*, Edith Wharton's *Sanctuary*), news stories (such as the mysterious disappearance of several nuns in the Brazilian jungle), signs of the zodiac, and his newborn daughter.[48] Herbie Hancock would blend his own fascination with African culture, electronics, groove music, and free improvisation over three albums with his *Mwandishi* band. Tony Williams would join forces with free-bop organist Larry Young and the British electric guitarist John McLaughlin to create a freewheeling form of electric jazz that was the true opening shot of what became jazz-rock fusion. Even Ron Carter, a sworn defender of acoustic jazz, would make a handful of influential recordings playing electric bass. Taken as a whole, this music was not the commercial contrivance that came to be known as "jazz-rock fusion" later in the 1970s. Rather, it embodied an interim period of electric textures, electronic soundscapes, exotic references, free improvisation, and alluring grooves that drew on the jazz avant-garde as a solvent to loosen the moorings of post-bop as it was gradually refashioned into the jazz-based musics of the 1970s. In short, the music of this period reflected all of the world (re)making strategies and utopian ideals of the late 1960s. It was an exciting, transformative period, and Miles was not about to be left behind. As usual, however, it was Shorter who expressed it most evocatively, his words presaging the imminent birth of the Lost Quintet.

> Form used to be simple, but as time went on . . . [p]eople started writing songs that sounded like nebuli—escaping gaseous substances in the universe . . . like rays of sunshine spreading out and it has no form around it . . . And then, something happened between that kind of nebulous stuff and what went into *In a Silent Way* and *Bitches Brew*.[49]

III: ANOTHER COLOR

> Miles chose specifically to work with the electric piano because first of all,
> you didn't have to strain to hear it, plus it was a new sound. Even today,
> people in jazz still like the Fender Rhodes because the mechanical part of it
> is still a piano—it has to be tuned, it has a weighted keyboard and it
> has a different sonority that lends itself to coloring the music.[50]
>
> *Jack DeJohnette*

Sandy McLean might easily have been referring to Harold Rhodes's new electric piano within the soundscape of the late 1960s when she wrote, "You can tell when a color is taking off. You can spot it all over the place."[51] Indeed, Rhodes's instrument went on to be one of the signature sonic colors of the 1970s, helping to transform the culture of keyboard playing (figure 5.8). Like much post–World War II musical technology, the Fender Rhodes story actually begins in the American military in the late 1940s, where the instrument's namesake was a pianist, music teacher, and inventor employed by the US War Department.[52] Rhodes's assigned task was to raise the morale of injured Air Force soldiers by teaching them music (he was later awarded a Medal of Honor for his therapeutic work). He elected to teach the soldiers piano but was hampered by the lack of available instruments. Shipping in dozens of acoustic pianos was not a viable option, besides the fact that most of the soldiers were bedridden in any case and could not sit upright to play. Rhodes's ingenious solution was to salvage and repurpose aluminum hydraulic tubes from the wings of disabled B-17 fighter jets, stagger their lengths to create a series of tuned pitches, and lay them horizontally in a vibraphone-like rack in which the individual tubes were struck by keyboard-operated hammers. This early version of the instrument was known as the "Army Air Corps Lap Model Piano," a keyboard spanning a mere two and a half octaves and built to be played by the soldiers in bed. It was not electrified, but Rhodes would refine the design over the next two decades as he developed a version that could be mass produced and commercially marketed—most significantly, by replacing the aluminum tubes with amplified tuning forks. This new and electrified version of the instrument sounded like a piano, in a way, but was essentially an electric, keyboard-operated thumb piano with a soft, alluring sonority that also evoked the keyed percussion instruments like the xylophone, marimba, and vibraphone, as well as the metallophones and gong-chimes of the Javanese gamelan. By the mid-1960s the Rhodes piano was being mass produced by the Fender Instrument Company (hence the common appellation "Fender Rhodes"), which was in turn bought out by CBS Musical Instruments in 1965 (with the Fender trademark retained), raising the instrument's design and availability to a peak. The Fender Rhodes subsequently became the electric piano of choice among musicians— "the 747 of electric keyboards" in the words of pianist Ramsey Lewis, rendering the competing Wurlitzer and RMI electric pianos to secondary status.[53] By 1968, Miles had become fascinated with the instrument, once even flying as far as Mexico City in 1966 to witness Joe Zawinul and his Rhodes in action with the Cannonball Adderley group. The pianist in fact remembered that, in New York, "[Miles] used to come to the clubs constantly where we played with Cannonball and record only the parts with the Rhodes."[54]

It is entirely appropriate that the *Electric Miles* documentary devotes an entire section to Miles's adoption of the Fender Rhodes.[55] Like the electric guitar, the electric piano was an instrument that referred backward to the pitch-based ma-nipulations of the old system, and forward, to the textural explorations of rock, electronic music, world music, and the jazz avant-garde. Like other instances of military-derived design in the 1960s, it was also an instrument that evoked the Space Age in its sound and physical construction. In a subtle way, the sound of the Rhodes resonated with the electronic beeps and blips that were defining the Space Age in sonic terms, as heard on the soundtracks of science fiction movies and television shows. The curved top of its housing mimicked the aesthetic of space capsule interiors and exteriors, avoiding edges and corners in favor of the rounded surfaces and bubble shapes that were the basis of design for zero-gravity

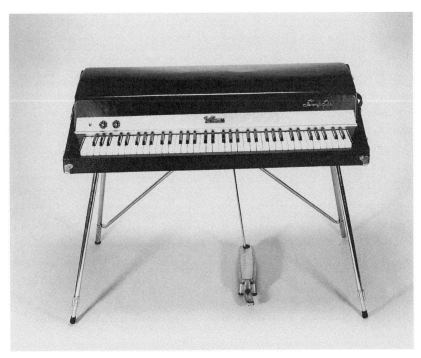

FIGURE 5.8 Smithsonian National Museum of American History,
Fender Rhodes Electric Piano. CCO.

environments. This was fitting given that Miles embraced the sound of this instrument just as he moved his own music into the flotation space of free meter,
simultaneously instructing an interior designer to redesign his New York apart-
ment in the curvilinear contours of the times, without corners or hard angles.[56]

For an instrument with such an immediately recognizable sound, the Rhodes
was remarkably flexible in its capabilities. At the top of the ensemble, it provided
a shimmering, bell-like lead voice. In the middle of the ensemble, it accentuated
voicings and bathed chordal colors in a warm aura. It also fattened up the ensemble bottom, and could easily function as a bass instrument (indeed, one early
version of the instrument was a low-register keyboard intended as a substitute
for the upright bass). In popular music, several well-known musicians helped
popularize the Rhodes during these early years, including Ray Manzarek of the
Doors (who, in the absence of a bassist, made its low end a defining feature of all
of the band's recordings) and Billy Preston (who used it for his famous solo on
"Get Back" by the Beatles). Many jazz pianists eventually embraced the Rhodes

as well, although almost all of them initially viewed it as a purely pragmatic (and inferior) solution for two common problems—it was at times a portable replacement for the poorly maintained acoustic pianos found in many nightclubs, and at other times, a way to be heard above the volume of drummers.

All of these considerations factored into the way the Rhodes was integrated into Miles's music, an integration that paralleled the change in personnel in his band that began when Ron Carter left in June 1968. According to Miles, Carter was generally reluctant to tour and wanted to focus on studio work, and was also resistant to playing the electric bass full time with the band at a time when Miles's fascination with the instrument was growing.[57] Carter was replaced by August 1968 by the British bassist Dave Holland, who would play upright with the Lost Quintet before adding electric to his arsenal as the band expanded during 1970. Herbie Hancock was the next to leave, also in August. Hancock was on vacation at the time and his temporary replacement, Chick Corea, became a permanent member of the quintet.[58] While Hancock and Corea would go on to define the sound of the Rhodes in the 1970s, both had to overcome their own initial suspicion of the instrument. Hancock, for example, remembered:

> I walked into the studio and I was looking for the acoustic piano, and I didn't see one. So I just kind of waited around and I thought, "What does Miles want me to play . . . ?" And he said, "Play that over there!" And I looked over in the corner, there was a Fender Rhodes electric piano. And so I thought, "He wants me to play that *toy*?" Mind you, I had never played a Fender Rhodes piano. So I turned the thing on and I played a chord on it. And to my great surprise, I thought it sounded beautiful—I *loved* the sound of it. It was rich, it was mellow, and it was a nice kind of blending sound.[59]

As their comments below show, Hancock's and Corea's gradual embrace of the instrument was also partially expedited by the fact that they were playing with one of the loudest drummers in the history of jazz. In Hancock's words, "I could turn up the volume and be just as loud as Tony Williams, that's what I was thinking! So he wouldn't have to lighten up on the sticks when I was playing a solo . . . I was kind of intrigued by that idea."[60] Meanwhile Corea, who remembered that he "absolutely hated" the Rhodes the first time he encountered it,[61] made his definitive transition onstage. He had been playing acoustic piano for his first several months after he joined the quintet, but found a surprise waiting for him when they arrived at Boston's Jazz Workshop in December 1968:

As I was walking toward the bandstand, I was behind Miles, and we were reaching the bandstand and I was headed toward the acoustic piano—the regular piano—and Miles just turned around and said "Play *that*!" (pointing at the electric piano). And that was it . . . The first thing I noticed about the instrument was the fact that I could play *louder*. And at that time, Tony Williams was one of the first drummers that began to play in an acoustic small group really vigorously . . . And with just the acoustic piano and the acoustic bass, there was no match.[62]

Corea eventually warmed to the instrument and its possibilities, telling Pete Gershon, "I started trying to get a sound out of it, fooling around with attachments that distorted the sound. I kind of got into electronics from there, fooling with a ring modulator and an Echoplex, various echo devices, different amplifier settings, that sort of thing."[63] The anecdotes of Hancock and Corea are borne out by the surviving recorded documents of Miles in concert at this time. For example, the recording of the Quintet's Jazz Workshop performance (with Williams still on drums) is a cloudy, lo-fi audience recording with a very truncated frequency range in general and, in particular, a very limited high end. Microphone placement is obviously far from ideal, but the anomalies of this crude audio snapshot seem to verify the recollections of Hancock and Corea, conveying some sense of what the evolving quintet sounded like in concert at this time. Suffice to say that even when the entire group was playing at full volume, they sound like they are essentially accompanying Williams, whose playing is so loud that it completely dominates the soundscape. As the drummer Mike Clark once remarked, "It seemed like the whole band was playing inside of his ride cymbal."[64]

―――――

Recorded during this period of transition between his old and new quintets and between acoustic and electric jazz, Miles's *Filles de Kilimanjaro* (1968) uses the sound of the Rhodes to give an electric resurfacing to the cerebral music of the Second Quintet (recorded in June) and a warm, intimate aura to romantically themed tracks featuring Corea and Holland recorded in September. Three tracks—Gil Evans's "Petits Machins" and "Tout de Suite" (June) and Miles's "Frelon Brun" (September)—mix R&B ideas with the highly cerebral and/or atmospheric approach of the recent Second Quintet albums such as *Miles in the Sky*. On the album's title track (June) and "Mademoiselle Mabry" (September), by contrast, the cerebral quality is tempered by a warmer, earthier sensibility anchored by steady bass figures (composed by an uncredited Gil Evans), with the adventurous harmonies of the Second Quintet scaled back toward less ambiguous, more folky sonorities. These latter tracks provided the clearest indication of where Miles's music was heading. "Mademoiselle Mabry," for example, is Evans's uncredited adaptation of Jimi Hendrix's 1967 ballad "The Wind Cries Mary," built around a reharmonization of the original song's ascending, stepwise chordal figure.[65] "Mademoiselle Mabry" almost seems a sideways glance at minimalism, its cyclical riff/chord sequence and controlled ensemble interaction occupying a conceptual space vaguely comparable to a tape loop. One of the defining features of *Filles de Kilimanjaro*, in fact, is its juxtaposition of repetition and metric ambiguity, and the net impression created by these tracks is of a layered music in which riffs on the bottom of the ensemble anchor fluid and/or metrically complex strategies on the top. But the sonic elements that unite the two styles here are the sound of the electric piano and the use of repeating riffs, and, in this way, *Filles* provided a proverbial launch pad for the freer excursions of the Lost Quintet while hinting at positive developments in Miles's personal life since an image of Betty, partially obscured by Hiro's photomontage, graces the cover of the record. The music on this album signaled a new and exciting direction for Miles, and it was even chosen as *DownBeat* magazine's "Jazz Album of the Year" for 1968. But released in the midst of this period of rapid transformation, it was a direction that he touched on and seemingly abandoned. Although it was an important turning point in his music, none of its material is known to have ever been performed live, and it has generally been afforded a fairly low profile in histories and surveys of his career.

The volume level was rising, but Miles, Hancock, and Corea were merely three of many musicians who were using the electric piano to channel the electric energy of the era while remaining true to the stylistic norms of acoustic jazz. And while some musicians, scholars, and journalists have demonized their choices as the beginning of the corruptive influence of so-called "fusion," the reality of what was taking place was more complex. The Rhodes was also adopted at various times, for example, by several musicians who were not at all associated with fusion, but who were actually vigorous defenders of acoustic jazz. Saxophonist and composer Joe Henderson, for example, remains one of the most canonized jazz composers of his generation, but he was also one of the early artists to embrace the sound of the new instrument. On albums such as *Power to the People*[66] (1969) and *Live at the Lighthouse* (1970), Henderson used the Rhodes to beef up the bottom of his new music with funky bass vamps ("Gazelle," "Afro-Centric,"252and

"Power to the People") while it also provided an exciting, electric resurfacing to the harmonies of his older compositions such as "A Shade of Jade," "Mode for Joe," and "Punjab."[67] Henderson always maintained that he was a fundamentally straight-ahead player but, like Sonny Rollins, he was such a master of his instrument that there was always a free subtext in his playing in the sense that he had the facility to go anywhere his imagination led him, on the spur of the moment. Combined with the freer approaches of younger musicians who accompanied him on these recordings such as Hancock, DeJohnette, drummer Lenny White, pianist George Cables, and trumpeter Woody Shaw, albums like *Power to the People* embraced the achievements of post-bop while they bristled with the electricity and exuberance that the younger players were bringing to the music.

After playing his way across jazz's progressive sphere in the sixties, virtuoso trumpeter Woody Shaw came into his own voice as a player and composer around the same time as the Henderson recordings in which he participated. This maturation was symbolized by the 1970 release of *Blackstone Legacy*—his first album under his own name—and its 1972 follow-up, *Song of Songs*. Both of these utilize a mixture of acoustic and electric piano (although for the rest of his career, encompassing many brilliant albums, Shaw would prefer the acoustic piano). As with the Henderson albums, the Rhodes merely colorizes compositions that are firmly in the stylistic vein of late-'60s acoustic jazz. Were Henderson and Shaw capitulating to commercial trends? Although these albums feature electric piano and repeating riff figures, neither could be considered "jazz-rock fusion" by any stretch of the imagination; rather, they cast the post-bop aesthetic through compelling prisms of freedom and electricity.[68] The Rhodes even made its way into the avant-garde; a lovely recording of a solo Sun Ra performance on Fender Rhodes has recently been unearthed,[69] and AACM violinist/composer Leroy Jenkins, whose stylistic orbit was set firmly in the second-wave avant-garde, made inventive use of the Rhodes on his 1978 work *Space Minds, New Worlds, Survival of America*, which blended free improvisation with precomposed music for chamber ensemble.[70]

In the jazz soundscape of the late 1960s and 1970s, then, the electric piano was literally "just another color." But in its nod to popular culture and the younger generation, it was a color that also sometimes carried a political aura. As their titles suggest, works like Henderson's *Power to the People*, Shaw's *Blackstone Legacy*, and Jenkins's *Space Minds* cast jazz in the heroic stance of instrumental music that could be understood as a form of racial, cultural, and political commentary. Saxophonist Gary Bartz, who participated in the recording of Shaw's *Blackstone Legacy* and would later join Miles's band, recalled:

We all were [thinking about social justice issues] in the '60s. I mean, they killed the president, they killed our leaders. Our leaders were assassinated in the '60s, and we act like it was just a footnote in history. But that was traumatic. I was going to stop playing music because I didn't think the world needed another musician. I thought, we got more problems than what a musician can solve, even though as I got to know [Charles] Mingus and Max [Roach] and different people, I saw that you can address social ills through music. That's the only thing that kept me out of the Black Panthers.[71]

———

The period spanning 1968–1972 can be understood as a laboratory for the new electric jazz that Miles and members of the younger generation were bringing into being. If Coltrane and other free musicians had loosened the rhythmic moorings of jazz in the mid-1960s by moving it into metrically free space, Miles and members of the younger generation would use the Fender Rhodes to ground those spaces with touches of the rhythm-and-blues and funk concepts of James Brown, Sly Stone, and others, and set everything simultaneously afloat and afire with the free structure derived from the avant-garde and the electric hues of Jimi Hendrix. The February 1969 recording of *In a Silent Way* marked the last time Miles and Tony Williams would work together, arguably symbolizing the spiritual end of the Second Quintet. While Wayne Shorter would remain for one more year, Jack DeJohnette would take over the drum chair shortly thereafter, solidifying a lineup that included Miles, Shorter, Chick Corea, and Dave Holland—the "Lost Quintet." Because they never recorded an official album, the surviving archive of unofficial recordings, concert reviews, and interviews vividly chronicle the brief, comet-like trajectory of a quintet that burned its way through the utopian space at the intersection of sixties post-bop and free jazz, and seventies jazz-rock fusion.

In Miles's own constellation, it was the influences of Betty Mabry, the Austrian pianist Joe Zawinul (discussed later in this essay), and Jimi Hendrix who helped electrify, funkify, and stylize a music that was becoming increasingly abstract, while the increasingly philosophical Shorter provided the solvent—the fluid sonic sensibility within which all the disparate stylistic elements could be dissolved and recombined in new ways. Gradually, a music that had been about declaration became a music of imagination, giving another dimension to the system that had been codified by Charlie Parker and liberated by Ornette Coleman. In a few years' time, the ideas germinating in this moment would be commercialized into what became known as "jazz-rock fusion." For the moment, however, it remained more about questions than answers.

With a new quintet, a new wife, and a new wardrobe, things were changing rapidly in the world of Miles Davis. Earlier in 1968 he had titled his previous album *Miles in the Sky* (an apparent reference to the Beatles's 1967 psychedelic anthem "Lucy in the Sky with Diamonds") and had included a song called "Paraphernalia," giving two knowing winks to the counterculture.[72] With the album titled *In a Silent Way* to be released in July, he and the other members of the quintet loaded the Rhodes and the rest of the band equipment onto a Volkswagen bus—that automotive symbol of countercultural adventure in the 1960s—and headed to upstate New York for the first formal gig with the new lineup.

IV: FOUND

> After we finished *In a Silent Way*, I took the band out on the road;
> Wayne, Dave, Chick and Jack were now my working band. Man,
> I wish this band had been recorded live because it was really a bad
> motherfucker. I think Chick Corea and a few other people recorded
> some of our performances live, but Columbia missed out
> on the whole fucking thing.[73]
>
> *Miles Davis*

The audience at Duffy's Backstage Tavern in Rochester, New York, must have been mildly shocked at the sound of the new Miles Davis Quintet. Miles and Wayne Shorter had traveled many musical miles together by this point, but this first documented gig made it clear that, from its very beginning, the new quintet had a sound and identity that was very distinct from the one that existed just a few months earlier. The percussive, distorted sound of Corea's electric piano, very different from Herbie Hancock's Impressionist sensibility, was a major part of the quintet's sound, strongly defining its colors, textures, and spatial contours. Corea's playing reflected the influences of pianists such as Horace Silver, Red Garland, Wynton Kelly, and Bud Powell, weighted with a percussive touch that would be perfectly suited to the textural sensibility of this band, while his background in Latin music (gained while working with Latin jazz luminaries such as Mongo Santamaria and Willie Bobo) lent a funky, syncopated angle to his phrasing that he very effectively transposed into free-meter space. Corea had obviously overcome any resistance to the electric piano by this point, as well as any idea of it being incompatible with free improvisation. Not only was he playing it with the quintet but he was also playing it on some of his own albums, and he would soon begin tweaking the instrument's sound with processing devices such as a ring modulator. The resulting sound seemed to owe as much to Karlheinz Stockhausen's ring-modulated piano pieces like *Mantra* and to Cecil Taylor's improvisations as they did to his earlier influences of Silver, Powell, and Kelly.

Like Corea, Dave Holland could move effortlessly between swing playing, free playing, and the new riff-based material that Miles had begun working into the set list. His playing juxtaposed a solid command of the bottom with an adventurous, melodic upper register that recalled Charles Mingus and Scott LaFaro. Holland provided the ideal counterpoint between Corea and Jack DeJohnette, whose intense, polyrhythmic style in this band can be compared to Elvin Jones in the sense that it kept the quintet in constant, swirling motion—whether in meter or free meter. DeJohnette's free jazz credentials were solid. Not only had he developed out of Chicago's AACM collective but he had also been one of the local musicians to sit in with John Coltrane several times during the saxophonist's March 1966 run at Chicago's Plugged Nickel, and this experience prepared him for the increasingly free trajectory he would take with Miles: "I worked with Coltrane in Chicago at the Plugged Nickel, with Rashied [Ali], us playing next to each other. He was really physically fit to do that gig, he'd built up stamina to do that. And it wore me out every night, playing with Trane! But I learned a lot about stamina, doing that gig with Rashied. It really helped me a lot in terms of influencing the way I play free drums, a looser way of playing."[74] But DeJohnette wasn't only bringing the experimentalism of the AACM; he was also bringing the populist groove of his previous employer, the saxophonist Charles Lloyd, who had recorded a string of best-selling albums that brought jazz into dialogue with the rock and world music influences of the counterculture. Lloyd's album *Love In*, for example, had been recorded live at the Fillmore West in 1967.[75] Finally, DeJohnette had an ear cocked toward the abandon of jazz-influenced rock drummers such as the Who's Keith Moon, Cream's Ginger Baker, and especially, Jimi Hendrix's drummer Mitch Mitchell, for whom he had high words of praise: "I thought Mitch was the unsung hero of [Hendrix's band]. Mitch was great; he could really play. He never really got the credit he was due."[76] As the band embraced the freedoms of the avant-garde and the counterculture, Wayne Shorter adventurously responded to and shaped those freedoms on his own idiosyncratic terms, pushing his saxophone playing over the border into New Thing territory with solos that referenced late Coltrane, Pharoah Sanders, and Albert Ayler, while quoting liberally from his recent albums such as *Super Nova*, *Odyssey of Iska*, and *Moto Grosso Feio* in his solos. Even more surprisingly, this freewheeling approach to the music included Miles, whose well-known antipathy toward the avant-garde would seem to have inclined him, as bandleader, to tighten the reins on these younger players. But Miles was gushing enthusiastically about the band and lamenting the fact that, in 1969's rush of activity, a proposed live album (provisionally titled *Live at the Village Vanguard and the Spectrum*) was never completed.[77]

The set lists from two performances at Duffy's (documented sometime between February 25 and March 2, 1969, by an unidentified recorder) seem fairly conservative at first glance, comprising mostly familiar tunes stretching back through the 1960s into the late 1950s—including "Gingerbread Boy," "Green Dolphin Street," and "So What"—alongside tunes recorded by the Second Quintet that had never been performed live by that band, such as "Nefertiti" and "Paraphernalia." Like the Plugged Nickel recordings of 1965, however, these recordings depict Miles once again at the helm of a band that was about to radically rewrite the rules and procedures of his music, regardless of the repertoire. This quintet's rhythmic sense, in particular, was as flexible as a rubber band—they swung as hard as any band had ever swung, but frequently pushed that swing into all kinds of unusual rhythmic shapes and spaces. They swung so hard and with such turbulent, polyrhythmic invention, in fact, that it was sometimes difficult to tell whether or not they were actually playing time. Miles alluded to this in an interview conducted in New York with a Japanese interviewer that was published in a Japanese magazine that summer. "We play four tempos at once, and you can hear a tempo but you also can hear another one within that. And you can either play on that one or that one."[78] For the most part, the quintet did actually remain within the bounds of metered swing at this early stage, but their dizzyingly fast tempi often resulted in the kind of surreal experience of the beat that Larry Kart described:

Outside of Charlie Parker's best units, I don't think there's ever been a group so at ease at up tempos as Miles Davis's current quintet. Their relaxation at top speed enables them to move at will from the "hotness" up-tempo playing usually implies to a serene lyricism in the midst of turmoil . . . This "inside-out" quality arises from the nature of human hearing, since, at a certain point, musical speed becomes slow motion or stillness (in the same way the eye reacts to a stroboscope) . . . They generally stay right on the edge, and, when the rhythm does seem ready to spin endlessly like a Tibetan prayer wheel, one prodding note from Davis or Shorter is enough to send them hurtling into "our" time world, where speed means forward motion.[79]

Kart's comments, echoing Alan Silva's earlier observations about the innovations of Sunny Murray, are an accurate description of the rhythmic world that the quintet generated. If the Second Quintet had moved like magic between discrete tempi, the new quintet—even at this early stage—took things a step further, sometimes stacking different tempi, and at other times moving in and out of free-meter spaces with a deftness that made them seem like magicians of morphing structure. On the Duffy's recordings, some of these liquid moments might be heard as "bracketing devices"—subtle but dramatic shifts between songs—or tempo changes hinted at or executed. Yet others exist as moments of repose when the band is collectively "exhaling" after a particularly intense passage, in a way that causes them to relax out of meter. Like the rhythmic ebb and flow of the Coltrane quartet's performance of "Acknowledgement" at Antibes, what is remarkable here is the amount of dynamic tension that these juxtapositions of meter and free meter generate within the overall song form. And as with Coltrane, the quintet's mastery of the more traditional conceptions of time enabled discerning listeners to follow them through this dynamic of musical tension and release in the same way viewers might follow the trajectory of a given painter's work across a trajectory from representational painting to full abstraction and back. Overall, the exhilarating experience of time when listening to this quintet results from the absolute confidence of the band's collective rhythmic compass, which gives them an extraordinary ability to mold the music in plastic terms. Jack DeJohnette himself said it best when he explained, "We were playing the music as shapes, not as time. That kind of ebb-and-flow playing was a way of allowing the music to breathe."[80]

Taking its cue from the last days of the Second Quintet, the Lost Quintet played its music in freely associative, uninterrupted suites, with Miles cueing the next tune by playing a fragment of its theme. The band would then take off on the next tune without pause, regardless of whether it was in a different key, tempo, or time signature. In a reflection of their awareness of the ground they were breaking, and of Miles's time spent with sonic innovators such as Jimi Hendrix, Miles had bought a sound system for the band's club dates, as DeJohnette remembered:

Miles bought a sound system which the band took around. Because he wanted to make sure everybody heard the details of what was going on. So we had this portable sound system that we carried around in a Volkswagen bus. And sometimes Dave would drive it to gigs and set it up. It was just two speakers—one on each side—and then there was a head and we would just set it up. So everybody was hearing the detail."[81]

One wonders to what extent a personalized sound system would have made a difference in the presentation and reception of John Coltrane's later music. As a result of this heightened sonic clarity, many of the reviews of the new quintet began to narrate not a progression of songs, but a continuous suite of magically changing moods and structures: "Miles and his alter ego, Wayne Shorter, are gravitating ever closer to a free Nirvana, basing their improvisations on arbitrary scales and/or modes, rendering all conventional frames of reference obsolete. Tempos change and moods shift almost subliminally. The rhythm section follows with an uncanny instinct."[82] Even the reviews were becoming more impressionistic, colorful, and effusive.

The structural complexity of the Duffy's recordings is intensified by the anomalies of the crude audience recording, which alternately obscure or clarify the details of the music. This was in all likelihood a monaural recording originally made on someone's personal cassette recorder, but after many generations of duplication there are now notable differences between the left and right sides of the sound space. And while there is substantial bass presence in the 100–500hz range, a substantial chunk of frequencies is missing between 1,000 and 3,000hz. Thus, while all of the instruments can be heard, they are audible to differing extents. Miles and Shorter are fairly audible for most of the recording, and Corea's Rhodes is likely more prominent on the recording than it actually sounded in the venue—the most prominent instrument on the recording, in fact. His percussive touch, amplified by the distortion of the recording, occasionally makes the instrument sound like a Hammond B-3 organ in a neighborhood organ trio. With the sizzling sound of DeJohnette's oversaturated ride cymbal oscillating across the soundscape due to excessive compression and phase-cancellation issues, the recording as a whole presents a humid, in-your-face sound portrait that intensifies the overall sound of the band. And given the quintet's tense muscularity, this soundscape is also a very valuable portrait of a time when jazz bands came to *burn*, sublimating the physicality of the urban black experience into musical sound. Recorded on the cusp of the age of jazz-rock fusion in early 1969, it is also an instructive showcase for the glorious heritage of bebop drumming and specifically, the incredible amount of ensemble gravity that a mere ride cymbal can command on its own, with DeJohnette holding the entire ensemble together and driving them forward with much less low-end information than would be expected today.

This mechanically distorted document of the Lost Quintet, ironically set in the heart of America's Rust Belt in 1969, is a funky, textured excursion through postindustrial aesthetics, with the sound of a semi-electric jazz quintet projected through the aesthetics of decayed magnetic tape. In the visual sphere, the sound world of this recording might provide perfect accompaniment to some of the images of the Japanese street photographer Daido Moriyama, images that were also generated during a late-1960s period of social unrest in postwar Japan (figure 5.9). Moriyama's rough, heavily textured, sensual excursions burn with a haphazard energy through Tokyo's industrial districts such as Shinjuku.[83] Across traffic intersections, railroad and subway platforms, alleyways, rooftops, mirror reflections, and building facades, humans are often reduced to shadowed, spectral presences while over- or underexposed light, textures, objects, and spaces take center stage. Like Francis Wolff's cover of the 1959 album *At the Jazz Corner of the World* by Art Blakey and the Jazz Messengers but pushed a few aggressive steps further into the realm of abstraction, Moriyama's fevered black-and-white narratives transform daytime into a blinding haze of light, and nighttime into a blurred play of animate and inanimate phantoms, defined by stark contrasts of black and white, with industrial gray as the chromatic solvent: "[Cities] are alive with a breakneck momentum, with a vitality like an incredible creature or monster," Moriyama told Bree Drucker in 2017. "[M]y photographs are all about the gray, they're gray tones."[84] Photographic collections such as *Shashin Yo Sayonara* (Farewell to Photography) are dramatic problematizations of photography as a medium of realist documentary, with images cropped and distorted until familiar sights are reduced to the most abstract, indeterminate gestures.[85] Moriyama discussed his photographic process in ways that are directly resonant with the alter-archives of the Lost Quintet and its distressed textures of industrially produced sound: "When I see something discarded, be it mine or someone else's, on the darkroom floor or elsewhere in the world, and discern a certain reality or actuality in it, for me that is photography. Discarded things are beautiful. They're emotional."[86]

FIGURE 5.9 Daido Moriyama. *Riot, Tokyo, Japan 1969.* Reproduced courtesy
of the Daido Moriyama Photo Foundation.

Halfway through Corea's solo on "No Blues" in Rochester, the rhythm section begins to float away from hard swinging into a free-meter space. Miles
had been selectively toying with Don Cherry-isms on the trumpet, but now
Corea, Holland, and DeJohnette were forging an entirely new environment
around him. And while Miles had recently prodded Corea toward the Fender
Rhodes, the pianist was now channeling Bud Powell's percussive touch to make
the instrument sound as if he were transmitting Morse code instead of playing
bebop lines. So as the rhythm section ventured deeper and deeper into the free
zone (with Shorter a willing participant), Miles now had no choice but to go
with their flow. Even without LSD and light shows, these young musicians were
making Coltrane's free jazz sound like the new, psychedelic sounds coming out
of the Fillmore. Run tell that.

V: "WHAT IS SOUL?"

It's like we would go to another planet or another galaxy to get
an idea to expand and explore: different sonic things, different rhythmic
things, different coloring things—I think the band became more of a colorist
band. And I think Miles got really freer in it as well. I mean during that
period he was going for a lot of different things.[87]

Jack DeJohnette

I've been thinking—what would happen if we were on the moon and
wouldn't have any gravity and we had to play some music? 'Cause there
wouldn't be no downbeat . . . What would we be thinking of? The gravity's
no barrier. Then everything you do has to begin with an "and," know what
I mean . . . ? It's just a natural thing down here with the gravity, you know.
It doesn't go the other way. The other way is weird. It's like the back of
something. I would really like to take a flight to outer space.[88]

Miles Davis

As 1969 unfolded, Miles was clearly excited about his new quintet, and for good
reason. It has often been noted that the Lost Quintet was unique in that it performed music associated with each of Miles's three successive quintets, and in
fact the summer's set list was richly varied, encompassing abstract, gestural
themes ("Agitation," "Paraphernalia," Chick Corea's "This"), funk-rock vamps
("Directions," "Miles Runs the Voodoo Down," "It's about That Time"), blues ("No
Blues," "Gingerbread Boy"), rubato ballads ("Sanctuary," "I Fall in Love Too Easily"), standards ("'Round about Midnight," "On Green Dolphin Street"), rhythm
changes ("The Theme"), and modal pieces ("So What," "Footprints," "Nefertiti,"
"Milestones," "Masqualero," "Spanish Key"). More significant than the music they
played, however, was the *way* they played it. These songs—many of them among
Miles's most popular in their recorded versions—were rendered only fleetingly
recognizable; obliquely rendered themes spun by in a dizzying tapestry of continuously shifting moods. The composed harmonies remained as nebulous as they
had been in the Second Quintet but now opened up into completely chromatic
improvisation, sometimes anchored by funky vamps that deconstructed into
free-meter environments. With Chick Corea's electric piano and Dave Holland's
occasional riff figures, the new quintet's sound refracted Miles's older repertoire
through subtle prisms of rock and funk. But while it was relatively easy for the
progressive listener to discern the auras of musicians such as Jimi Hendrix and

Sly Stone in the Lost Quintet's new music (especially as they found themselves sharing the stage with many of these musicians on the summer festival circuit), one overlooked aspect of the electric influence was that it provided a subtle cover for the integration of experimental sounds and textures usually associated with the jazz avant-garde. After all—the sound of an overdriven electric guitar was not very different from the sound of an overblown saxophone, and once Miles started using electric piano, it was natural to blend all of these colors. At the same time that he moved into dialogue with the most sonically innovative currents in popular music, his music began to sound much more influenced by the innovations of musicians such as Cecil Taylor and Sun Ra. Ironically, then, it was the cloak of popular music that helped move Miles's music closer to free jazz than he would have ever openly admitted, and the imminent controversy over his transition into what came to be called "jazz-rock fusion" clouded the realization that the Lost Quintet was by far the freest group he had ever led. As Chick Corea described it, their music was "like free music with an occasional vamp in it."[89]

Even without a studio album of their own to sell them, the quintet was making a mark on the concert trail. The spring/summer itinerary included documented performances in Washington, DC (March 10–15), Stony Brook, New York (March 21), West Peabody, Massachusetts (May 5–11), Philadelphia, Pennsylvania (May 11), Chicago, Illinois (June 4–14), Brooklyn, New York (June 21–29), Baltimore, Maryland (June 22), Newport, Rhode Island (July 5), New York City's Central Park (July 7), and Dallas, Texas (July 18).[90] A surprisingly effusive Leonard Feather caught them in action at the Manne Hole in Los Angeles:

> A far from quiet revolution has been taking place in the world of Miles Dewey Davis. The concepts of the group he led from 1963–7 are as dead as Buddy Bolden . . . The orientation of the present unit is even more abstract than that of its predecessor . . . One set ran uninterruptedly for 90 minutes, with at least a dozen changes of tempo, meter and dynamics . . . In this group, as in life, there are some sensations that are sublime, even ecstatic, while others rack the mind almost beyond the point of endurance. The surrealist pleasure and pain, beauty and shock treatment of the new Miles Davis Quintet provide a devastating encounter, a palpable augury of the coming decade in American music.[91]

These summer performances definitely served notice that there was a new Miles Davis Quintet and a new Miles Davis sound. But as the group hit the summer festivals, they met a mixed reception. Some listeners had a negative response to the electric piano or the free elements, but the more fundamental split seemed to be between those listeners who could hear the new quintet within the ongoing continuum of Miles's music, and those who could only compare it (generally, negatively) to *Kind of Blue*, *Sketches of Spain*, and other, earlier moments of his highest commercial visibility.

The reviews of those who could hear continuity with Miles's earlier work were typically brimming with superlatives. For example, Harvey Siders reviewed the quintet's summer performance at the Monterey Jazz Festival (September 20) and reported:

> Miles is indeed fortunate: few combos as tight-knit as his could let a Herbie Hancock and a Tony Williams go and come up with replacements of equal caliber. But in Corea, he has a brilliant keyboard artist, a bit wilder and some-what freer in his comping; and in Jack DeJohnette a drummer of less intensity but no less imagination . . . The group, as a whole, is an intellectual experience from start to non-stop . . . Miles's chops were as firm as ever, and his ideas cut through with clarity . . . even though the familiar yardstick of following changes had been discarded.[92]

Larry Kart caught the quintet at the Plugged Nickel on June 14 and depicted Miles in *DownBeat* as:

> The leader in the best sense of the term. Playing almost constantly at the limit of his great ability, he inspires the others by his example. There is no shuck-ing in this band . . . With this version of the Miles Davis Quintet, one aspect of jazz has been brought to a degree of ripeness that has few parallels in the history of the music.[93]

One of the most effusive accounts came from Chris Albertson, who caught the quintet at the Garden State Jazz Festival on September 7:

> The Miles Davis quintet played an extended piece that lasted the whole set. It was one of the most exciting performances I had heard . . . Davis and Wayne Shorter expressed themselves eloquently, stepping to the back of the huge stage between chill-provoking solos . . . During the second minute of the tumultu-ous ovation that followed, the young lady seated behind me was still gasping, "Oh God, oh God, oh God!" Her reaction was understandable. She had just witnessed contemporary jazz at its peak of perfection.[94]

But the quintet was more difficult to digest for those who insisted on hearing (or seeing) Miles frozen in the moments of recordings like *Kind of Blue* or even

Miles Smiles. Karl Arnett reported in Baltimore, "Dressed in fringed buckskin, the master was accompanied by electric piano and soprano saxophone, and it was a different music. This observer found himself wishing for the old group of Herbie Hancock and Ron Carter."[95] Alistair Lawrie, in a review of the quintet's Toronto set later in the year, noted that "Davis's playing indicates that he regards coolness as passé. With his five [*sic*] collaborators and a terrifying battery of electronic gadgets, he exults today in the jagged, tearing sounds of what is referred to as the new jazz. The lyrical, thoughtful Davis has yielded to a savage thrusting style which is anything but introspective. Mostly it sounds angry, sometimes demented."[96] Some of the harshest reactions came at the very same Monterey performance that Harvey Siders had reviewed with glowing words, a festival where the quintet shared the bill with a bevy of blues and rhythm-and-blues acts. Siders himself admitted toward the end of his piece that the quintet "left many of his listeners behind, and some Neanderthal types, who can only fathom the visceral, spoiled it for the others with their dumb jeers."[97] *Billboard* reported of the same performance that "Miles Davis, 'Mr. Cool' of modern jazz trumpeting, also debuted his new quintet, with less rewarding results. Davis's group played a one-number set of music Saturday night which was fast, full of assertive anger and more convulsive than cool. There were even some boos from people unprepared for this new sound."[98] This was echoed by Leonard Feather: "Pure jazz played by the Miles Davis Quintet and the Modern Jazz Quintet were met with apathetic reactions. After Davis's performance, there was even a little booing. A couple of malcontents yelled 'We want some music!'"[99]

Miles had built a large part of his reputation as a master player of ballads, and in reality, it had only been a few years since he made cherished ballad recordings like "Blue in Green," "Someday My Prince Will Come," "Flamenco Sketches," and "My Funny Valentine." Implicit in some of this criticism was a bemoaning of the relative lack of ballads in the group's performance. With the exception of Thelonious Monk's "Round Midnight" (which itself switched to up-tempo after its rubato introduction) and Shorter's "Sanctuary" (the latter occasionally prefaced with a brief reference to Miles's 1963 recording of "I Fall in Love Too Easily"), most of the tunes were up-tempo swing tunes or abstracted funk vamps, and even these ballads seemed to function mainly as transitional interludes to cool down or refocus the band after its turbulent excursions into free playing. "Now and then," as Lucien Malson observed, "Miles gets back on stage [to] impose a tragic calm ... with that deeply dull timbre that is his alone."[100] More fundamental, though, was the ever-present issue of exactly what "modern jazz" *was*—what it should sound like, look like, and signify and, perhaps most importantly, *whose* cultural priorities it should address.

Unsurprisingly, given the state of America in the late 1960s, these reactions were often divided along racial lines. The pro-quintet reactions generally came from white American jazz journalists such as Kart, Siders, and Albertson, who were invested in the construction of jazz modernism traceable to Charlie Parker and the bebop revolution, and who could appreciate the quintet's aggressive abstraction. But for the African American jazz audience who were less beholden to the cult of bebop as it had been constructed by white jazz critics and who expected their jazz to sound a more direct dialogue with soul, jazz, and blues (as opposed to black hippie-bohemian experimentalists such as Hendrix and Sly), the music represented somewhat of a sonic and social affront. While Harvey Siders glowed about the quintet at Monterey, for example, Edith Austin wrote of "A Soul-Less Weekend in Monterey":

> Saturday night we met for the first time a Washingtonian by the name of Roberta Flack. The girl's got soul and knows exactly what to do with soul songs. Not so with the Saturday night's star attraction—Miles Davis. "Miles oughta be shot," jazz enthusiast Herbert Mims told us after the show . . . Had it not been for Sly and the Family Stones [*sic*], Sarah Vaughan, Little Esther Philips, Mr. Cannonball Adderley and Buddy Guy, you could have racked this one up as another NO![101]

White jazz critics such as Leonard Feather, meanwhile, had nothing but harsh and sarcastic words for Sly and the Family Stone:

> Ominous vibrations threatened the festival during the 90 minutes allotted to Sly and the Family Stone . . . Apparently irked because the sound was only twice as strong as necessary instead of ten times too loud, Sly stopped the show, threw a four-letter word at the crowd, and wouldn't resume until the alleged trouble had been resolved.[102]

Billboard took a similar position:

> Sly's raw outbursts of amplified power completely engulfed and dominated the opening night show, much to the chagrin of the jazz purists who kept shaking their heads (while others shook their hips) and asking "What is this

group doing here at a jazz festival . . . ?" Sly's performance, maddening in its loudness and poor musicianship, but totally motivating the audience to stand up and dance anywhere there was room, was in stark contrast to the polished excitement which Miss [Sarah] Vaughan, [Cannonball] Adderley and [Buddy] Rich generated.[103]

That Sly was one of the main musicians who had inspired the recent changes in Miles's music was apparently lost on these jazz critics, who were too consumed with resentment at the presence of rock and soul music in festivals ostensibly devoted to jazz (a programming change deemed necessary because of the declining audience for jazz and the booming audience for rock music) to recognize the innovation of his work.[104] The influence of Hendrix and Sly on jazz musicians such as Miles also implied that, whereas jazz had typically been a music led by horn players, the music's cutting edge was being increasingly shaped by a younger generation of rhythm-section players. But this was irrelevant to audiences for whom the fleeting appearance of a riff in the midst of free improvisation was not enough to root the music in anything familiar. This dichotomy between those who could hear the musical and cultural continuities in Miles's music and those who could or would not, would shape the reception of the quintet's performances as the summer unfolded. If it was the "general audience's" lack of tolerance for the high abstraction of modern jazz that inspired Miles to begin remaking his music in the first place, reviews like these must have stung. But these concerns were largely reflective of the particular dynamics of American culture, and the quintet would simultaneously confirm and confound a different set of expectations when they traveled to Europe in July.

VI: MAGNETIC

It'll feel maybe like floating at first
And then a great current gets under you[105]
Tracy K. Smith

The Austrian pianist/keyboardist Josef Zawinul was never a member of Miles's working band, but he was nonetheless a central figure in the electrification of the trumpeter's music. In the accounts of both men, their conversations tended to center around the themes of cars, boxing, and bass lines.[106] But in practical terms, Zawinul's blend of the earthy and the ethereal was the same blend that the trumpeter would seek to distill for his own new music as he gradually infused his quintet with an electric sensibility. Zawinul had emigrated to New York City in 1959 and had cut his teeth with the progressive big band of trumpeter Maynard Ferguson and the vocalist Dinah Washington, before landing a major gig with saxophonist Cannonball Adderley, whose quintet/sextet he would play in for almost a decade.[107] The Adderley band, boasting the bebop pedigree of the Adderley brothers along with (at different times) the Afro-exoticism of multiwoodwind player Yusef Lateef, the harmonic inventiveness of Zawinul, and propulsive, hard swinging rhythm-section players such as Sam Jones, Louis Hayes, Victor Gaskin, and Walter Booker, essentially functioned as a laboratory in which developments in twentieth-century Western harmony were refracted through the blues aesthetic and, as their sound evolved, expressed atop a soul groove, and occasionally inflected by exotic, world music influences. The net effect was a band sound that was simultaneously earthy and harmonically imaginative, down-home, and cosmopolitan, making the Adderley band one of the most commercially successful *and* artistically respected jazz groups of the 1960s.

Zawinul was one of the key players throughout his tenure with Adderley but his own breakthrough moment came in 1966, when he composed the soul-jazz hit "Mercy, Mercy, Mercy," adapting the gospel-soul piano stylings of Ray Charles to an instrumental jazz format and colorizing them with a newly acquired Wurlitzer electric piano (Charles had been among the first to popularize the Wurlitzer on his 1959 hit "What'd I Say," and Sun Ra had been recording with it since the 1950s). "Mercy" struck a resonant chord; it mined a similar vein as Herbie Hancock's "Watermelon Man" or Art Blakey's "Moanin'" while, similar to Wayne Shorter's stint with Miles, it also represented the beginning of an extremely productive streak in which Zawinul's compositional vision came into sharp focus. The heavier low end of the electric piano (especially after he switched to the Fender Rhodes) inspired him to expand his compositional palette to encompass catchy bass vamps on the bottom and even more adventurous, ambiguous harmonies on top. Despite its earthy, soul-jazz image, then, it is perhaps unsurprising that by 1970, one of the Adderley quintet's last albums with Zawinul was described as "music that floats and dreams like dust motes in a sun streak."[108] The Fender Rhodes was a crucial ingredient of that flotation.

While Zawinul would contribute several pieces to Miles's repertoire during 1969 and 1970, two stood out as clarion calls for the trumpeter's new direction. The first, "Directions," was one of Zawinul's most significant contributions to the

Davis band but actually had a peculiar recorded history. It had only been released in truncated form, buried as a one-minute-long, set-closing theme on Cannonball Adderley's 1970 album *The Price You Got to Pay to Be Free*.[109] And although it would later be frequently performed in concert by Zawinul and Shorter's fusion supergroup Weather Report, that group's own 1971 studio recording of the song remained unreleased until 2006.[110] Undoubtedly, then, it was through Miles's live performances that the tune received its widest exposure.

Miles recorded two excellent studio takes of "Directions" in November 1968, but they remained unreleased until 1981, and another Zawinul contribution would bring the changes in Miles's music to the attention of a much wider audience more immediately.[111] "In a Silent Way" was a meditative piece composed by Zawinul during a visit to Zurich and recorded by Miles in February 1969 (Zawinul would release his own version in 1971).[112] Several previous authors have recounted the way Miles removed most of the chords from "In a Silent Way," leaving only a repeating bass riff and a static harmonic environment of E dominant, bracketed by guitarist John McLaughlin's rubato statements of the theme. This key was eminently comfortable for guitarists, implying that from this point the harmonic complexity in Miles's music would be achieved less through chordal sequences, and more through the chromatic coloration of static vamps. Reportedly inspired by the majestic mountains ringing the city of Zurich, the warm sonority of three electric pianos is bathed in a pool of synthetic reverberation. "In a Silent Way" offers a mood of pastoral reflection updated for the psychedelic era—a guitar- and organ-driven idyll that seems to exist apart from the everyday world of jazz, and whose closest counterparts would probably be the extended, electro-pastoral readings of the Grateful Dead,[113] the shimmering textures of Roger McGuinn's guitar-driven group the Byrds, and the meditative spaces of the Indian classical traditions, especially as played on stringed instruments like the sitar, vina, sarod, and sarangi. "In a Silent Way" was released in July 1969 on an album of the same name, backed with "It's about That Time," an atmospheric treatment of a riff that would have fit perfectly on one of Cannonball Adderley's late-sixties albums.[114] The music on *In a Silent Way* was less a *clue* about Miles's new music than a full-on mission statement. In its embrace of the electric guitar and its harmonically droning nod to the Indophilia of the counterculture, the album was also a tacit admission that Jimi Hendrix's psychedelic blues was the guiding spirit of Miles's new phase, in the way that Bird, Gil, Coltrane, Wayne, and Tony Williams had been to his previous phases. And if the electric post-bop of "Directions" and *Kilimanjaro* borrowed ideas from pop and increased their harmonic complexity, the music on *In a Silent Way* represented a more dramatic paradigm shift that—unlike the earlier, muted experiments with straight-ahead jazz guitarists like George Benson, Joe Beck, and Bucky Pizzarelli—foregrounded the sound and sensibility of the electric guitar.

———

"Directions" and "In a Silent Way" both figured prominently in the two sets the quintet played at Juan Les Pins, France, on July 25 and 26, 1969. Tucked away in the commune of Antibes on the French Riviera, the seaside village has hosted one the world's most cherished jazz festivals since 1960. When Coltrane played there with his quartet in 1965, their set was described as having blown through the tranquil setting "with the force of a cyclone."[115] Now Miles, who had last played the festival in 1963 as he was assembling the Second Quintet,[116] was back with a new band to unleash his own storm, an electroacoustic conflagration that the photographer Guy Kopelowicz was on hand to document. Kopelowicz probably bought an almost-perfect set of ears to Antibes that evening given that he was a big fan of Miles's music, and had heard Cecil Taylor's Unit at the Fondation Maeght[117] in nearby St. Paul de Vence earlier the same day:

> I went to the Riviera for two reasons: Miles and Cecil Taylor. Cecil was playing with his quartet with Sam Rivers, Andrew Cyrille and Jimmy Lyons, at Fondation Maeght in Saint Paul de Vence. Then, in the evening, we headed to Antibes for the Miles concerts. Beautiful! The setting was absolutely perfect.
>
> A number of fans were very eager to hear whatever new sound Miles Davis would bring. I knew that Chick Corea had replaced Herbie Hancock in the band and I knew that he was playing electric piano . . . When the set started, the sound of the band was overwhelming. I was really stunned by the volume.[118]

Both shows were recorded and broadcast by the Office de Radiodiffusion-Télévision Française (ORTF) with the first show later released in 1991 as the Japanese album *1969 Miles*, the only official document of the Lost Quintet until Sony released more live recordings of the group in 2010 and 2013.[119] These Antibes gigs were significant because, although the quintet had been playing club dates, college dates, and summer festivals across the US during 1969, this was their European coming out of sorts. The set lists from the two nights reflected this; alongside remodelings of older staples, they also presented game-changing material from 1968 and 1969 (including material from *In a Silent Way* and the yet-to-be-recorded *Bitches Brew*).

The quintet even presented a new look, with the band members following the transformation Miles had undergone around the time he married Betty Mabry, albeit more casually. Of Corea, Holland, and DeJohnette in France, Lucian Malson observed,

> The three makers of rhythm exhibit the modern antibourgeois dress. Scruffily clad in t-shirts or a sleeveless fur vest, they let their naked arms hang. Miles Davis poses in the opposite way, refined. He appears, decked out in pink and olive green velour suits, and moves on stage with the same majesty of a prince of the old Indies.[120]

It appeared that Miles was going to have to leverage not only that princely aura but also his very musical credibility now that he was openly breaking rank and entering into a creative dialogue with ideas drawn from funk, rock, and free jazz. But the band was making no concessions at this stage and, as Guy Kopelowicz remembered, "those of us wondering about Miles's new sound were not disappointed; he was well received. Of all the concerts that he played in France that year, I think those Antibes concerts were the best."[121]

At Antibes, the quintet started things off with Zawinul's "Directions." In this live arrangement, the tune has been simultaneously simplified, accelerated, and given a jet-speed remodeling that imparts a heroic feel. Its metrically tricky opening statement has been removed (ostensibly to make the opening more aerodynamic) while the rhythm-section figure preceding the main theme is looped and repeated until a cue is given from Miles to proceed to the head. A dissonant cluster from Corea prefaces the horns' entry and, as in most of the Lost Quintet's versions of "Directions," the song is taken at such a fast pace that it takes a few seconds for the horns to sync up properly with the rhythm section; invariably, they enter hanging a bit behind the beat.

The studio take of "Directions" (recorded in November 1968) was significant in that it marked the first appearance of Jack DeJohnette on a Miles Davis recording. After arriving in New York DeJohnette had, among other gigs, played bona fide straight-ahead jazz with Jackie McLean, learned how to give both the free and straight-ahead jazz a populist inflection while playing in the band of saxophonist Charles Lloyd, and subbed for Tony Williams with Miles. He remembered: "I had played with Miles previously before officially joining the band. I had filled in for

Tony a couple of times. So I actually played from around '67 . . . Miles heard me playing with Jackie McLean, same way he heard Tony. And Jackie said to me, 'Miles is checking you out, you're probably gonna end up playing with Miles one day, because me and Miles got the same taste in drummers.'"[122]

If Tony Williams had played "Directions" at the Jazz Workshop as if he were "throwing a tantrum," Jack DeJohnette's performance of the same tune at Antibes sounds as if he is wholeheartedly embracing the concept of a drumming tantrum as his own point of departure. Writers have often contrasted Williams and DeJohnette by claiming that the latter was more willing to give Miles the "steady beat" that the trumpeter desired.[123] But while it is certainly true that DeJohnette references the swung-eighth and straight-sixteenth-note feels of jazz and rock music more often than Williams, these observations ignore the fact that these are typically mere points of departure and most of the time, DeJohnette is playing at a level of abandon that exceeds most jazz *and* rock drummers. In contrast with his measured, anchoring performance on the studio take of "Directions," the video of the Antibes set on July 26 and 27 shows DeJohnette working unbelievably hard and virtually without respite to create a maelstrom of drumming from the very beginning of the set to the very end. And while the two currently available audio documents of this performance paint very different sound pictures—the bright, cavernous soundscape of *1969 Miles* or the dry, close-mic'ed sound of the same concert as presented on *The Bootleg Series*—only players or listeners with the most deeply ingrained metronome sense could remain metrically oriented within the firestorm of DeJohnette's drumming here. His wild abstracting of the pulse makes the quintet sound as if they're hanging together by the sheer centrifugal force of the song's repeating riff although, strictly speaking, Corea and Holland depart from strict repetitions of the riff within thirty seconds after the head. The visceral effect of DeJohnette's playing here is as if the drums are spilling out around the edges of the riff like water spills from the edges of a bowl on a shaking table, like a child colors outside the lines of a figure in a coloring book, or as if circles of varying circumference have been lofted from the rotating edge of a spinning top and juxtaposed.

Trumpeters and drummers have always enjoyed a special synergy in jazz, and Miles, his playing here spurred on by DeJohnette, is improvising at a level of daring and athleticism never before heard in his career. From his opening shriek, he rips through his solo in a manner that can only be described as heroic—darting in and around the rhythm with chromatic streams of syncopated sixteenth notes sprayed across the middle and upper ranges of the horn, punctuated by his characteristic trill figures, high shrieks, and slurs—in all, definitely dispelling the stereotype of himself as a resolutely middle-range player. In fact, one might use the term "pugilistic" to describe Miles's playing here, as he audibly bounces phrases off of the whirlwind of DeJohnette's drumming and the rest of the band. If the churning rhythm section functions as his "opponent," Miles peppers them with jabs, hurls taunting shrieks and slurs at them, and finally pummels them with acidic chromatic runs and patterns that burn around the edges of the tempo. Miles's playing had long been considered the introverted compared to Dizzy Gillespie's extroverted, but even Lucien Malson made mention on this occasion of Miles's "zigzags, those piercing highs and those thundering lines that bring his recent language fleetingly close to Gillespie's."[124]

Equally surprising here is the playing of Wayne Shorter. In the early days of the Lost Quintet, Shorter seemed to retreat from the verbal cadences of his playing in the last days of the Second Quintet, reaching back into a more muscular hard-bop approach that was tightly wedded to the underlying swing, albeit given a highly chromatic resurfacing. Most of his solos on the Duffy's gigs, for example, feature a stream of chromatic lines alternately riding atop and burning through the dense ensemble textures of Corea, Holland, and DeJohnette. But the Shorter that stepped up to the mic on tenor and soprano saxophones at Antibes was a different Shorter than the one of just a few months earlier. After Corea and Holland reestablish the original ostinato at the end of Miles's solo, Shorter enters on tenor in very muscular style around 2:00. Introducing his solo with a string of thematic fragments from "It's about That Time," Shorter shapes his solo around a fracturing of the language of hard bop. His tone is harsh, as if he's playing in a 1950s rhythm-and-blues band, his Blakey experience (and Newark roots) audible in the terse muscularity of his tone. But the logic of his solo becomes progressively fragmented, disjointed, and discontinuous, a muscularity rendered full of conflict and self-critique. Initially playing within the established meter and the tonality, he soon begins to pull the band in and out of meter and tonality with his frenzied "egg scrambling" phrasing. By approximately 3:15, they have entered an environment of complete chromaticism and high-density free meter. Shorter is stoking the intensity using a combination of swirling phrases and tense, jagged statements that sound—especially in combination with DeJohnette's drums—as if he's playing himself into the center of a tornado. The solo ends with a shriek from Shorter atop a cascade of cymbal and snare from DeJohnette.

With the quintet still set squarely within a free-meter space, Chick Corea begins his solo just before 4:00, sprinkling a layer of chromatic lines over a lighter but busy texture by Holland and DeJohnette, the latter's drumming momentarily recalling Rashied Ali on John Coltrane's *Interstellar Space* sessions. The tone of Corea's instrument is not particularly well represented on *1969 Miles*, most likely due to limitations in recording quality. Besides being somewhat overshadowed by the drum set, his instrument sounds as if it has been treated with a ring-modulating unit, with the high partials consequently more apparent than the fundamentals; this detracts from the full-bodied sound the instrument is known for and gives it less presence in this particular mix. The ensemble gradually builds in intensity as Corea moves into a percussive, clashing free-meter space around 4:30, his left hand syncing up remarkably with Holland through a series of interjected clusters and fourths (a la McCoy Tyner), while his right continues to spray chromatic lines across the upper register. The piece builds in intensity from around 4:40 as Corea embarks upon a fevered progression of ascending lines and clusters, until the structure explodes around 4:50, with Corea spinning out a wild cascade of notes against a jagged ascent of chromatic figures in his right hand that open momentarily into a clearer soundscape around 4:55; this is the climax of his solo and arguably, of the entire piece. The structure intensifies again in a manner of seconds, with a second climactic passage occurring between 5:07 and 5:30.

Around 5:45 the rhythm section, seemingly magically, reconsolidates into the original meter, tempo, and tonality of "Directions" in anticipation of Miles's reentry. With Corea feeding him funky, dissonant clusters, Miles fires off an aggressive phrase that suggests a second, exciting solo. Instead, however, he quickly cools the band off with the laconic, descending blues motif that signaled the transition to the as-yet-unrecorded "Miles Runs the Voodoo Down."

How does this quintet create such a compelling sense of structural "gravity" and forward motion when all of the tension-and-release devices associated with tonality and meter have been deconstructed? One analytical model can be found in Patrik Schumacher's essay in *Digital Hadid*, in which he introduces a language to narrate the experience of an architecture in which "the inhabitant . . . no longer orients by means of prominent figures, axes, edges and clearly bounded realms. Instead, the distribution of densities, directional bias, scalar grains and gradient vectors of transformation constitute the new ontology defining what it means to be somewhere."[125] In this context of an architecture that avoids right angles, regularized spacing, and rectilinearity, Schumacher essentially narrates the flow of design energy through curvilinear space, with *density* now being the central parameter of measurement and curvilinearity being a way of charting the effect of gravity upon density. This allows him to draw a set of distinctions between *differing qualities* of curvilinear space, delineating the states of *continuously distorted space, magnetic field space,* and *particle space.* Without being too rigid and dogmatic in application, Schumacher provides a useful model for this performance of "Directions" as it unfolds through a series of metrically free states.

Of Schumacher's three qualities of curvilinear space, "magnetic field space" is particularly relevant to Holland's treatment of the bass riff that forms the basis of this piece. That riff functions here as the central "magnetizing" element—the key conceptual guidepost in the minds of the players, even as it is deconstructed in actual performance. Holland, in fact, repeatedly accesses motivic fragments of the riff as signposts in the midst of his otherwise very free accompaniment. Thus, even as they deconstruct the riff in free-meter time, it remains within arm's reach, able to be reconstituted at any moment. This concept of form can be likened to a rubber band, alternately pulled taught and left loosened, able to be pulled back into a state of tension at will. This process of building a collective improvisation by referring to increasingly remote thematic material—one of the core concepts of the game of obscuration that is modern jazz—is what provides the rhythm section with its coherence in this ostensibly "free" musical landscape. We can refer to this process as "deformation of the riff," a process very similar to what occurs in the version of "Acknowledgement" that was performed four years earlier by the Coltrane quartet on this same stage, and the gravitational element around which the tune's curvilinear rhythmic space coheres. What is fascinating in the case of the Lost Quintet is how quickly this "deformed" structure is reconstituted back into to its original form as Miles reenters, a testament to the elevated musicianship—and especially, acute listening skills—of the quintet's members. In the end, all of this can be boiled down to the same concept around which jazz has cohered since its very beginnings: motivic improvisation. And what we might refer to as the "bell-shaped" form of the quintet's performance of "Directions" here—playing metered time under Miles, expanding into free meter under Shorter and Corea, and contracting back into meter for Miles's reentry—is a form they used for most of their songs at Antibes and thereafter.

———

In addition to Zawinul's two tunes and older songs associated with Miles's First and Second quintets, the quintet played a handful of newer songs at Antibes (such as "Sanctuary," "Spanish Key," and "Miles Runs the Voodoo Down") that were in development for upcoming recording sessions scheduled for August.[126]

These sessions would be the true test of whether Miles, producer Teo Macero, and the other musicians could find the right variables to solve the musical, cultural, and marketplace equations of looseness and tightness that he and the quintet had spent the spring and summer tinkering with. More than any other musical parameter, the rhythmic dialects of groove and free meter became signifiers of this negotiation. "Looseness," as in the improvised ensemble "conversations" of small-band jazz. "Tightness," as in the repetitive structures of funk and rock. "Looseness," as in expanding the dwindling audience for jazz. "Tightness," as in remaining true to the core principles of that music. "Looseness," as in the utopian freedoms of the counterculture. "Tightness," as in the spirit of rhythmic coordination imbued with political struggle. Transcending these dichotomies would imbue the melting distinction between meter and free meter with the spirit of a new age of jazz.

VII: WORKING THE HEAVY BAG

> We wanted to make a contribution to the advancement of this music. For some people it was a peak of music. But for some other people it might have been the downfall, because Miles wasn't swinging anymore.[127]
>
> *Jack DeJohnette*

"I could put together the greatest rock and roll band you ever heard," Miles boasted to *Rolling Stone*'s Don DeMichael in late 1969, in a statement of calculated competition aimed mischievously at Jimi Hendrix, more abstractly at the new generation of improvising rock musicians, and strategically, as a way of building a bit of hype around his forthcoming album *Bitches Brew*.[128] One of the combined consequences of the psychedelic exploration, better-quality instruments, and the adventurous ethos of the time was that rock musicians were devoting more and more space to improvisation in their music, with some—guitarists such as Carlos Santana and the Grateful Dead's Jerry Garcia—openly acknowledging jazz musicians such as John Coltrane and Ornette Coleman as inspirations. But the flip side of this equation—of jazz musicians acknowledging rock musicians—was much rarer, sometimes even in the cases of the jazz-rock fusion musicians whose work was clearly indebted to the innovations of the rock musicians. Miles, by contrast, had been effusive in his public praise of Hendrix, whose chart-topping double album *Electric Ladyland* had been one of the visionary works of rock music released in 1968.[129] A sprawling mélange of hard rock, blues rock, funk, soul, and jazz filtered through a psychedelic sensibility and tied together by Hendrix's virtuoso guitar work, imaginative songwriting, and visionary approach to studio production, the album in fact offered a cornucopia of possibilities for open-minded jazz musicians. As improvisational as Hendrix's own music was becoming, however, he himself never presumed to be a jazz player, and, in fact, he had a somewhat ambivalent relationship with the rank-and-file jazz musicians of his day, most of whom could not or would not distinguish between his music and the wave of rock, soul, and funk music that seemed to be rendering jazz increasingly irrelevant as a market presence. In this light, Miles's high-profile praise of Hendrix was not only an acknowledgment of the guitarist's influence on his own new music, it also had the effect of conferring a huge amount of cultural capital on Hendrix in the jazz world while simultaneously serving definitive notice that the trumpeter himself was now aggressively separating himself from the proverbial pack.

If Hendrix's music was a transformative influence on Miles, it was because, like jazz, it was an improvisation-based practice that had developed out of the blues idiom. And the fact that Hendrix was articulating these concepts through an electric aesthetic provided a medium for the more open-minded jazz musicians to interface with the cutting edge of 1960s popular music. But there were other ties connecting the two musicians that drew their sonic and social worlds closer together as 1969 unfolded. Miles's wife Betty, for example, was a very close friend of both Hendrix and his charismatic-but-troubled live-in girlfriend, Devon Wilson, and Miles and Betty often shopped at the same East Village boutique frequented by Hendrix, a boutique co-owned by Betty's friends Colette Mimram and Stella Douglas, wife of the jazz producer Alan Douglas. Douglas himself had previously produced influential jazz recordings by John Coltrane, Cecil Taylor, Duke Ellington, Charles Mingus, Eric Dolphy, and other luminaries, and was spending more and more time with Hendrix in the studio, providing the guitarist a direct interface with the jazz world, while running interference between him and his increasingly estranged management.[130] The Douglas connection gradually drew Hendrix and Miles closer musically, while the connection with Betty drew them together socially.

The fact that jazz musicians of the stature of Miles and Gil Evans would even consider such collaborations indicates not only their imagined commercial prospects but also the musical bond that they felt with Hendrix, which Miles and Evans both acknowledged for the rest of their careers. Miles felt that "Jimi was just a great, natural musician—self-taught. He would pick up things from whoever he was around, and he picked up things quick . . . He had a natural ear for hearing music. So I'd play different shit for him, show him that way . . . It was great. He influenced me, and I influenced him, and that's the way great music is always made."[131] Unsurprisingly, many of the jazz players who valued Hendrix's innovations early on tended to be electric guitarists such as Larry Coryell and especially John McLaughlin, who remembered that "Jimi was a revolutionary like Coltrane. He could do things with the guitar that nobody had ever done before. We all owe him a great deal."[132] Dave Holland, meanwhile, remarked, "I love Jimi Hendrix . . . He was the most amazing musician, and improviser."[133] As more and more jazz musicians warmed to the possibilities opened by Hendrix, his orbit increasingly intersected with other open-minded players including McLaughlin (who would record an album with Hendrix's rhythm section the following year), Holland, Larry Young, Tony Williams, Jack DeJohnette, Sam Rivers, Rahsaan Roland Kirk, Quincy Jones, and others.[134] Eventually, Alan Douglas would attempt to broker studio collaborations between Hendrix and Miles, as well as between Hendrix and Gil Evans, projects unfortunately aborted by Hendrix's unexpected passing in September 1970. Evans, in fact, had planned to duplicate the format of his collaborations with Miles, writing an album of orchestral arrangements that featured Hendrix as soloist: "Alan Douglas had arranged for us to meet . . . He'd given [Jimi] the *Sketches of Spain* album. And the idea was for him to make a guitar record—not to sing. Because Alan felt, as I felt, too, he wasn't appreciated, even by himself."[135]

Sketches of Spain was an intriguing choice for Douglas to present to Hendrix. Conceived by Miles and Evans, it was built around a reimagining of Joaquín Rodrigo's 1939 "Concierto de Aranjuez," a piece that filtered the melodies and rhythms of traditional Spanish music through the harmonic prism of Impressionism. The album's other pieces were similar in design, contemporary works from or inspired by the music of Spain and the Iberian diaspora, including Evans's adaptations of music by the Brazilian composer Heitor Villa-Lobos, and three of his own original compositions based on Andalusian and Peruvian sources.[136] But these musical ideas did not only evoke Spanish culture for Miles. With their historical roots in North Africa and the Muslim world, they also helped open his music more explicitly to images of "Africa" and of "the East," tapping into a subtle cultural undercurrent in jazz that had grown since the 1940s and that had helped definitively shape the music of Coltrane and many others of their generation.[137] In the case of Miles, these were ideas he would revisit in 1969, as central reference points for the new music he was imagining. Even the African

American women with whom he was associated during this period—Betty Davis, Marguerite Eskridge, Jackie Battle—could, with a slight squint of the eyes, be exotically reimagined as Moorish princesses or Saharan nomads. In Hendrix's case (he had recently returned from a trip to Morocco), *Sketches of Spain* would help him articulate a more adventurous cultural sensibility, draping his blues with exotic scales and harmonies, and cloaking them thematically with images of gypsies, nomads, and caravans.

Friendships and border crossings aside, the new rock music was essentially virgin territory for Miles and the musicians around him, and, as such, it was probably no coincidence that Don Hunstein's photos for the *Rolling Stone* story built the hype by depicting Miles in full challenge mode. Hunstein presented the trumpeter as a musical don, with huge wrap-around shades and a patchwork suede vest, while the article itself is accompanied by several photos of him working out at a New York City boxing gym—crouching beneath the heavy bag, drumming the speed bag, and weighing himself on the scales with the concentration of a championship weigh-in, as his concerned trainer looks over his shoulder. The message was clear: Miles was out to conquer new territory, and his musical exchanges with Hendrix were crucial keys to that territory. These exchanges also happened to be keys to the new territory Hendrix was exploring in his own music, providing among other things a link to Coltrane's way of thinking, as Miles recalled: "I'd play [Hendrix] a record of mine or Trane's and explain to him what we were doing. Then he started incorporating things I told him into his albums."[138]

———

It might have been the spirit of Coltrane that was animating Hendrix at the Woodstock Festival in upstate New York on the morning of August 18 when—after a rambling, two-hour set with a group of underrehearsed musicians, he suddenly turned his amplifiers up full blast and catapulted into a legendary deconstruction of "The Star Spangled Banner" as his drummer Mitch Mitchell played free meter behind him as if they had suddenly transported themselves into a parallel, electrified sphere of Coltrane and Ali's *Interstellar Space*. In this three-and-a-half-minute performance—arguably the defining moment of Hendrix's career *and* one of the defining sonic-political statements of the late 1960s—the guitarist seemed to push the existential crises of the blues to their peak intensity, using his instrument to channel the most extreme sonic aspects of Coltrane,

Albert Ayler, and Sun Ra into a fully frontal critique of American militarism and a harrowing depiction of the soundscape of war. As with his virtuoso improvisation "Machine Gun" recorded later the same year, the political mood provided the context for Hendrix's most visionary statements of 1969, as noted by several reviewers who were also able to hear his music in dialogue with other currents of jazz and experimental music. In his review of Hendrix's 1969 concert in Frankfurt, Germany, for example, Wolfgang Vogel offered a characterization that could have been equally applied to any number of avant-garde jazz artists: "Musically [Hendrix] reaches far beyond the listening habits of his audience who is familiar with occidental harmonies. He doesn't abide by scales, and it isn't the proper blues he plays, but music with a different harmony pattern; never does he stick to the given time signature during his chorus. He goes over and under, exactly as it suits him . . . This is utopian music . . . Here we can hear music which one day will enter the history of music as a revolution like bop or free jazz."[139] Vogel's words were prophetic; Hendrix's 1969 performances arguably set the tone for Miles's music for the next six years; by the time of Miles's "retirement" in 1976, his avant-funk band would feature a trio of screaming, Hendrix-influenced electric guitarists who took performances like "The Star-Spangled Banner" and "Machine Gun" as their own points of departure. In the summer of 1969, however, the Hendrix influence remained subtle, mainly manifesting in Miles's music via funk and rock rhythms, repetitive bass lines, and the ambient stacking of distorted, ring-modulated electric pianos.

———

The same weekend that Hendrix was deconstructing the national anthem at Woodstock, Miles took the Lost Quintet—augmented by John McLaughlin on guitar, Bennie Maupin on bass clarinet, Joe Zawinul on electric piano, Larry Young on organ, Harvey Brooks on electric bass, percussionist Jim Riley (a.k.a. Jumma Santos), and drummers Lenny White and Don Alias—into Columbia Records' Studio B on West 52nd Street in Manhattan, to lay down tracks for the monumental album that would be titled *Bitches Brew*. *Bitches Brew* is probably the most written about Miles Davis work after *Kind of Blue*, with articles, essays, chapters, and blogs devoted to the album, not to mention several entire books.[140] My goal in this section is not a comprehensive discussion of the album but rather to bring it into proper dialogue with the Lost Quintet, without which it could never have assumed its ultimate form.

Bitches Brew would be released in March 1970, its six extended tracks spanning Zawinul's Afro-Egyptian evocation "Pharaoh's Dance," the "Spanish Phrygian" harmonies of the title track, the amorphous, ectoplasmic ensemble shapes of McLaughlin's eponymous feature, the Andalusian shades of "Spanish Key," the slow, gutbucket Hendrix-taunting "Miles Runs the Voodoo Down," and a floating, technicolor revision of Shorter's "Sanctuary" (originally recorded by the Second Quintet in early 1968). Taken as a whole, the album suggests a churning, aqueous, funked-up fusion of the sensibilities of *Sketches of Spain* and Hendrix's *Electric Ladyland* in which castanets are replaced by congas and West African drums, woodwinds and brass are replaced with electric pianos, harp and acoustic guitar are replaced with electric guitar, while Miles and the other soloists play over the top, blending the heroic stance of the *toreador* with the street heroism of the boxer. Like the relationship between Coltrane's *Crescent* and *A Love Supreme*, the album made good on the implied promise of *In a Silent Way* by delivering in chromaticized and spatialized terms what the earlier album merely sketched out in pleasantly hued pastel harmonies and a warm, cozy ambience.

Bitches Brew was transformative for jazz in several respects, one of the most far-reaching of which was in its embrace of recording technology as a *creative* medium, a moment that—as the numerous edits, loops and splices demonstrate—was as significant as Ornette Coleman's "Lonely Woman" or Coltrane's *Meditations* in its catalyzing of a new generation of design thinking in jazz—one, in fact, whose most profound implications for jazz would remain incompletely realized for another two decades, until the age of digital music production. Miles and his producer Teo Macero created a fantasia of vamp forms that collaged passages of real-time playing with tape loops excerpted from the recorded jams. The centrality of Macero's postproduction work is reflected in the anecdotes of the players, many of whom left the studio unsure of what they'd produced, only to be surprised and impressed when hearing the final results months later after the album was mixed.[141]

While the use of tape editing to mold compositions out of what were essentially open-ended jams resonated in the broadest view with the tape-splicing procedures of musique concrète, the concept of an album constructed from fragments and vignettes also brought *Bitches Brew* into dialogue with contemporaneous rock and pop albums of similarly collagist construction such as the Beach Boys's *Pet Sounds* and SMiLE projects,[142] the early recordings of Frank Zappa and the Mothers of Invention,[143] and Nico's *Marble Index*.[144] But none of this is meant to suggest, by any means, that *Bitches Brew* was merely a studio creation; rather, the relationship between the freely improvising Lost Quintet and their recorded representation on the album makes clear that the album's distinctive soundscape would not have been possible without the prior "research" done by the quintet on the concert trail. Of the album's six tracks, in fact, four had already been played at the Lost Quintet's summer 1969 concerts.

As a work conceived equally as funk, experimental jazz, and psychedelic rock, *Bitches Brew* can be experienced as both a collection of grooves and a succession of immersive environments. The album's groove sensibility represented a crossroads of several musical worlds. If the summer's performances of songs intended for the album had involved the Lost Quintet's typical seesawing between the metered grooves of funk and rock and fluid free meter, the rhythmic design of the *Bitches Brew* album, by contrast, tended to deemphasize the metrical seesawing in favor of a more complex juxtaposition of free and metered groove playing that could only have been executed with such clarity through the use of multitrack and multichannel technology. A comparison of the evolution of "Miles Runs the Voodoo Down" renders their process fairly transparent. The album version of the song, for example, is solidly grounded in a medium-slow funk pocket for all of its fourteen minutes. But what deserves particular attention is the ensemble's playing under Chick Corea's solo (beginning around 8:00 until approximately 10:30), which—unlike the reined-in playing of the other soloists—is as free as anything he was playing on the Lost Quintet's live gigs. What is remarkable is that, while the bottom of the groove remains funky underneath Corea's solo, an upper stratum of free meter flows over the top.

This juxtaposition was clearly by the design of Miles and Macero, since the ensemble rehearsed many takes of "Miles Runs the Voodoo Down" before achieving a master take. And the take that most clearly illuminates the gradual refinement of their process is "Rehearsal Take 9," released on an unofficial, two-volume set titled *Deep Brew*.[145] The take unfolds as a successive juxtaposition of two distinct metric environments, one metered and one in free meter. It opens with a very free electric piano solo by Corea, played over a steady groove maintained by the primary electric bass (played by Brooks) and Don Alias on drum set. Gradually, as Corea's solo develops in complexity, its increasingly free rhythmic movement is supported by DeJohnette and Holland (playing upright bass), who move freely in tandem with Corea's piano improvisation. Essentially, a layer of free playing was grafted on top of the basic layer of metered-groove playing in order to articulate the song surface in a particularly "open" way, rendered especially transparent by Macero's moving of the two rhythm sections to opposite channels of the stereo mix.

In the *Meditations* section of this book's essay on John Coltrane, I used Peter Eisenman's *Church of the Year 2000* project to illustrate the way a complex, composite structure could be generated from the juxtaposition of structurally static and structurally fluid strata. Another digital project by Eisenman called *Virtual House* (1997) uses a similar process of juxtaposition while arriving at a result that is more specifically relevant to the rhythm concepts of "Miles Runs the Voodoo Down" (and much of the rest of *Bitches Brew*). The illustrations for *Virtual House* depict a process in which a complex of cubes within a three-dimensional grid are set into vibrating motion, their movement gradually "deforming" their respective contours (figure 5.10). The final version of the "house" emerges out of the mutual deformation of the cubes, appearing as a region of flux within an otherwise symmetrical grid structure. Eisenman's diagrams relate to the song in this sense: while the juxtaposition of the Lost Quintet's curvilinear rhythmic

TABLE 5.2 Miles Davis Studio Ensemble
Recording session for Bitches Brew: *"Miles Runs the Voodoo Down" (August 20, 1969, rehearsal take 9)*

PERSONNEL	
Miles Davis: trumpet	*Harvey Brooks*: electric bass
Wayne Shorter: soprano saxophone	*Dave Holland*: acoustic bass
Bennie Maupin: bass clarinet	*Jack DeJohnette (right channel) and Don Alias*
John McLaughlin: electric guitar	*(left channel): drums*
Chick Corea (right channel) and Josef Zawinul	*Jumma Santos (Jim Riley)*: congas
(left channel): electric pianos	

TIME	EVENT
0:00	Alias (?) begins piece with drum pattern.
0:04	Brooks enters with primary ostinato (electric bass).
0:16	McLaughlin enters with rhythm-guitar accents.
0:20	Corea (?) enters with very free electric-piano improvisation.
0:24	DeJohnette (?) enters with free drum-set playing, in tandem with Corea's solo.
0:30 (appx.)	Holland enters with free-time (acoustic) bass playing, in tandem with Corea and DeJohnette.
2:25 (appx.)	Corea, Holland, and DeJohnette gradually resolve their parts metrically, fusing in tempo with Alias, Brooks, and McLaughlin.
2:55 (appx.)	Corea, Holland, and DeJohnette diverge from Alias, Brooks, and McLaughlin, back into a free metric space.
3:45	Take 9 ends.

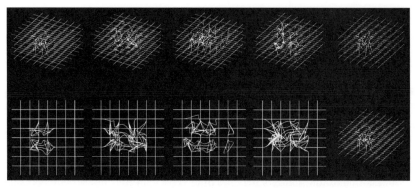

FIGURE 5.10 Peter Eisenman, *Virtual House* (1997). Copyright Eisenman Architects.

surfaces with an underlying layer of static, symmetrical repetition results in a complex and distorted composite, the outer contours of the underlying grid referent remain intact in the final illustration, retaining both the original grid referent and the emergent form. Like Eisenman's *Virtual House*, the metric freedom of the surface layer threatens to destabilize the solidity of the underlying groove but merely renders it more complex. Unfortunately, while *Bitches Brew* has been hailed and canonized as the generative work of jazz-rock fusion, scant attention has been paid to the seminal contributions the album made to the evolution of jazz drumming. Perhaps this is why the March 1999 issue of DRUM! magazine devoted an entire feature to the drummers of *Bitches Brew*, titled "The Album That Changed Drumming Forever . . ."[146]

That the "free" element has been underacknowledged as a crucial element in the construction of *Bitches Brew* is a testament to how seamlessly Macero integrated it into the fabric of the album. And those musicians and listeners involved in playing free music who were less ideological and more flexible in their thinking could hear the substantial free component. Sam Rivers, for example, offered his own take on the album, while dispelling long-standing rumors of a stylistic conflict between him and Miles: "Miles was just as advanced. In certain ways he wanted to produce his free stuff, which is what he did in *Bitches Brew* and everything. All these things are pretty much free over the static rhythm."[147]

To the extent that *Bitches Brew* has partial roots in the progressive hard-bop designs of the 1960s, it can be heard as part of a cluster of other, similarly conceived albums. Four notable works in this regard, all recorded and released between 1969 and 1971 (and perhaps, not coincidentally, all led by horn players), include Joe Henderson's *Power to the People* (recorded May 1969),[148] Donald Byrd's

Electric Byrd (recorded May 1970),[149] Woody Shaw's *Blackstone Legacy* (recorded December 1970),[150] and Lee Morgan's *The Last Session* (recorded September 1971).[151] All of these albums feature electric piano and extended songs that strike a balance between progressive hard bop, the vamp forms inspired by *Bitches Brew*, and subtle tinges of free jazz. The closest contender would probably be Henderson's *Power to the People*, recorded two months before *Bitches Brew*, and which happens to feature Miles's sidemen Ron Carter (on electric bass), Herbie Hancock, and Jack DeJohnette.

What arguably separates *Bitches Brew* from these albums is that it is a collection not only of songs and/or grooves but also of *environments*. And if the "disorienting effects" of *Electric Ladyland* were created by Hendrix's and his engineer Eddie Kramer's use of atmospheric sound processing, Miles and Teo Macero achieved the same effect by the above-mentioned juxtaposition of metered and free-meter passages, with a sense of wholeness achieved in the end through Macero's bathing of the entire album in a pool of synthetic reverberation. Not only did this render *Bitches Brew* as much about atmosphere and soundscape as it was about "jazz" performance in any traditional sense but it also liquefied and ultimately unified the various strata of activity in a way that made the album an integrative, immersive sonic experience. Producer Brian Eno explained:

> [The recording was done] by a group of musicians in a room, all sitting quite close to another . . . But they were all close-miked, which meant that their sounds were quite separate from each other. And when Teo Macero mixed the record, he put them miles apart . . . Everybody is far away, and so the impression that you have immediately, is not that you are in a little place with a group of people playing, but that you're on a huge plateau, and all of these things are going on sort of almost on the horizon.[152]

In this light—choosing for the sake of argument to hear *Bitches Brew* as a dialogue between *Sketches of Spain* and *Electric Ladyland*—we are also able to understand how the orchestral sensibility of the former was recreated via the mixing-board vision of the latter, and then expanded to cinematic dimensions. This played out in three ways across the span of the album. In terms of studio craft, one lesson Miles and Teo Macero seemed to have gleaned from *Electric Ladyland* was that the mixing process could be used to create a cinematic dimension in the music; but this lesson could have been learned just as easily from other producers and engineers of the time such as Phil Spector, Geoff Emerick, and

George Martin, or Brian Wilson, not to mention some of the panoramic 1950s jazz productions of George Avakian and Irving Townsend in the same Columbia studio, such as Duke Ellington's *Uptown* and *Ellington Indigos* albums.[153] What Miles and Macero really learned from *Electric Ladyland* was how, as in Jamaican *dub* music, the mixing process could be a form of composition and improvisation in and of itself.[154]

As a studio work, in fact, *Bitches Brew* might be considered a generative point for what might be called a stream of "ambient jazz" in which strongly stated ostinati essentially anchor music that is otherwise devoted to spatial exploration. The most thoroughly conceived projects in this vein were arguably produced by Herbie Hancock during his "Mwandishi" phase of 1970–1972.[155] Like *Bitches Brew*, Hancock's albums such as *Mwandishi*, *Crossings*, and *Sextant* (as well as side projects by band members like Eddie Henderson and Julian Priester) extended the "ambient" aspects of *Bitches Brew*, exulting in the studio's ability to contribute a dramatic spatial dimension to the music. And the particular success of Hancock's albums results from their being crafted by a rhythm-section player who orchestrated the groove of the music in a way that powerfully anchored its atmospheric aspects.

———

For several years after hallucinogens began making their way through popular culture, immersive environments became all the rage. Inspired by the synesthesia that often accompanies psychedelic experiences, these environments sprang up at the multimedia intersection of architecture, film, photography, art, and sound design. Their goals varied, but overall, they were united by a stream-of-consciousness strategy of overwhelming the senses with stimuli in the hopes of breaking through normative consciousness and opening the way for higher insights to emerge. In New York alone, they included Timothy Leary's ongoing "Psychedelic Religious Celebrations" at the Village East Theater, Billy Kluver's "9 Evenings: Theater and Engineering" at the 96th Street Armory, US Company's "Brain Activating Light Show" at the New Theater, the "Tie Dyed Cave" at the Riverside Museum, and Stan VanDerBeek's "Movie Drome" in Stony Point.[156]

Bitches Brew didn't share these projects' goal of overwhelming the mind of the listener to the same point of disorientation; the traditional narrative elements of modern jazz form and improvisation remained largely in place. But what the album (and *In a Silent Way*) did share with them was the goal, catalyzed by recent developments in studio technology, of immersing the listener in a *space*, a *vibe*, an *environment*. Armed with filters, channel switchers, and synthetic reverberation, the cinematic scope that Macero created exponentially expanded the spatial acuity of a musician whose sense of space had previously been most eloquently expressed in the phrasing of his trumpet solos and his praise of/collaborations with space-sensitive pianists like Red Garland, Bill Evans, and Ahmad Jamal. This, in fact, is what made *Bitches Brew* categorically different from Miles's recent albums like *Filles de Kilimanjaro* or *Miles in the Sky*. As much as the tracks may have been *songs*, they were also exploratory environments that opened a space for more open-ended, imaginative journeys through a musical terrain that, despite the new rhythmic language, was still strongly grounded in the progressive jazz trends of the 1960s. And while the album's sculpted street rhythms were less overtly oriented toward the kinds of dramatic alterations of consciousness that John Coltrane had been producing three years earlier, its spatialized juxtaposition of metered and nonmetered rhythms was certainly capable of generating its own psychic impact. As the *Village Voice* critic Jill Johnston wrote in her survey of the psychedelic-environmental experiments, "The name of the game is dislocation."[157] And this rhythmic dislocation, and the expanded sound mix, helped project the sound picture of recorded jazz beyond simulations of the small jazz club, to a new Space Age vision of the solar system, anchored by a newly aggressive embrace of Afro-inflected rhythm.

Finally, *Bitches Brew* is also significant as a jazz concept album of the 1960s and 1970s. Although it is probably easier to hear it in the context of rock and/or soul concept albums such as *Electric Ladyland*, the Beatles's *Sergeant Pepper's Lonely Hearts Club Band*, Sly and the Family Stone's *There's a Riot Going On*, Frank Zappa's *We're Only In It for the Money*, the Rolling Stones's *Her Satanic Majesty's Request*, and Marvin Gaye's *What's Going On*, there had been previous concept albums in jazz, suites such as Coltrane's *A Love Supreme*, Charles Mingus's *Black Saint and the Sinner Lady*, and any number of Duke Ellington's extended suites such as *Such Sweet Thunder*, the *Far East Suite*, and the *Afro-Eurasian Eclipse*, and many others, including works by Cannonball Adderley, Mary Lou Williams, and Randy Weston. Its extensive studio crafting and packaging reflect a production budget far beyond the reach of any other jazz artist of the time, placing Miles in closer dialogue with the concept album as it was being elaborated in popular music.

———

The jazz critic Bill Meyer once wrote of *Bitches Brew* that the album "drew a line in the sand that some jazz fans have never crossed, or even forgiven Davis for drawing."[158] Like the debates around free jazz, the debate around jazz-rock fusion is well-worn territory that need not be revisited here. Suffice to say that as a phenomenon, fusion generally evolved as a result of the dynamic tension between two priorities: (a) musicians' organic and sincere response to the changing soundscape of the time, and (b) a top-down mandate from recording companies encouraging jazz musicians to adapt to the new sounds in popular music that were making the corporations so much money. As such, the outcomes were as diverse as the motivations, spanning a wide spectrum of electrified jazz. *Bitches Brew* simultaneously offered a more accessible streamlining and a radical expansion of what the Lost Quintet had been offering its audiences in concert. Following the recording sessions, in fact, the quintet continued to play the music in the highly abstract way they always had while, like Coltrane's *Ascension*, the finished album waited six months in the can before wreaking its explosive transformation in the jazz world. Bringing the album and live quintet into dialogue makes clear, then, that *Bitches Brew* represented not an abrupt break but rather a logical extension of ideas Miles had been working with for some time. It also makes clear that, in the end, the album did not represent a *negation of* the jazz tradition so much as a *major transformation within* the jazz tradition.

Close musical analysis of *Bitches Brew* has an important role to play in the histories of Miles Davis and modern jazz, revealing the oft-repeated descriptions of the magical, mystical processes guiding the album's creation to be largely music industry myth making rather than accurate history. The various commercial necessities—of marketing *Bitches Brew* as a revolutionary musical statement and a definitive break with the jazz past, of creating a market demand for the musicians of the "new" musical movement (jazz-rock fusion) that followed in its wake, and later, for the mythologizing of Miles Davis and the cyclical repackaging of his recordings—have all contributed to this hype-driven warp in the historical fabric. And this is precisely why the Third Miles Davis Quintet remained "lost" for so many years: controversy and mythologizing obscured the fact that their radical rhythmic geometries helped catalyze one of the most momentous transformations in the history of jazz.

VIII: "ALMOST PURE VAPOR"

Tone is history.
Tone is memory.
Tone is heritage.
No tone, no meaning.[159]
Woody Shaw III

Son of one of the most brilliantly innovative trumpeters in the history of jazz, Woody Shaw III's meditation fundamentally reflects a *jazz philosophy of sound*— the idea that a player's musical identity is manifest first and foremost in the distinctive texture/timbre/tone color of their instrument's sound. This idea has been echoed by many of the music's greatest improvisers, including saxophonist Sonny Rollins, whose own style had ironically been forged in the idea-heavy, information-dense furnace of bebop. Surprisingly, however, Rollins told Eric Nisenson in 2000, "I think that *sound* is overall the biggest component. It's more important than ideas, really. My experience has been that the production of a certain sound supersedes what you are actually playing."[160] And while Rollins's ideas can be expanded beyond the domain of traditional instrumentalism into a broader sonic-philosophical assertion about the nature of jazz sound in general, I will focus them here on a particular assertion about the potentialities of recorded jazz sound.

For the record, these types of ideas are by no means exclusive to jazz. Writing his 2013 essay "The Metaphysics of Crackle" in the wake of 1990s electronica, for example, Mark Fisher critiqued two tendencies in much writing about popular music.[161] The first was the tendency to define that music's "authenticity" in terms of bodily presence and performances fixed in space and time; music, in this view, is something always created by human musicians playing together in real time. Fisher identifies the second tendency as "the quest to eliminate surface noise" in sound recording—in other words, the idea that playback media should be inaudible, with musical performances' instruments reproduced on recordings as faithfully and transparently as possible. Without uncritically subjecting jazz to the more extreme disembodiment tropes of electronica and digital culture, we can nonetheless observe in the jazz discourse an even more dogged insistence on the constructed authenticities of bodily presence, and on the jazz recording as a sonically faithful document of a real-time/space performance, with all of its attendant values of sonic "purity" and "fidelity." And we can combine

Fisher's ideas to observe that one unfortunate by-product of these attitudes has been that the shapers of the jazz discourse have generally remained resistant to understanding the centrality of *production* (i.e., studio craft disembodied from real-time/space performances) to the music's creative process. This, in turn, has broader implications for our understanding of jazz sound.

In fact, Fisher's critique of these ways of understanding instrumentalism and sonic fidelity can be easily applied to the culture and values of recorded jazz. And acknowledging the relevance of these critiques is a way of (to quote Fisher) "restor[ing] the uncanniness of recording by making the recorded surface audible again"[162]—in other words, of embracing all of the accidents and anomalies of the recorded medium as components of the artwork. Having been addressed in earlier sections of this essay (and in chapter 4), the artistry of the recording studio is not a primary concern of this section. But it is absolutely relevant as a point of comparison and departure into an alternate vision of recorded jazz, and a prerequisite for this section's dive into the alter-archive of the Lost Quintet.

"[B]ack-to-nature pastoralism is intrinsically reactionary," Fisher writes, and "only ways of technological interaction inherited from the jazz and now the rap avant-gardes can reintegrate humanity with the runaway machine age."[163] The flow of his argument suggests that, in his view, the torch of music's sonic cutting edge had been passed over the course of the twentieth century from jazz, to rock, and on to hip-hop and its electronic dance music descendants.[164] This lineage is predicated on the idea that jazz, in the decades of its emergence, occupied a sonic cutting edge of popular music culture due largely to its emergence at the dawn of the recording age, and its radical reconfiguration of the sonic potentials of instruments historically associated with the European marching band and symphonic traditions. That torch was subsequently passed to rock music in the mid-1960s, the electric soundscape of which exploded just as jazz seemed to have exhausted its own sonic possibilities. By the 1980s the torch was passed on to hip-hop, with its protodigital embrace of sonic values that creatively violated the sonic orthodoxies of the forms of popular music that had solidified in the 1970s, as the music became increasingly shaped by corporate priorities. Bringing the implications of this history to bear on the specific example of the Lost Quintet, then, is essentially a digital-age gambit that, like the expansion of meter into free meter, reimagines the band's alter-archives as a (retroactive) explosion of the sound world of *Bitches Brew* into a more complex set of sonic possibilities.

———

As it happens, Sonny Rollins's ideas about the psycho-emotional affect of sonic timbre and texture correlate very strongly with the work and words of photographers, who have manipulated parameters such as light, texture, and surface toward similarly expressive ends. Most photographers, for example, speak of their craft as more a manipulation of light than a depiction of a putative "subject." "If you want something to look interesting," quipped photographer John Loengard, "don't light all of it."[165] This idea, of the utility and poetry of obscuration, of the artwork shaped by varying shadings of perceptibility, is useful for the way I bring photography and recorded sound into dialogue with each other in an attempt to generate new ways of hearing the alter-archive of the Lost Quintet and other (jazz) recordings that would necessarily be considered partial and/or deficient according to mainstream standards of sound recording. And the fact that so many photographic discoveries were (circumstantially or technically) accidental not only provides a conceptual link with jazz's improvisation-driven evolution, but also provides a framework for pondering the "alternate" aesthetics of informal jazz recordings which, having degraded in fidelity as they moved across social and technological locations, might be thought of as the products of a different, albeit parallel, process of accidenting.

————

Photographically, the accident became the center relatively early in the career of the French photographer Christoph Jacrot, who received an assignment to shoot images for a photo book about Paris, his ambitions unexpectedly thwarted by the protracted spell of inclement weather the city suffered during the spring of 2006. Jacrot's resulting frustration proved to be the catalyst for a career spent photographing cityscapes partially obscured by weather disturbances (rainstorms, snowstorms, fog) or other unusual circumstances. In works such as *Meteores* (a photographic survey of weather-disturbed cities around the world),[166] *New York in Black* (documenting the blackout in New York City that followed Hurricane Sandy in 2012),[167] and *Snjór* (a portrait of Icelandic snowscapes),[168] his ambient, atmospheric images chronicle the ongoing dialogue between the constructed human environment and the elemental forces of nature, also helping him to evoke the fragility and ephemerality of the human condition. The aesthetic of obscuration in Jacrot's work is, of course, deliberate and not a consequence of technical mishap or malfunction. But his embrace of nature's defamiliarization of human habitats also springs from an initial accident, so to speak, that can inspire us to reconsider the play of presence and absence in the construction of the photographic (and phonographic) subject.

Procedures of defamiliarization-by-accident are embraced—not forced—in the photographic work of Sally Mann.[169] Innovative, imaginative, and at times controversial, much of her work would not typically come to mind as a reference point for anything having to do with jazz. But her moody landscapes (figure 5.11), shot in the American South, are in some ways closer than Jacrot to the elemental spirits that also gave birth to African American musics, while her pictorial distortions inspire a language that helps us colorize our discussion of alter-archives like those of the Lost Quintet. Mann's stylistic evolution is in many ways quite similar to Keith Calhoun and Chandra McCormack in New Orleans, while her aesthetic results are at times equally similar to a more culturally distant figure such as Miroslav Tichý or even more historically distant figures such as the nineteenth-century British photographer Julia Margaret Cameron.[170] As far back as the 1970s, Mann was experimenting with late nineteenth-century developing procedures such as the use of wet collodion negatives. Historically, collodion negatives were considered preferable to earlier developing techniques (such as the daguerreotype) that could only produce one, single-use negative at a time. The collodion process, on the other hand, produced glass-based negatives that could be reused. Their main disadvantage was the nitrate solution used to develop images, which was volatile and often resulted in stains and smears on the printed image. The nitrate solution also tended to attract foreign matter such as dust and salt that could cause the image to streak, fade, or even entirely disappear. But this volatile chemistry led to the revival of the collodion process in the hands of Mann and other contemporary photographers who exploited its visual anomalies. "You pray 'please don't let me totally screw it up,'" Mann once explained, "but still . . . screw it up enough to make it interesting."[171]

In 1975, she stumbled upon thousands of glass negatives at Washington and Lee University that had been abandoned in a state of disrepair—cracked, broken, scratched, coated with dust, and scattered across the floor. She spent the next few years cleaning, cataloguing, and printing the disfigured negatives, and while it was impossible to completely restore them, she learned profound lessons from their haphazard photographic dialect that she eventually integrated into her own work. The results were ultimately quite similar to Tichý's work, deliberately making use of a myriad of visual distortion effects such as solarization, light streaks, smudges and over-/underexposure, all of which infused her ghostlike portraits

FIGURE 5.11   Sally Mann, *Deep South, Untitled (Three Drips)* (1998). Tea-toned gelatin silver print, 40 x 50 inches/101.6 x 127 cm. Copyright Sally Mann, reproduced courtesy of Sally Mann and Gagosian.

and spooky landscapes with a sense of nostalgia, history, and loss, while also eroticizing them as sites of fertility and fecundity.

If Christoph Jacrot's visual narratives of the city disappearing into nature prepare us aesthetically for a sonic encounter with musical information obscured by clouds of tape hiss and ghosted frequencies, Mann's embrace of photography's errant chemistries inspires us tease the sonic poetry out of musical sounds that become increasingly disfigured as tapes shed their magnetic oxides, as their substrates decay, as their signal-to-noise ratio is upended by multiple duplication, or as their information is glitched out by malfunctioning digital devices. Her romantic, nostalgic commentary on the disappearing rural culture of the "old South" may not exactly align politically with the urban African American culture out of which jazz was generated, but she once described the desired effect of her work as "almost pure vapor: the whiff of dark loss and neglect,"[172] and this visual "blues sensibility" is where her specks, streaks, and light flares become aesthetically and even existentially relevant as analogues to the alter-archive of the Lost Quintet.

———

The mercurial history of that archive has only recently begun to be acknowledged as documenting a crucial chapter in the evolution of Miles Davis. Due mainly to circumstances beyond his control, the Lost Quintet never made a formal studio recording, nor were any concert recordings of them officially released during Miles's lifetime (or for decades afterward). Despite this, there are sound and/or video recordings of most of the performances given on the quintet's European tours of July and October/November 1969, as well as a handful of American performances given during the spring and summer of the same year. Some are sourced from broadcasts made by national or regional broadcast networks, while others are traceable to amateur audience recordings made by intrepid listeners who surreptitiously recorded concerts with hand-held equipment. Taken together, these recordings provide the bulk of the recorded documentation of the band's work. But herein also lies the challenge. The hodgepodge of Lost Quintet recordings, captured under a wide variety of institutional and technological circumstances, does not have the same fidelity or consistency of presentation as officially released albums or box sets of live Miles Davis performances such as *In Person at the Blackhawk*, *Live at the Plugged Nickel*, *Seven Steps*, *Pangaea*, or *We Want Miles*. The audio and visual documents of the band vary dramatically in fidelity, ranging from professional (Newport, Berlin, Rome, Paris, Rotterdam, Copenhagen) to quite challenging (Milano, Central Park, Hammersmith Odeon). Over the intervening decades, these recordings became the province of tape traders who duplicated and traded recordings via home recording equipment or file-sharing sites. Increasingly degraded in fidelity as they passed from hand to hand and across multiple generations of analog tape duplication, these recordings have become further disfigured as a result of glitches, editing, and other anomalies of their transmutation into the worlds of digitized sound.

As a result, the quintet's alter-archive is encountered through diverse and complex aesthetic prisms—their electric ethos of rhythmic flotation amplified by the glitched and corroded aesthetics of information floating in analog and digital transit—and their varying sonic fidelity presents the main analytical challenge to an accurate accounting of the Lost Quintet's brief traversal of the firmament of late-1960s jazz. Any study of their sonic legacy is thus a de facto exploration of how archival limitations might be turned to analytical and/or interpretive advantages. If the sonic-psychedelic splendor of *Bitches Brew* marked a new high-water mark for studio production in jazz, the alter-archive of the Lost Quintet exists in potent sonic counterpoint to the album, challenging accepted notions of jazz fidelity in an equally provocative way and ultimately fusing with—and, I propose, *extending*—the imaginative parameters proposed by that exalted and game-changing work of studio craft.

Some of the recordings discussed in this section were downloaded from now-defunct blog sites, while others are drawn from a cluster of recordings I received from the late producer Bob Belden, who curated several box-set reissues of Miles's music for Sony Records. Their provenance is in almost all cases unclear, the identities of the original recordists having become obscured with time. They also exist in many versions as a result of their wide circulation, making it difficult to identify a single, shared version as a credible point of departure for discussion. However, most of the recordings I cite in this section can be found on the blog *The Heat Warps: Live Miles 69–75*, and I believe these are the most widely disseminated (and easily available) versions of the Lost Quintet's live recordings.[173]

———

An audience recording made by an unidentified recordist at the Schaefer Music Festival in New York's Central Park on July 7 fades in on a distorted maelstrom of the quintet in the midst of a transition between "No Blues" and "Miles Runs the Voodoo Down" and continues through a set that is very similar in spirit to the Antibes dates, with Miles playing boldly on top, Shorter quoting liberally from his constellation of "Super Nova" themes, and the rhythm section superimposing all kinds of rhythmic and harmonic slopes against the riff-based conception of the music. Recorded under similar acoustic circumstances as the Antibes dates (i.e., an outdoor venue with a semi-enclosed stage area), the reverberant soundscape is generally similar in spatial character to the *1969 Miles* depiction of the quintet.

But here the similarities end. Although this particular recording presents a fairly balanced sound spectrum in the middle-high range, the low frequencies are barely audible, the ambient sound of the venue has fused with a layer of tape hiss accruing from generations of duplication, and the entire recording is marked by a substantial amount of distortion. There are also phase-cancellation issues, due either to improper microphone placement onstage, or anomalies of the recording equipment; the stereo microphones may be out of phase, or the heads of the recording deck may have been misaligned. In music-analytical terms, this recording is most revealing as a dramatic presentation of the counterpoint between DeJohnette and the horns. Even though the drummer's bass drum and tom-toms are for the most part inaudible, his snare and cymbals are very prominent, detailed (and distorted) in the soundscape, making the inner workings of the horns-drum dialogue vividly apparent. But with the specificity of the drum sound often lost in the mix, metric markers are obscured and whether the band is spiraling out into high-energy free-meter passages or traversing quieter, transitional moments, the overall saturation of the recording fuses the band's playing, the audience applause, the ambient sound of the venue, and the tape hiss into a relatively indistinct sound that cascades outward toward the listener in waves of edgy distortion.

An audience recording made by an unidentified recordist on October 26 at the Teatro Lirica in Milano features a spirited performance by the quintet received by an enthusiastic and appreciative audience. The Teatro Lirica had been built in 1779 as a venue primarily devoted to opera with a capacity of 1,500 (both Donizetti and Giordano had premiered works there), and in this spacious environment the quintet opened their set with the bewitching flotation space of "Bitches Brew." The rubato introduction is given a particularly probing, pointillistic treatment, its effects intensified by the anomalies of the surviving audience recording. Overall, the quintet is portrayed in a more sonically uniform manner on this recording, with the band sound seeming to emanate from a relatively confined point of acoustic origin, and all of the instruments occupying the same location in acoustic space. The balanced frequency range suggests that this was once a professional-quality recording or broadcast that became distressed over generations of duplication. There is a substantial amount of reverberant room sound here, which implies that the recording device was either located farther away from the stage (likely), or that synthetic reverberation was added after the fact (less likely). Either way, the band on this recording is portrayed in a much more indistinct character. DeJohnette's snare drum, for example, is a distinct presence but the rest of his drum set is reduced to an atmospheric turbulence, with the cymbals ceasing to function as metric markers and distilled to a droning, metallic glow. The attack of Holland's bass can be intermittently felt, though the recognition of specific pitches becomes challenging once the ensemble activity intensifies. Corea's distorted and detuned electric piano gains an additional level of texture from the poor fidelity, his playing providing the usual counterpoint between the turbulent atmospherics of the rhythm section and the horn solos above.

As usual the horns rise above the fray, with Miles and Shorter pulling the entire band into storm clouds of turbulence within which only a bit of rhythm-section detail is discernible. Corea, Holland, and DeJohnette combine in the soundscape to produce a thick, floating cloud of distorted sound that intermittently consolidates and dissolves, held together by the ectoplasmic texture, densely chromatic harmonies, and spooky psycho-emotional effect of Corea's electric piano. With the distinction between meter and free meter rendered virtually imperceptible by the fidelity and the extremely "wet" room sound, this version of "Bitches Brew" unfolds as an atmospherically enhanced voyage across a series of rhythmic reefs intermittently strewn across free-floating space, its iridescent distortion marking it as a document of "sonic fiction" equal to anything created by Sun Ra's Crumar organ, King Tubby's hi-pass filter, or Coltrane's late-period tenor saxophone.

On November 2, the quintet played its second London gig (independently of the Newport tour) at Ronnie Scott's famous basement club on Frith Street, with a recording made by the BBC. Unfortunately, the original tapes were wiped in the 1970s.[174] The recording that survives (apparently captured by an unidentified recordist from a BBC broadcast) presents a dry soundscape that is the atmospheric opposite of the cavernous Teatro Lirico recording. The fairly balanced frequency spectrum and reasonably balanced stereo field suggest that this was originally a well-executed audience recording. But the minimal room sound, in conjunction with a recorded signal once again compromised by generations of compounded tape hiss, results in a document that depicts the space as almost claustrophobically tight.[175] The spatial qualities of the quintet's performance must then be experienced less through their sound's resonance in an acoustic space, and more as a consequence of the internal construction of their rhythms.

Like the Milano recording, the Ronnie Scott recording is incomplete, and fades in with the quintet once again exploring the fragmented flotation space of the "Bitches Brew" outro. Miles, playing with a Harmon mute, navigates the space economically and somewhat laconically, making the room ebb and flow like an aquatic environment before cueing "It's about That Time" at around 2:10. There follows a rowdy, pugilistic trumpet solo that gradually tightens up the room, with DeJohnette driving Miles higher and higher, Corea improvising figures that alternately punctuate and cascade across the groove, and Holland holding down the bass line as it was originally recorded, before exploding into a funky, syncopated sixteenth-note line around 4:31. Coming out of Miles's solo and into Shorter's, the band relaxes into a free-meter space around 4:58, which Corea measures out with an ascending chordal figure that seems derived from

Gil Evans's "Eleven" (recorded by the Second Quintet as "Petits Machins" on *Filles De Kilimanjaro*). Its particular placement against the ongoing, turbulent motion of Holland and DeJohnette gives the impression of intermittently slashing against the underlying rhythm at a diagonal, creating a tense soundscape that opens up the space by pulling it in two directions simultaneously. The recording of this exciting set continues for another thirty-two minutes, but in these first five minutes, the quintet has taken the audience on a spatial journey via their continuous rhythmic transformations, and the varying interlocking of ensemble parts, to mold the listener's acoustic experience of the room. And the aesthetics of this recording, which all but eliminate the presence of ambient room sound, dramatize the spatiality of the band's rhythmic journey.

———

"The poor image tends toward abstraction," writes Hito Steyerl in her digital-age meditation on glitch aesthetics, and certainly none of these recordings of the Lost Quintet conform to what is typically expected of commercial jazz record-ings.[176] And while hearing them through the conceptual prism of experimental photography and engaging them as objects of sound art potentially intensifies the ethos of abstraction that led to their marginalization from jazz history in the first place, there are nonetheless photographers who have, in their work, directly responded to the call of free jazz. Culturally closer than Christian Jacrot and Sally Mann to the spirit and history of free jazz is the work of a quartet of photographers—Roy De Carava, Hart Leroy Bibbs, Spencer Richards (figure 5.12), and Ming Smith—whose work was contemporaneous with free jazz as an emergent movement, and for whom the sensation of *blurring* has been central to their visual representations of that music's affect. De Carava's fevered images of the John Coltrane quartet in performance,[177] Richards's action shots on Ce-cil Taylor's late-1970s albums like *One Too Many Salty Swift and Not Goodbye* (1980),[178] Bibbs's blurred portraits of Steve Lacy on albums like *The Flame* (1982)[179] and *Scratching the Seventies* (1997),[180] and Smith's legendary images of Sun Ra and her urban landscapes that adorned the cover of David Murray's two-volume *Live at Sweet Basil* (1984)[181] arguably bring the sonic and the visual closer in political, aesthetic, and cultural terms.

Other artists and thinkers have sensed deeper cultural and historical reso-nances in this photographic romancing of the blur. Arthur Jafa and Fred Moten, for example, have embraced low fidelity, low resolution, and the blur at different

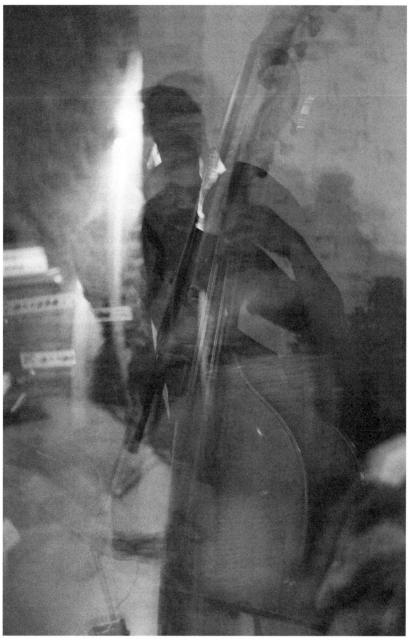

FIGURE 5.12 Spencer Richards, *Sirone Digs* (late 1970s).
Reproduced courtesy of Spencer Richards.

times in their respective cultural commentaries. Jafa achieved widespread acclaim with his 2016 art film *Love Is the Message, the Message Is Death*, which deliberately repurposed low-resolution YouTube videos into a meditation on the triumphant and tragic dimensions of African American life in the new millennium and is as much a commentary on archives as it is on culture.[182] Moten, meanwhile, has explored this idea in his 2017 book *Black and Blur*, which uses the blur trope to bring music, philosophy, and Afro-diasporic history into dialogue in a meditation on the continued necessity of indeterminacy and fugitivity for Afro-diasporic cultural survival.[183] Both of these artists, in fact, interpret the blur as a fugitive strategy of escaping surveillance.[184] But even Hito Steyerl, writing far beyond the span of the African diaspora, has produced a video titled *How Not to Be Seen*, suggesting that, in the age of the digital panopticon, glitch aesthetics can be strategically harnessed as a midpoint on the spectrum spanning invisibility and ubiquity.[185] While many of these psycho-historical interpretations lean toward the speculative, they do evoke psychic states fundamental to both Afro-diasporic cultural experience and the general human experience of digital-age paranoia. Meanwhile, these ideas of fugitivity intersect most literally with the glitched and blurred alter-archive of the Lost Quintet in its decades-long obscuration, itself a consequence not only of Davis's stylistic restlessness and the indifference of his record label, but also of the demonization of the utopian strivings of the 1960s, as well as the neoliberal, digital restructuring of media industries that began in the 1980s. Miles Davis was by no means an icon of the jazz avant-garde, but, given his important place within those strivings, it is perhaps no coincidence that sonic distortion and historical marginalization intersect in the documentation of this provocative moment in his career.

IX: SHOOTING ROCKETS

The records like *In a Silent Way* and *Bitches Brew* now get talked about a lot because they are well-documented recordings, but to me were really just "wisps in the wind" as far as "the meat of the process" from that era. The "meat of the process" was our live performances and what Miles did in front of people. That music was some of the wildest, strongest and most free music that Miles ever played.[186]

Chick Corea

It was fantastic for all of us, playing with the greatest living trumpet
player in the world . . . I think in that period the music really expanded, and
the music reflected the times . . . Young people felt that they could actually
have some power and change the policies of the government. People were
trying everything—sex, drugs, rock and roll. So we were trying things in the
music. We had the Cream, we had Jefferson Airplane, we had Hendrix,
we had Sly and the Family Stone. The Vietnam War was going on. They were
shooting rockets off of Cape Canaveral. So people felt that they could make
a difference, and they felt they could shoot rockets off in the music as well.[187]

Jack DeJohnette

For Miles and the musicians around him, 1969 was a year of building momentum that culminated with the recording of *Bitches Brew* in August. It might
seem logical, then, to conclude this extended essay on the Lost Quintet with
the recording, release, and commercial success of that album. In one way of
thinking, after all, the sun seemed to be setting on the dynamic quintets that
had reigned since the days of bebop. But *Bitches Brew*, with its expanded ensemble and its extensive postproduction, was a special, one-off project that
had more in common with Miles's earlier orchestral collaborations with Gil
Evans than it did with how the quintet was playing the same music in concert.
And if that music had needed to be reined in, in some ways, for *Bitches Brew*,
the live performances allowed the quintet much more latitude to explore and
reinterpret it from night to night. And reinterpret it they did. As a jazz musician, Miles wasn't nearly as constrained by the pop audience's expectation that
he would faithfully reproduce the material from his recordings. Although he
would occasionally face audiences yelling out for "So What" and "My Funny
Valentine" well into the 1970s, the general operating procedures of modern
jazz had broadened the field of possibility in his music to a degree that left his
creative horizons wide open in 1969.

Secure in the knowledge that he had a game-changing album in the works,
Miles took the quintet back out on the road through the late summer and fall
of 1969 (unfortunately, a Japanese tour planned for this time was cancelled at
the last minute). And as much as his eyes were now increasingly trained on the
horizon beyond the world of *jazz-as-it-had-been*, he remained excited about
the quintet, which he praised in interviews (and later, in his autobiography),
while lamenting the fact that a proposed live album (provisionally titled *Live*

at the Village Vanguard and the Spectrum) was never completed.[188] After their return from Antibes, the quintet is documented as having played gigs at Rutgers University (July 27), French Lick, Indiana (July 31), Philadelphia, Pennsylvania (August 15), Chicago's Grant Park Theater (August 22), Crosley Field in Cincinnati (August 23), and Shelly Manne's Manne Hole in Los Angeles (September).[189] But their highest-profile performances took place during late October and early November, as part of George Wein's Newport Jazz Festival in Europe, a package tour that also included the Duke Ellington Orchestra, the Cecil Taylor Unit, and Nina Simone. Unlike the two-night appearance at Antibes, the tour of late 1969 gave the Europeans more sustained exposure to Miles's latest music.[190] And at a time when, as Dave Holland remembered, the quintet was playing to American nightclub audiences that were sometimes as small as thirty or forty people, recordings of the European tour afford us the opportunity to hear and see them in front of sizeable and appreciative audiences.[191]

The Newport tour included stops in Milan (October 26), Rome (October 27, two shows), Vienna (October 31), London (November 1 and 2), Paris (November 3, two shows), Copenhagen (November 4), Stockholm (November 6, two shows), Berlin (November 7), and Rotterdam (November 9), and all of these performances were documented in one form or another. As on the summer festival tour in the US, reviews of the quintet's performances were generally rendered with superlatives. Ian Carr recounted the group's performance at London's Hammersmith Odeon (November 1) with enthusiasm:

[The quintet] created music at an extraordinarily brilliant level of intensity . . . and they offered long sets of continuous music. The musical transitions seemed magically achieved, and some people wondered if there were visual signals, such as when Miles rested his trumpet on his shoulder, but this was not the case. The cues were all musical and Miles's playing was awesome (in the full sense of the word) that night.[192]

Ian Breach reviewed the same Hammersmith concert and, like the other writers, heard this quintet as a clear extension of the Second Quintet:

For all its sparse, fragmented sound the newest quintet has a unity that few groups could claim after many more years together than this one . . . The surprise comes in finding that pianist Armando [Chick] Corea takes over precisely where Herbie Hancock left off, amplifying the somnolent slow passages and forcing the pace on teeth-rattling upper-register runs . . . Like bassist Dave Holland and drummer Jack DeJohnette, he is young enough to underline Davis's apparent determination to keep well ahead.[193]

DownBeat's correspondent Ronald Akins was suitably impressed with the quintet's Berlin performance and compared their achievement with John Coltrane's: "This is the first time we'd heard Davis play in a style well in advance of anything he has recorded, and the impact he made was equaled in my experience only by John Coltrane."[194] As with the American reviewers, however, not everyone was equally moved. What some listeners heard as the proverbial "next level," others heard as cold, cerebral, sometimes even intimidating detachment, the ultimate refinement and abstraction of the cool, detached musical codes of the beboppers. Back in the heat of the Newport summer, for example, Ira Gitler had observed that "Miles Davis was in a dark brooding mood, blowing steel rivets from his black and orange horn and soldering them to the girders of the uninterrupted pieces that comprised his set."[195] Reviews of this type continued in Europe. Despite his glowing review of the London show, Ian Carr also noted that "the Hammersmith Odeon was only at seventy-five percent capacity, and the audience gave [Davis] only a lukewarm reception. Many people were seen to walk out."[196] Miles Kington described the quintet's Hammersmith set as offering "an hour of arrogantly good music," but he added, "I would willingly forego some of the brilliance for more warmth, more humanity."[197] Breach similarly noted this quality in his review of the quintet's Hammersmith performance:

> For half his life Miles Davis has moved quickly as soon as each of his styles has become accepted . . . Which is a way of saying that his performance on Saturday was a disappointment for anyone who expected him to play a selection from *Milestones, Kind of Blue,* or even *Nefertiti.* The concert ran exceedingly late, and there were trains and buses to catch, but many of the deserters who left around midnight would, I am sure, gladly have walked home if Davis and tenor man Wayne Shorter had been swapping solos of the kind they did until recently.[198]

The irony here is that, at the concert Breach reviewed, the quintet *did*, in fact, perform several pieces from the earlier periods he evokes, including "No Blues" (1961–62), "I Fall in Love Too Easily" (1963), "Masqualero" (1967), and "Paraphernalia" (1968). But, typically for this band, they were played in a fashion that rendered them only fleetingly recognizable to all but the most committed listeners. Of course, this was par for the course for post–Second Quintet Miles. Even after the release of *Bitches Brew*, some of the most astute listeners attending a concert with the intention of hearing the type of riff-based, rhythmically accessible music offered on that album might still have had difficulty recognizing familiar themes, since the live performances unfolded as if the studio takes were distant points of departure. Miles admitted as much—with characteristic exaggeration—in a Japanese interview in August, when *Filles de Kilimanjaro* had been out for a mere six months, and *In a Silent Way* less than a month: "I don't know what to say about those albums now. They seem like they're fifteen years old to me. It's a nice way to play but there's something else happening now . . . The records, those are like plastic thoughts. It's nice, but it'll sound different when we play it in person."[199]

Part of the challenge for some listeners was the fact that the quintet performed the music on this tour in the same oblique, rhythmically elastic way they had been performing it since the spring of 1969, making the identification of discrete songs challenging. On most of these performances, the order of solos remained Miles > Shorter > Corea (with an occasional drum or bass solo interpolated) with the rhythm section playing time under Miles's solo, moving gradually into free meter for the solos of Shorter and Corea, before returning to metered time that may or may not include a restatement of the head. This expectation of return to the original form, in fact, probably helps imbue the music with its formal and structural tension as the metric "rubber band" is alternately loosened and tightened. Malson noted this quality:

> From the first seconds until the last, the luxurious rhythms, the continuous rattle of Jack DeJohnette's drum, the imperative pulsation of Dave Holland's bass . . . the nervous statements of Chick Corea's electric piano have the permanent scansion necessary for the "free" aesthetic not to fall into chaos.[200]

"Scansion," a term that refers to the measuring of the rhythm of a poetic verse as it unfolds, is rooted in the Latin verb *scandere* (to climb), while "permanent" reflects the continuity that Malson perceived in the midst of the quintet's structural transformations. His choice of words reveals that he not only perceived a linear continuity and cohesion but also that the tension and release of swing existed for him without the reference points of meter.

But perceptions like these would only be available to the most advanced jazz listeners; the fact is that all of this was taking place within a conception of music that was remarkably free for someone who had previously voiced such harsh and dismissive words for the jazz avant-garde. Wayne Shorter told Oliver Bremond, "You can't really hear it on [Miles's] albums . . . [b]ut in public, we really played very *free*, particularly with the group with Jack DeJohnette and Chick Corea."[201] Corea himself described the quintet's music as "free jazz with an occasional vamp in it."[202] DeJohnette recalled that the band's style—freely flowing but tight—also benefitted from the opportunity to check out the internal workings of Cecil Taylor's group on a nightly basis: "We went on the Newport tour in Europe—it was Duke's band and Cecil Taylor's band when he had Jimmy Lyons, Andrew Cyrille, and Sam Rivers. So they would open up for us. So we were around that and we were exposed to these guys."[203] It was a measure of how much freedom Miles allowed the group that, for a period, Corea sometimes even left the electric piano to play a second drum set alongside DeJohnette:

> Chick just turned up one day and said to Miles, "Do you mind if I bring a drum set . . .?" He carried a drum set around with him, and sometimes instead of me playing a drum solo, we would play two-drum stuff. But we only did that for a little while. Miles kind of got tired of that. But to his credit, he was open to us experimenting and trying stuff like that.[204]

———

The European concerts are arguably as compelling in visual terms as they are in sonic terms. Miles had been in the habit of touring Europe every two or three years, with each visit presenting a dramatic change in his music. This particular tour also presented a dramatic change in his self-presentation. The last time most of Europe (with the exception of the Antibes audiences in July) had seen him was in 1967, when the Second Quintet toured the continent dressed in the dark suits of jazz modernism, still asserting bop and its derivations as a black art music of the American metropolis. But things had changed dramatically by 1969. The widely circulated photos of the quintet's appearance at Ronnie Scott's in London (November 2), for example, are nothing if not period pieces of high-end, exotic hippie chic framed by typical late-sixties nightclub decor. Against a faux-psychedelic, zig-zag patterned stage backdrop, Davis appears in an indigo shirt, long rainbow-colored scarf, and black leather pants, while the rest of the band are in loosely flowing shirts with vests, the silver-black electric rectangle of the Fender Rhodes symbolically and sonically dominating stage right and pointing the way toward the 1970s. The quintet's sartorial choices might seem like fairly innocuous reflections of the fashion trends of the time. But with western Europe reeling from political turmoil in the universities, struggling with its legacy of colonialism, and with the continent's ongoing valorization of jazz being challenged by a younger generation's suspicion of the assumption that a virtuoso art music—albeit one improvised by African American musicians—was inherently politically progressive, the quintet's hippie chic was also a complex signifier of jazz's changing social and cultural capital on both sides of the Atlantic. This was especially true on the stages of Europe's concert halls, many originally built for the performance of Western art music. Guy Le Querrec's iconic images of Miles onstage at the Salle Pleyel (built in 1927) portray the trumpeter as elegantly as ever, but his embroidered Moroccan shirt, multi colored scarf, snakeskin pants, and leather boots represent a new sartorial equation that gestured more toward the non-West as center of taste than it did toward Western Europe. Or even central Harlem.

———

I think nightclubs as a whole are passé. They have served their purpose and
I don't think they are functional anymore as far as jazz is concerned, that is
not unless the whole concept of architecture has changed.[205]

Elvin Jones

A catenoid is a curve defined as a hanging weighted string.[206]

Greg Lynn

The quintet's performance in Hans Scharoun's Berlin Philharmonie (built 1963) is probably the cleanest visual document of the tour. Originally broadcast by Sender Freies TV in Berlin, it is also one of the few Lost Quintet performances that has been given an officially sanctioned release.[207] Despite the passage of time and the vaguely blurry resolution, the sonic and visual clarity would have been considered first-rate at the time of the performance. The stage is bathed in bright light as in a concert of classical music, highlighting not only the musicians' fashion choices for the evening but also the highly technological environment of the Berlin Philharmonie. The musicians enter the brightly lit stage among a maze of wires and with a studied insouciance, barely acknowledging the audience's applause as their names are introduced. Miles himself appears in an embroidered black Moroccan shirt and black fringed-leather vest, with a flowing red-and-yellow scarf and crimson pants, with the other musicians only slightly more muted in their attire. But the turbulent, ephemeral music they played belied their subdued demeanors, and it was fittingly framed by the unique geometry of Scharoun's staggered balconies that wrapped all the way around the stage.

Scharoun's stage-in-the-round concert hall is often referred to as a "vineyard" design, a departure from the rectangular "shoebox" that had been the standard for European concert halls since the end of the eighteenth century.[208] The rectangular form, which had been devised as a way of channeling the linearized flow of energy from a symphony orchestra, through the intermediary figure of the conductor, and on to a seated audience, was encoded with power and hierarchy. The "vineyard" arrangement, by contrast, was an attempt at a more egalitarian experience of the concert hall, one of many ways that the past was being challenged in post–World War II (West) Germany. Viewing the video of the quintet performing against Scharoun's backdrop is in fact a welcome change from the typical jazz scenery of nightclubs and open-air festival venues such as Newport, and a visually rare and compelling backdrop for the quintet's fluid, deconstructive sound world. After all, jazz musicians have not only fantasized about specially designed venues in which to present their music but have also acted on this whenever possible, from the sacred concerts that Duke Ellington presented at Grace Cathedral in San Francisco and the Cathedral of St. John the Divine in New York, to Don and Moki Cherry's "Utopia and Vision" geodesic dome at Stockholm's Moderna Museet, to the numerous loft spaces in downtown Manhattan of the 1970s, to Rose Hall, the auditorium specially designed for Jazz at Lincoln Center in New York City. The irony, of course, is that although several of Europe's post–World War II concert halls abandoned the traditional interiors for more dynamic, circular forms, they continued to overwhelmingly showcase Western art music of the eighteenth and nineteenth centuries.

Challenges to this status quo were being mounted, however. At the 1970 Worlds' Fair in Osaka, Japan, for example, the experimental composer Karlheinz Stockhausen premiered a number of works that he had specially composed for the "Garden of Music," a specially constructed geodesic dome in which the pieces were being performed. The "performance" was a number of live and prerecorded electronic and electro-acoustic works, mixed by Stockhausen himself from a centrally located mixing board and designed to immerse the audience in what Michael Fowler referred to as a series of "ephemeral sonic architectures."[209] In possibly the pinnacle project of the his late-1960s/early-1970s work, Stockhausen was drawing on the legacy of composers such as Iannis Xenakis and the architect Le Corbusier, whose Phillips Pavilion at Expo '58 in Brussels was one of the first high-profile collaborations between a musical composer and an architect, showcasing canonical works of post–World War II experimental music such as Xenakis's *Concret PH* and Edgar Varèse's *Poème électronique*. Stockhausen's spatial preoccupations arguably began in the 1950s with the abstract pitch spaces of serialism, expanded in the early 1960s with pieces such as *Momente* that incorporated physical movement of the performers, extended into sonic-architectural thinking with pieces composed for specific spatial configurations such as *Pole* and *Spiral*, expanded into a vision of global musical unity with pieces such as *Hymnen* (1966–67), projected into celestial and/or cosmological scale with pieces such as *Kurzwellen* (1968), *Sternklang* (1971), and *Sirius* (1975), and culminated with *Helikopter Streichquartett* (1995), a string quartet in which the musicians played while suspended in midair in four separate helicopters.

Miles and his musicians had neither geodesic domes nor helicopters at their disposal, but like John Coltrane's recordings from Europe or Japan, many of the European recordings give the quintet's music a much more expansive spatial identity by merely lifting it out of the acoustic space of the nightclub. Across spacious concert halls like Paris's Salle Pleyel, Berlin's Philharmonie, or London's Hammersmith Odeon, not only are layers of sonic detail revealed, but the group's playing also articulates the sonic spaces in different ways. On a hypercharged revamping of "It's about That Time" played in Berlin, for example, Miles's phrasing is like a boxer, darting around the insistent riff of the tune in a way that alternately seems as if he is shouting across a valley or playing against a solid wall. Shorter's solos, as the band morphs into free meter, sometimes flow like liquid, sometimes stutter like Morse code, and at other times unfold as sermons, making the space seem to expand and contract in response to his different improvisational dialects. In particular, these reverberant spaces demonstrate just how central Chick Corea is to the band's sound. His pointillistic phrasing, bouncing around the acoustic space, seems to render the entire hall a porous sponge. With his background in drumming and his general percussive sensibility, he was the perfect architect to weave free-meter flotation and funk gravity into a unified rhythmic narrative, stretching a flexible trampoline for Davis and Shorter over the rolling, shifting counterpoint that these spaces reveal in the interplay between Holland and DeJohnette. And even though the debates surrounding jazz-rock fusion were emerging on the horizon, listeners like Ronald Akins and Lucien Malson were appreciative of the music's newly electric resurfacing, with the latter enthusing, "We were touched by Chick

Corea's playing, whose—electric—instrument expressed a splendid sound, full of clarity and density. Chick Corea *interrogates* the piano, *searches* in front of us . . . and almost continuously *finds* figures of great relief."[210]

While the bulk of this performance is situated in various articulations of free-meter space, the film's framing shows Miles in command, keeping the band as tight as a military unit, his sidemen waiting in taut anticipation of the leader's "coded phrases" that abruptly and dramatically redirect the music.[211] Of the five songs played during the quintet's short set in Berlin, only two ("Directions" and "It's about That Time") are truly up-tempo while one ("Bitches Brew") unfolds at a funky midtempo (albeit with rubato introduction and conclusion), and the other two ("I Fall in Love Too Easily" and "Sanctuary") are entirely rendered in freely floating rubato. On this night, as on most of the others, the performance as a whole passes as a highly cerebral, highly evocative dream sequence occasionally underpinned by funky rhythms. The quintet's music likely seemed puzzling to some of the audience who had followed Miles's music over the years, but it was intriguing for listeners such as Ronald Akins, who could hear the quintet's place within the electrifying soundscape of the late 1960s:

> For the first time, this highly-rated jazz musician got away from the bop idea of coupling trumpet and tenor saxophone. The electric piano provides the ideal for the wind instruments and determines the tonal color. In this way Miles Davis and his saxophonist Wayne Shorter produced improvisations with a degree of maturity and melodic beauty which can have few parallels in the history of jazz.[212]

While Scharoun's "vineyard" was a fascinating setting in which to experience the quintet, there were other settings in Germany that, like Stockhausen's geodesic dome, might arguably have framed their sound in an even more resonant way. At the same time that the quintet was triumphing in Berlin, the architect Frei Otto (1925–2015) was challenging the more problematic aspects of Germany's twentieth-century history by creating lightweight structures—"cable-net structures," "tensile structures," and "membrane structures," as they were variously called—that were modeled on minimal, organic forms such as spider webs, sand dunes, and soap film and that, he claimed, "free[d] architecture from simple geometry."[213] Otto's innovations, which were awarded the Pritzker Prize in 2015, did not materialize out of nowhere. He was born in 1925 to a family of stonemasons and spent his childhood obsessed with flotation and flight, devoting most of his free time to building model airplanes. While studying architecture in Berlin he was drafted into the Nazi Luftwaffe in the final years of World War II. After the war he was held in a French prisoner-of-war camp, where he was forced to repair damaged structures (especially bridges) using only natural materials available in the local environment. Otto's architectural vision emerged out of these diverse and turbulent experiences. His working motto "with lightness against brutality" reflected the fact that these structures were also at least partially conceived as a rejection of the monumental architecture of the Nazi era,[214] embracing the ephemeral tent forms and states of pervasive postwar homelessness that surrounded him and resignifying them as icons of openness and mobility. Arguing that "a light, flexible architecture might bring about a new and open society," Otto helped pioneer a form of architecture that emphasized the sensations of floating and sailing, creating for its inhabitants a sense of buoyancy, transparency, freedom, and flexibility and a dialogue with the organic forms of the natural world.[215]

We can safely assume that Otto was not concerned with concepts such as the "Africanist Grid" in 1969 as he planned the stadium for the 1972 Olympics in Munich, the capstone project of his career (figure 5.13). But his suspended nets that, in one way of thinking, redeployed flowing splines from ground surfaces to roofs and coverings, proved that structural integrity could be maintained without a heavy, imposing system of rigid columns and beams. And while there is a clear metric regularity to both the support structure and the floating nets, Otto's innovations remain in this sense compelling structural analogues for the way the Lost Quintet stretched and distorted the contours of the Africanist Grid into a more metrically flexible space, retaining the tension and release of swing without the cyclical strong and weak beats of meter. Back in 1962 Otto had edited *Tensile Structures*, a manual that might be thought of as his technical manifesto, and his projects are, in their own ways, studies in the manipulation of an aesthetic of tension and release that might be considered their own form of "swing."[216] A key element of his style (for example, in the Munich stadium) is the *catenoid*, a curve articulated by hanging weighted strings. And if the spline surface is one of the iconic symbols of the way digital architecture has rendered our understanding of surface more flexible and fluid at the dawn of the new millennium, Frei Otto had arguably anticipated this design element thirty years earlier with his structures built from catenoidal curves.[217] In embracing the organic forms of nature as an antidote to the human urge to impose power,

his "celestial tents" essentially made splines airborne and, in the process, made his buildings "swing" in the rhythmic language of freedom.

Reflecting on his formative years as an architect in wartime Germany, Frei Otto once commented that "burning cities are a hard introductory course for young architects."[218] Here he was simultaneously evoking the circumstances out of which his artistic vision had been birthed, while placing himself in a twentieth-century tradition of "dematerializing" architecture. This "tradition" has dotted the history of the field at least as far back as the end of World War I, as architects fought to distance themselves from the ethos of fascism and authoritarianism as they had been concretized within architectural form, while transmuting wartime energies of destruction and dissolution. It would be irresponsible to claim that Otto's dematerialization of architecture and the dematerialization of jazz rhythm in the 1960s sprang from the exact same sources and intentions. But with experimental jazz musicians pushing back against a beat that to them represented commerce and control, and with America's own cities burning in the late 1960s as a by-product of racial and political strife, the morphological similarities between the quintet's distorted, free-meter grid and Otto's cable-net structures might be said to reflect their mutual genesis within a project of pushing back against oppressive configurations of political power, and a social quest for freedom, mobility, and levity. Herein lies the resonance with Miles and the Lost Quintet, who blended the empowering rhythms of the street with the free-meter rhythms of Coltrane, alternately fragmenting and liquefying the Africanist Grid in order to fuse street-level politics with a utopian vision of freedom and limitless possibility.

———

We might borrow an architectural metaphor to loosely ponder musical sounds in their relationship to space, by contrasting the operating procedures of Miles's two quintets of the late 1960s. If we think of a structure as an open space bounded by four walls and a roof, we think of that structure as *enclosing space*. If, on the other hand, we think of a structure as something created out of a preexisting mass, we might think of *sculpting out* a shape or surface. Using this line of thinking we might say that, framed by the ambient timeline of Tony Williams's ride cymbal, the Second Quintet's airy soundscape implied a variety of open spatial configurations, whereas the much denser surface of the Lost Quintet was a sound mass out of which various rhythmic shapes and spaces were carved or sculpted. Keeping these images in mind, I end this passage of music-analytical thinking the way I began this Miles Davis essay, using the concept of the "warp" to explore the inner workings of the Lost Quintet's rhythm section in finer detail. As in the beginning of the essay, I return to the tune "Agitation"—in this case, a version documented by Radio Televisione Italian at the Teatro Sistina in Rome on October 27, 1969, on the opening night of the Newport tour (table 5.3). Like the loosening and tightening of the proverbial rubber band, my goal here is to explore the questions of how a rhythm section can sculpt the metrically free song surface to imply different experiences of time and momentum.

Unlike the Second Quintet's "warp" that was defined by the entire ensemble's sudden deceleration of tempo (for example, the studio, Stockholm, and Karl-sruhe versions) or the collaging of discrete, warping tempi played by different musicians (as in the Plugged Nickel version from 1965), the "warp" in the Rome version of "Agitation" is defined by two linked elements. One is DeJohnette de-

TABLE 5.3 Miles Davis Quintet, "Agitation"
Teatro Sistina, Milano, Italy (October 27, 1969)

Personnel	
Miles Davis: trumpet	*Dave Holland*: acoustic bass
Wayne Shorter: tenor saxophone	*Jack De Johnette*: drums
Chick Corea: electric piano	

TIMING	EVENT
0:00 (4:10 of entire track)	Wayne Shorter ends tenor-sax solo with thematic fragments from "Agitation."
0:12	Chick Corea begins electric-piano solo; bass and drums in meter (up-tempo swing at quarter note = 368).
1:03	WARP #1 (into free meter).
1:09	Band consolidates back into metered swing.
1:11	WARP #2 (into free meter).
1:25	DeJohnette's cymbal washes, fast tempo implied within free meter.
1:32	WARP #3 (deceleration into an implied tempo of quarter note = 208).
1:40	Reconsolidation of fast feel within free meter.
1:50	WARP #4.
2:03	WARP #5.
3:03	Corea refers to "Agitation" theme, ensemble texture thins.
3:39	Holland emphasizes scale degree 5 (per the original recording) to prepare Davis's reentry.
3:45	Corea refers obliquely to "Agitation" theme to end solo.
3:54	Davis reenters with theme from "I Fall in Love Too Easily."

celerating while switching momentarily from the ride cymbal to the snare, *or* by decreasing the density of the ride cymbal pattern. The other is a characteristic descending figure played on the electric piano by Corea, in conjunction with DeJohnette's decelerations.

Fashioned from shards and fragments of the grammar of swing, Corea, Holland, and DeJohnette have de- and reconstructed these fragments as a heavily textured *surface* in which the quintet moves in and out—and then definitively out—of meter, producing a continuous but curvilinear distortion of the symmetrical Africanist Grid. Within this texture, these moments of "warp" imply multiple ways of experiencing musical motion. On one hand, they can be horizontally experienced as periodic surface distortions intermittently distributed throughout the ongoing fabric of the song surface, as if a sheet of paper has been crumpled up and then unraveled to result in a surface of myriad variations in depression, elevation, available paths of navigation, and hence, tempi. If three different vehicles were to move across this crumpled surface, the surface variations would create discrepancies in their respective rates of progress. On the other hand, the warps can be vertically experienced as "breakages" or "portals" within a continuous field, providing fleeting access to different experiences of time. Regardless of which way we hear them, these moments reflect a momentary change in the textural density of the ensemble, which in turn implies a change in momentum. In such an environment, fast tempi can be implied within slow tempi, and vice versa (there are many such fluctuations here, I've merely noted the more obvious ones). Essentially, the Lost Quintet engaged in a sculpting of metrically free space that was a very fluid distortion of the interlocking dynamics of the Africanist Grid. This inspired Jack DeJohnette to narrate the "warping" passages with a succession of metaphors, with *breath*, *waves*, *spirals*, and *speech* being perhaps the most potent:

> Everybody's playing in terms of shapes, in terms of phrases, like painting a picture, instead of bar lines. There are no bar lines, it's just telling a story with phrases. And so we're collectively doing this. Coloring the music and playing ideas—not randomly. There's an architecture to it, but it's in the moment, it's happening on the spot. We're feeding each other. And the music keeps feeding on itself and it becomes a spiral. It's just the chemistry between us. On an inter-conscious level we're speaking a language that we understand, but it's nonverbal. Those phrases you're pointing out, that's where we're breaking it down, that's where it's breathing. You know, like it's waves.[219]

Most of the European sets ended with "The Theme," which was for Miles's First Quintet in the 1950s what Joe Zawinul's "Directions" was for the Lost Quintet in 1969—a slick, urbane arrangement of hard-hitting, syncopated accents that worked perfectly as a show opener or closer. Miles's earliest recorded version of "The Theme" dates from 1955 but from its earliest performances, the band had already reduced the melody to the series of long tones that follow the round-robin statement of the opening riff, and this oblique way of playing the melody continued through the days of the Second Quintet and the Lost Quintet as well. Nevertheless, it is tempting to conclude that, by this point in his career, Miles's retention of this piece was—when juxtaposed against all of the highly cerebral, free improvisation in the set—as much a perverse gesture as anything else, cal-culated to tease the audience with a fleeting fragment of "jazz" as it faded into the mists of Miles's musical history.

The band headed home after the final gig of the tour in Rotterdam on November 9, apparently also the last gig played with the quintet configuration. Aside from a handful of low-profile gigs in the interim during which Miles tinkered with the personnel (including a stint in Toronto with guitarist Sonny Greenwich sitting in and another in Ann Arbor, Michigan, with John McLaughlin guest-ing), the band generally laid low until the release of *Bitches Brew* in March 1970, promoted by high-profile stints at Bill Graham's Fillmore auditoriums in March and June (Fillmore East) and in April and October (Fillmore West). The March 1970 gigs were the real "coming out" of the "newly" electrified Miles, and the last with Wayne Shorter (replaced thereafter by Steve Grossman), who left to form Weather Report with Joe Zawinul, while the Brazilian percussionist Airto Moreira joined as a sixth member. From this point, Miles would continue to tinker with both the personnel and the musical formula for another three years, until he settled fully into his radical take on the riff-based Jimi Hendrix/Sly Stone/James Brown music that had originally inspired him, with his so-called "rhythm band" of 1972–1975.[220]

———

The Lost Quintet was one of the most exciting bands Miles Davis ever led, but one reason it was short-lived was because Miles himself ultimately had his eyes on a different prize. In Jack DeJohnette's estimation,

> It got, for Miles's tastes, too free. It was Chick and Dave who were really kind of tight in that way of playing. And sometimes I would lay out when they played, and Miles would come over to me and say, "Hey man, can't you make 'em swing?" And then I'd drop out and just let Chick and Dave have a dialogue. And then eventually they left and Miles decided he wanted to do more groove-oriented stuff, and that was the end of the group.[221]

From the perspective of an artist attempting to remain on the cutting edge of jazz while simultaneously broadening his audience, perhaps the most disconcerting observation came from Lucien Malson, who reviewed the quintet's Paris concert of November 3:

The striking Miles, now flanked by his four stevedores, no longer attracts the swanky public to the front rows of the room as he once did. The 50-franc seats, which used to go first (as it is most important to be seen), are no longer snatched up at this price. Miles Davis's concerts have become what they once were before he was in vogue in the posh areas of town: a gathering of music buffs.[222]

Meanwhile, Guy Kopelowicz felt the quintet's French performances to be the end of an era: "I had seen almost all of Miles Davis's concerts in Paris over the years. [The Lost Quintet] were great, but those were the last truly great concerts that Miles gave in France. It was never really the same after that."[223] What Miles and many of the other pioneers of jazz-rock fusion were learning was that merely substituting electric instruments for acoustic ones would not garner the larger audiences they were after as long as the music remained as complex as his had been during the heady days of acoustic jazz in the mid-1960s.

Miles Davis had always been a hyper status- and fashion-conscious jazz musician, and part of his allure was the fact that the fashion always worked in tandem with the music to signify sonic innovation while resonating in broader social spheres having to do with race, culture, and politics. The critical comments of observers such as Ian Breach and Lucien Malson implied that either the music and fashion were now detaching into separate priorities, or that they continued to work together in the service of a message that some audiences were reluctant to hear. Malson, for example, remarked that "the resources of violence that these black Americans have certainly surpass those of their colleagues of festivals of aggression of the—recent—European tradition," going on to note that "Davis's young musicians had, like [Pharoah] Sanders last year, imposed the violent image of 'new jazz.'"[224] Clearly, Malson heard this music as free jazz with all of its stereotyped political associations intact. In truth, the intellectual demands the music made on its audience sidestepped some of the reductive articulations of Black Power and Negritude that were then fashionable in the cosmopolitan centers of both the United States and Europe. In the United States, the music existed in a space between free jazz, psychedelia, and funk while in Europe, it existed in the netherworld between the transplanted polemics of the New Thing and the various nostalgias of pre–World War II European jazz.[225] This placed it outside of the jazz fashion cycles of the day. Touring the various Western European capitals with a quintet that simultaneously referenced Jimi Hendrix and Cecil Taylor made quite a challenging cultural assertion: that black modernity could be simultaneously earthy and hyperintellectual, experimental and accessible, and funky and abstract, and that it could be delivered with a depth, elegance, and intensity that was simultaneously answerable to the new music brewing in the lofts of lower Manhattan, the funky boutiques of Greenwich Village, the political battles taking place in the streets, the prestige venues of Western Europe, and the postcolonial cultural shifts that were global in scope. If Coltrane's move into free meter was shaped by the ascetic priorities of prayer and meditation, the aura of Miles's Lost Quintet showed that his own move was resolutely worldly: a funky, cosmopolitan intersection of experimental jazz and popular music, clashed together and exploded into rhythmic kaleidoscopy by the political priorities implicit in Miles's mission.

———

As with John and Alice Coltrane, the love dynamic supplied a crucial variable to the creative equation. Betty Davis had never presented herself as an activist, but she had played a catalytic role in *Filles de Kilimanjaro*, *In a Silent Way*, and *Bitches Brew*—as muse for the former two and somewhat of a co-conspirator for the third. If Jimi Hendrix's *Electric Ladyland* had been the guitarist's psychedelic-cinematic celebration of the sexuality he shared with so many women, *Bitches Brew* represented the full flowering of the vision that Betty had inspired for Miles. She was apparently in the studio for some of the sessions, and Wayne Shorter felt her presence was instrumental in shaping the album: "He was bringing to the table her generation which he knew about, but with her being right there with him, he could see her reaction to the music. If she was moved by some idea he had musically, he dug that."[226] Betty even claimed to have coined the title *Bitches Brew* (Miles had initially titled it *Witches Brew*)[227] while Shorter considers "Miles Runs the Voodoo Down"—one of the centerpiece grooves of the album—to be an adaptation of one of Betty's unreleased songs.[228]

But we might also speculate that the harmonic trajectory from *In a Silent Way* to *Bitches Brew* paralleled the emotional contours of Miles and Betty's relationship. Which is to say that the shimmering, pastoral idyll of *In a Silent Way* had now given way to the more structurally complex, chromaticized sensibility of *Bitches Brew*. In Miles's own account, it was during the summer of 1969 that the relationship between he and Betty began to take a downturn, and by 1970 their marriage was unraveling following (among other things) Miles's accusations that Betty had had an affair with Jimi Hendrix, and Mabry's counteraccusations that, among other things, Davis had been physically abusive toward her and had deliberately sabotaged the release of her debut album.[229] It is possibly telling that by the European tour of late 1969, Miles was regularly inserting brief references to "I Fall in Love Too Easily" into his concert performances (usually as a preface to "Sanctuary") even though he had trimmed most of the other standards from his concert repertoire by this time. Of course, the chemistry between two highly creative people can often be as volatile as it is inspiring and, ultimately, what took place between Miles and Mabry was most likely a charged encounter between two highly competitive and creative spirits; fireworks were inevitable. Nonetheless, Miles's karmic debt as an abuser of women continues to hang like a cloud over all his profound transformations of the jazz language.

The relationship between Miles and Betty was obviously profoundly transformative for both of them, while it lasted. Even interpreted as a "midlife crisis" relationship for Miles (who turned forty-three in 1969), it surely was one of the most productive on record (pun intended), redirecting his career and personal habits in ways that were initially very beneficial, while providing Betty a foundation for her own career as an acknowledged musical innovator. Betty went on to release a series of influential funk-rock albums,[230] while Miles embarked on a trajectory in the 1970s that maximized the musical and extramusical influences of his funk and rock star inspirations, for better and for worse. Just prior to the fall tour, in fact, he was arrested in the company of his new girlfriend Marguerite Eskridge, following a shooting incident after an October engagement at the Blue Coronet club on Fulton Street in Brooklyn.[231] The noirish overtones of this incident set the template for his 1970s, a decade of the "blaxploitation Miles" of much drug and personal excess punctuated by music that was sometimes visionary and sometimes the soundtrack to a remarkably dramatic trajectory of personal dissolution. What the "Lost Quintet year" seems to represent is a year-long interregnum of inspired balance and inspiration—in terms of music, fashion, health, and lifestyle—in which a woman was an openly acknowledged figure in Davis's musical life—not only as mere muse or victim, but also as mentor and guide. Like Alice Coltrane, Betty Davis's crucial contribution to one of jazz's most innovative phases complicates, clarifies, and ultimately enriches the narrative.

NOTES

1. Liebman, David, and Larry Fisher. *Miles Davis and David Liebman: Jazz Connections.* Lewiston, NY: Edward Mellon Press, 1996, 74–76.

2. Macero quoted in Mandel, Howard. "Sketches of Miles." *DownBeat* 58, no. 12 (December 1991). Reprinted in Alkyer, Frank, ed. *The Miles Davis Reader.* Milwaukee, WI: Hal Leonard Books, 2007.

3. Although there are conflicting accounts, most consider the Original Dixieland Jass Band's "Dixie Jass Band One Step/Livery Stable Blues" to be the first commercially released jazz recording. Original Dixieland Jass Band. "Dixie Jass Band One-Step/Livery Stable Blues." Victor 18-255A. Originally released 1917.

4. The footage of Hendrix's Monterey performance is available on the Jimi Hendrix Experience, *Live at Monterey* (Universal Music Group, 2008).

5. See McLaughlin's comments in the afterword to Moriarty, Frank. *Jimi Hendrix.* Pennsauken, NJ: Bookbaby, 2018.

6. Shorter in Oulette, Dan. "*Bitches Brew*: The Making of the Most Revolutionary Jazz Album in History." *DownBeat* 66, no. 12 (December 1999): 36.

7. Davis, Miles, and Quincy Troupe. *Miles: The Autobiography.* New York: Simon and Schuster, 1989, 291.

8. The Chambers Brothers. *Time Has Come.* Columbia CL 2722 [Mono] CS 9522 [Stereo]. Originally released 1967.

9. I take it as a positive omen that enormously helpful materials serendipitously appear in the midst of a writing project. When I was writing my book on Fela Kuti, for example, a disc of previously lost recordings of his was released, and this allowed me to complete the stylistic chronology of his musical development. My book on Jamaican dub music was aided immeasurably by the reissue campaigns of several labels, which began just after I started writing. The same is true for this book, the spirit of which was aided considerably by the fact that it was begun concurrently with a publicity blitz surrounding the reissue of Betty Davis's funk-rock albums of the early 1970s. Recent articles include Ballon, John. "Liberated Sister." *Wax Poetics* 22 (April/May 2007); Mahon, Maureen. "Betty's Back." *Ebony/Jet.com*, 2007. https://as.nyu.edu/content/dam/nyu-as/music/documents/Betty%27s%20Back%20ebonyjet.pdf; and Chang, Jeff. "A Funk Queen Steps Out of the Shadows." *San Francisco Chronicle*, May 18, 2007. https://www.sfgate.com/entertainment/article/A-FUNK-QUEEN-STEPS-OUT-OF-THE-SHADOWS-Betty-2593729.php. For older articles, see Richard, Sue, and Bob Weinstein. "Betty Davis: Bawdy Bombshell." *High Society* (October 1976); Ledbetter, Les. "Mood Isn't Candlelight in Betty Davis's Songs." *New York Times*, June 21, 1974; Gibbs, Vernon. "Betty Davis: Singin' to the Max." *Essence* (July 1974); and Adderton, Donald. "Her Act Too Spicy for U.S. Tastes; Betty Davis Finds Success in Europe." *Jet* (April 5, 1976): 57.

10. See Betty Davis's albums *The Columbia Years, 1968–1969* (Light in the Attic LITA 135, 88843048152, 2018), *Betty Davis* (Just Sunshine JSS-5, 1973), *They Say I'm Different* (Just Sunshine JSS-3500, 1974), *Nasty Gal* (Island ILPS-9329, 1975), *Crashin' from Passion* (P-Vine PCD-1993, 1993), *Is It Love or Desire?* (Just Sunshine LP 5313, 2009). See also the 2017 documentary *Betty Davis: They Say I'm Different* (directed by Phil Cox, Native Voice Films and La Compaigne des Taxi Brousse).

11. A podcast recording of Betty Davis's interview with Jesse Thorn is available at http://www.maximumfun.org/blog/2007/06/podcast-tsoya-betty-davis.html.

12. Betty Davis as interviewed in Chang, "A Funk Queen Steps Out of the Shadows."

13. Hancock quoted in Murray Lerne, dir. *Miles Electric: A Different Kind of Blue*. Eagle Vision Media, 2004.

14. Herbie Hancock and Carlos Santana as interviewed in *Miles Electric*.

15. Betty Davis as interviewed in Thorn, 2007.

16. DeJohnette, as quoted in Milkowski, Bill. "In Search of Jack DeJohnette." *Traps* 5 (Spring 2008): 38.

17. See Miles's comments in Gleason, Ralph. "I Could Put Together the Greatest Rock and Roll Band You Ever Heard." *Rolling Stone* 48 (December 27, 1969): 17–21.

18. Keepnews was the first writer to use the term "Lost Quintet." See his essay "The Lost Quintet." In *A Miles Davis Reader*, edited by Bill Kirchner. Washington, DC: Smithsonian Institution Press, 1997.

19. Shorter, as quoted in Mercer, Michelle. *Footprints: The Life and Work of Wayne Shorter*. New York: Tarcher, 2004, 157.

20. Stettner, Louis. *Louis Stettner: Penn Station*. London: Thames and Hudson, 2015.

21. Davis, Miles. *In Person Friday and Saturday Nights at the Blackhawk, Complete*. Columbia/Legacy C4K 87106. Originally released 2003.

22. See Kelley, Robin D. G. "Miles Davis: The Chameleon of Cool; a Jazz Genius in the Guise of a Hustler." *New York Times*, May 13, 2001. https://www.nytimes.com/2001/05/13/arts/miles-davis-the-chameleon-of-cool-a-jazz-genius-in-the-guise-of-a-hustler.html. See also Cleage, Pearl. *Mad at Miles: A Black Woman's Guide to Truth*. New York: Cleage Group, 1990; and Carby, Hazel. "Playing the Changes." In *Race Men*. Cambridge, MA: Harvard University Press, 2009.

23. As quoted in Kelley, "Miles Davis: The Chameleon of Cool."

24. See, for example: Martin, Waldo E. "Miles Davis and the 1960s Avant-Garde." In *Miles Davis and American Culture*, edited by Gerald Early. St. Louis: Missouri Historical Society Press, 2001.

25. Jack DeJohnette, interview with the author, Woodstock, NY, November 2009.

26. See Mercer, *Footprints*, 111.

27. See the following sources: Waters, Keith. *The Studio Recordings of the Miles Davis*

Quintet, 1965–68. New York: Oxford University Press, 2011; Yudkin, Jeremy. *Miles Davis, Miles Smiles, and the Invention of Post Bop*. Bloomington: Indiana University Press, 2008; Coolman, Todd F. "The Miles Davis Quintet of the Mid-1960s: Synthesis of Improvisational and Compositional Elements." PhD Dissertation, New York University, 1997.

28. Shorter, as quoted in Mercer, *Footprints*, 100.

29. Davis, as quoted in Davis and Troupe, *Miles*, 274.

30. Bob Belden's notes in *The Miles Davis Quintet, 1965–'68* box set (Columbia/Legacy C6K 67398, 1998) offer a somewhat more complicated take on the form of "Agitation."

31. From https://www.dictionary.com/browse/warp.

32. Even though I came upon it independently, I am not the first person to use the term "warp" to refer to a process of rhythmic transformation. For example, David F. Garcia (citing the earlier work of the ethnologist Fernando Ortiz) has used the term to refer to the interwoven rhythmic matrices shaping the *son montuno* style of the highly influential Cuban composer and bandleader Arsenio Rodriquez. See chapter 2 ("Negro y Macho") of Garcia, David F. *Arsenio Rodríguez and the Transnational Flows of Latin Popular Music*. Philadelphia: Temple University Press, 2006.

33. The Stockholm and Karlsruhe concerts are both available on Miles Davis. *Live in Europe 1967 (The Bootleg Series, Volume 1)*. Columbia/Legacy 88697 94053 2. Originally released 2011.

34. Miles Davis. *The Complete Live at the Plugged Nickel*. Columbia/Legacy 66955. Originally released 1995.

35. Davis, as quoted in Davis and Troupe, *Miles*, 283.

36. Shorter, as quoted in Szwed, John. *So What: The Life of Miles Davis*. New York: Simon and Schuster, 2002, 256.

37. See Yudkin, *Miles Davis, Miles Smiles, and the Invention of Post Bop*. The "Time No Changes" approach is extensively discussed in chapters 9 and 10.

38. Kolatan, Ferda, and Jenny Sabin, eds. *Meander: Variegating Architecture*. Bentley Institute Press, 2010, 12.

39. Schumacher quoted in Singstedt, Niklas. "Exhibition Design, Interview with Patrik Schumacher." *Future Exhibitions*, No. 2 (Spatial Encounters), March 2010, https://www.patrikschumacher.com/Texts/Exhibition%20Design.htm.

40. Shorter, as quoted in Nemeyer, Eric. "The Magical Journey: An Interview with Wayne Shorter." *Jazz Improv* 2, no. 3 (2000): 75.

41. Davis, *Miles Davis Quintet, 1965–'68*.

42. See Dean, Roger, with Dominy Hamilton and Carla Capalbo. *Views*. New York: Collins Design, 2009. See also Smith, Ming, with Emmanuel Iduma, Janet Hill Talbert, M. Neelika Jayawardane, Namwali Serpell, Greg Tate, and Arthur Jafa. *Ming Smith: An Aperture Monograph*. New York: Aperture Books, 2020.

43. Both of the Cartier-Bresson images discussed in this section can be found on page 89 of Galassi, Peter. *Henri Cartier-Bresson: The Modern Century*. New York: Museum of Modern Art, 2010. Interestingly, Cartier-Bresson produced a variation—an "alternate take," if you will—of the first image, which shows the same bespectacled man gazing through the same opening in the foreground, his eyes now trained in the opposite direction. Another man, different from the one in the previous image, is visible inside of the enclosure, his head turned backward toward the photographer. The panel on the far left is no longer visible in the picture. Titled "Bullring, Valencia, Spain, 1933," this image simultaneously clarifies and further obscures the context of the photograph. This image can be found on page 63 of Clair, Jean. *Henri Cartier-Bresson: Europeans*. London: Thames and Hudson, 1997.

44. See the discussion of this photograph in Chéroux, Clément. *Henri Cartier-Bresson: Here and Now*. London and New York: Thames and Hudson, 2014.

45. I will return to this theme of photography evolving by accident. See Davey, Moyra. "Notes on Photography and Accident." In *Long Life Cool White*. Cambridge, MA: Harvard Art Museums, 2008. See also Kelsey, Robin. *Photography and the Art of Chance*. Cambridge, MA: Harvard/Belknap, 2015.

46. Sudek, Josef. *The Window of My Studio*. Prague: Torst, 2007.

47. Footage of the quintet's Milano performance can be found at https://www.youtube.com/watch?v=fBoHkB92SUo.

48. Ekwensi, Cyprian. *Iska*. Lagos: Spectrum, 1966. Kingsley, Charles. *The Water Babies: Fairy Tale for a Land Baby*. London: Macmillan, 1863. Wharton, Edith. *Sanctuary*. Glasgow: Good Press, 1903.

49. Shorter, as quoted in Darrock, Lynn. "Wayne Shorter." *Jazz Times* 15 (December 1985): 14. The first part of this quote originally came from Liska, A. James. "Wayne Shorter: Coming Home." *DownBeat* 49, no. 7 (July 1982): 20. The two comments were later combined in the Liska article. To avoid the confusion of two citations for one quote, I have taken the liberty of using a little bit more of Shorter's original comments (to Liska).

50. DeJohnette, interview with the author, 2009.

51. As quoted in Garfield, Simon. *Mauve: How One Man Invented a Color That Changed the World*. New York: W. W. Norton, 2000, 86.

52. The primary source for biographical information on Harold Rhodes is the film *Down the Rhodes: The Fender Rhodes Story* (Triads Music, 2011). There are also several relevant websites, including *Fender Rhodes: The Piano That Changed the History of Music*, http://www.fenderrhodes.com/history/narrative.html.

53. See Lewis's comments in *Down the Rhodes*.

54. See Zawinul's comments in the notes to Miles Davis, *The Complete "In a Silent Way" Sessions* (Columbia/Legacy C3K 65362, 2001).

55. *Miles Electric*.

56. See Miles's comments in Davis and Troupe, *Miles*, 314.

57. See Miles's comments in Davis and Troupe, *Miles*, 293.

58. For more detailed accounts of the departures of Carter and Hancock, see: Tingen, Paul. *Miles Beyond: The Electric Explorations of Miles Davis, 1967–1991*. New York: Billboard Books, 2001, 47. The section "Miles Davis Live-Band Personnel, 1963–1991," included in the book's appendix, is also a very helpful source of this information.

59. Hancock, as quoted in *Miles Electric*.

60. Hancock, as quoted in *Miles Electric*.

61. See Corea's comments in *Down the Rhodes*.

62. Corea, as quoted in *Down the Rhodes*.

63. Corea in Gershon, Pete. "Class of '69." *Signal to Noise* (November/December 1998): 21–22.

64. Drummer Mike Clark, as quoted in "Tony Williams Interview, Part 1," https://www.youtube.com/watch?v=Sroumdzu3c4.

65. The Jimi Hendrix Experience. "The Wind Cries Mary." *Are You Experienced*. Reprise 6261. Originally released 1967.

66. Henderson, Joe. *Power to the People*. Milestone MSP-9024. Originally released 1970.

67. The Lighthouse material was previously spread out over several releases, but is now available in one collection on *Joe Henderson Quintet at the Lighthouse* (Milestone MCD 47104-2, 2004). Additional tracks recorded at the Lighthouse but not released on Milestone can be found on the 1982 release *Jazz Patterns* (Everest 363). This bootleg release includes two mistitled Henderson compositions: "Lofty" (actually "Punjab") and "What's Mine Is Yours" (actually "Power to the People").

68. Shaw, Woody. *Blackstone Legacy*. Contemporary S 7627/8. Originally released 1970.

69. Sun Ra. *Haverford College, January 25, 1980 Solo Piano*. Bandcamp download. 2019.

70. Jenkins, Leroy. *Space Minds, New Worlds, Survival of America*. Tomato 8001. Originally released 1979.

71. Bartz, as quoted in Haga, Evan. "Bright Moments with Gary Bartz." *Jazz Times* 49 (July 2019). https://jazztimes.com/features/interviews/bright-moments-with-gary-bartz/.

72. "Paraphernalia." *Miles in the Sky*. Columbia 9628. Originally released 1968.

73. Davis, as quoted in Davis and Troupe, *Miles*, 297.

74. DeJohnette, interview with the author, 2009.

75. Charles Lloyd Quartet. *Love-In*. Atlantic 1481. Originally released 1967.

76. DeJohnette, interview with the author, 2009.

77. See Szwed, *So What*, 291.

78. Miles, quoted in "The Miles Davis Interview." CBS/Sony 01502, August 4, 1969.

79. Kart, Larry. "The Lost Quintet." In *Jazz in Search of Itself*. New Haven, CT: Yale University Press, 2004, 210–12.

80. DeJohnette, interview with the author, 2009.

81. DeJohnette, interview with the author, 2009.

82. Siders, Harvey. "Caught in the Act: Monterey Jazz Festival." from *DownBeat* 36, no. 24 (November 27, 1969): 25–28.

83. Moriyama, Daido. *Shinjuku*. Tucson, AZ: Nazraeli Press, 2002.

84. Moriyama quoted in Drucker, Bree. "Daido Moriyama." *Bomb*, January 4, 2017, https://bombmagazine.org/articles/daido-moriyama/.

85. Moriyama, Daido. *Shashin Yo Sayonara*. Tokyo: Power Shovel Ltd, 2006.

86. Moriyama quoted in Drucker, "Daido Moriyama."

87. DeJohnette, interview with the author, 2009.

88. Davis, as quoted in Harrington, Richard. "Miles Davis: Well-Tempered Trumpet." *Washington Post*, June 2, 1985: G1.

89. Corea, as quoted Tingen, *Miles Beyond*, 112.

90. These dates taken from Peter Losin's *Miles Ahead* website: http://www.plosin.com/MilesAhead/Sessions.aspx?s=690600.

91. Feather, Leonard. "Miles Davis Quintet Plays at Manne-Hole." *Los Angeles Times*, September 12, 1969: F13.

92. Siders, "Caught in the Act."

93. Kart, "Miles Davis: 1969," in *Jazz in Search of Itself*, 211–12.

94. Albertson, Chris. "Caught: Garden State Jazz Festival." *DownBeat* 36, no. 25 (December 11, 1969): 29–31.

95. Arnett, Karl. "Morgan Festival Succeeds, Despite Disappointing Attendance." *Baltimore Sun*, June 24, 1969: B6.

96. Lawrie, Alistair. "No Lonely Trumpet Notes for the New Miles Davis." *Boston Globe*, December 3, 1969: 15.

97. Siders, "Caught in the Act."

98. (Author uncredited). "Monterey Jazz Fest: Rhythm Carnival." *Billboard* 81, no. 40 (October 4, 1969).

99. Feather, Leonard. "Monterey Musicians Present Mixed Bag." *Seattle Times*, September 24, 1969, 62.

100. Malson, Lucien. "Miles Davis et le jeune garde á Antibes." *Le Monde*, July 29, 1969: 14. Translated by Matthew Landry.

101. Austin, Edith M. "A Soul-Less Weekend in Monterey." *Sun Reporter*, September 27, 1969: 18.

102. Feather, Leonard. "Monterey Jazz Fest Amplifies Rock Aspects." *Los Angeles Times*, November 22, 1969.

103. (Author uncredited), "Monterey Jazz Fest: Rhythm Carnival."

104. For an in-depth discussion of this tension between jazz and rock as played out in

the summer 1969 festivals, see: Brennan, Matt. "Failure to Fuse: The Jazz-Rock Culture War at the 1969 Newport Jazz Festival." *Jazz Research Journal* 1, no. 1 (2007). https://journal.equinoxpub.com/JAZZ/article/view/12291.

105. From Smith, Tracy K. "They May Love All That He Has Chosen, and Hate All That He Has Rejected." In *Life on Mars*. Minneapolis: Graywolf Press, 2011.

106. See Davis and Troupe, *Miles*; and Glasser, Brian. *In a Silent Way: A Portrait of Joe Zawinul*. London: Sanctuary, 2001.

107. For a biography of Zawinul, see Glasser, *In a Silent Way*.

108. From the notes to the Cannonball Adderley Quintet album, *The Price You Got to Pay to Be Free* (Capitol SWBB-636, 1970).

109. Adderley, *The Price You Got to Pay to Be Free*.

110. Weather Report's version of "Directions" is available on the 2006 box set *Forecast: Tomorrow* (Columbia/Legacy 82876 85575 2).

111. Davis, Miles. *Directions*. Columbia RO2 36472. Originally released 1981. See also *The Complete "In a Silent Way" Sessions*.

112. See Zawinul. *Zawinul*. Atlantic SD 1579. Originally released 1971. For the circumstances around the creation of "In a Silent Way," see the chapter "Silent Beauty" in Glasser, *In a Silent Way*.

113. A good example for comparison here might be the well-known version of "Dark Star" contained on: The Grateful Dead. *Dick's Picks: Fillmore East: 2/13–14/70*. Grateful Dead/Rhino Originally released 1996.

114. Davis, Miles. *In a Silent Way*. Columbia CS 9875. Originally released 1969.

115. Polillo, Arrigo. "Successo a Juan-Les-Pins." *Musica Jazz* (October 1965). Reprinted in Kahn, Ashley. *A Love Supreme: The Story of John Coltrane's Signature Album*. New York: Penguin, 2002.

116. Davis, Miles. *Miles Davis in Europe*. Columbia CS 8983. Originally released 1964.

117. Taylor's performance was released as *Nuits de la Fondation Maeght, Volume 1* (Shandar SR 10.011, 1971) and *Volume 2* (Shandar 83.508, 1972).

118. Guy Kopelowicz, interview with the author, January 19, 2010.

119. In 2010, Columbia/Legacy issued a DVD of the quintet's concert in Copenhagen, Denmark (November 4, 1969) as part of two releases: the Legacy Edition of the *Bitches Brew* album (Columbia/Legacy 88697-54519-2) and a 40th-anniversary box set of the same album (Columbia/Legacy 88697-70274-2-MC). In 2013, they released a box set of the quintet's performances at Antibes (July 25 and 26, 1969), Stockholm, Sweden (November 5, 1969), and Berlin, Germany (November 7, 1969) as the second volume of the *Miles Davis Bootleg Series* (Columbia/Legacy 88725 41853 2).

120. Malson, "Miles Davis et le jeune garde á Antibes."

121. Kopelowicz, interview with the author, 2010.

122. DeJohnette, interview with the author, 2009.

123. For an example of this characterization of DeJohnette: Chambers, Jack. *Milestones: The Music and Times of Miles Davis.* Toronto: University of Toronto Press, 1985, 153.

124. Malson, "Miles Davis et le jeune garde á Antibes," 14.

125. See Schumacher's essay in the pamphlet *Digital Hadid* at https://www.patrikschu macher.com/Texts/digitalhadid.htm.

126. Pre-Antibes versions of "Miles Runs the Voodoo Down" also survive on recordings from the Village Gate (May), the Blue Coronet (June), and Central Park (July).

127. DeJohnette, interview with the author, 2009.

128. DeMicheal, Don. "Miles Davis: The Rolling Stone Interview." *Rolling Stone* 48 (December 13, 1969).

129. The Jimi Hendrix Experience. *Electric Ladyland.* Reprise RS 6307. Originally released 1968.

130. See chapters 11, 12, and 13 of McDermott, John, and Eddie Kramer. *Hendrix: Setting the Record Straight.* New York: Grand Central, 1992.

131. Davis, as quoted in Davis and Troupe, *Miles*, 292–93.

132. McLaughlin, as quoted in Roby, Steven. *Black Gold: The Lost Archives of Jimi Hendrix.* New York: Billboard Books, 2002, 143.

133. Holland, as quoted in "It's the Spirit of the Music That Matters." *JazzWise*, September 1, 2021. https://www.jazzwise.com/features/article/it-s-the-spirit-of-the-music-that -matters-and-that-s-been-true-since-my-very-early-days-dave-holland-interview.

134. See McLaughlin's album *Devotion* (Douglas 4, 1970), recorded with Larry Young, drummer Buddy Miles, and bassist Billy Rich. Rich had been the alternate bassist in Hendrix's *Band of Gypsys* project of late 1969/early 1970. See also McDermott and Kramer, *Hendrix: Setting the Record Straight.*

135. Evans, interview with Les Tomkins. Quoted in Hicock, Larry. *Castles Made of Sound: The Story of Gil Evans.* New York: Da Capo, 2002, 190.

136. For background on *Sketches of Spain*, see Hicock, *Castles Made of Sound*, 108.

137. See, for example: Kelley, Robin D. G. *Africa Speaks, America Answers: Modern Jazz in Revolutionary Times.* Cambridge, MA: Harvard University Press, 2012; Monson, Ingrid. *Freedom Sounds: Civil Rights Call Out to Jazz and Africa.* London: Oxford University Press, 2007; and Turner, Richard Brent. *Soundtrack to a Movement: African American Islam, Jazz, and Black Internationalism.* New York: New York University Press, 2021.

138. Davis and Troupe, *Miles*, 293.

139. Vogel, "Sounds from Utopia: Jimi Hendrix Experience at Jarhunderthalle," 1969. Reprinted in Valkhoff, Ben. *Foxy Papers, Volume 6.* Self-published, 2018, 32.

140. See Grella, George Jr. *Bitches Brew.* New York: Bloomsbury, 2015. Svorinich, Victor. *Listen to This: Miles Davis and Bitches Brew.* Jackson: University of Mississippi Press, 2015.

141. See, for example, Maupin's comments in Grella, *Bitches Brew*, 62.

142. Beach Boys. *Pet Sounds*. Capitol T 2458. Originally released 1966; *The Smile Sessions*. Capitol T-2850. Originally released 2011.

143. Frank Zappa and the Mothers of Invention. *We're Only in It for the Money*. Verve V6-5045X. Originally released 1968.

144. Nico. *The Marble Index*. Elektra EKS-74029. Originally released 1968.

145. Miles Davis. *Deep Brew, Volume 1*. Megadisc. 2005.

146. Doerschuk, Andy, Rick Mattingly, Tony Davis, Wally Schmalle, and David Weiss. "*Bitches Brew*: The Album That Changed Drumming Forever." *DRUM!* 8, no. 1 (February, 1999): 54–64.

147. Sam Rivers, interview with Ted Panken, 1997. https://tedpanken.wordpress.com /2011/12/27/sam-rivers-1923-2011-r-i-p-a-downbeat-article-from-1999-and-interviews/.

148. Henderson, *Power to the People*.

149. Byrd, Donald. *Electric Byrd*. Blue Note EKS-74029. Originally released 1970.

150. Shaw, *Blackstone Legacy*.

151. Morgan, Lee. *The Last Session*. Blue Note BST-84901. Originally released 1972.

152. Brian Eno, as quoted in Grella, *Bitches Brew*.

153. Duke Ellington and His Orchestra. *Ellington Indigos*. Columbia CK44444. Originally released 1956; and *Ellington Uptown*. Columbia/Legacy CK 87066. Originally released 1957.

154. For a comprehensive study of dub music, see: Veal, Michael. *Dub: Soundscapes and Shattered Songs in Jamaican Reggae*. Middletown, CT: Wesleyan University Press, 2007.

155. For a comprehensive discussion of Hancock's "Mwandishi" period, see: Gluck, Bob. *You'll Know When You Get There: Herbie Hancock and the Mwandishi Band*. Chicago: University of Chicago Press, 2014.

156. These projects are discussed in Gordon, Alistair. "Infinity Machines." In *Spaced Out: Radical Environments of the Psychedelic Sixties*. New York: Rizzoli, 2008.

157. Jill Johnston, quoted in Gordon, *Spaced Out*, 42.

158. This comment is taken from Meyer's review of *The Complete Bitches Brew Sessions*, http://www.inkblotmagazine.com/rev-archive/Miles_Davis_Bitches_Complete.htm.

159. Instagram post, used with permission.

160. Rollins quoted in Nisenson, Eric. *Open Sky: Sonny Rollins and his World of Improvisation*. New York: Da Capo, 2000, 53.

161. Fisher, Mark. "The Metaphysics of Crackle: Afrofuturism and Hauntology." *Dancecult: Journal of Electronic Dance Music Culture* 5, no. 2 (2013). https://doi.org/10.12801/1947-5403 .2013.05.02.03.

162. Fisher, "The Metaphysics of Crackle," 7.

163. Fisher, "The Metaphysics of Crackle," 42–55.

164. The quotes are all taken from Fisher, "The Metaphysics of Crackle."

165. For a discussion of Loengard's photographic techniques, see: (Author uncredited). "Don't Light All of It." https://www.apogeephoto.com/dont-light-all-of-it/.

166. Jacrot, Christoph. *Meteores*. Paris: Hartpon, 2015.

167. Jacrot, Christoph. *New York in Black*. Paris: Hartpon, 2017.

168. Jacrot, Christoph. *Snjör*. Paris: Hartpon, 2016.

169. For a comprehensive survey of Mann's work, see: Mann, Sally. *Sally Mann: A Thousand Crossings*. New York: Abrams, 2018.

170. See chapter 3 of Kelsey, *Photography and the Art of Chance*.

171. Mann, *A Thousand Crossings*, 245.

172. Mann, *A Thousand Crossings*, 247.

173. See https://theheatwarps.com.

174. See the entry for this gig on Peter Losin's website, http://www.plosin.com/miles Ahead/Sessions.aspx?s=691102.

175. A video excerpt of this performance, filmed by the BBC, can be seen at https://www.youtube.com/watch?v=5uWoSRgmxkY.

176. Steyerl, Hito. "In Defense of the Poor Image." *e-flux journal* 10 (November 2009). https://www.e-flux.com/journal/10/61362/in-defense-of-the-poor-image/.

177. De Carava, Roy, Sherry Turner de Carava, and Radiclani Clytus. *The Sound I Saw*. New York: David Zwirner, 2019.

178. Cecil Taylor Unit. *One Too Many Salty Swift and Not Goodbye*. Hut TWO 3R02. Originally released 1980.

179. Lacy, Steve, featuring Bobby Few and Dennis Charles. *The Flame*. Soul Note SN 1035. Originally released 1982.

180. Lacy, Steve. *Scratching the Seventies*. Saravah SHL 2082. Originally released 1997.

181. All of the images discussed can be found in Smith, et al., *Ming Smith*.

182. Jafa, Arthur. *Love Is the Message, the Message is Death*. Commercially unreleased 2016. No company credits available.

183. Moten, Fred. *Black and Blur: Consent Not to Be a Single Being*. Durham, NC: Duke University Press, 2017.

184. See the conversation between Jafa and Greg Tate in Smith, *Ming Smith*.

185. Steyerl, Hito. *How Not to Be Seen: A Fucking Didactic Educational*. 2013. Video, 14:00.

186. Corea, as quoted in: (Author uncredited). "Miles Ahead of His Time." *Fuse* 4 (1999): 16.

187. DeJohnette, interview with the author, 2009.

188. See Szwed, *So What*, 291.

189. These dates documented on the Speakeasy blog page, http://speakeasyjazzat theclub.blogspot.com/2010_09_01_archive.html, as well as on Peter Losin's Miles Ahead website, http://www.plosin.com/MilesAhead/Sessions.aspx?s=690600.

190. In my interview with him, the photographer Guy Kopelowicz was insistent that the quintet played another gig elsewhere in southern France the day after Antibes, but I haven't been able to find any documentation of this performance. His claim also conflicts with the documented gig at Rutgers University in New Jersey which, assuming the date is correct, took place on July 27, one day after the second Antibes gig.

191. See Holland's comments in Tingen, *Miles Beyond*, 82.

192. Carr, Ian. *Miles Davis: The Definitive Biography*. Paris: Hachette, 2009, 271.

193. Breach, Ian. "Miles Davis at Jazz Expo." *Guardian*, November 3, 1969: 6.

194. This uncredited review excerpted in the liner notes for the *Bitches Brew* box set. See Davis, Miles. *The Complete Bitches Brew Sessions*. Columbia/Legacy C4K 65570. Originally released 1998.

195. Gitler, Ira. "Newport '69: Bad Trip." *DownBeat* 36, no. 17 (August 21, 1969): 25.

196. Carr, *Miles Davis: The Definitive Biography*, 271.

197. Kington, Miles. "Giant and His Heir." *Times* (London), November 3, 1969: 11.

198. Breach, "Miles Davis at Jazz Expo."

199. Miles, quoted in "The Miles Davis Interview."

200. Malson, "Miles Davis et le jeune garde á Antibes," 14.

201. Shorter, as quoted in Brémond, Olivier. "Wayne Shorter: A Mystic in the Computer Age." *Jazz Hot* 412 (1984): 16.

202. Corea, as quoted in Tingen, *Miles Beyond*, 112.

203. DeJohnette, interview with the author, 2009.

204. DeJohnette, interview with the author, 2009. One such "double drum" passage can be heard during the quintet's second set in Stockholm, Sweden on November 5.

205. Jones to Herb Noan, as quoted in: Howland, Harold. "Elvin Jones." *Modern Drummer* 3, no. 4 (September 1979). Accessed July 19, 2019. https://www.moderndrummer.com/article/august-september-1979-elvin-jones/.

206. Lynn, Greg. *Animate Form*. Princeton, NJ: Princeton Architectural Press, 1999, 43.

207. The Berlin footage is included on: Davis, Miles. *Live in Europe 1969: The Bootleg Series, Volume 2*. Columbia/Legacy 88725 41853 2. Originally released 2013.

208. For a discussion of this history, see: Vermeil, Jean. "Chant du Cygne?" *Techniques and Architecture: Programme Musiques* 489 (April–May 2007).

209. Fowler, Michael. "The Ephemeral Architecture of Stockhausen's *Pole für 2*." *Organised Sound* 15, no. 3 (2010): 185–97.

210. Mason, Lucien. "Miles Davis et Cecil Taylor." *Le Monde*, November 6, 1969.

211. See Merlin, Enrico. "Code MD: Coded Phrases in the First 'Electric Period.'" 1969. http://www.plosin.com/MilesAhead/CodeMD.html.

212. This uncredited review excerpted in the liner notes for *The Complete Bitches Brew Sessions* box set.

213. See Murphy, Douglas. "Frei Otto (1925–2015)." *Architectural Review* (April 21, 2015).

214. See Nerdinger, Winfried. "Working for a Better 'Earth for Mankind.'" In *Frei Otto: Complete Works*, 11. Basel: Birkhauser, 2005.

215. Frei Otto quoted in Whitehead, Rob. *Structures by Design: Thinking, Making, Breaking*. New York: Taylor and Francis, 2019, 291.

216. Otto, Frei, ed. *Tensile Structures*. Cambridge, MA: MIT Press, 1967.

217. Douglas Murphy, in fact, discusses Otto as prefiguring "the anti-architecture that accompanied cybernetics and the post-industrial society." See Murphy, "Frei Otto (1925–2015)."

218. Otto quoted in Nerdinger, "Frei Otto: Working for a Better 'Earth for Mankind,'" 9.

219. DeJohnette, interview with the author, 2009.

220. For a discussion of Davis's "rhythm band," see: Veal, Michael. "The Complete On the Corner Sessions." *Jazz Perspectives* 3, no. 3 (2009): 265–73.

221. DeJohnette, interview with the author, 2009.

222. Malson, "Miles Davis and Cecil Taylor," 21.

223. Kopelowicz, interview with the author, 2010.

224. Malson, "Miles Davis and Cecil Taylor," 21. For sources on Miles's "rhythm band" of the 1970s, see the following: Freeman, Phil. *Running the Voodoo Down: The Electric Music of Miles Davis*. New York: Backbeat Books, 2005; Tingen, *Miles Beyond*; Tate, Greg. "The Electric Miles." In *Flyboy in the Buttermilk: Essays on Contemporary America*. New York: Simon and Schuster, 1992; Veal, Michael. "The Complete On the Corner Sessions." *Jazz Perspectives* 3, no. 3 (2009): 265–73.

225. See Drott, Eric. "Free Jazz and the French Critic." *Journal of the American Musicological Society* 61, no. 3 (2008): 541–82.

226. Shorter in Oulette, "*Bitches Brew*: The Making of the Most Revolutionary Jazz Album in History."

227. See Ballon, "Liberated Sister," 114.

228. From Michelle Mercer's biography of Shorter: "Wayne couldn't help noticing how another *Bitches Brew* tune, 'Miles Runs the Voodoo Down,' bore suspiciously close resemblance to a song recorded by Betty Mabry on a demo that summer. 'That was his wife Betty's tune, called "Down Home Girl,"' Wayne said. 'Miles took it and broke it down with no beat, like he was hearing it through water.' Betty's demo, which perhaps coincidentally went unreleased, was produced by Miles and featured John McLaughlin, Hendrix's drummer Mitch Mitchell, Harvey Brooks, and Larry Young. She and Miles split up shortly after the recording." Mercer, *Footprints*, 135. McLaughlin, Brooks, and Young all went on to perform on the *Bitches Brew* album. Betty's "Down Home Girl" was later released on *Betty Davis: The Columbia Years, 1968–1969* (Light in the Attic LITA 135, 88843048152, 2016).

229. See Ballon, "Liberated Sister," 114–15. The material was eventually released in 2016 as *Betty Davis: The Columbia Years, 1968–1969*.

230. See Betty Davis's albums: *Betty Davis*. Just Sunshine JSS-5. Originally released 1973; *They Say I'm Different*. Just Sunshine JSS-3500. Originally released 1974; and *Nasty Gal*. Island ILPS 9329. Originally released 1975.

231. See Granger, Greg. "50 Years Ago: Who Tried to Kill Miles Davis on a New York City Street?" *Something Else!* October 10, 2019. https://somethingelsereviews.com/2019/10/10/miles-davis-shot-1969/.

CONCLUSION

"A Liquid Feeling Emerges"

Free Meter and Distortion as Generators

of Black Pasts and Futures

The great New York *conguero* Felix Sanabria once claimed to me that he (and other congueros like him) could produce twelve distinct tones from the head of a single conga drum. This same idea, of generating complexity from a seemingly simple surface, is a helpful metaphor for sounding out the relationship between the basic idea of rhythm and its many complex articulations throughout the Black Atlantic. Martin Munro's 2010 book *Different Drummers* explores the varying ways that the trope of "black rhythm" has been manipulated through-out the history of the African diaspora to generate a constellation of cultural meanings and experiences.[1] In this book, I think of myself as having extended a trajectory outward from Munro, positioning free meter—as articulated in the music of John Coltrane, Miles Davis, and the other musicians discussed—as a more provocative point on the rhythm-culture continuum that Munro mapped out so vividly in his study. Meanwhile, Sanabria's "twelve tones" image can also be used to evoke the alter-archives of jazz and the ways that its varying sonic fidelities might be used as prisms through which we can imagine alternate cultural pasts and futures.

The musicologist Kofi Agawu has produced some of his most influential work in the process of deconstructing the simplistic stereotype of rhythm as the con-ceptual cornerstone of African music.[2] Yet even Agawu was eventually moved to claim the experience of *groove* as the distinguishing factor of most African musics.[3] This observation extends to the music of the African diaspora, the grooves of which—blues, jazz, soul, funk, hip-hop, son, mambo, salsa, calypso, soca, ska, reggae, ragga, etc.—largely defined the global twentieth century in musical terms. As the work of Munro, Agawu, and legions of ethnomusicologists narrates so vividly, a groove (or any musical element) is more than a mere rhythmic construction. It is a type of cultural narrative that provides a window into how a particular society experienced, organized, and expressed reality in a given historical moment. And while no era can be encapsulated by any single rhythmic sensibility, certain idioms do seem paradigmatic of their particular points in cultural space and time. Within the history of African American dance music in the twentieth century, for example, the legendary big bands of the swing era roared with a loping, swinging groove that was an unmistakable reflection of their time—a black American inflection on industry, the city, and American upswing. In the 1960s and 1970s, the era of great funk bands adapted the machinist discipline of the swing bands to more foursquare rhythms that emphasized the downbeat thump of a blackness made newly explicit in the context of Civil Rights, Black Power, and Pan-Africanism. That thump was later distilled into the stubborn rhythmic cadences of hip-hop, a digitally freeze-framed take on the funk that pushed back against the rightward drift of America's political culture in the 1980s. But the unusual rhythmic designs created in the 1960s by jazz musicians like Coltrane in his late period and Miles's Lost Quintet during 1969 are much more complex propositions that seem, at first glance, to stand outside of this evolutionary narrative. Like the contestations of the 1960s in general, their radical structure demands that they either be written out of the historical narrative as disruptions and aberrations, or acknowledged as constituting a radically transformative evolutionary plateau, the full implications of which remain incompletely implemented and fiercely contested. How then do we embrace these complex rhythmic geometries that seem to represent a profound paradigm shift in the body's relationship to space and time, and seek (to use Coltrane's term) new, "multidirectional" experiences of the groove? If, as Ralph Ellison claimed, the artist's role is to "reset society's clock by imposing upon it his own method of defining the times,"[4] what do these rhythmic constructions tell us about how society's clock was ticking in the particular moment of their emergence, and how it might tick in the future? And how might our experience of that ticking be shaped by refracting it through the alter-archive of jazz?

URBAN SPACES

AN EDGE

A CITY IS

A CITY A PLACE WITHOUT

ENTRAPMENT

CONTAINMENT

A PRISON BEING DEMOLISHED[5]

Gordon Matta-Clark

When Le Corbusier asserted Louis Armstrong's music in 1947 as constituted from the energies of prewar Manhattan (and conversely, Manhattan of 1947 as "hot jazz in stone and steel"), he was implicitly asserting the city as a viable mode of musical analysis, while also generating a mode of urban-rhythmic insight that we can apply transhistorically.[6] As architectural theorists Mabel Wilson and Rashaad Shabazz have noted, Le Corbusier was not particularly progressive when it came to using architecture as a way of addressing America's racial complexities.[7] Nonetheless, his comments represent one productive point of departure for an alternate take on the idea of the twentieth- and twenty-first-century city, one that happens to stand in contrast to many prevailing Western interpretations of the urban condition, and one that posits rhythm as a potent mode of interpreting the urban.

During the course of this project, I have encountered many examples of physical shapes manifesting from sonic stimuli, aesthetic shapes manifesting from cultural stimuli, and vice versa: So-called "Lissajous curves" created by ink pens set into motion by tuning forks vibrating at different frequencies or pendulums rotating at particular rates.[8] Geometric patterns of salt formed by table surfaces vibrating at different frequencies.[9] Buildings digitally "printed" in three dimensions from sonic stimuli. Moving into more speculative ideas about the relationship between manifestations of patterns of cultural behavior in different artistic media, I brought Ghanaian drumming and textile traditions into dialogue in the chapter titled "Curvilinearity, Swing, and the Spline." Stepping even further out on a speculative limb, we might use the relationship between jazz and the city to hear more deeply into the 1960s and 1970s, flipping Le Corbusier's 1947 proposition to think of free jazz—with its fragmentation of regimented, regular rhythms that can be at least partially considered the products of industry—as a manifestation of the vibratory pattern of the deindustrializing city. This current period (2020) has witnessed a retrospective interest in the generation of (visual) artists who chronicled and/or interpreted the forms, cultures, and energies of postindustrial New York City, whether Robert Smithson, Eva Hesse, Gordon Matta-Clark, Alvin Baltrop, Richard Serra, or the legions of subway graffiti artists documented by Henry Chalfant, Martha Cooper, Paul Calvieri, and others. Meanwhile, Michael Heller's excellent *Loft Jazz* narrates a more concrete link between the deindustrializing city and the jazz experimentation that flourished within it.[10] The work of Heller and David P. Brown notwithstanding, there is a larger place for jazz within these discussions.

Throughout the history of their field, after all, architects have taken an ambivalent view of the city, embracing it on one hand as a site of endless practical possibilities for their craft while often remaining suspicious of it as a distortion of more "natural" modes of human living (for example, the architectural theorist Anthony Vidler's take on digital architecture is based on a psychoanalytic interpretation of its eccentric forms as manifestations of underlying social phobias).[11] The entire history of jazz tells us, by contrast, that for African Americans, the city has generally been a site of liberation and experimentation. So even if a case can be made for Vidler's pathological interpretation, the city, like all environments, will always necessarily reflect the varied experiences of its diverse inhabitants, subject to equally varied interpretations. In fact, Le Corbusier's own interpretation of the relationship between jazz and New York City can, when brought into dialogue with free jazz, provide a corrective to pathological readings of the fin-de-siecle city, and his seminal insight in this light was probably that, in their transmutation of urban forms and energies, jazz musicians not only digested the American city, but found a way to make it *swing*. And if high-modernist New York City of 1947 swung, in Le Corbusier's hearing, to a conception of rhythm typified by Louis Armstrong, we can hear the curvilinear rhythms of free jazz of the late 1960s as a language that made the *postindustrial* city swing.

———

While musicians and architects were equally obliged to respond to the increasingly dissolute forms of the postindustrial environment, the responses of the two fields were not, strictly speaking, concurrent. Whereas John Coltrane and Miles Davis were working in the heart of deindustrializing the New York of the 1960s and 1970s, architects such as Peter Eisenman, Zaha Hadid, and Greg Lynn, although trained between the 1950s and the 1970s, respectively, mainly established their professional reputations in the digital, neoliberal 1980s and 1990s (although Eisenman had enjoyed a previous period of prominence in the 1960s). To the extent that there are shared morphological and sociocultural resonances between the two creative spheres and historical moments, then, the jazz musicians working in the postindustrial era might be said to have prefigured some of the formal developments of digital-age architecture. In fact, Le Corbusier himself declared in 1947, "The jazz is more advanced than the architecture. If architecture were at the point reached by jazz, it would be an incredible spectacle."[12]

That the musicians were able to transmute the prevailing energies into art earlier than the architects is probably less a reflection of any conceptual disparity than of the relative ease of manipulating the amorphous physicality of sound over the hard physicality of built structures. Paul Goldberger suggested in his biography of Frank Gehry that different art forms evolve at different rates, due partially to the technical factors involved in their realization: "The challenges of getting a building built meant that architectural ideas rarely bore fruit as rapidly as artistic ones; it was one thing for a painter to put a dashing brushstroke across a canvas, and quite another for an architect to make a vast, flowing, irregular, geometrically complex space real."[13] Nonetheless, we can reflect the two practices back at each other across the span of the twentieth century and, if I have used architecture to think through jazz, this also provides a preliminary portal through which jazz can be used reciprocally, to think through architecture.

Of course, the "invisible art" of music is difficult for most people to conceptualize in plastic terms and given most architects' lack of musical training, it is unrealistic to expect them to understand the types of morphological and conceptual correspondences I have asserted throughout this text—architectural musings such as Steven Holl's "Architectonics of Music" and Marcos Novak's "Liquid Architecture" notwithstanding.[14] Difficult, for example, for them to hear Ornette Coleman's "Lonely Woman," with its disjunct metric layers stabilized by a continuous cymbal drone, as a study in structural stability based on an ingenious interweaving of a fragmented foreground, disjunct layering, and a continuous, textural foundation. Or to articulate the dichotomy between painstaking design and the swirling, centrifugal motion that provided the structural stability at the heart of Cecil Taylor's convulsive marathons of improvisation.

Nonetheless, jazz—one of the primary aesthetic shapers of late modernity—deserves acknowledgment for the sonic commentaries it has potentially made on the principles of structural engineering and urban planning.[15] The West's interaction with African musical forms has transformed the former since at least the sixteenth century, with manipulations of the Africanist Grid providing a very effective tool for measuring Africa's contribution to, and commentary on, our spatial understanding of the industrial and the postindustrial, of the modern and the postmodern. This idea might seem fanciful but it is not at all unprecedented. It was, after all, one of the main ideas that Laszlo Moholy-Nagy brought to the Bauhaus Academy: that practical design solutions could be achieved by understanding the concepts and principles being investigated in the various cutting-edge arts of the day.[16] The principles of black engineering are conclusively embodied in African and Afro-diasporic music and these sonic constructions, when successively turned out on the world at large since the centuries of colonization and the trans-Atlantic slave trade, have proven to be extremely durable mediums for transformations of political, spiritual, and social consciousness within and far beyond the Black Atlantic. Furthermore, as Matias Del Campo has observed, the aesthetic and social impact of contemporary and experimental architecture has sometimes been volatile, with architects moving beyond issues of mere form and function, to begin pondering the cultural implications and ramifications of their work:

> The debate on computational design thinking over the last two decades has focused mainly on techniques, technologies and tools—on how things are done, and not what they do or what they emanate. This has left very little breathing space to contemplate what those computationally driven chunks, pieces, objects and things actually imprint on the world in terms of cultural agency. What traces do they leave? How do they relate to each other, and the rest of the world? How do carved patterns, translucent patterns, ultra-black asteroids, massive lacerated blocks and flocks of colorful boulders create an alternative frame for realism?[17]

In this way of thinking, free jazz created its own "alternative frame," as society transitioned between technological eras. Which is to say that if Coltrane, Miles, and the other musicians of their generation came of age during the era of bebop as a high-velocity art music of America's industrial age, they, and the younger musicians who emerged after them, were the first to use jazz to investigate the ways that energy would flow along the fragmented contours of the postindustrial and in doing so, set the stage for the curvilinear rhythms of the information age. But amidst the ongoing debates about the social impact of experimental forms and new technologies, the most profound lesson emerging from the jazz-architecture dialogue is probably that even the most eccentric shapes, surfaces, and spaces can be made to "swing" as long as they remain accountable to social rhythms and priorities.

POLITICAL SPACES

> We were talking about freedom, and getting out of jails. Bar lines [measure lines] was like going to jail for us. So everyone wanted to escape from that. There was a general feeling that everyone wanted to be free.[18]
>
> *Pianist Mal Waldron*

The comments of the musicians in this book regarding free meter are in the end quite varied. Considered collectively, Rashied Ali's "multidirectional" rhythms, Jack DeJohnette's idea of *rhythm-as-shape*, and even the (dis)continuous "pulse(s)" felt by the Indian *khyal* and *thumri* singers during their ostensibly free meter *alaps*, seem to suggest that free meter can be considered as much a philosophical orientation as a practical musical or music-theoretical one. What unites them is the idea that there is no such thing as a *suspension* of time; there are only *infinitely varied elaborations* of time. And if that idea seems self-evident to any human being, Mal Waldron's comments in the previous epigraph further suggest that the particular application of that philosophical orientation in jazz of the 1960s was both utopian and pointedly political.

What are the spaces, shapes, and surfaces of liberation, of utopia? What do the ways we sculpt space, form, and time tell us about the relationship between sound and society? In *Animate Form*, Greg Lynn adapts the ideas of the Scottish zoologist Sir D'Arcy Thompson to suggest deformation as "an index of contextual forces acting on an organism."[19] In jazz of the 1960s, as with all music of any time, those deforming forces encompassed politics, culture, spirituality, technology, and cosmology, with the music made by free jazz musicians reflecting the transformations of those phenomena that were taking place after World War II.

The language and imagery of architecture have provided a number of analytical metaphors throughout this book, helping on one hand to narrate ideas of rhythm and structure while also narrating the way that arrangements of sounds are able to imply different configurations of physical space. The second idea, in particular, also helps us understand the way that configurations of sonic space can sublimate experiences of the body in physical space. That physical space extends directly into political space. In *Contagious Architecture*, Luciana Parisi ponders the idea that "spatial perception is derived from experiential movement . . . The geometrical shape of space and ultimately the idea of space are not defined according to Euclidean postulates of absolute and eternal form, but rather are produced by the sensorimotor activities that generate (as it were) the knowledge of shifting angles, volumes, and contours."[20] Meanwhile, spatial thinkers from the architect Lebbeus Woods to the philosopher Henri Lefebvre have argued that changes in our conception of space are, among other things, fundamentally political, with Lefebvre also arguing for an understanding of space *not* as a naturally occurring substance or void but rather a culturally produced phenomenon that takes its contours from society and the activities therein.[21] Space in this understanding is not absolute but improvised, and the way we improvise rhythmic energies across space is potentially a compelling way of determining whether the world is experienced as expanding outward to liberate the human body, or contracting to confine it.

As demonstrated by the tortured histories of Tulsa's famed "Black Wall Street" (1921) or Congressman Floyd McKissick's "Soul City" project in North Carolina (1969), there has been a pronounced history of Euro-Americans excluding African Americans from their spaces while being profoundly threatened by, and sometimes destroying, spaces of African American political, economic, and cultural autonomy.[22] Thus, the entire trajectory of the African American struggle can be understood in spatial terms, and we can use rhythm as a way of measuring the freedom quotient in society at a given time—hence Mal Waldron's commentary on his generation's resistance to an experience of rhythm constrained by measures and bar lines. It is probably no coincidence, for example, that the eruption of free jazz was concurrent with musicians' efforts to escape the control, conformity, and exploitation of nightclubs by establishing autonomous performance spaces in the decommissioned industrial spaces of downtown Manhattan.[23]

I have used the concept of the "Africanist Grid" throughout this book not only to make cultural and historical assertions about musical structure but also more pragmatically as a mode of abstract measurement, a way of charting the changing spatial configurations implied within the music of Coltrane, Miles, and other musicians. Of course, to refer to the grid as "Africanist" merely gives a particular cultural-historical inflection to one of the key conceptual tools of modernity, one that in the words of grid theorist Hannah Higgins represents "a visualization of modernity's faith in rational thought and industrial progress comprising everything from the urban landscape to the power grid, from modernist painting to the forms of modern physics."[24] The grid has, in fact, had its own sociopolitical applications across cultures and artistic media. Far away from the world of jazz rhythm, for example, the graphic designer Timothy Samara discussed the grid as a form that facilitates both freedom and constraint, an,

> organizing principle . . . whose influence is simultaneously ingrained in current practice and fought over . . . revered and reviled for the absolutes inherent in its conception . . . For some . . . it has become an unquestioned part of the working process that yields precision, order, and clarity . . . For others, it is symbolic of old guard aesthetic oppression, a stifling cage that hinders the search for expression.[25]

Samara went on to ponder the grid's sociopolitical implications: "Amid discussions of race and gender, conservation, political empowerment, and civil rights, perhaps a simple conversation about where to put things—the 'mundane housekeeping' of grid-based design—might have value again."[26]

"Where to put things" is another way of acknowledging *where things can go*, and in this sense, we can hear in the curvilinear grids of drummers such as Rashied Ali, Sunny Murray, Jack DeJohnette, and others sonic reflections of the reality that radical reorganizations of society called for radical reorganizations of musical sound, as African Americans moved into new social, political, cultural, and physical spaces. In this sense, Coltrane's spiritually conceived work can be thought of as what the architect Mies van der Rohe once described as "the spatial execution of spiritual decisions,"[27] with the proviso that, in the context of his time and place, those "spiritual decisions" carried an added political dimension to them. If (as discussed in chapter 3) these and other musicians were aspiring to a "fourth dimension" of rhythmic awareness, that rhythmic awareness correlated with a new dimension of political awareness at that time.

As a long-standing symbol of rhythm, remembrance, and revolt, the drum has long been asserted as a primary sonic marker of racial and cultural distinction. We might argue that the drum exploded into its ultimate revolution in the 1960s; on one side of the coin, musicians like James Brown and Sly Stone were reasserting and extending a very traditional articulation of the Africanist Grid, their percussive rhythmic constructions orchestrating communal joy and euphoria for a new and unprecedented age of African American agency. On the other side of the coin, jazz musicians like Coltrane, Miles, and their respective drummers were using free meter to leverage (what initially seemed like) rhythmic disorder into a new, utopian configuration of musical, cultural, and political power. Thus, the apparently divergent rhythmic visions of dance music and free meter need not be considered mutually exclusive; both encoded complementary

FIGURE 6.1

visions of freedom and liberation. Ashon Crawley has written powerfully of the centrality of *breath* to the process of liberation, and if Coltrane and Miles were the horn-playing figureheads breathing liberation via the syntaxes of free jazz and electric jazz, their respective drummers stood side by side with them in the sonic-social exhalations of the 1960s.[28]

The theorist Kodwo Eshun coined the formulation "chronopolitical intervention" to discuss the way that the discourse of Afrofuturism challenges notions of linear time in order to resignify African and Afro-diasporic pasts and futures.[29] Eshun was not concerned with the analysis of musical structures per se, but his term can itself be resignified to do music-analytical work. In this resignification, "chronopolitical intervention" dramatizes the fact that as a particular articulation of musical time, free meter was also a political intervention—a reconfiguration of musical time born of the liberation impulse in a volatile and transformative political moment. In our current moment, when a range of phenomena—from music-production software to the grids of prison cells in the age of mass incarceration—have imposed the most rigid and controlling articulations of the grid on African American people, it is crucial that people of African descent, and *all* human beings, have access to as many different and flexible articulations of the grid as possible.

(PAN-)AFRICAN SPACES

Understood in the broader context of the Black Atlantic cultural sphere, then, the curvilinear distortions of the Africanist Grid innovated in the 1960s can be heard as one very local articulation of the global struggles for black political and cultural freedom. But with the image of decolonizing Africa newly rehabilitated in the constellation of global cultures, Afro-diasporic musicians also used these new rhythmic constructions to imagine a radically reconfigured "Africa" that, while nominally in dialogue with African sonic and cultural realities, ultimately served their own purposes in the diaspora. If free meter has been argued in this book as partially a reflection of diasporic experience, how then does this reconfiguration of the Africanist Grid resonate on the African continent itself?

In the end, and taking 400 years of cultural dispersal and dislocation into account, it may not fundamentally be a reconfiguration after all, at least, in one way of hearing. To take an example: a well-known ethnographic recording of the music of Nigeria's Hausa people, released by Barenreiter-Musicaphon in the mid-1960s under the title *Nigeria: Hausa Music I*, contains a track that is strikingly reminiscent of some of the music discussed in this book. "Fanfare for the Sultan of Sokoto" features a traditional ensemble of drummers and horn players saluting a visiting dignitary with a cacophonous public fanfare. This type of drum-and-horn processional music, quite common across the Muslim areas of the West African Sahel and savannah, presents a soundscape that most unfamiliar Westerners might easily mistake for a traffic jam, the blaring sirens of emergency vehicles . . . or possibly a piece of free jazz along the lines of Coltrane's *Ascension*, Ornette Coleman's *Free Jazz*, or any number of collective improvisations by the Sun Ra Arkestra. And while the drummers maintain a constant underlying pulse in "traditional" (i.e., 12/8) meter, the horns are playing rhythmically free, motivic phrases over the drummers' pulse. In fact, the musicians' practical purpose is threefold: the steady, underlying rhythm takes authoritative command of the physical space while the horn players' riotous sound helps announce the arrival of the dignitary and clear pedestrians from the path to the Sultan's compound. But given that Hausa is a tonal language, the horn players' free-meter phrasing also indicates that they are in "speech mode," using linguistic phrases as royal salutations, their melodies properly understood as a multiplicity of (literally) speaking voices.[30] This is an important distinction to make in relation to African cultures that speak tonal languages, and in which musical instruments function as "linguistic surrogates," replicating the melodic contours of the spoken language:

when musical parts are played in free meter, it is generally because they have moved into "speech mode."[31]

Through this concept of *speech*, this particular genre of Hausa music invites close comparison with works of collective improvisation discussed throughout in this book, and in fact, the horn-and-drum ensembles of the West African savannah have appealed to many of the more adventurous jazz musicians. Both Ornette Coleman and the multi-woodwind player Yusef Lateef traveled to Nigeria and performed/recorded with Hausa musicians like these, while Coltrane's plans to do the same were scuttled by his passing, and this attests to the sonic resonances the musicians themselves felt between these sounds and some of those being made back home in the jazz spaces of the United States.[32] Without claiming any kind of direct and uncomplicated ancestral inheritance, we can nonetheless draw a loosely functional connection between both cultural spheres. This lies in their use of flexible, "speech rhythms"—to give "testimony" of one kind or another and to perform a similar social function of *clearing a space*. If the Hausa musicians were clearing a space in the immediate physical area of a dignitary's compound in Nigeria, the musicians discussed in this book were clearing political space in the United States. Scholars such as Norman Weinstein and Jonathan Rowlands have seized upon the spiritual imperatives of Coltrane's later music to variously interpret it as a form of communal, spiritual testimony (Weinstein) or glossolalia (Rowlands).[33] But it is also important to acknowledge that Coltrane and Miles used musical elements like free-meter rhythm to articulate a moment when political testimony was an urgent priority, hence the liquification of dance rhythms into speech rhythms, with the latter proclaiming new freedoms that resonated and reverberated throughout American society and the wider world.

————

> The main difference between *son, bomba, plena, merengue, samba* and the blues—aside from the use of different Western European languages—is that the blues aesthetic developed severed away from drum culture.[34]
>
> *Jay Hoggard*

This discourse of music as/interpolated by speech might also explain why many African listeners who relate to "free jazz" often hear it as much in dialogue with various African traditional musics as with anything putatively related to what is typically considered "jazz," "experimental," or even "Western" music. Perhaps unsurprisingly, it follows that many of these African musicians also process the music as much through the conceptual prisms of African drumming and/or languages as they do through the prism of Western harmony. The Ghanaian woodwind player Nii Noi Nortey, for example, is an avowed disciple of *late-period* John Coltrane and expressed his feeling to Steven Feld that:

> [Coltrane's] drummers . . . were playing something nearer to what I heard in Africa, in terms of complexities and tonalities and all kinds of things. I heard more of the African things in these drummers. I heard the drums overlapping and hooking up like our drummers do, and over that I can hear Coltrane as a drummer playing the saxophone, working his rhythms too. I heard more of the African thing in these drummers. So Coltrane's music for me is just a sound that he projects and the image of Africa that we get in his music, first and foremost, before the sheets of sound. I hear the sheets of sound rhythmically. Others may hear it harmonically. I hear it as the drums overlapping each other, I see Coltrane as a drummer playing the saxophone.[35]

Nortey's drum-based way of hearing Coltrane's complex pitch arrays becomes less metaphorical once we understand the close relationship between drumming and language in the West African cultures that speak tonal languages. And this is why, echoing Pete Cosey's earlier vision of *linguata dakinda* (see the Coltrane essay), jazz improvisations are as often heard by African listeners as deeply encoded with African linguistic traits as much as they are associated with the Western harmonic system. Nii Nortey continued: "In Coltrane's music you can hear the various African language groups . . . even if he couldn't speak an African language, he tried as much as possible to vocalize it in his instrument . . . Coltrane leapt from the American language idiom into an African idiom, and I think he did it very, very successfully."[36] In this light, Coltrane's and Miles's music can be partially understood as a project of African cultural reclamation. The Coltrane of *Interstellar Space* imagines Africa as a constellation of incredibly complex rhythmic and pitch-driven equations, an Afro-hyperintellectualism accessed via the spiritually driven technologies of trance and/or possession, speaking in tongues that fuse submerged and fragmented linguistic traits of traditional Africa with channeled dialects of extraterrestrials to warp the twelve tones of the Western chromatic scale into new, hybrid expressions. And even though Miles's Lost Quintet didn't seem as immediately invested in the Africa concept as Coltrane, it was undeniably the opening gambit of his own evolving Africanist orientation as he gradually digested the influence of Jimi Hendrix throughout the 1970s, ultimately fielding an avant-funk band with three Hendrix-influenced guitarists, while titling their pieces after iconic and historical African locations (such as Ife, in Nigeria), African liberation movements (such as the *Frente de Libertação de Moçambique* [Frelimo] in Mozambique), or emergent African nations such as Zimbabwe (still known by its settler-colonial name Rhodesia in 1975). But the Lost Quintet and, by extension, the magnum opus *Bitches Brew*, moved much more fluidly between body rhythms and speech rhythms, conforming most closely to the fluid Africanist symbiosis of music and speech. And it in fact it is this entire, Hendrix-inspired trajectory that makes the distorted alter-archives of the Lost Quintet all the more relevant and resonant.

The cultural practices of the African diaspora have often suggested that one role of its cultures has been not only the preservation but also the *recombination* and *reconfiguration* of the inherited African codes and concepts. *Music as speech* is one Africanist concept that has had particularly potent refractions throughout the diaspora, with even the ostensibly "experimental" extremes of the African American tradition found to have cognates in some African cultural practices. But the continuum of sound from Sokoto to Coltrane to Nortey to Miles also attests to the fact that flexible articulations of the Africanist Grid need not be only understood as a function of diasporic dislocations or transformations—they are also common throughout sub-Saharan Africa whenever musicians shift into functions requiring musical instruments to replicate speech. Jazz musicians of the 1960s shifted into speech mode in order to proclaim new spaces of African American agency, to give urgent testimony to 500 years of Afro-diasporic struggle and triumph, and to proclaim a vision of black freedom and limitless possibility that extended all the way to the cosmic realm.[37]

OUTER SPACES

The free-meter rhythms of free jazz were not only too urgent to be confined to bar lines and measures, they were too urgent to be confined to the home planet, and Afrofuturism becomes particularly relevant at this intersection of rhythm and cosmology. The prominence of Afrofuturism across various modes of Black Atlantic artistic production and scholarship is at least partly a reflection of the fact that the advent of digital culture has recycled the outer-space tropes of "classic" science fiction through the more recent infinities of cyberspace, and because the multiworld perspectives of Afrofuturism continue to illuminate the multidimensional challenges of black life in the early twenty-first century. With the exception of Sun Ra, however, jazz music and jazz musicians actually appear very infrequently in Afrofuturist discussions. The reasons for Sun Ra's appeal are obvious: with his costumes, poetry, lyrics, and cosmically garbed dancers, he is a convenient point of interface for people interested in the thematic expression of Afrofuturism in music but not so interested in its articulation within the arcane intricacies of jazz improvisation. But with its endless improvised pathways through internal spaces of the mind and heart, modern jazz in general (and free jazz in particular) seems a perfect fit for the chronopolitical odysseys of the Afrofuturists, their themes of time travel, time capsules, time machines, and riddles of time all manifesting as sonic analogues within the forms and structures of free jazz. Works such as *Interstellar Space* (possibly the clearest presentation of Rashied Ali's "multidirectional" rhythms) and *1969 Miles* (with every song time-stretched by Jack DeJohnette from straight-ahead jazz or funk-rock into the kaleidoscopic curvilinearity of free meter) stand head to head with authors such as Octavia Butler, Nalo Hopkinson, and Ytasha Womack in subjecting the concept of time to all kinds of dramatic reformulations and reinterpretations.

Given that the manipulation of time in the Afrofuturist project has generally reinflected the historical past of slavery, exile, and colonization in order to generate alternate black futures, the chronopolitical and cosmological narratives implied in the curvilinear rhythms of free jazz might inspire us to reflect on the continued viability of the political and cultural visions of the post–World War II era and to ponder the central temporal question of post–World War II Black Atlantic culture: In terms of agency, self-determination, and vision, are people of African descent moving forward? Backward? Were Civil Rights, Black Power, and African independence the labor pains of a new order being birthed? Were they historical mirages, as distant from our current reality as the alien worlds depicted in science fiction? Or are these movements merely the cyclical return of an ever-changing same? Whether that history is experienced as a line, a circle, or a spiral, the chronopolitical interventions of works like *Interstellar Space* and *Bitches Brew* stand as preeminent sonic documents of Black Atlantic world (re-)making in the age(s) of outer-space exploration, Civil Rights/Black Power, and African/Caribbean independence that are ultimately transhistorical in their resonance. Hearing them today offers the same lessons as a work like Octavia Butler's *Kindred*, allowing us to understand the time-stretched dialects of the digital age as merely now-generation iterations of the ever-present strategy of fighting the power by manipulating the experience of time.

These experiences of space and time had rhythmic consequences that were also felt in architecture. For example, Greg Lynn fused his professional interest in architecture with his personal interest in science fiction in works such as *Form*,[38] *Animate Form*,[39] and *Outer-Space Odysseys*,[40] suggesting that the proliferation of new architectural forms in the digital age was at least partially a reflection of new understandings of gravity resulting from the human exploration of outer space. And whereas his free-floating, curvilinear "blob" forms represent Space Age manifestations in the sphere of design, curvilinear rhythms represent their manifestation in the sphere of jazz rhythm. Thus the idea of *antigravity*, as a conscious design element, was prominent in the 1960s and fundamental to most of the music chronicled in this book. Works such as *Meditations* and *Bitches Brew*, with their fractured, collaged rhythmic structures and passages of free-floating, curvilinear rhythms, are as compelling commentaries on new experiences of gravity as are any canonical works of science fiction. While the ecstatic rubatos of the Afro-Baptist liturgy or the meditative *alaps* of Hindustani music have typically been understood through the lens of devotional experience as an escape from worldly rhythms, the flotation spaces of free jazz can be equally heard as a Space Age reversal of the gravities of oppression and containment.

Ultimately, this unmooring of the traditional gravities offered new ways of channeling cosmic energy through terrestrial form in both jazz and architecture. Sean Lally's book *The Air from Other Planets* envisions a new kind of "architecture" that replaces walls and roofs with manipulated energies (electromagnetic, thermodynamic, acoustic, chemical) of the natural world.[41] The visionary designer Buckminster Fuller in the 1960s radically reframed "architecture" as a discourse that would address not only built structures but *any* medium that served to transmit or contain energies.[42] Meanwhile, a subgenre of projects over the years has been devoted to the "dematerialization" of architecture, from Fuller's aforementioned idea of architecture as energy, to Coop Himmelblau's *Architecture Must Burn* (1980), to Marcos Novak's ideas of a "Liquid Architecture,"[43] and on to Diller Scofidio + Renfro's *Blur Building* (2002). With free jazz musicians themselves reconceptualizing the 1960s song as "energy music," jazz, architecture, and science fiction all pursued radical dematerializations of traditional forms as the twentieth century morphed into the twenty-first.

———

Finally, engaging the concept of *distortion* in free jazz with digital-age ears suggests that the imperative of sonic world making took an additional and unexpected leap when, aided by the explosion of domestic tape-duplication technology, the music arguably transcended the conscious intentions of its creators. Heard in the context of the Space Age with which this was concurrent, all of the sonic idiosyncrasies of these recordings—frequency-range distortion, tape hiss, compression, etc.—have played their own role in creating a dialogue between free jazz/jazz-rock fusion and the imaginings of a generation raised on science fiction. Today, in fact, complex (and costly) sound-processing devices, frequently used in science fiction soundtracks, replicate the same distressed textures found throughout the alter-archives of jazz (and other recorded traditions). And if, throughout this book, I have discussed the ability of these sonic anomalies to evoke the historical past and cultural others, I invoke them here in their ability to evoke historical futures—of jazz, and even of cultures yet to be discovered. In this, the innovators of hip-hop deserve credit for creating a context in which the aesthetics of previous eras were resuscitated and repurposed as samples, their quality of lo-fi sonic abjection now hitched to the forward-looking impulse of innovation. Once again, photography also provides a helpful parallel. The accidents through which that field evolved gave birth not only to new photographic techniques and genres, but led to new ways of seeing and understanding the existing world while stumbling upon entirely novel and previously unimagined potential realities.

As a technology that emerged simultaneously with Europe's colonization of the wider world, photography seemed to hold revolutionary potential as a means of representing the world's peoples for the Western gaze. What few people understood at the time was the emergent technology's ability to *create* new understandings of the human.[44] And as much as I have emphasized photography's evolution-by-accident, it is equally true that the stylistic idiosyncrasies of photography in the colonial period were as much the result of manipulation of the medium with the intent of manufacturing otherness as they were the result of technical accidents. Overexposure could make humans appear as if they were spirit beings constituted out of pure sunlight. Underexposure made everyday landscapes look like gateways to infinity, and made ordinary humans look like spectral presences. Eyes glistened like lasers, breasts and buttocks protruded like planets about to be slung across the solar system, and scarification appeared like the charred surfaces of distant planets.[45] It is ironic but unsurprising, then, that the creators of science fiction films eventually came to use the photo-captured iconography of non-Western peoples to fashion futuristic depictions of extraterrestrial beings.[46]

So it might be with the alternate archive of jazz. These bootleg recordings not only resonate with the spatial thinking of digital architecture in their sonic simulation of unusual spatial dimensions that are absent from more conventionally produced jazz recordings; they also resonate with photography to the extent that their eccentric spatialities can evoke other worlds for the listener. This interpretation is not as fanciful as it might initially seem. In 2021, the *Jazz Research Journal* issued a call for papers on the topic of "Speculative Histories of Jazz," implying at the very least a fatigue with the well-worn narratives of the music and a desire for new narratives, including fictional narratives completely generated from the imagination.[47] Like the forced photographic collaboration between Chandra McCormack, Keith Calhoun, and Hurricane Katrina, the new worlds proposed by Coltrane, Miles, and other musicians were inadvertently refracted into even more radical sonic worlds than their creators had ever imagined. "People believe what they see in photographs," wrote the art historian David Levi Strauss in 2005. "The imagination is thought to be yoked to the material world."[48] Do people equally believe what they hear in sound recordings? Heard with ears that bridge the eras of analog/digital sound and tape trading/file sharing, they provide what Rosa Menkman referred to as an "exoskeleton for progress,"[49] allowing us to counteract the oft-proclaimed obsolescence of jazz by forcing the music into accountability to contemporary sound values of distortion, glitch, circuit bending, and other vernaculars of the sound-signal-in-transmission process. Their alter-archives now offering a blend of gritty, street-level texture and exotic Space Age fantasia, there is no more compelling sonic resource for the Afrofuturists than the alter-archive of 1960s jazz.

"A LIQUID FEELING"

The notions of space and time have also been influenced by the arrival of electronics and are now drastically compressed: far from being a merely technological question, digitalization has implied a difference in cultural reorganization. For this to happen, it is vital to adopt the attitude of being willing to undertake this reorganization. You must be willing to support the creation of a different world, one that never existed before.[50]

Luca Galofaro

The digital is the unknown presence of the Other at the table of postcolonial possibilities.[51]

John Akomfrah

"How Long 'til Black Future Month?" asked science fiction author N. K. Jemisin in the title of her 2018 collection of short stories.[52] Earlier, in 2013, the cultural theorist Kodwo Eshun had similarly noted the erasure of blackness from what he termed the "futures industry" of science fiction, fantasy, and their related genres. "African social reality," Eshun writes, "is overdetermined by intimidating global scenarios, doomsday economic projections, weather predictions, medical reports on AIDS, and life-expectancy forecasts, all of which predict decades of immiseration."[53] Viewed from the African American side of the Black Atlantic, then, it didn't seem coincidental that America's long, predictable slide from Ronald Reagan to Donald Trump had culminated in the cinematic trending of black suffering: an ever-growing cluster of films devoted to the topics of enslavement, police brutality, mass incarceration, ghetto life, African dystopias and warlords, and the like. The 2018 film *Black Panther* notwithstanding, films of black visionaries, liberators, paradigm shifters, and problem solvers seemed in woefully short supply, and almost always flew below the radar.

Jazz was by no means immune. Like Civil Rights, Black Power, African independence, second-wave feminism, antimilitarism, and environmentalism, the utopian visions of 1960s jazz were profoundly under siege by the 1980s, as right-wing fervor swept across the land and jazz's functionaries of the Reagan era used an ideology of classicism to collapse the music's spatial and cultural scope from other cultures and other worlds down to the "old-time" iconography of second-line parades, jazz funerals, country roads, cotton fields, steam trains, the Christian church, and an extremely reductive understanding of the concept of "swing." But it only (seemed to) work for a short time because the digital revolution was already underway and would transform music making—across genres—in ways those musicians could neither imagine, anticipate, nor integrate. And while that revolution initially seemed relevant only to hip-hop, electronica, and various experimental musics, the new digital reality would gradually open up new ways of creating and understanding jazz that were as vast and varied as the outer-space reality that had transformed the jazz imaginings of the 1960s.

The early hip-hop producers worked in miniature, by looping breakbeats manually excerpted from vinyl records by scratching and later, excerpted by digital sampling. Like photographers, they understood that by staging the right combination of thematic and atmospheric material, the loop/breakbeat/sample could exist as an audio vignette as sonically colorful and spatially compelling as any equivalent length of traditionally orchestrated "music." This, in fact, gave birth to a sonic science of lo-fi in which samples were valued on the basis of the spatial and textural qualities of their original recorded environments, with various degrees of signal degradation and distortion valued in the ways that filters might be in the world of film.[54] But aside from some early, preliminary attempts to blend them, jazz and hip-hop seemed to spring from irreconcilably different methodologies—one based on real-time interaction between improvising human musicians and the other on the interplay between improvised human vocalizing and static, mechanized rhythms.[55]

Simultaneously, however, the music of saxophonist and "M-Base" pioneer Steve Coleman (and others in his orbit) was heralding a new era in which the digital reality was slowly manifesting in jazz. A child of the Space Age (born in 1956) and a self-described computer obsessive, Coleman initially made his name playing on the streets of deindustrializing New York City, eventually becoming a paradigm-shifting influence on his and subsequent jazz generations. Harmonically, his composing and improvising are a hyperchromatic extension of the bebop paradigm from Bird to the esotericisms of Coltrane. Rhythmically, it is formed from a broad, global awareness of Black Atlantic (and other) musical traditions, expanding the traditional symmetries of the Africanist Grid into more complex states through the stacking of different time signatures. The resulting compositions are circular complexes of competing metric gravities that resemble funky, sonic analogues of M. C. Escher's perspective-scrambling woodcuts. Too complex to be heard in the mind's inner ear before they have first been programmed on a computer and heard aloud (at least by most people), Coleman's metrically complex equations of hyperchromaticized jazz-funk arguably comprised an early, profound shot in jazz's transformation from the postindustrial age to the information age.

As in architecture, the aesthetics of postindustrial jazz held the key to at least certain core aesthetics of jazz in the information age. In one way of hearing, Coleman and others of his artistic sensibility represented a gnostic order for a new jazz generation, offering their own generational refraction of the esoteric, experimental music that had thrived in John Coltrane's wake, in the lofts of postindustrial New York City during the 1970s. But it was really hip-hop, itself a product of deindustrializing New York City, that was the (unacknowledged) handmaiden of jazz's transition to the digital era. And if Coleman had fired the opening shot in that process, the release of D'Angelo's 1996 neo-soul album *Voodoo*, with live musicians imitating the glitches and stutters that resulted from the imprecise manual beat matching of the hip-hop deejays, was a subsequent turning point that proved that live players could embrace the rhythmic anomalies of hip-hop and make them swing.[56] In turn, a generation of jazz drummers would emerge who had been raised not only on Coleman's metric stacking but also on the microtiming experiments of D'Angelo and hip-hop-influenced producers such as Madlib, DJ Premier, and especially J. Dilla, who stylized the rhythmic traits that had emerged out of turntablism.[57] These rhythmic limps and stutters would impart an ironically human quality to the digital mechanization of rhythm, and younger jazz drummers from Tyshawn Sorey to Makaya McCraven and Chris Dave would, in their various ways, import the rhythmic sensibility of scratching into jazz. The result was a seemingly new syntax of staggered, slipping counterrhythms and accelerating/decelerating tempo slopes—often juxtaposed against static, repetitive groove elements—that gave a new, digital-age inflection to the process of juxtaposing fluid and repetitive rhythms that had been at the heart of works such as Coltrane's *Meditations*, Miles's *Bitches Brew*, and Ornette's "Lonely Woman."

The rhythmic transformations and renegotiated values that hip-hop bequeathed to jazz seemed to reaffirm the idea that forward movement in the music would be predicated less on traditional considerations of pitch, and more on various reconfigurations of space, structure, texture, and pure sound. And the spinning off of a new vector of rhythmic ellipsis from the regimented grid of hip-hop rhythm suggested that the process of generating pleasure from within the tension between liberation and constraint is a cyclical process of history and culture. It is these contributions that also allow us, in the digital age, to not only reassess the jazz avant-garde, but also to recuperate the alter-archive of the music in all of its low-fidelity glory. And this, in a way, returns jazz to some of the values that had emerged in the late 1960s, before horn players of the Reagan era began their desperate attempt to wrest control of the music back from the rhythm-section players who had defined jazz-rock fusion. Unfortunately for them, the new digital paradigm was already rendering traditional conceptions of instrumentalism irrelevant across instrumental categories. Players of instruments, implicitly or explicitly, were now responding to that new paradigm, using digitally mediated speech and body rhythms, and lo-fi audio snapshots of recorded history, to liquefy and colorize the Africanist Grid in the twentieth century.

When does the issue of fidelity become ideologically loaded? David Novak has identified distortion (as a negative value within an ideology of signal purity) as one means by which Western cultures have reinforced the technological divide between the West and the non-West.[58] But it is also true that there are Western aficionados of non-Western music who embrace distortion as a means of imagining a sonic path *forward* for Western music. More significantly, the very history of hip-hop has demonstrated that future aesthetics and orientations can be generated from within the distressed aesthetics of obsolete formats. Applied to jazz, this value of distortion counters forty years of conservative drift during which jazz musicians' insistence on "high" fidelity functioned as a means of gaining social respectability. Given that, by the 1980s, that respectability was being gained at the expense of the imaginative horizons of the music, distortion has become a means through which those imaginative horizons can be pushed back, via the anomalies of the analog and digital eras.

This is to say that the alter-archive of jazz offers an alternate construction of musical history and a potential underground of sonic practice, and its aesthetics hint at the politics behind it all, its insights transportable across contemporaneous artistic media. John Akomfrah's 1988 film *Testament*, for example, focuses on its protagonist's attempt to reconstruct the history of newly independent Ghana under president Kwame Nkrumah and his Convention People's Party. Frustrated at every turn by interview subjects who (for various reasons) refuse to engage with that transformative, turbulent, and troubled chapter of Ghana's and Africa's post-independence history, the film partially becomes a philosophical meditation on the concept of archives, dramatizing the difficulty of reconstructing the lost and submerged histories of post–World War II black liberation. In fact, *Testament*'s lo-res/lo-fi presentation is itself a reflection of the fact that Akomfrah had to rely on archives that were by turns disfigured or partially destroyed by Ghana's subsequent political regimes. That lo-fi/lo-res aesthetic, then, is not merely an aesthetic preference for Akomfrah; it is a concrete result of the tragedies that befell the utopian dreams of the liberation generation. And as he recounted in 2013, building a history from partial archives became a practical and philosophical cornerstone of the body of work he created with the Black Audio Film Collective:

> Given the fact that the archival has mattered for so long in our work . . . it was absolutely critical to see whether by means of just the archival . . . one could construct a narrative . . . Over the years we've said over and over again how much diasporic identity is being structured by absences, specifically of tangible monuments, [that] find themselves increasingly brought into being, almost, by the archive. And so if the archive can't have a voice, if it can't speak in a way that's legible, then what it says about diasporic history is pretty serious. So what might feel like a simple exercise of splicing bits together became ethically and philosophically a really important project for us.[59]

Akomfrah's comments are absolutely relevant to the alter-archive of jazz. Shot through with its own distortions and absences and inextricably connected to the impulse toward liberation on the American side of the Black Atlantic, the recorded archives of late Coltrane and Miles's Lost Quintet are a local microcosm of the same factors of erasure and distortion.

Surveying the history of postcolonial film throughout Africa and the diaspora, Akomfrah coined the term "digitopia" to refer to a technological moment in which the digital consolidation of older analog aesthetics creates the conditions for a resurgence of post-/anticolonial imagining.[60] Even though the sound recordings I discuss in this book (unlike the distressed visual aesthetic of Akomfrah's cinematic output) were not deliberately fashioned to sound the way they now sound, their protracted existence on the margins of jazz commerce is no coincidence since both Coltrane's late music and Miles's Lost Quintet were conceived at the very heart of the contestations of the 1960s. "[The] unofficial history of the digital," Akomfrah writes, "is merely the more known version of a now forgotten narrative that played across a series of postcolonial spaces throughout the sixties and seventies."[61] And if hip-hop, Jamaican dub music, and free jazz created a space for the politicized linkage of sonic experimentation and politics, digital-age jazz can now benefit retroactively from the advance work done in the analog era.

———

Frank Gehry may well be the most famous architect of the digital era. His legendary facades, from the Guggenheim Museum in Bilbao to the Walt Disney Concert Hall in Los Angeles, reflect a self-consciously "trashy" aesthetic of sharp, angular forms often violently juxtaposed against organic, biomorphic protuberances, demonstrating the abilities of digital drafting and animation technology to dramatically reconfigure architectural surfaces.[62] But despite his use of collage, fragmentation, and juxtaposition, Gehry—like John Coltrane, Miles Davis, and Cecil Taylor before him—is ultimately striving for a feeling that the architect Bruce Lindsey has evoked in particularly fluid terms: "Interior and exterior, space and volumes, atmosphere and material, are now all conceived in a fluid, continuous movement: *an underwater, liquid feeling emerges*" (my italics).[63]

Like Gehry, the jazz musicians chronicled throughout this book also utilized fragmentation, distortion, collage, and similar processes to fashion their own liquid realities. And as David S. Ware's comments (cited in the opening chapter) suggest, their deconstruction of rhythms rooted in social dancing—swing, funk, or otherwise—might seem to have violated the social contract implied by the cyclically repeating, interwoven, and hocketed dance rhythms of the traditional Africanist Grid that underpinned most of the history of jazz. However, we can take a cue from the insights of Amiri Baraka while spinning the jazz-classicist arguments of Albert Murray and Stanley Crouch into a more flexible understanding of the jazz tradition, arguing that it is the emotional/existential imperatives of the blues, and the grounding, bodily philosophy of swing, that demand that metrically free space be experienced *not* nihilistically (i.e., as atomized, fragmented, and unresponsive to social concerns), but rather as charged and curvilinear—i.e., as radical formal decisions made *gravitationally* accountable to the human social rhythms of dance, speech, sex, spirituality, politics, and community. This is the true essence of "swing." Like Rashied Ali's comment that he was merely playing in "the higher regions of 4/4," this idea of social gravity allows us an alternate, "liquid" way of hearing of the shapes of the 1960s, whether sonic or plastic. It acknowledges the radically deconstructive nature of the formal transformations while hearing them not as violations, but rather as radical *extensions* or *revisions* of the social contract. What the musicians were striving for was not a state of disunity but, rather, a more flexible sense of unity and flow. And as America plunges back into a sociopolitical dynamic as volatile and racially contested as the 1960s tempest that gave birth to free jazz, the rearticulated rhythms of curvilinearity suggest a space in which African American strength and survival manifests not only as frontal resistance but equally as strategically amorphous, just like every style of black music and dance that has unexpectedly shape shifted American culture as a whole down unexpected and regenerative corridors.

NOTES

1. Munro, Martin. *Different Drummers: Rhythm and Race in the Americas*. Berkeley: University of California Press, 2010.

2. See Agawu's seminal essay, "The Invention of African Rhythm." Agawu, Kofi. *Representing African Music: Postcolonial Notes, Queries, Positions*. London: Taylor and Francis, 2003.

3. For example, in his book *The African Imagination in Music* (Oxford University Press, 2016), Agawu has written: "Groove and associated repetition are the ultimate guarantors of meaningfulness in musical performance" (17).

4. Ellison from his essay, "The Art of Romare Bearden." Reprinted in *The Romare*

Bearden Reader, edited by Robert O'Meally, 198. Durham, NC: Duke University Press, 2019.

5. An excerpt from the notes of artist Gordon Matta-Clark, as reprinted in Bessa, Antonio Sergio, and Jessamyn Fiore. *Gordon Matta-Clark: Anarchitect*. New Haven, CT: Yale University Press, 2018, 134.

6. Le Corbusier. *When the Cathedrals Were White*. New York: McGraw-Hill, 1947, 158.

7. See Shabazz's historical account (and Wilson's quoted comments) of Le Corbusier's involvement in the planning of urban architectural projects in Chicago, in Shabazz, Rashad. *Spatializing Blackness: Architectures of Confinement and Black Masculinity in Chicago*. Chicago: University of Illinois Press, 2015, 58–59.

8. See, for example, "Three Pendulum Harmonograph," https://www.youtube.com/watch?v=bXAWXoew9mM.

9. See, for example, "Resonance Experiment! (Full Version—With Tones)," https://www.youtube.com/watch?v=1yaqUI4b974&t=155s.

10. Heller, Michael. *Loft Jazz: Improvising New York in the 1970s*. Berkeley: University of California Press, 2017.

11. See Vidler, Anthony. *Warped Space: Art, Architecture, and Anxiety in Modern Culture*. Cambridge, MA: MIT Press, 2000.

12. Le Corbusier, *When the Cathedrals Were White*, 161.

13. From Goldberger, Paul. *Building Art: The Life and Work of Frank Gehry*. New York: Knopf, 2015, 6.

14. Holl and Novak are two architects who have consciously explored correspondences between the two fields. See, for example: Holl, Steven. "The Architectonics of Music." http://architectonicsofmusic.com; and Novak, Marcos. "Liquid Architectures of Cyberspace." In *Cyberspace: First Steps*, edited by Michael Benedikt. Cambridge, MA: MIT Press, 1992.

15. It is, however, the primary focus of David Brown's *Noise Orders*, which I have cited throughout this text.

16. See, for example: Moholoy-Nagy, Laszlo. *Telehor: The International Review New Vision*. Brno (Czechoslovakia): Fr. Kalivoda, 1936.

17. Del Campo, Matias. "Moods and Other Ontological Catastrophes," *Architectural Design* 86, no. 6 (November/December 2016): 7.

18. Waldron, as quoted in Saul, Scott. *Freedom Is, Freedom Ain't: Jazz and the Making of the Sixties*. Cambridge, MA: Harvard University Press, 2003, 33.

19. Lynn, Greg. "Animate Form." In *Animate Form*, 26. Princeton, NJ: Princeton Architectural Press, 1999.

20. Parisi, Luciana. *Contagious Architecture: Computation, Aesthetics, and Space*. Cambridge, MA: MIT Press, 2013.

21. See chapter 2 of: Lefebvre, Henri. "Social Space." In *The Production of Space*, esp. 71–73. London: Blackwell, 1974.

22. See Healy, Thomas. *Soul City: Race, Equality, and the Lost Dream of an American Utopia*. New York: Henry Holt, 2021.

23. See Heller, *Loft Jazz*.

24. Higgins, Hannah. *The Grid Book*. Cambridge, MA: MIT Press, 2009, 6.

25. From Samara, Timothy. *Making and Breaking the Grid: A Graphic Design Layout Workshop*. Gloucester, MA: Rockport Publishing, 2002, 9.

26. Samara, *Making and Breaking the Grid*, 10.

27. Mies van der Rohe, as quoted in the introduction to Lambert, Phyllis. *Mies van der Rohe: The Difficult Art of the Simple*. Montreal: Canadian Center for Architecture, 2001, 9.

28. Crawley, Ashon. *Blackpentecostal Breath: The Aesthetics of Possibility*. New York: Fordham University Press, 2017. See especially chapter 1, "Breath."

29. See Eshun, Kodwo. "Further Considerations on Afrofuturism." *New Centennial Review* 33, no. 2 (Summer 2003): 292.

30. Ames writes in the album notes: "In this recording the musicians of the Sultan of Sokoto praise their patron with their instruments but without words . . . Court musicians of all the Emirs traditionally play these horn and drum fanfares called *sara* on the 'eve of Friday.' Though there is no singing, all the instruments are 'talking.' These wind instruments are played only for high officials in the Hausa government and thus emphasize their position in the ruling aristocracy." See, Various Artists. *An Anthology of African Music: Nigeria-Hausa Music I*. Barenreiter Musicaphon BM 30 L 2306. n.d.

31. For an introduction to the concept of "linguistic surrogates," see chapter 16: Nketia, J. H. Kwabena. "Speech and Melody." In *The Music of Africa*. New York: W. W. Norton, 1974.

32. Coleman's recordings with the Nigerian musicians have never been commercially released, but footage of their collaboration appears in Shirley Clarke's film *Ornette: Made in America* (Milestone Video, 1986). Yusef Lateef's collaborations were released on his 1985 album *Yusef Lateef in Nigeria* (Landmark LLP-502).

33. Rowlands, Jonathan. "John Coltrane's *A Love Supreme* as Prayed Glossolalia," *Journal of Pentecostal Theology* 28 (2019): 84–102.

34. Jay Hoggard quoted on Facebook, December 12, 2018.

35. Nortey, as quoted in Feld, Steven. *Jazz Cosmopolitanism in Accra: Five Musical Years in Ghana*. Durham, NC: Duke University Press, 2012.

36. Nortey in Feld, *Jazz Cosmopolitanism in Accra*, 104.

37. These are, of course, long-standing tropes of African American culture, but in this section I am generally responding to points raised by Martin Munro in *Different Drummers*, 11–15.

38. See Lynn, Greg. "Fictions." In *Form*. New York: Rizzoli, 2008. This connection

between science fiction and architectural thought is elaborated further in: Lynn, Greg, Michael Maltzan, and Alessandro Poli. *Other Space Odysseys*. Edited by Giovanna Borasi and Mirko Zardini Baden: Lars Müller, 2010.

39. Lynn, Greg. *Animate Form*. Princeton, NJ. Princeton Architectural Press, 2009.

40. Lynn, Maltzan, and Poli, *Other Space Odysseys*.

41. Lally, Sean. *The Air from Other Planets: A Brief History of Architecture to Come*. Baden: Lars Müller, 2014.

42. See Wigley, Mark. "Broadcasting Shelter." In *Buckminster Fuller Inc.: Architecture in the Age of Radio*. Zurich: Lars Muller, 2015.

43. Silva, Camile. *Liquid Architectures: Marcos Novak's Territory of Information*. Baton Rouge: Louisiana State University Press, 2005.

44. See Pinney, Christopher, and Nicolas Peterson, eds. *Photography's Other Histories*. Durham, NC: Duke University Press, 2003.

45. Sources helpful in this discussion would include: Hight, Eleanor M., and Gary D. Sampson, eds. *Colonialist Photography: Imag(in)ing Race and Place*. New York: Routledge, 2013; and Pinney and Peterson, *Photography's Other Histories*.

46. Rieder, John. *Colonialism and the Emergence of Science Fiction*. Middletown, CT: Wesleyan University Press, 2012.

47. See the *Jazz Research Journal* call for papers, https://journal.equinoxpub.com /JAZZ/announcement/view/247?fbclid=IwAR1eHqIuEQ3mAg9YjH51Oom7wnajckeXV 41DOCnyTBLryjqDRfJeYUvrVzo.

48. Strauss, David Levi. *Between the Eyes: Essays on Photography and Politics*. New York: Aperture, 2005.

49. Menkman, Rosa. *The Glitch Moment(um)*. Amsterdam: Network Notebooks 04, 2011, 11.

50. From Galofaro, Luca, and Peter Eisenman. *Digital Eisenman: An Office of the Electronic Era*. Basel: Birkhauser, 1999, 55.

51. From Akomfrah, John. "Digitopia and the Spectres of Diaspora." *Journal of Media Practice* 11, no. 1 (2010): 23.

52. Jemisin, N. K. *How Long 'til Black Future Month?* London: Orbit, 2018.

53. Eshun, "Further Considerations on Afrofuturism," 291–92.

54. For music-analytical studies of hip-hop, see Schloss, Joseph G. *Making Beats: The Art of Sample-Based Hip-Hop*. Middletown, CT: Wesleyan University Press, 2014. See also chapter 3 of: Rose, Tricia. "Soul Sonic Forces." In *Black Noise: Rap Music and Black Culture in Contemporary America*. Middletown, CT: Wesleyan University Press, 1994.

55. Early examples of this fusion would include Branford Marsalis's *Buckshot Le Fonque* project, a handful of early recordings by saxophonist Greg Osby, and DJ Guru's Jazzmatazz project.

56. D'Angelo. *Voodoo*. Virgin 7243 8 48499 2 4. Originally released 2000.

57. Charnas, Dan. *Dilla Time: The Life and Afterlife of J. Dilla, the Hip-Hop Producer Who Reinvented Rhythm*. New York: Farrar, Straus and Giroux, 2022.

58. See Novak, David. "The Sublime Frequencies of New Old Media." In *Punk Ethnography: Artists and Scholars Listen to Sublime Frequencies*, edited by Michael Veal and E. Tammy Kim. Middletown, CT: Wesleyan University Press, 2015.

59. Akomfrah in "John Akomfrah and Lina Gopaul," https://www.youtube.com /watch?v=bXUbGuN0QOQ. See also Mercer, Kobena. "Post-Colonial Trauerspiel." In *The Ghosts of Songs: The Film Art of the Black Audio Film Collective*, edited by Kodwo Eshun and Anjalika Sagar. Liverpool: Liverpool University Press, 2007.

60. Akomfrah, "Digitopia and the Spectres of Diaspora," 23.

61. Akomfrah, "Digitopia and the Spectres of Diaspora," 23.

62. See Saggoi, Antonino. "Flying Carpets." In *Digital Gehry: Material Resistance, Digital Construction*, edited by Bruce Lindsey. Basel: Birkhauser, 2001.

63. Saggoi, "Flying Carpets," 6.

INDEX

Page numbers in *italic* refer to illustrations.

audience recordings. *See* sound recordings, audience

audiocassette culture. *See* cassette culture and tape trading

Austerlitz, Paul, 64

Austin, Edith, 258

authenticity, 82, 83, 90, 91, 281

Ayler, Albert, 99, 125, 139, 156, 163, 189; Collin documentary, 163; influence on Coltrane, 144, 163; influence on Shorter, 249; Silva and, 179

Bair, Paul, 102

Balmond, Cecil, 232

Baltrop, Alvin, 42

Banham, Reyner: *The Architecture of the Well-Tempered Environment*, 48

Barron, Bill, 103

Bartz, Gary, 245–46

bata drums and drummers, 181–83

Bates, Eliot, 17, 18

Bearden, Romare, 13, 90, 127–30, *129*

Belden, Bob, 224, 287

Bernstein, Jack, 173–74, 185

Bibbs, Hart Leroy, 290

Bird at St. Nick's (Parker), 87–88

Birdland (New York club), 109, 118

Bird Lives (Russell), 91

Bird's Eyes (Parker), 88

Bitches Brew (Davis), 8, 11, 267–68, 272–80, 287, 293, 337–39; architectural model, 47; Betty Davis role, 309; concerts before and after, 263, 267, 296; *Deep Brew*, 274; implied interstellar theme, 28; Miles photo in gatefold cover, 223; Shorter on, 239; Young, 196, 272

"Bitches Brew" (Davis), 273, 288–89, 301

black dance music, 14, 38, 82, 325

Blackstone Legacy (Henderson), 245, 277

Blackwell, Edward, 67

Blakey, Art, 53, 178, 265; *At the Jazz Corner of the World*, 252; "Moanin'," 260

Blesser, Barry, 48

Bley, Paul, 39, 40, 125

Blue Note album covers, 52

blur (aesthetic), 234, 252, 290, 292; in album cover portraits, 234; in side slipping 101

Boccioni, Umberto, 73

Bolletino, Dante, 83

bootleg recordings, 16–17, 18, 83, 95–96n17, 110, *111*, 112, 264

Borges, Jorge Luis, 28

Braxton, Anthony, 40–41, 150

"Brazilia" (Coltrane), 107, 120–21

Breach, Ian, 294, 295

Brooks, Harvey, 272, 274, 275

Brown, David P., 49

Brown, James, 37, 38, 307, 332

Brown, Marion, 139, 156

Butler, Octavia, 338

Calhoun, Keith, 79–81

Captain Beefheart, 40–41

Carles, Philippe, 61

Carr, Ian, 294, 295

Carter, Ron, 226, 238, 242, 277; "Agitation," 230–31; live performance, 230–31

Cartier-Bresson, Henri, 234–35, *235*, 314n43

cassette culture and tape trading, 18, 91, 92, 286

"catastrophe theory" (Thom), 196–97

Chambers, Paul, 1

Charles, Ray, 260

"Chasin' the Trane" (Coltrane), 117, 136

Chéroux, Clément, 235

Cherry, Don, 24, 53, 67, 159, 227, 228, 253, 299

"Chim Chim Cheree" (Sherman Brothers): Coltrane version, 45, 46, 113

Choma, Joseph: *Morphing*, 46–47

Clarke, Kenny, 105–6

Cobb, Jimmy, 1

Cohn, Richard, 14, 39

Coleman, Ornette, 43, 47, 138, 159, 171–72; drummers, 180, 238; *Free Jazz*, 139; influence on Coltrane, 101, 166; influence on Miles, 227, 231; influence on Sun Ra, 131; "Lonely Woman," 47, 67, 72, 89, 121, 134, 166, 172, 328; Nigeria visit, 335; Silva and, 179

Coleman, Steve, 47, 72, 343, 344

collage, 41, 127, 128; architectural, 168; musical, 67, 125, 142, 273

collectives: architectural, 50; film, 20, 345; musical, 50, 248

Collin, Kasper: *My Name Is Albert Ayler*, 163

Coltrane, Alice, 24–27, *151*, 151–52, 173, 178, 192–94; on audience possession, 183–84; Betty Davis compared, 220, 309, 310; harp, 173, 178; "Leo," 176; management of John's estate, 4, 163; replacing Tyner, 168; solo work, 99, 123, 162, 193, 198; *Stellar Regions*, 186

Coltrane, John, 2–7, 40–41, 72, 74, 128–30,

Dance, Stanley, 174
dance music, 39, 40, 60–61, 62, 105; live, 88. *See also* black dance music; mambo
D'Angelo, 344; *Voodoo*, 343
Davis, Betty Mabry, 24, 220–23, *221*, 246, 271, 309–10; *Filles de Kilimanjaro*, 244; Hendrix and, 269; "Miles Runs the Voodoo Down," 322n228
Davis, Frances Taylor, 25, 226
Davis, Miles, 5–11, 20, 74, 216–82 passim, *222*, 286–323 passim; addiction and abstinence, 54, 223; Africa and, 38; Antibes concerts, 262–67; arrest, 310; on Coltrane death, 198; Cosey and, 108; Douglas and, 269; dress, 221–22, 236, 263, 297–99; family, 25; Hendrix and, 216–24, 268–70; live performance, 9, 94, 109, 228–32, 236, 242–43, 247–58, 262–65, 274, 286–308; mistakes and, 94; wives, 24, 25, 220–23, 244, 246, 269, 271, 309–10, 322n228
Davis, Miles, albums: *Bitches Brew*, 8, 11, 28, 47, 196, 223, 239, 263, 267–68, 272–80, 287, 293, 296, 309, 337–39; *Filles de Kilimanjaro*, 243–44, 262, 279, 290, 296, 309; *In a Silent Way*, 25, 239, 246, 247, 261–63, 273, 275, 296, 309; *Kind of Blue*, 1, 100, 132, 236, 256, 295; *Miles in the Sky*, 243, 247, 279; *1969 Miles*, 262, 264, 338; *Sketches of Spain*, 270–71, 273, 277
Davis, Miles, songs (compositions): "Agitation," 228–33, 254, 304–5; "Bitches Brew," 273, 288–89, 301; "Frelon Brun," 243; "It's about That Time," 254, 261, 265, 289, 300, 301; "Mademoiselle Mabry," 243–44; "Miles Runs the Voodoo Down," 254, 266, 267, 273, 274, 287, 309, 322n228; "No Blues," 252, 254, 287, 295; "So What," 249, 254, 293; "Spanish Key," 254, 267, 273; "The Theme," 254, 306
Davis, Miles, songs (covers): "Gingerbread Boy," 249, 254; "I Fall in Love Too Easily," 254, 257, 295, 301, 305, 310
De Carava, Roy, 290
degradation and decay: of audio signals, 18, 20, 86–93, 119, 176, 283, 286, 289, 343; of photo prints, 79–81, *80*, 284–86
DeJohnette, Jack, 8, 46, 246, 263–66, 295, 307; *Bitches Brew*, 11, 274, 275; Henderson and, 245; live performance, 250–56, 263–66, 288–90, 296, 297, 300, 304–5; on Miles's health-consciousness, 223; on Miles's influences,

227; *1969 Miles*, 338; on other drummers, 179, 248; *Power to the People*, 277; Siders on, 256; on "warping" passages, 306
Delany, Samuel, 3, 28
Del Campo, Matias, 329
Delorme, Michel, 150
Delue, Rachel, 128
digital architecture, 45, 47, 49, 70, 302, 327, 341
"digitopia" (Akomfrah), 346
"Directions" (Zawinul), 254, 260–67, 301, 306
distortion devices, 18, 195, 196, 243, 340
"Dogon jazz," 206n61
Dolphy, Eric, 47, 72, 155, 156, 269
Douglas, Alan, 269
drone, 7, 100, 102–3, 113, 120, 129, 177–82; electric guitar, 261; in "Lonely Woman," 67, 328
drugs: heroin, 99, 112, 136, 158–59, 198; Mile's addiction and abstinence, 54, 223; psychedelics/hallucinogens, 157–64, 278
Duffy's Backstage Tavern (Rochester, New York), 247, 249, 250, 251, 252, 265
"Dusk Dawn" (Coltrane), 123

Edensor, Tim, 42
Eisenman, Peter, 35, 47, 49, 71; Alteka Office Building, Tokyo (unbuilt), 114, *115*, 116; Church of the Year 2000 project, 166–68, *167*, 275; Staten Island Institute for Arts and Sciences (unbuilt), 68, *69*; *Virtual House*, 275–76, *276*; Wexner Center for the Visual Arts and Fine Arts Library, 65, *65*
electric bass, 218, 238; *Bitches Brew*, 272, 274, 275; *Power to the People*, 277
electric guitar, 38, 216–19, 223, 255, 261–62, 270, 272. *See also* Hendrix, Jimi; McLaughlin, John
Electric Ladyland (Hendrix), 268–69, 273, 277, 278, 279, 309
electric piano, 244–48, 254–62, 272–77, 289, 297, 300–301; "Agitation," 305; *Bitches Brew*, 274, 275; distorted and detuned, 288; ring-modulated, 272; Sun Ra, 132, 245. *See also* Fender Rhodes electric piano
electric saxophone, 196
Ellington, Duke, 99, 131, 269, 278, 279, 294, 299
Ellis, Don, 201
Ellison, Ralph, 325; *Invisible Man*, 54
Eno, Brian, 94
Eshun, Kodwo, 27, 82, 333, 342

MUSIC / CULTURE

A series from Wesleyan University Press
Edited by Deborah Wong, Sherrie Tucker, and Jeremy Wallach
Originating editors: George Lipsitz, Susan McClary, and Robert Walser

The Music/Culture series has consistently reshaped and redirected music scholarship. Founded in 1993 by George Lipsitz, Susan McClary, and Robert Walser, the series features outstanding critical work on music. Unconstrained by disciplinary divides, the series addresses music and power through a range of times, places, and approaches. Music/Culture strives to integrate a variety of approaches to the study of music, linking analysis of musical significance to larger issues of power—what is permitted and forbidden, who is included and excluded, who speaks and who gets silenced. From ethnographic classics to cutting-edge studies, Music/Culture zeroes in on how musicians articulate social needs, conflicts, coalitions, and hope. Books in the series investigate the cultural work of music in urgent and sometimes experimental ways, from the radical fringe to the quotidian. Music/Culture asks deep and broad questions about music through the framework of the most restless and rigorous critical theory.

Harris M. Berger
*Stance: Ideas about Emotion, Style,
and Meaning for the Study
of Expressive Culture*

Harris M. Berger and
Giovanna P. Del Negro
*Identity and Everyday Life:
Essays in the Study of Folklore,
Music, and Popular Culture*

Franya J. Berkman
*Monument Eternal: The Music
of Alice Coltrane*

Dick Blau, Angeliki Vellou Keil,
and Charles Keil
*Bright Balkan Morning: Romani Lives and
the Power of Music in Greek Macedonia*

Susan Boynton and Roe-Min Kok, editors
*Musical Childhoods and the Cultures
of Youth*

James Buhler, Caryl Flinn,
and David Neumeyer, editors
Music and Cinema

Patrick Burkart
Music and Cyberliberties

Thomas Burkhalter, Kay Dickinson,
and Benjamin J. Harbert, editors
*The Arab Avant-Garde: Music,
Politics, Modernity*

Julia Byl
*Antiphonal Histories: Resonant Pasts
in the Toba Batak Musical Present*

Corinna Campbell
*The Cultural Work:
Maroon Performance in
Paramaribo, Suriname*

Alexander Cannon
*Seeding the Tradition: Musical Creativity
in Southern Vietnam*

Daniel Cavicchi
*Listening and Longing: Music Lovers
in the Age of Barnum*

Susan D. Crafts, Daniel Cavicchi,
Charles Keil, and the
Music in Daily Life Project
*My Music: Explorations
of Music in Daily Life*

Jim Cullen
*Born in the USA: Bruce Springsteen
and the American Tradition*

Anne Danielsen
*Presence and Pleasure: The Funk Grooves
of James Brown and Parliament*

Peter Doyle
*Echo and Reverb: Fabricating Space
in Popular Music Recording,
1900–1960*

Andrew Eisenberg
*Sounds of Other Shores:
The Musical Poetics of Identity
on Kenya's Swahili Coast*

Ron Emoff
*Recollecting from the Past:
Musical Practice and Spirit Possession
on the East Coast of Madagascar*

Yayoi Uno Everett and
Frederick Lau, editors
*Locating East Asia
in Western Art Music*

Susan Fast and Kip Pegley, editors
Music, Politics, and Violence

Running with the Devil: Power, Gender, and Madness in Heavy Metal Music

Dennis Waring
Manufacturing the Muse: Estey Organs and Consumer Culture in Victorian America

Lise A. Waxer
The City of Musical Memory: Salsa, Record Grooves, and Popular Culture in Cali, Colombia

Mina Yang
Planet Beethoven: Classical Music at the Turn of the Millennium

ABOUT THE AUTHOR

Michael E. Veal is Henry L. and Lucy G. Moses Professor of Music at Yale University. His work has typically addressed musical topics within the cultural sphere of Africa and the African diaspora. His books include *Fela: The Life and Times of an African Musical Icon* (Temple University Press, 2000), *Dub: Soundscapes and Shattered Songs in Jamaican Reggae* (Wesleyan University Press, 2007), *Tony Allen: Master Drummer of Afrobeat* (Duke University Press, 2013), and *Punk Ethnography: Artists and Scholars Listen to Sublime Frequencies* (co-edited with E. Tammy Kim) (Wesleyan University Press, 2017).